WEST FROM APPOMATTOX

West from Appomattox

The Reconstruction of
America after the Civil War

HEATHER COX RICHARDSON

Yale University Press   New Haven & London

Published with assistance from the Mary Cady Tew Memorial Fund.

Photo on p. iii: Rough Rider on bucking horse, Long Island, New York. Theodore Roosevelt Collection, Harvard College Library.

Designed by James J. Johnson and set in Adobe Caslon by Keystone Typesetting, Inc.
Printed in the United States of America.

The Library of Congress has cataloged the hardcover edition as follows:

Richardson, Heather Cox.
West from Appomattox : the reconstruction of America after the Civil War / Heather Cox Richardson.
p. cm.
Includes bibliographical references and index.
ISBN: 978-0-300-11052-4 (cloth : alk. paper)
1. United States—Politics and government—1865–1900. 2. Reconstruction (U.S. history, 1865–1877) 3. United States—History—1865–1898—Biography. 4. National characteristics, American. 5. Political culture—United States—History—19th century. 6. Middle class—United States—Political activity—History—19th century. 7. United States—Social conditions—1865–1918. I. Title.
E661.R53 2007
973.8—dc22

2006024633

ISBN: 978-0-300-13630-2 (pbk. : alk. paper)

A catalogue record for this book is available from the British Library.

The paper in this book meets the guidelines for permanence and durability of the Committee on Production Guidelines for Book Longevity of the Council on Library Resources.

10 9 8 7 6 5 4 3 2 1

For David Herbert Donald and William E. Gienapp

Contents

Acknowledgments

At a time when I was disenchanted with academia and almost ready to quit the profession, a colleague urged me to give it another try, insisting that no people were as generous as scholars. I was skeptical, but the last few years have proved him right. Colleagues and friends have nurtured this book from the time of my first e-mail to Jim Huston, asking if the project sounded workable, to the arrival of the final manuscript draft, which Eric Arnesen took time to edit days before he left for a semester abroad. Much of what is good in this book is thanks to the wonderful people who helped along the way; all the faults that remain are my own responsibility.

Special thanks are due to those who reviewed the final manuscript, whose detailed comments improved the final product immensely. They are Eric Arnesen, Thomas J. Brown, James West Davidson, Michael Green, Mitchell Snay, and Mark Summers.

So many other nineteenth-century historians have asked or answered questions, commented on drafts, or discussed pieces of this book with me that thanking them by name runs the risk of seeming to try to hide behind other people's reputations. Instead, I will thank as generally as possible people directly in my field, hoping that individuals recognize themselves where reviewers won't. Various colleagues at Columbia University, Kansas State University, Louisiana State University, Oklahoma State University, Princeton University, the University of Arkansas, the University of Florida, and the University of Pennsylvania have been insightful critics of this project. At my home university, BL has been a frequent source of support and information. Scholars at the Southern Intellectual History Circle gave an early version of this manuscript careful criticism that helped it mature; thanks are especially due to BWB and DMH. The scholars whom the Institute for Southern Studies invited to talk about recent trends in reconstruction historiography offered an insightful discussion of the state of reconstruction studies; I thank them for our stimulating debate.

Scholars outside of reconstruction history have also contributed to this project. Henry Bolter, Jonathan Hansen, Daniel Kryder, Geoff Tegnell, Andrea Walsh, Michael Willrich, and Richard Young, with whom I worked for a number of years on the Teaching American History grant project, "Defining Justice," will see their influence here. At UMass Amherst, women's historian Laura Lovett and Latin Americanist Jane Rauch offered advice and translations and generously produced documents I couldn't find myself. Also at UMass, classicist Carlin Barton explained the importance of moderation to Roman society so lucidly she made me approach my American moderates more sympathetically; and political scientist Michael T. Hannahan ran a critical eye over material on a moment's notice.

This book also benefited enormously from students at MIT, Suffolk University, and UMass Amherst. It was sparked in 2001 when an MIT student challenged me to explain why the image of the cowboy has come to represent America. As my ideas developed, I tried them out on students at Suffolk University and UMass Amherst, who were most helpful in identifying weaknesses and applauding strengths. On more than one occasion, I have rewritten sections—and in one case a whole chapter—when student responses indicated I had organized material badly. I thank all of you and hope you learned as much from me as I did from you.

A number of people outside academia have lent their expertise to this project. Engineer Klint Rose figured out whether or not an arrow really could go through a bison. Dr. Charles A. Garabedian explained obscure medical issues and made some guesses about what really killed Theodore Roosevelt's wife. Bill Klein at Sandy Lake Implement Company in Pennsylvania explained spring tooth harrows. Guy Crosby of Vermont showed me an army worm moth and impressed on me the devastation the worms had wreaked on his fields.

Others worked to bring this book to fruition. My agent, Lisa Adams, helped me to whip the idea into a workable project. Lara Heimert, then at Yale University Press, recognized the potential of my ideas and gave me the space to develop them. PJ, FW, and PB provided writing tutorials when I couldn't make my material fit together. Stalwart editor Chris Rogers cut my prose in a mainstream way, and copy editor Eliza Childs did a brilliant job of making the manuscript both grammatically correct and readable. Finally, Margaret Otzel managed the book's final stages with both professionalism and humor. I thank them all.

There are also personal debts to be acknowledged when a book is finished. Mitchell Snay has always been at the other end of a telephone or an e-mail as we both struggled to write books that threatened sometimes to devour us. Jo Calnan, Ann Corcoran, Beth LaDow, Jim and Sarah Matel, Gillian Pearson, Karina Pinella, and Mary Jean and Walther T. Weylman cheered this project on, read drafts, provided information, lent books, and asked questions. Devon, Jillian, and Rachel Murphy kept an eye on my children, playing capture the flag and drawing pictures with endless patience. Robert, Marshall, and Eva made my work easier by their comforting acceptance of a mother who kept disappearing with a pen and a manuscript; on a more practical level, their concrete approach to history has taught me to keep my prose from straying into theoretical tangents. Michael R. Pontrelli pretended to believe me when I assured him that this one would be a small project. I thank him for managing to refrain (mostly) from saying "I told you so" when it grew into an all-consuming big book, for taking the kids on weekend trips so I could work, and for keeping the book (and me) balanced.

Finally, I owe profound thanks to the two men to whom this book is dedicated. David Herbert Donald and William E. Gienapp were unstinting in their efforts to train me to be a historian and then supported me no matter what happened. I owe them more than any book can ever repay.

Figure 1. America in 1865 with featured people.

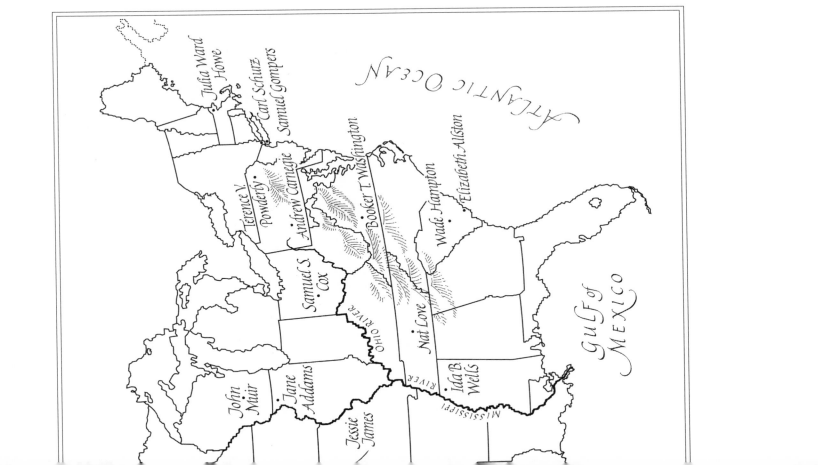

Julia Ward Howe

Carl Schurz

Samuel Gompers

ATLANTIC OCEAN

Terence V. Powderly

Andrew Carnegie

Booker T. Washington

Wade Hampton

Elizabeth Allston

Samuel S. Cox

OHIO RIVER

Nat Love

GULF of MEXICO

John Muir

Jane Addams

Ida B. Wells

MISSISSIPPI RIVER

Jessie James

Introduction

A week after the 2004 presidential election, a friend sent me a map of America with the red and blue states superimposed over the Confederate and Union states of the Civil War years. The Republican red states fit almost perfectly over the southern states that supported the Confederacy and the western plains that were territories during the 1860s, and the Democratic blue states fit closely over the states that had supported the Union. The caption of the map suggested that today's voters were still fighting the same issues over which they went to war in 1861. I was fascinated by the map, but not convinced by the caption. "This is exactly what my new book is about," I wrote back. "But it's not the Civil War that made today's map match the earlier one. The story is all about reconstruction."

This is the book that explains why today's political map looks like a map of the 1860s. It argues that in the years between 1865 and 1901, a new definition of what it meant to be an American developed from a heated debate over the proper relationship of the government to its citizens. In spring 1865, Americans everywhere had to ask themselves how the different sections of the country could reconstruct themselves into a nation that offered individuals economic opportunity and political freedom at the same time that it protected private property. By 1901, a newly formed "middle class" had answered that question by embracing a worldview that divided the nation into two groups. On one hand, they believed, were hardworking Americans—those who believed that success came through hard work and that all Americans were working their way up together. On the other hand were special interests—those who believed that there were fundamental conflicts in society that must be adjusted by the federal government. Regardless of how much money they made, those who believed they could make it on their own themselves as part of "the great middle" between rich monopolists and the lazy poor who were trying to harness the government to their own needs. They distrusted certain suffragists, African Americans, and veterans, as well as certain kinds of businessmen and workers, believing that they wanted special government aid, which, if given, would destroy the American system of evenhanded government. At the same time, because they defined themselves as true Americans, members of this middle class willingly harnessed a growing national government to their own interest, for it was the government's job, they believed, to promote the good of all Americans. Paradoxically, American individualists came to depend on government support while denying it to others.

This process was not as simple as today's politicians would have us think, with small-government Republicans fighting against big-government Democrats who wanted to create a welfare state. In fact, in the mid-1800s, it was the Republicans, not the Democrats, who stood for big government and Democrats who insisted on government limitations. Instead, the process was a complicated story in which sectional animosities, racial tensions, industrialization, women's activism, and westward expansion cut across party lines to create both a new definition of what it meant to be an American and a new vision of the government's role in the lives of its citizens.

The stark division that contemporaries saw in nineteenth-century America was not as simple as they thought, either. From the very beginning of the postwar era, the government that Republicans had constructed to benefit everyone equally actually privileged eastern businessmen over southern and western farmers and laborers. Laws, the economy, and tradition firmly placed whites over blacks and most immigrants, and men over women. Then, too, protesters of these conditions were not all radicals attempting to monopolize the state, as their opponents claimed. Many, in fact, adopted the mainstream ideology and wanted relatively mild adjustments to society to make that dream a reality for them.

Although questions about the relationship between the government and its citizens were hardly new in 1865, one thing made the post–Civil War years critical for American identity: during the war, for the first time in American history, Congress had imposed national taxes. After the war, individuals—taxpayers—had a new and powerful interest in their government and were concerned about who should be able to vote about how their money was spent. The correct sphere of government was no longer an academic question, but of personal financial interest to every American. This new relationship between government and citizens meant that the question of who should have a voice in government took on great practical meaning. Who was, or should be, a citizen of the new nation? Should African Americans vote? Women? Immigrants? The poor? Would they make reasonable decisions about the expenditure of tax dollars?

These were not academic questions either, for during the war the Republican Congress had strengthened the national government, expanding its power dramatically with an army and a navy of more than a million men, and increasing its role in the economy with new legislation to develop the nation. Then, in January 1865, the Thirteenth Amendment, ending slavery, indicated the firm intention of Republican congressmen to strengthen the national government. With its second section declaring that "Congress shall have the power to enforce this article by appropriate legislation," it was the first amendment in the history of the American Constitution that increased, rather than limited, the power of the national government. Nineteenth-century attempts to balance freedom, taxation, and government power were the central story of post–Civil War America. Their ultimate outcome defined a desirable American citizen and an ideal American state.

My interest in this process was sparked by the disparity between the way people a century and a half ago disparaged the government at the same time they developed it. I knew that for all their fervent talk about "self-made men" and "laissez-faire government," late nineteenth-century Americans did not, in fact, decrease the size and activity of the national government. They increased it. How did they justify this contradiction? This question interested me deeply, for the Reagan Revolution of the 1980s brought this same paradox to the fore in modern American political rhetoric. It gives us antigovernment rhetoric from the South and western plains, regions that receive far more in federal aid than they pay in taxes. At the same time, the Northeast and West Coast support government activism although they receive back from the national government considerably less money than they pay in. In 2003, for example, taxpayers in Mississippi received a federal outlay of $1.83 for every dollar of federal tax they paid, while taxpayers from Massachusetts saw only $.78 come back to the state for every dollar they gave to Uncle Sam. Yet in 2004, Mississippi voters spoke firmly against government activism and Massachusetts voters spoke strongly in favor of it. Clearly there is a stark regional contrast in American thought between the reality of government activism and Americans' image of it. How did nineteenth-century Americans negotiate this contrast?[1]

In order to find out, I tried to put myself as closely as I could into the position of an educated nineteenth-century American, worried about the future of the nation, my family, and myself. I read newspapers, novels, memoirs, and histories of the late 1800s; looked at paintings; and listened to music. As I did so, the world I saw around me appeared very different from the one I had read about in history books. Most histories of "Reconstruction" focus on the South and its morass of racial problems. But nineteenth-century Americans never focused on racial problems in the postwar South to the exclusion of the issues of postwar industrialization and urbanization that appeared dramatically as early as 1866. Also, women were prominent in postwar records, exercising an increasingly visible role in American life and causing plenty of comment, both positive and negative. It seemed to me that the mindset of the era must have somehow incorporated the growing public activities of women, and that histories of the period that pushed women's actions into their own sphere, divorced from American society in general, were missing an important part of the story.

Finally, it was evident that the reconstruction years could not be understood without acknowledging the central importance of the American West. The postwar years were the heyday of westward expansion, miners, the American cowboy, Plains Indians, and gunfighters. These events and characters were everywhere in the historical record. Indeed, as I worked, the obvious suddenly dawned on me: the nation's strongest cultural images of the postwar years came from the West. Only a few of us could pick out a photograph of even the most prominent African Americans or industrialists—let alone a labor organizer or women's activist—but most Americans have heard of Jesse James and Geronimo, and few people in the world wouldn't recognize the American cowboy. The history of the West was part and parcel of the story of the reconstruction years and must be put back into it. Postwar "reconstruction" was the literal reconstruction of the North, South, and West into a nation in the aftermath of the Civil War. That rebuilding stretched from the end of the Civil War until the start of the twentieth century.

How did nineteenth-century Americans justify the expansion of government activism and still retain their wholehearted belief in individualism? Upwardly mobile members of American society opposed government activism to promote the interests of workers, big businessmen, minorities, and certain activist women, perceiving their demands as an attempt to advance a view of America as a land of class conflict rather than of economic harmony. Those in "the middle" between rich and poor firmly opposed government action on behalf of such "special interests," insisting instead that the government should promote the good of all Americans. By skillfully defining those who believed in economic and social harmony—themselves—as true Americans rather than a special interest, while denigrating activist workers, African Americans, Populists, robber barons, and so on as un-American, middle-class Americans could argue for government intervention on their own behalf without fearing the destruction of the American system of government.

Workers had demanded government activism on behalf of labor since at least 1866, but when the government first curbed the excesses of business and established the principle of intervention in the economy at the end of the century, it did not do so to protect organized labor. Denying that government must balance the interests of workers and farmers against those of big business, the same congressmen who opposed labor activism for its apparent suppression of individual liberty undercut certain business practices on the grounds that businessmen were trampling on the American ideal of a level playing field in the economy. Intervention in the economy went on to become even more active, venturing into social welfare legislation, when middle-class women activists argued that the government must protect the ideal middle-class family.

Yet even as members of the American middle class deliberately harnessed a newly active national government to their own interests, they retained a vision of America as a land of individualism. This contradiction was possible because of the blinding postwar image of the American West. Regardless of the harsh realities of the late nineteenth-century West, the peculiarities of the postwar years made it represent economic opportunity, political purity, and social equality. When a Republican government dominated by northeasterners and far westerners tried to impose freedom on the South, ex-Confederates immediately developed antigovernment rhetoric. This antigovernment stance spread to the plains and mountain West despite the region's complete dependence on the government, as angry settlers opposed a range of federal actions, from the awarding of army beef contracts to Indian policies. Then, as the Republican Party became loathed by its opponents as a patronage-spewing behemoth acting in the interests of African Americans and rich eastern businessmen, antigovernment protesters across the nation idealized the rural West as the opposite of the urban Northeast. This western antigovernment mindset flexed its muscles in the Spanish-American War when Theodore Roosevelt pointedly led a "cowboy" regiment up San Juan Hill to fight a conflict popularly justified as an attempt to take the nation away from eastern politicians and money-grubbing businessmen, returning it to independence, self-reliance, and morality. After the Spanish-American War, America was a land where an activist government supported individualism, and those who endorsed this contradictory ideology exported it to other nations through both trade and military conflict. In 1901, Theodore Roosevelt—that "damned cowboy," as a spokesman for the eastern establishment called him—sat in the White House, directing an activist government that served a peculiarly American middle class.

The pages that follow try to show what the nation looked like to nineteenth-century Americans. In order to do that, I have attempted to avoid portraying the era as one of abstract Forces—industry, labor, suffragists, immigrants, African Americans—conflicting over Big Issues. I have written this book as a narrative history about the experiences of a number of actual Americans who lived in the era from 1865 to 1901. When choosing my characters, I required that they lived through almost the entire period and that they left behind enough of their own words to tell their own stories. Ex-Confederate Wade Hampton and western scout Buffalo Bill, poet Julia Ward Howe, educator Booker T. Washington, and Sioux leader Sitting Bull, among others, fulfilled my requirements; labor pioneer William Sylvis, who died in 1869, and leading black politician W. Beverly Nash, who left few records, did not. As I researched these individuals, I was astonished at how often the lives of those who embraced a developing middle-class ideology crossed, suggesting that they recognized an affinity for those who thought like themselves and actively worked to spread their worldview across the country. Less prominent Americans who left fewer records aren't introduced as individuals; rather, they show up on the shores of New York Harbor watching the illumination of the Statue of Liberty, in a New Orleans freedmen's meeting, in Missouri helping Jesse James hide from government agents, in a California mining camp trying to make a fortune. They are William Graham Sumner's "forgotten Americans" who hated the idea of welfare legislation, the people who cheered when Ida B. Wells got dragged out of a white railroad car or applauded President Grover Cleveland's use of the army against the Pullman strikers. They are also Theodore Roosevelt's ideal hardworking citizens, black cowboy Nat Love's race-blind westerners, Americans who begged the government to go to war to save the lives of Cuban women and children.

They are both the worst and the best of America. This book is designed to tell the story of the construction of their worldview.

This middle-class ideology was both the greatest triumph and the greatest tragedy of reconstruction. It was an astonishingly inclusive way to run a country, making certain former slaves and impoverished immigrants welcomed participants in middle-class America, offering to them opportunities they could not have imagined in other countries, and it advanced women's position in a dramatically short time. But this ideology also rendered Americans unable to recognize systematic inequalities in American society. Anyone who embraced the mainstream vision came to believe he or she was on the road to a middle-class life, no matter what the reality of his or her position actually was. When things went wrong, individuals had no one but themselves to blame for failure, even if its causes lay outside their control. A man unemployed during a recession or a woman beaten by her husband could find little sympathy in the middle-class worldview. More strikingly, though, this mindset deliberately repressed anyone who called for government action to level the American economic, social, or political playing field. If a group as a whole came to be perceived as looking for government handouts its members were aggressively prohibited from participating equally in American society, and all of the self-help in the world wasn't going to change that. This middle-class vision also limited women's role in society by basing their power on their positions as wives and mothers, not as independent, equal individuals. The powerful new American identity permitted many individuals to succeed far beyond what they might have achieved elsewhere, but that exceptional openness depended on class, gender, and racial bias.

The political contours of this division have changed over the decades, but the divided vision of the nation is still a potent part of Americans' current mindset. It was certainly part of the 2004 electoral puzzle that made the red states, with their large government subsidies, vote so vehemently against what they perceived as government aid to "special interests." And red staters who trumpet America's greatness as a land of opportunity are right: the American ideology is truly great. This mindset is also, though, what made blue staters vote for a government that would level the economic, social, and political playing fields between different groups. The blue staters, too, are right; America has serious systematic inequalities embedded in its society. America is neither excellent nor oppressive; rather, it is both at the same time. In 1865, Americans had to reconstruct their shattered nation. Their solution "reconstructed" America into what it is today.

CHAPTER ONE

Spring 1865

The View from the Civil War

After an uneasy night, Lieutenant General Ulysses S. Grant awoke on April 9, 1865, still suffering from a migraine that had hit the day before. Tired and aching, he pulled on rough army clothes, mounted his horse, and rode out toward Appomattox Station, Virginia, where his men had engaged an advance column of soldiers from General Robert E. Lee's Army of Northern Virginia. On the way to the head of the column, Grant received a message from Lee, who requested an interview for the purpose of surrendering his army. "When the officer reached me I was still suffering with the sick headache," Grant recalled, "but the instant I saw the contents of the note I was cured."[1]

Grant found the Confederate general, painstakingly clothed in full dress uniform, waiting for him at the small village of Appomattox Court House in the substantial home of Wilmer McLean. The elegant, white-haired Lee and the weathered bulldog from the North commiserated on the terrible cost of the war and agreed that the bloodshed should end. As terms for surrender, Grant required only that the officers give their word that neither they nor their men would fight against the United States again, and that they turn over their military arms and artillery. The men could keep their own side arms and horses. Grant wanted them "to be able to put in a crop to carry themselves and their families through the next winter."[2]

Lee could surrender only his own men, but his army was the pride of the Confederacy and its demise signaled the end of the war. It was simply a question of time until the estranged sections of the country would have to begin to build a new postwar nation. The South, devastated and despairing, the North, bustling and proud, and the West, rich in resources but deeply embattled in a war between Native Americans and eastern settlers, somehow would have to create a unified America.[3]

Of course, not everyone saw it this way. For his part, Lieutenant General Wade Hampton III of South Carolina was not willing to abandon the Confederacy. Serving with Joseph E. Johnston's crumbling army in North Carolina, he gathered his men and angrily told them that the report of Lee's surrender was "a rumor he did not believe." In any case, Lee's Army of Northern Virginia was only one of three major Confederate armies, and its surrender did not end the war. With the Army of the Mississippi and the Army of the Tennessee still in the field, Wade Hampton begged Jefferson Davis not to give up. Hampton promised his president that he could find almost 100,000 men still willing to fight; they could force their way over the Mississippi River to Texas and launch a guerrilla war from there. The *Montgomery Advertiser* agreed: "As the crushing wheel of invasion rolls onward, behind it life and hope rise anew amidst the smoking ruins, and patriotism, torn and bleeding but still defiant, girds its loins for new struggles and new sufferings." When his commanding officer surrendered to General Sherman, Hampton carefully noted that since he had not been present, he was not bound by his superior's actions. "Those . . . who were absent can either accept or reject the terms. Nothing can be done at present, either here, or elsewhere, so I advise quiet for a time. If any opportunity offers, later, we can avail ourselves of it," he wrote. He remained hopeful of continuing the war until Union soldiers captured Jefferson Davis on May 10. The tall, squarely muscular Hampton had poured his vast wealth, his prestige, his blood, and the lives of his brother and son into the Confederate cause. He clung to the belief that his sacrifices had a purpose.[4]

For many Americans, Hampton seemed to represent the South. He was born into a powerful plantation family, graduated from the elite South Carolina College, and married Margaret Preston and then, after her death, Mary McDuffie, both from prominent planter families. In 1860, Hampton owned over 10,000 acres of land, which were carved into five plantations worked by more than 900 slaves. The rice, cotton, sugar, and corn that grew in Hampton's fields made him the richest man in South Carolina; a good year before the war brought a gross income of more than $200,000. Hampton sat in the antebellum state legislature, but his influence from Millwood, his beautiful home outside of Columbia, was probably more politically important. There, he regularly entertained the nation's leading men—governors, congressmen, cabinet officers, and army brass—expounding upon the issues of the day over gourmet food and fine wines.[5]

Central to Hampton's antebellum way of life were white southern ideas about the way society worked. Proud of their Revolutionary inheritance, white southerners believed their way of life was the culmination of the ideals of the founding fathers. Those august men had thrown off the yoke of monarchy and aristocracy and embraced the liberalism of eighteenth-century philosopher John Locke, who argued that individuals were inherently equal at birth. The hierarchical political and economic systems of Europe, where tenants farmed the land of noblemen and had no say in their government, distorted natural law, Locke maintained. Each individual had a right to "the fruits of his labor" and to determine the government under which he lived. America's Revolutionary generation had combined this Lockean liberalism with a profound distrust of the English ministers to the king, whom they saw as misrepresenting the colonists and misleading their sovereign for their own political ends. They came to believe that power—economic, political, or social—was inherently predatory and an enemy of liberty. Powerful people arranged to keep themselves in power by ruling against their opponents and distributing government largesse to their political friends.[6]

Once the Revolutionary generation had rid itself of monarchy—the most stable form of government the world had ever known—in the 1770s, it had to figure out how to create a government for a nation of Lockean individuals. It was all well and good to declare that "all men are created equal; that they are endowed by their Creator with certain unalienable rights; that among these are life, liberty, and pursuit of happiness," but how could that be translated into an actual form of government? The founding fathers tried to create a republican government based on the votes of economically independent individuals who owned their own land and were therefore able to act without fear of reprisal from an employer. The men constructing the new nation's government believed that by voting for measures that benefited themselves, economically self-sufficient and politically independent voters would also do what was right for the nation. The founding fathers were determined to keep government small so that it could not develop an office-holding class that lived on taxes sucked from hardworking producers. Large government invited corruption, they thought, as officeholders used tax dollars for pork-barrel projects to buy political support. If this were permitted, the government would become independent of its constituents, and the nation would have a new, European-style aristocracy, mercilessly taxing the average person to maintain its political and economic power.

Antebellum southern whites took their heritage firmly to heart, but they looked around them and saw that the realities of human nature and a capitalist economy meant that there would always be propertyless people dependent on others. Poor voters would corrupt the republic, it seemed, for they would be controlled by more powerful men who could make jobs or sustenance depend on a man's willingness to vote as his superior directed. White southerners sought to solve the problem of class divisions in society by enslaving its dependent members. This was especially easy in the South, of course, for race provided an obvious division around which to organize society. Safely under the control and protection of a white patriarch, black slaves could contribute economically to society without "contaminating" the government. Ironically, white southerners believed that a republican society of equals could not survive without slavery. For Hampton, American society rested on the idea that all *white* men were created equal.[7]

Plantations were worlds in themselves, their white inhabitants convinced that they belonged to an interdependent community that offered the best for everyone. Enslaved black men and women provided the labor that supported the community while white masters and mistresses "cared for" them. The life of a plantation mistress "is a very noble life . . . the life of a missionary, really; one must teach, train, uplift, encourage," planter's daughter Elizabeth Allston recorded. "It is a life of effort; but . . . it is . . . the life of those who have the great responsibility of owning human beings."[8]

White plantation women were protected and idealized by white men. While in reality most southern white women worked in the fields or as domestic servants in wealthier homes, the image of the white southern women was of sexless, delicate creatures completely dependent on the men around them, who would provide for them and manage society. Never married, Wade Hampton's three sisters lived at Millwood, a potent reminder of how completely they depended on their brother. "I feel that you . . . belong to me," Hampton wrote to his youngest sister, "& that it is my duty as well as my happiness to care for you always; to be to you a father as well as a brother." Planters modeled themselves on European aristocrats, managing and protecting those beneath them.[9]

Southern planters owned more than 50 percent of the region's slaves, their lands produced all of the region's rice and sugar and most of its tobacco and cotton, they dominated southern politics, and they determined its social mores. But only 4 percent of white southern men, clustered mainly on the coastlands of South Carolina, Georgia, and Mississippi, owned the twenty or more slaves necessary to be considered a member of the planter class. Most southern whites worked smaller inland farms with a handful of slaves, growing short-staple cotton or tobacco in addition to the hogs and corn that fed their families. Whites on the upland hill country of North Carolina, Arkansas, and Virginia were poorer still, scratching out of infertile soil corn and cotton in addition to the family's food. Rough settlements in Alabama, Mississippi, Louisiana, Texas, and Arkansas, begun in the 1830s, produced rich crops to replace declining production in the East, but in 1860 they were still plagued by malaria, yellow fever, and the drinking and violence of the frontier.[10]

Over on the coast near Charleston, Elizabeth Allston enjoyed the European masterpieces, including a Rembrandt, hanging on the walls of her father's six plantations; learned French at a private school; wore silk gowns to fancy dress balls; and ate meals of "delicious things . . . shrimp, fish, and rice-birds, and green corn, and lima beans." But the families of white yeomen farmers lived in two-room cabins, and poor whites lived in shacks. Most white southerners would never go to school, would never see a city, and would eat a diet of corn, game, pork, molasses, and greens. Some of the poorest "white trash" would struggle endlessly with hookworm, malaria, and pellagra that sapped their strength and gave them a reputation for laziness.[11]

The idealized image of the slave plantation also ignored the realities of forced labor and human slavery. On the large cotton and rice plantations, where more than half of all slaves worked, slaves worked in gangs run by an overseer. Dehumanized by white masters, housed in cabins, fed basic rations, sold at will, and held to work with physical threats, field slaves were hardly a contented peasantry enjoying an enlightened patriarchy. Grouped together far from contact with the big house, field hands were able to develop their own culture, but they were cut off from the house slaves who were often lighter skinned and educated in trades. On smaller inland farms, slaves and masters often worked together in the fields, and slaves there developed a wider range of skills. Reminiscing about the more than 600 slaves her father owned, Elizabeth Allston recalled that her father's plantations "were models of organization and management" and treasured fond memories of "Daddy Thomas," who ran the establishment's large carpenter's shop. "He was a great person in my eyes. He was so dignified, and treated us young daughters of the house as though we were princesses; just the self-respecting manner of a noble courtier." But Nat Love, a young plantation slave in Tennessee, saw the system more clearly. His master was "kind and indulgent," but Love still believed that while slaves in such conditions were "lucky," "their lot was the same as a horse or a cow."[12]

About one-quarter of all southern white families owned slaves, but almost all southern whites bought into the ideology of slavery. Slavery fed the psychological and economic needs of poor whites as it supported the social, economic, and political power of planters. For the yeoman farmers who made up the majority of the southern population, increasingly squeezed in the booming market of the late 1850s, slavery reinforced the idea that all whites, rich and poor, were equals. White yeomen understood, as one man commented, "that . . . where Capital rules, where there are no black slaves, there must be white ones." This "slave-labor republicanism," as one historian put it, meant that a barefoot country man could hold up his head in the presence of a wealthy planter, convinced that they were equals, independent and wielding a vote that supported a pure republican government.[13]

Before the war, white southerners contrasted their society with that of the North, whose growing industrialism threatened to undermine the republic by forcing propertyless wage earners to depend on capitalists while still permitting them to participate in politics. Economically and thus politically dependent, northern workers were not equals to their fellow citizens but rather were "wage-slaves," according to southern critics. Because slavery was essentially a paternalistic system, such southerners argued, northern workers were worse off than southern slaves. "The Southern slave is . . . well clothed, well fed, well treated, in every way comfortable beyond the labouring class of any country," wrote a southern woman, "and, although not enjoying the luxuries of life, is as far from starvation as his master." White southerners pointed to northern laborers "with withered forms and haggard faces" as dependent on the vagaries of the economy and the whim of employers for their very survival. "Our slaves are black, of another and inferior race. . . . Yours are white, of your own race," southern thinkers insisted.[14]

White southerners believed in 1860 that "fools and fanatics of the North," the radical abolitionists who were determined to achieve black freedom at any cost, sought to destroy the southern system. The dramatic growth of northern cities and the flood of farmers west into Wisconsin, Minnesota, Illinois, and Iowa fed white southern fears that an antislavery North would take over the federal government and then carve away at slavery until it withered and died. Each sectional crisis in the 1850s became, for southerners, a test of their strength. The northern backlash against southern attempts to protect slavery seemed to prove that the South was under attack. The organization of the Republican Party as a sectional party dedicated to preventing the westward expansion of slavery indicated a crisis was at hand. The South had long ago lost its parity in the House of Representatives, where representation was apportioned by population. If new slave states did not balance the new free states forming in the West, the South would lose its parity in the Senate and go down on the ruins of slavery, destroyed by the powerful hand of a Republican-controlled government. Determined to protect slavery at all costs, southern whites stood adamantly for states' rights and argued that the entire American government would be destroyed if the Republicans came to power. If the Republicans won the 1860 election, the South would lose slavery and, the *Charleston Mercury* warned, "the patronage resulting from the control of ninety-four thousand offices, and the expenditure of eighty millions of money annually" would make the Republicans "irresistible in controlling the General Government." Tyranny would replace republicanism.[15]

In response to Lincoln's election, South Carolina left the Union on December 20, 1860. "The whole town [of Charleston] was in an uproar," Elizabeth Allston recalled. "Parades, shouting, firecrackers, bells ringing, cannon on the first booming, flags waving, and excited people thronging the streets." On December 24, South Carolina issued a "Declaration of the Immediate Causes which Induce and Justify the Secession of South Carolina from the Federal Union." This document explained the state's anger at the Union for its threats to slavery and insisted upon South Carolina's state sovereignty and the right of secession to protect the South's slave system. By February 1, the six states of the lower South—Mississippi, Florida, Alabama, Georgia, Louisiana, and Texas—had followed South Carolina. Over the next few weeks, delegates meeting in Montgomery, Alabama, set up a provisional government, selected Jefferson Davis as president, and adopted a Confederate constitution. Based upon the U.S. Constitution, the new document had some key differences: it protected slavery, insisted upon each state's "sovereign and independent character," and reduced the spending powers of the Confederate government. Each of these new provisions would check the ability of a large government to interfere with white liberties, as southerners thought was happening in the old Union.[16]

Men like Hampton were lords within their own lands, self-sufficient and isolated from the world. Looking from their verandas down the majestic oak alleys that led to the palings of their estates, they could not imagine their world invaded by Yankee shopkeepers. Hampton believed that southerners would easily defend their homeland. The rural South, with its large territory, lack of roads, hills, swamps, heat, and disease, would defeat invaders, just as Russia had defeated Napoleon in 1812. Receiving a colonel's commission upon the outbreak of the Civil War, Hampton raised the Hampton Legion—with infantry, cavalry, and artillery—in May 1861. In less than a week he had more than the 1,000 volunteers he had requested. Out of his own purse he bought British guns for his men and supplemented the cavalry with horses from his own stables. He gathered his regiment from the southern elite, elegant young men like Elizabeth Allston's brother Charley, proud to be seen in the light gray uniform of the legion, with its gilt buttons and braid, and rich enough to bring their own slaves—like the Allston's Sam Galant—with them to camp. In Richmond by early July, the legion was, one man recalled, "recognized as the elite of the regiments, and obtained the best of the social honors that were then so profusely distributed among the military men. Its associations were aristocratic; . . . and as a corps of gentlemen soldiers, they were perfect in every appointment."[17]

Hampton's men first saw battle at Bull Run in July 1861, and although the Confederates ultimately routed the Union soldiers, Hampton's men were shocked. "Never have I conceived," one recalled, "of such a continuous, rushing hailstorm of shot, shell, and musketry as fell around and among us for hours together. We who escaped are constantly wondering how we could possibly have come out of the action alive." At the end of the fight, the legion had 19 dead, 100 wounded, and 2 missing. The casualties would continue to mount as disease and northern bullets claimed the lives of about 258,000 white southerners and left scars in at least 100,000 others. In June 1862, Hampton's beloved brother Frank fell at Brandy Station, and by October 1864, Hampton reflected in sorrow: "We gain successes but after every fight there comes in to me an ominous paper, marked 'Casualties' and in this I often find long lists of 'killed' and 'wounded.' Sad, sad words which carry anguish to so many hearts. And we have scarcely time to bury the dead ere we press on in the same deadly strife." In 1864, at Burgess Mill, Hampton watched his son Preston fall from his horse with a bullet in his groin. When Wade IV ran to his brother, a Union sniper put a bullet in young Wade's back. Wade eventually recovered, but Preston died a few hours later. As his son lay dying, the general held him in his arms and cried.[18]

Those back home suffered, too, from shortages, wildly spiraling inflation —compounded by the depreciation of Confederate paper money—and, by

1863, hunger. Troops absorbed food, clothing, and manufactured goods, and the northern blockade stopped European imports. The southern economy sagged as invasion and lack of manpower decreased production. Chicken and ham became luxuries, and, with flour up to $75 a barrel and butter at $2 a pound, families eked by on cornbread, rice, and milk. Scrimping to buy food, many white southerners found new clothes out of reach. Elizabeth Allston recalled that "the price of every article of clothing was enormous, and shoes were impossible." She made clothes from her sister's faded pink bedroom curtains.[19]

The shortages were hard, but they were easier to bear than the loss of homes, abandoned either in fear of northern invaders or in the devastation that followed their arrival. The shelling of Charleston drove Allston and her mother into the country, leaving behind "many things of great value." They fled into the path that Sherman would take in 1864, when, Elizabeth recalled, "I became an expert in burying. Three sheets were a necessity; one to put the top earth on, with moss and leaves and everything to look natural, then one to put the second colored earth near the surface, and one to put every grain of the yellow clay below, one little pellet of which would tell the tale that a hole had been dug."[20]

And always, there were the deaths. "I can't bear to think of Preston," sobbed a young southern belle as she ran away from the young Hampton's funeral. "I can't bear to hear any more moaning and weeping and wailing. If I do I shall die."[21]

The loss of his son made Hampton determined never to stop fighting the Union, and he became more desperately certain of victory the more the South suffered. In the 1863 reorganization of Lee's army, Hampton was put in charge of a cavalry brigade; by the end of the war he had been promoted to lieutenant general. By 1865, as William Tecumseh Sherman's 60,000 men smashed their way through North Carolina, Hampton's fury at the North had become frantic. The Union soldiers had devastated a sixty-mile-wide swath that stretched three hundred miles from Nashville to Savannah, before fanning out through South Carolina, where they did so much damage that even Sherman worried. They continued up the coast to North Carolina. Hampton's men were some of only 22,000 soldiers who could be mustered to stop the Union army. Their efforts were futile. They could do little as the soldiers came on relentlessly, ten miles a day, despite armed resistance and torrential rains that swelled rivers and forced even Sherman to sleep in a tree. Hampton, galled at his inability to protect his land, writhed as the enemy burned homes, killed livestock, and destroyed railroads and the region's productivity. "I have directed my men to shoot down all of your men who are caught burning houses," Hampton wrote to the Union general. He insisted upon "the right that every man has to defend his home, and to protect those that are dependent upon him. And from my heart I wish that every old man and boy in my country who can fire a gun, would shoot down, as he would a wild beast, the men who are desolating their land, burning their houses, and insulting their women." Although Elizabeth Allston noted that the Yankees who sacked her home "seemed to be in great dread of being surprised by Hampton's cavalry, whom they spoke of as 'the devil, for you never knew where he was,'" Hampton was unable to do much but keep Sherman's men from wandering too far from their main army.[22]

By 1865, the land that proud Confederates had thought was unconquerable was devastated. Two-thirds of the assessed value of southern wealth had evaporated; two-fifths of the livestock—horses and draft animals for tilling fields as well as pigs and sheep for food—were dead. Over half the region's farm machinery had been destroyed, most factories were burned, and railroads were gone, for even where they had not been torn up, they had received such heavy wartime use that they were worn out. Now refugees, Elizabeth Allston and her mother struggled along a typical road. "We were never out of the sight of dead things, and the stench was almost unbearable. Dead horses all along the way and, here and there, a leg or an arm sticking out of a hastily made too-shallow grave. Along the way ten cows dead in one pen, and then eight or ten calves dead in another. Dead hogs everywhere; the effort being to starve the inhabitants out, no living thing was left." Destroyed homes would no longer welcome residents: two of Wade Hampton's grand homes had been ruined, one had become the headquarters of Union General John A. Logan. "The breaking up of our railroad system, the destruction of our machine shops and factories and the spoliation of the people at large who lose their animals and crops" was the heart of the North's military plan, the *Montgomery Advertiser* wailed. "We have no mails, no telegraph; our means of communication are interrupted . . . even in the city," the newspaper explained when it stopped publication in April 1865.[23]

Hampton had watched his world crumble. Southern whites were demoralized and citizens of the dying Confederacy drank, whored, and stole. "A spirit of lawlessness seems to pervade the town," warned the *Montgomery Advertiser* in mid-April 1865. "Men seem the prey of reckless despair, and, forgetting the laws of God and man, to give way to the phrensy of wild beasts." The *Houston Telegraph* warned its despairing readers to beware that "much of the liquor sold is called by some people 'rifle whiskey,' and will kill at a thousand yards distance." The editors of the *Atlanta New Era* reported a crime wave of "rape, murder, suicide, theft, burglary, garroting, pocket picking, embezzlement, elopements, bigamy, adultery" and insisted "that a great moral reform must be begun, and at once, or the great social fabric on which we have prided ourselves, will be sapped to the foundation, and he who can commit the most hideous crimes will find little difficulty in evading the punishment inflicted by the law." Cities were crippled by a lack of police and the physical damage of the war. Derelict buildings hid criminals. Inability to light gas streetlights meant that cities were dangerous after dark, when pedestrians had to worry about both broken pavement and thugs. Things had turned upside down. In March 1865, the *Richmond Whig* reported that when Wade Hampton had tried to stop some Confederate cavalrymen from looting a store in Columbia, two of the men "drew pistols on Gen. Hampton . . . and threatened his life."[24]

No longer were planters the unchallenged patriarchs of the South. While Hampton insisted that he fought to defend the ideal of southern womanhood, Elizabeth Allston's elegant mother chatted with Julius Pringle, Elizabeth's future husband, "about her success with the rye crop" and the problems of crop storage. The war had forced women to manage plantations and households, to work as government clerks or in the South's new war industries. They had entered traditionally male spheres, becoming nurses exposed to the raw indelicacy of men's wounds; spies, whose bodies were subject to searches by Union army personnel; and even, occasionally, soldiers, fighting in disguise alongside men. For women unwilling to take such dramatic action, it was still almost impossible not to step out of traditional social roles during the war, assuming paternal authority toward children when fathers left and masterly authority over slaves when white men were at the front. "It was perfectly wonderful to see how she rose to the requirement of the moment," recalled Allston of her mother's expanded wartime role, "and how strong and level her mind was. In a little while she had grasped the full extent of the situation, and was perfectly equal to her new position."[25]

Women also took on new political roles during the war. "I longed to take part in the work going on everywhere for our soldiers," recalled Elizabeth Allston. Women began by knitting socks and sewing shirts for the soldiers and supplied the mustering soldiers with coffee and hot food. As supplies became scarce, women directly petitioned government officials for aid when their men went to war. Then, as their homes were overrun, they complained bitterly about war strategy. When food ran short, women took to the streets of southern cities demanding bread. Horrified by their actions, Jefferson Davis repressed the story from the newspapers. In spring 1865, women begged their men not to stay and fight but come home and save their families from starvation. By 1865, southern white women were competent, outspoken, and disgusted with the Confederacy, a far cry from the dependent loyal Confederate women of legend.[26]

Planters like Hampton had also lost their slaves. Proslavery propaganda insisted that the paternalism of southern slave society kept slaves contented and loyal to their owners, but when the circumstances of the war and emancipation permitted slaves to indicate their support for that happy paternalism, they voted with their feet. Long before Abraham Lincoln signed the Preliminary Emancipation Proclamation in September 1862, slaves knew what was at stake. "The Union was 'IT,' and we were all 'Yankees,'" recalled Nat Love, a Tennessee slave ten years old in 1861. Beginning as early as 1861, when slaves seized the confusion of the early war to escape into Union army camps, about 30 percent of planters' prewar assessed value melted away into the woods and roads that led away from plantations. Ex-slaves fought bravely for the Union, asserting their manhood as soldiers, and in January 1865, Congress passed and sent off to the states for ratification the Thirteenth Amendment to the Constitution declaring that "neither slavery nor involuntary servitude, except as a punishment for crime . . . shall exist within the United States." Desperate to maintain some agricultural production in the South, the U.S. Army often forced ex-slaves back into former masters' fields, but even when this happened, white southern men knew their authority had been eclipsed: the freed people had contracts and answered to army officers rather than southern whites. By 1865, freed black southerners demanded wages and respect from their white neighbors.[27]

Hampton no longer led all southern white men either, since the realities of war had stripped away the proslavery rhetoric that called all white men equal. Poorer southerners had never been happy converts to secession, and their weak Confederate sentiments had disappeared entirely as the war dragged on. It was a rich man's war and a poor man's fight, they declared, furious at Confederate laws that tried to prevent slave insurrections by exempting from military service any white man in charge of twenty or more slaves. Poor upcountry farmers blamed the aristocratic planters from the low country for precipitating the war and by 1865 hated them accordingly. A northern man traveling in the South in fall 1865 reported the recent murders of two Rebels by pro-Union southerners and the conviction of local leaders that "ex-Rebel soldiers, those who were in any sense leaders, will fare hard at the hands of the mountain Unionists."[28]

At the end of the war, Hampton bitterly lamented that "four years of war—a war savage, bloody, and cruel beyond nearly every other on record—left the South bleeding at every pore—her resources exhausted—her property stolen—her cities laid in ashes—her fields ravaged—her living sons ruined and many of her noblest sleeping under the soil they fought so bravely, though so fruitlessly to defend." With the ruins of their past smoldering at their feet, white southerners could look back proudly on one thing. They had fought a losing battle with grim determination until privation and death forced them into despair. Grant spoke for many northerners in April 1865 when he noted that the surrender, which had at first made him jubilant, left him "sad and depressed. I felt like anything rather than rejoicing at the downfall of a foe who had fought so long and valiantly, and had suffered so much for a cause, though that cause was, I believe, one of the worst for which a people ever fought, and one for which there was the least excuse. I do not question, however, the sincerity of the great mass of those who were opposed to us." General Lee symbolized Hampton's South when, dressed proudly for the surrender in a pristine uniform, he was obliged to tell General Grant "that his army was in a very bad condition for want of food, and . . . that his men had been living for some days on parched corn exclusively, and that he would have to ask . . . for rations."[29]

The North, too, had been transformed by the war, but in completely different ways from the devastated South. Grant indicated the great industrial power of the North in 1865 when he responded to Lee's request for food for his starving soldiers. "Certainly," Grant replied, before asking how many men were unsupplied. When Lee told him that about 25,000 needed rations, Grant did not hesitate. He immediately "authorized him to send his own commissary and quartermaster to Appomattox Station, two or three miles away, where he could have . . . all the provisions wanted." The northern army in 1861 would have been hard pressed to provide for an unexpected 25,000 starving men, but by 1865 it could do so automatically. The need to equip armies of hundreds of thousands of men with food, clothing, and munitions, as well as to move them from place to place and manage their warfare, shoved the North toward modern systems of capital, transportation, and industry. Critically, it also demanded a growing government.[30]

When the war began, northerners, like southerners, believed the conflict would be short and bloodless and would not demand any significant reworking of northern society. Indeed, northerners fought the war to defend their society just the way it was. Like southerners, they based their society on the Lockean and republican ideals they inherited from the founding fathers, but unlike southerners, they had come to rest their society not on slavery but on the idea that all men had the potential to become equal, independent citizens. They believed that America was a model of God's vision for mankind because its vast untouched natural resources and lack of an entrenched aristocracy would permit any individual to prosper, if only he tried.[31]

Carl Schurz staunchly believed in the North's free labor system, which was described to him before he set foot in America. On a boat entering New York harbor from Germany in September 1852, twenty-three-year-old Schurz asked a fellow passenger about the people who lived in the fine country homes he saw on Staten Island. They were "Rich New Yorkers," said he," Schurz recorded, "'who ha[ve] something like $150,000 or $200,000 or an assured income of $10,000 or $12,000. . . . Of course, there are men who have more than that—as much as a million or two, or even more . . . not many; perhaps a dozen. But the number of people who might be called "well to do" is large.' 'And are there many poor people in New York?" Schurz asked. "Yes, some, mostly newcomers, I think. But what is called poverty here would, in many cases, hardly be called poverty in London or Paris. There are scarcely any hopelessly poor here. It is generally thought here that nobody need be poor.'"[32]

The North to which Schurz came was largely rural and agricultural. In 1860, New York City was the only city in the country with more than a million people; Philadelphia had about a half a million; Baltimore and Boston around 200,000. In this period before steel frame construction or elevators, there were no high skylines. Travel depended not on cars or buses but on feet, boats, horses, and railroads, so cities were compact, without urban sprawl. Most people lived in the country, making a living from the land or the sea. Just by applying his labor to natural resources, a man could transform them into something useful: fields could be planted, wood and fish harvested, minerals mined. If he worked in an industry, it usually handled a natural product directly: milling lumber or weaving cloth. That labor created value from natural resources seemed obvious. God had given man land to farm and nature to harvest; this was the primary stage of economic development. With a strong agricultural base, society could develop trade and manufacturing.[33]

As his fellow passenger had told Schurz, most members of the upwardly mobile population believed that everyone could prosper since a benevolent God had provided that a man could produce more than he required to survive. Anyone willing to work could accumulate savings and better himself. Following economist Adam Smith, they believed that workers would become employers and, in turn, hire those just starting out, who would themselves become employers one day. In this harmonious economic world, workers and employers each benefited from increased production, for if labor indeed created value, more products meant higher wages for workers and greater profits for employers. In a world of small producers, such a rosy view of the relationship between employers and their workers was not unrealistic; workers in small shops knew their employer, greeted him on the street, and could effectively protest low wages or poor conditions.[34]

Schurz's informant had been largely right. In the North's booming economy, young men could earn a living, and many did rise. Thirteen-year-old Scottish immigrant Andrew Carnegie began work in Pittsburgh, Pennsylvania, in 1848 as a bobbin boy for $1.20 a week, but he quickly moved up to bookkeeping, and then, in 1850, into a telegraph office as a messenger boy. "From the dark cellar . . . begrimed with coal dirt . . . I was lifted into paradise . . . with newspapers, pens, pencils, and sunshine," he recalled. By 1853, the "white-haired boy" was a telegraph operator and clerk for Thomas A. Scott, a leading railroad entrepreneur; by 1860, he was in charge of the Pittsburgh Division of the Pennsylvania Railroad, making $1,500 a year.[35]

Northerners believed that their free labor economy created true republican government by guaranteeing that all men could become productive members of society. As they accumulated wealth, they would be interested in the protection of property and the preservation of good government. Many northern states had property requirements for suffrage—and all had residency requirements—but theoretically, any individual could attain a position where he could meet those requirements, which generally approximated self-sufficiency. Those at the bottom of society were viewed as having no stake in its stability and could not participate in its government. The poor, the lazy, the drunkards, the dull knives in the drawer—these dregs of society would not pollute government because they could not vote. But everyone had the potential to rise and become a voting member of society.

In 1860, northerners like Schurz were afraid that their free labor model of political economy was in danger from a "Slave Power" determined to expand slavery into the territories and eventually into northern states. Having carefully observed southern congressmen in debate, Schurz had concluded that southern slave owners were deliberately trying to control the government to force the nationalization of slavery. The spread of slavery would destroy the free labor system at the base of American society by undercutting the wages of free workers until they, too, became dependent on overlords. Schurz was watching from the Senate gallery in 1854 when northern Democrats voted the party line to pass the Kansas–Nebraska Act, overturning the tradition of a free Northwest established by the Missouri Compromise in 1820. "I had seen the slave power officially represented by some of its foremost champions—overbearing, defiant, dictatorial, vehemently demanding a chance for unlimited expansion, and, to secure its own existence, threatening . . . the National Republic itself," Schurz recalled. "I had seen standing against this tremendous array of forces a small band of anti-slavery men faithfully fighting the battle of freedom and civilization. I saw the decisive contest rapidly approaching, and I felt an irresistible impulse to prepare myself for useful ness . . . in the impending crisis." Schurz became a committed Republican, organizing German–American votes for the party.[36]

When the southern army fired on Fort Sumter, Schurz packed his pistols in his suitcase and rushed to Washington, passing throngs of "young men hurrying to the nearest enlistment place, and anxious only lest there be no room left for them in the regiments hastily forming." Volunteers poured into state militias to put down the bullying southerners. So convinced were northerners that the war would end in a single battle that Union residents of Washington—including a number of congressmen—packed picnics and took carriages out to Manassas, Virginia, to watch the Battle of Bull Run in July 1861. They decamped in panic as Union soldiers bolted past them, flinging haversacks and rifles as they fled. One congressman, New York's Alfred Ely, was captured by Confederate troops and spent six uneasy months as a prisoner-of-war, his empty desk in the House chamber a pointed reminder to lawmakers that the war would not be easy. Ultimately, fighting it would transform the Union.[37]

In 1861, the national government was small, but it was large enough to handle its few responsibilities. On a visit to Washington, D.C., in 1852, Schurz thought the town was "dismal." The Capitol was under construction, "the departments of State, of War, and of the Navy were quartered in small very insignificant-looking houses which might have been the dwellings of some well-to-do shopkeepers who did not care for show." Goosecreek Brook crossed Pennsylvania Avenue and was spanned only by a wooden bridge, which "fuddled" congressmen sometimes missed at night, falling into the water "to be fished out with difficulty." Cows, pigs, geese, and chickens strayed in the dirty streets; mosquitoes, cockroaches, bed bugs, and lice plagued inhabitants. The city had "a slouchy, unenterprising, unprogressive appearance." The government did little. It collected tariffs, handled land sales, managed the postal service, and maintained a small army on the western border. Few Americans had any contact with the national government. It was a distant enterprise that had little influence in daily affairs.[38]

As soon as the war broke out, the government exercised dramatic new powers to maintain the nation's integrity. Immediately, Washington became the center of the war effort, and people reoriented their thinking about the government as their sons, brothers, and husbands camped in the unfinished Capitol, guarded the heights above the city, or languished in hospital wards. Visiting from Boston at the end of 1861, forty-two-year-old mother and poet Julia Ward Howe sat at the window of her Washington hotel room and wrote of what she had seen on the previous day's tour of the army encampments around the city. "Mine eyes have seen the glory of the coming of the Lord," she wrote.

He is trampling out the vintage where the grapes of wrath are stored;
He hath loosed the fateful lightning of His terrible swift sword:
His truth is marching on.

She looked out into the darkness of the early dawn to see the flickering campfires of the troops bivouacked in sweeping circles around the city.

I have seen Him in the watch-fires of a hundred circling camps
They have builded Him an altar in the evening dews and damps
I can read His righteous sentence by the dim and flaring lamps
His day is marching on.

The *Atlantic Monthly* printed Howe's "Battle Hymn of the Republic" on its cover in February 1862. The popular battle song became a justification for the war. It also illustrated just how profoundly the struggle was strengthening the national government.[39]

The changes began as Lincoln called the Thirty-Seventh Congress into emergency session in July 1861. The Union could not fight the war without money, and Congress set out to find it. The legislators turned first to taxes and tariffs, traditional sources of income that would be the backbone of revenue throughout the war. Beginning with modest levies on coffee, tea, and sugar, Congress by 1865 had instituted a sweeping system of internal revenue that included not only taxes on manufactured goods that amounted to 5 percent of a product's value, but also a novel income tax, graduated at levels of 5 percent for incomes from $600 to $5,000, 7.5 percent for incomes from $5,000 to $10,000, and 10 percent for incomes over $10,000. By 1865, the federal government had raised more than $200 million from taxation.[40]

To make up the difference between income and the huge expenses of the war, Congress also floated a series of war bonds that eventually amounted to about $2.5 billion. People from cities to tiny hamlets bought these bonds. To facilitate their sale—and commerce in general in the Union—Congress developed a new national financial system based on two kinds of paper currency. Before the war, there was no national American money; state banks, operating under state charters, issued their own notoriously volatile currency backed by their own capital (or lack of it). New national currency, called "greenbacks" because the back was printed with green ink, was secured only by the promise that the government guaranteed their value. "National bank notes" were issued by a new system of national banks and were secured by national bonds, purchased with the banks' capital. Unlike greenbacks, national bank notes were ultimately backed with gold.[41]

The search for revenue for a war that came to cost more than a million dollars a day prompted Congress to pass legislation to develop the economy, believing that the greater production became, the more tax revenue would pour into the Treasury. To develop agriculture, which Republicans believed was the prime factor in economic growth, in 1862 Congress passed the Homestead Act, which provided 160 acres of land to anyone who would farm it, and the Land-Grant College Act, which created agricultural colleges designed to teach young farmers of middling prosperity to produce better crops. Farming land was no good without a way to reach it. In 1862 and 1864 Congress passed legislation chartering the Pacific Railroad to connect the East and West coasts by rail and provide branch roads into the farming regions of the plains and the mining regions of the mountains. This railroad would also connect the American East to the Pacific, opening up the huge markets of China and the Orient. Offering entrepreneurs free western land to sell for revenue and government securities to finance the railroad's construction, the act worked. So did the Homestead Act. Western fields produced so much grain that the Union actually exported grain during the war, sending it to Europeans plagued by repeated crop failures.[42]

Republicans in Congress also used tariffs—essentially taxes on imported products—in a new way to nurture the entire economy. Tariffs had traditionally been placed only on certain imports to protect fledgling American manufacturing. Farmers and workers forced to buy more expensive products hated tariffs, though, and by the time of the Civil War, their pressure had prevailed over manufacturers. By July 1861, the nation's lowest tariff ever protected only a few favored industries while it encouraged dependence on imports. During the war, Republicans broke away from the old justification for tariffs, insisting that general protection from foreign competition of all kinds would help develop the entire economy. By 1865, a sweeping new system placed tariff rates of an average of 47 percent on agricultural and manufactured goods to encourage American economic development. With European vacillation about the Union cause, it became, Andrew Carnegie recalled, "a patriotic duty to develop vital resources."[43]

During the war, the Republican Congress created an army and navy of more than a million men, invented national taxation and national money, distributed land to settlers and state governments for colleges, and protected American production. The government's increasing activity meant that government positions multiplied dramatically. By spring 1865, the Union army had more than a million men on the rolls, the navy more than 50,000. The military grew new departments and desk workers, and the civilian branches of government also flourished. Although tax collectors were perhaps the most visible government workers once Congress established the Bureau of Internal Revenue in 1862, civilians throughout the Union worked to maintain the war effort. When the fighting broke out Andrew Carnegie's boss Thomas A. Scott had been made assistant secretary of war in charge of transportation, and he called young Carnegie to Washington to help organize telegraph communications, a task that took eight months of such intense work that Carnegie's health broke down. Women, too, began to work directly for the government, as "government girls" kept records and cut the sheets of newly printed money into individual bills.[44]

The war fed the northern economy. Just as congressmen had hoped, farming boomed during the war as the productive western wheat farms of men like John Muir's father, a Scottish immigrant, fed both the troops and Europe. Industry made even more dramatic strides. "During the Civil War the price of iron went up to something like $130 a ton," Carnegie recalled, but manufacturers could not deliver their goods because "the railway lines . . . were fast becoming dangerous for want of new rails," and the tendency of wooden bridges to catch fire from the locomotive engine sparks meant that railroads were often shut down for weeks for repair. In 1862, Carnegie decided to launch a venture to build railroad bridges with iron. Two years later, he organized a rail-making company in Pittsburgh, Pennsylvania, financing the construction of the mill with a million dollars in cash and dividends from oil wells he bought in the newly discovered Pennsylvania oil fields. By 1865, Carnegie was a wealthy man.[45]

Entrepreneurs like Carnegie flourished during the war, fattening on government contracts and a general business boom that made the North bustle. In 1865, *Harper's Weekly* touted New York's "busy streets . . . the long ranges of stately houses radiating from Madison Square . . . [and its] nearly a million of people, who are remarkably comfortable." Although never in the wealthiest tier of society, Julia Ward Howe belonged to one of these comfortable families. While southerners were making due with fat pork and cornmeal, Howe recorded in her diary a "receipt"—as recipes were called then—for a luxurious plum pudding made with "layers of crackers and raisins, till the dish is nearly full, sweeten[ed] . . . milk with molasses . . . [and] five eggs."[46]

Wartime prosperity did not reach everyone. Working on Carnegie's shop floors stoking the brutally hot furnaces were hundreds of unskilled immigrants, hired for low wages and fired at will. Trapped in exhausting factory jobs and paid so little that it took a number of wage earners to support a family, unskilled workers often lived in squalor. Arriving from England during the war, thirteen-year-old Samuel Gompers worked making cigars in a New York City tenement between a slaughterhouse and a "dreadful" brewery. "All day long we could see the animals being driven into the slaughter-pens and could hear the turmoil and cries. . . . The neighborhood was filled with the penetrating, sickening odor. The suffering of the animals and the nauseating odor made it physically impossible for me to eat meat . . . [until] we had moved to another neighborhood," he recalled. In April 1865, *Harper's Weekly* reported that "78,000 [New Yorkers] live in damp, dark, dreary cellars, often under water, close to the most loathsome sinks, overcrowded, and reeking with filth and mortal disease. There is never sound health in them, and the sickness-rate ranges from 75 to 90 per cent. . . . Every hideous form of misery and vice, hunger, murder, lust, and despair, are found in every corner. There is nothing that makes human nature repulsive or human life intolerable that does not abound in . . . tenant-houses."[47]

Gompers and his fellow workers watched wartime inflation drain wages paid in greenbacks even as Carnegie's purse grew fatter on the need for wartime transportation and as financiers bought government bonds whose interest was paid in rock-solid gold. Since the early nineteenth century, some labor leaders had rejected the free labor ideal, insisting instead that class interests in society inevitably led to conflict. Following David Ricardo and Thomas Malthus rather than Adam Smith, they argued that America was no different from England or other industrialized nations and that the condition of workers in America would gradually decline, wealth would become polarized, and economic classes would clash. They launched fledgling labor organizations decades before the Civil War, but these did not flourish in wartime. It was hard for workers to combine to demand higher wages during a war for the very existence of the nation. Irish-American worker Terence V. Powderly recalled the resolution of a union whose entire membership enlisted in the army when the war broke out: "It having been resolved to enlist with Uncle Sam for the war, this union stands adjourned until either the Union is safe, or we are whipped." The drain of men to the battlefields meant that employment was high and few laborers were interested in activism. Those who did agitate were accused of disloyalty, and unscrupulous employers in places like the Pennsylvania coal mines justified their repression of striking laborers by accusing strikers of trying to injure the northern war effort. [48]

By 1865, the government's active promotion of economic development, its new financial instruments, and its growing role as an employer gave northerners a personal stake in the national government. By 1865, income taxes and national sales taxes literally made every northerner a Union supporter, while the new money and bonds spreading across the Union gave northerners a financial stake in the nation's survival. At the same time, the tariffs, the Homestead Act, the Land-Grant College Act, and the Pacific Railroad Act convinced individuals that the government was working directly for their benefit. More and more people looked to the government for a living, cementing their loyalty to the Union and becoming dependent on tax dollars for their livelihood. By the end of the war, northerners had died for their government, sacrificed for it, benefited from it, and had its money in their pockets. The government belonged, literally, to the people.

It was not just white men who owned the government, either; bankers had worked to make sure women felt comfortable buying bonds. Women's work itself became politicized as women worked so that husbands and sons could fight for the Union. As they supported their families, raised money for troops, picked lint for bandages, and nursed the wounded, northern women abandoned their reserved antebellum lives. Julia Ward Howe wrote that they learned to listen to "the still, small voice" inside themselves. "Met . . . Mrs. Peterson," recorded Howe in her 1864 diary, "and arranged to read at her home, for [a soldiers' aid society], if possible, otherwise, for my usual motive, to say my word as well as I can, and as often as circumstances call for it." "Life to me now means work of my best sort," Howe wrote that year, "and I value little else, except the comfort of my family." Women's new activism was not unchallenged, and some chafed under traditional norms. "Began today my essay on sex, which may run into a treatise on limitation," Howe wrote sadly in 1864, "as the two subjects run together in my mind."[49]

Black Unionists had at least as strong a relationship with the government as northern whites, for its boon to them and their sacrifice for it were both enormous. The national government took in southern African Americans first as "contrabands of war," confiscated to prevent their use in the Confederate army and then, after the Emancipation Proclamation of January 1, 1863, as free people. It provided rations and medical care to the refugees both in wartime contraband camps and in southern towns and cities occupied by the Union. In 1865, it declared the federal government would overrule state laws sanctioning slavery and with the Thirteenth Amendment guaranteed freedom to black slaves. Black Americans were not passive recipients of this government concern. Their sacrifices for the nation were those of people determined to earn their right to the nation's gratitude. Black southerners spied for the Union and obstructed southern war efforts, and those who stole north fed the Union's economy. One hundred and eighty thousand black soldiers fought for the Union's existence and their own liberty; at the battle of Fort Wagner, South Carolina, fully one-half of the black troops fell. African Americans had a special relationship with the federal government; while they could not look to states for protection, the federal government stood in their behalf.

Not all northerners approved of the new power of the federal government. True to their political heritage, northern Democrats feared the growth of the national government and, throughout the war, protested every piece of legislation that strengthened it. Ohio Congressman Samuel S. Cox, known as "Sunset," led the struggle of the Democrats against the Republicans' program. Conservative northern Democrats had joined with the Union to defend the integrity of the nation but had no interest in black rights. Many did not even oppose slavery; after the war, they continued to believe that African Americans were unfit for freedom and would either die out or rely on charity to survive. Northern Democrats were racists, but they were also passionately concerned with keeping the American government small to preserve the republic. They watched the expansion of government power under the Republicans with horror. Sharing many of the opinions of his fellow Democrats in the South, Cox charged that Massachusetts abolitionists had "wormed themselves and their plots into national affairs . . . to incite the conflicts and fan the flames of passion," in order to gain control of the national government. Lincoln was a tyrant, Cox insisted, suppressing dissent and attacking civil liberties as he permitted the arrest of key Democrats opposed to the war. Taxes, Cox fumed, were designed to funnel the meager earnings of working people into the pockets of Republican hangers-on, who filled the new government positions in return for supporting Republican leaders. Cold-blooded Republican politicians controlled the growing government in favor of the wealthy at the expense of the American workingman. To racist Democrats, utterly convinced that America was a "white man's government," emancipation and the arming of black soldiers proved dramatically that the Republicans were deliberately destroying the nation's political system to keep themselves in power.[50]

Democrats' dislike of the growing government was compounded by the nineteenth-century system of filling government offices. Known as the "spoils system"—for to the victors go the spoils—it allowed successful politicians to award government positions to their political supporters. This created a mutual dependency between politicians and the men who held jobs as government ministers, petty clerks, or day laborers digging a ditch for the road in front of a new county courthouse. In exchange for political support, a ward boss dispensed patronage to his constituents, a state leader provided support for local bosses, and the president cultivated state leaders. Failure to provide patronage meant a lost election. In exchange for patronage, a government worker owed his superior both his vote and a prescribed financial contribution to his party's election war chest. Failure to provide either meant a lost job. Under this system, Democrats watching the Republican-controlled government expand to provide large numbers of new jobs could not hope that any of those new jobs would go to Democrats. For them, the growth of government meant a huge boost for the political fortunes of their opponents. Indeed, it might even spell the death of the Democratic Party, as government largesse fed only Republicans. Under these circumstances, the founding fathers' warnings about big government took on apocalyptic meaning. For Democrats, the large government of the war years meant that the republic of the founding fathers, that of independent self-sufficient men voting for the good of all, was being eclipsed by a system in which increasing numbers of voters were dependent on politicians.

Northern Democratic opposition to Republican government did not prevent a Union triumph, and on April 10, 1865, Julia Ward Howe could record in her diary that she spent forty cents on "Ribbons for Victory." Northerners, for whom the triumph of victory was tempered with sadness for missing sons and brothers, comforted themselves with the belief that their loved ones died to establish an American republic based on the ideal of free labor. Their blood had been poured upon the altar of freedom, expiating the nation's guilty sin of slavery and permitting the nation to move forward as God's land, with freedom and prosperity for all. Truly, now, America could be an example to the rest of the world of the best possible human government. On May 23, 1865, the Union armies paraded through Washington, D.C., and although Schurz had resigned his commission, he rushed to the city nonetheless, proud to have served with "those valiant hosts swinging in broad-fronted column down Pennsylvania Avenue . . .—the men nothing but bone and muscle and skin— their tattered battle-flags fluttering victoriously over their heads in the full pride of achievement." But, true to his free labor principles, he reflected that "a spectacle far grander and more splendid" was the "transformation of a million soldiers into a million citizen-workers." He rejoiced that "every man that had wielded the sword or the musket or served the cannon in terrible conflict" was now "going home to his plow, or his anvil, or his loom, or his counting-room, as a peaceable citizen." Each northerner now had a personal stake in the free labor nation, having poured out blood and treasure for it.[51]

But in 1865, it was unclear exactly what a free labor nation was.

What was clear was that a free labor nation would include the West. It had been the spread of slavery into the western territories that had finally sparked the sectional conflict, and westward expansion continued during the war. Land was critically important to nineteenth-century Americans. As one woman recalled: "The land was a passion, magical in its influence upon human life. It produced people; nothing else at all, except trees and flowers and vegetable harvests. Life ran back and forth, land into people and people into land, until both were the same." The West seemed to offer exciting amounts of this precious resource. For northerners land meant the chance for economic mobility, resources to exploit, and a safety valve to relieve the pressures of cities. Always with an eye to finding good farms, northern soldiers looked with enthusiasm on the regions through which they marched.

Western land spelled riches to northerners, and they used it during the war to finance both colleges and railroads. To southern whites, land meant wealth and social status. It produced cotton and rice to fund white lifestyles, and it was the visible sign of an affluence that determined social and political power. For ex-slaves, a lifetime toiling yielded a connection to the land that had less to do with slavery than with sweat and blood and familiarity.[52]

When the war broke out, organized American settlement stretched only to Missouri, Iowa, Minnesota, Arkansas, and Texas before jumping across the Great Plains, the Rocky Mountains, and the Sierra Nevada Mountains to California and Oregon. During the war, both northerners and southerners looked to the West to bring money into their cash-starved treasuries. The South concentrated on pushing west into California, where gold mines offered quick money. Northerners looked to the established mines of California and to other western lands that congressmen eager for northern expansion quickly brought under the mantle of the Union. Colorado, which produced as much as $5 million in gold by 1860, was organized as a Territory in 1861. Nevada, also organized as a Territory in 1861, was where the legendary Comstock Lode of silver came to light right before the war, creating a mining rush that built the legendary Virginia City. In 1864, the year the state was admitted to the Union, it yielded $30 million in ore. Montana was "a trackless wilderness" until 1861, but it was organized as a Territory in 1864 after miners pulled gold out of Grasshopper Creek in July 1862. Montana was taken from Idaho, where gold was found in the Snake River Valley, and which was organized into a Territory in March 1863. Idaho yielded gold, too, and in 1864, an Idaho judge circulated an $800 gold nugget on the floor of Congress. New Mexico Territory was "rich in gold, silver, and copper" as well as anthracite coal. Its neighbor Arizona—organized as a Territory in 1863—contained "mines of precious metals unsurpassed in richness, number, and extent by any in the world," according to Brigadier General James H. Carleton, the army officer in charge of the area. At the end of the war, humorist Artemus Ward poked fun at the American fascination with the mineral-rich mountains, telling a British audience that "they are regarded as a great success and we all love to talk about them."[53]

Northerners also saw the West as a land rich for farmers. Word traveled that the fertile lands of the new state of Oregon—admitted to the Union in 1859, right before the war—produced "wheat, oats, barley, potatoes, and domestic animals" and excellent fruit. Nearby, Washington Territory had "exceedingly fertile" soil, producing the same crops its southern neighbor did.

The Territory of Nebraska had "quick and lively" soil, "producing Indian corn, wheat, oats, hemp, tobacco, and sorghum. Vegetables of all kinds thrive well, and it produces fine grapes." It also was prime grazing land. Dakota Territory, organized in 1861, promised great agriculture, too, although in 1865 there was little information coming from the 9,000 white Americans who had settled there.[54]

For northerners and southerners of all races, western lands were irresistible. Southerners had begun to press west into Texas in the 1820s, opening up the rich cotton lands in the eastern part of the state. In 1836, they had wrested Texas away from Mexico, established the Lone Star Republic, and applied for annexation to the United States, an application granted with state admission in 1845. Cotton farmers had begun American emigration to Texas, but cotton could not expand into the area that stretched between the southernmost point of Texas north to Canada—roughly along the ninety-eighth meridian—and the Rocky Mountains. This region of the country, known as the Great Plains, was generally treeless and flat and had less rainfall than the East. It stretched unbroken from Mexico to the Arctic Circle, making it a natural corridor for wind and for the storms that could sweep through the plains with withering heat in the summer and ferocious blizzards in the winter.[55]

Although it wasn't much good for cotton, this land was ideal for grazing animals. In 1866, the important southern magazine *De Bow's Review* rhapsodized that the land was "beautiful and rich beyond description, and watered by numerous streams flowing into the Rio Grande on both sides. On these streams are many fine mill sites, with excellent water-power. Large droves of wild horses, herds of thousands of black-tailed deer roam over the country. Game of nearly all kinds is abundant." It boasted of the country's grasses, which could support "any given number of cattle, sheep and goats. From the mildness of the climate, sheep, in this region . . . require no sheds during the winter months, as they can graze the entire year." Herds of the American bison—called "buffalo" but quite unlike the huge domesticated Asian water buffalo or fierce African Cape buffalo that define that species—roamed the prairies that bloomed with coneflowers, violets, and prairie grasses that needed little water.[56]

With its grasslands and low rainfall, Texas was ideal for cattle and horses, and by the time the Civil War broke out, the state was developing a valuable cattle industry. When the Union navy took the Mississippi River in 1863, it separated the Texas longhorn cattle range from southeastern markets. Over-worked southern railroads quickly deteriorated during the war, and they could not move the cattle east. Penned up in Texas, feral cattle multiplied until observers estimated there were eight cattle for every one person in Texas. By 1865, Texas cattlemen offered cattle to the Confederate military for free, if only the government would transport them. But it could not, and southern troops eked by on parched corn while cattle ran wild in Texas.[57]

In his later years, Charles Goodnight was proud that his history reflected that of the state. A handsome man with piercing eyes, a long face, a moustache and chin whiskers when he was grown, Goodnight was a ten-year-old boy when his family had moved to Texas in 1846. He spent some time as a young man overseeing slaves on nearby farms but recognized that the future lay in cattle. By 1856, Goodnight and his stepbrother were tending a herd of four hundred Texas longhorn cattle in exchange for 10 percent of the calves dropped. Goodnight left his growing business on the Texas frontier to fight with the Texas Rangers in the Civil War. As a member of the Frontier Regiment of the Confederate forces, he battled Indians and white bandits on the Texas border and on the plains, mastering the wilderness skills he had first picked up as a boy on the Texas frontier and honed while looking after his herd. Goodnight left the Confederate service in 1864 and went back home to Palo Pinto County, where he tried to rebuild the business the war had destroyed. "I suffered great losses," Goodnight lamented. "The confederate [sic] authorities had taken many of them without paying a cent. Indians had raided our herds and cattle thieves were branding them, to their own benefit without regard to our rights."[58]

Easterners saw the West as a land of plenty, but men like Goodnight knew it would not be theirs without a struggle. The plains were held by powerful Indian tribes whose enormous skill at warfare meant they could hold their land against unwelcome intruders. Spanish explorers had brought the horse to Plains tribes at what is now the Mexican border around 1700; by the time of the American Revolution horses had spread north to the Sarsi tribes in what is now Montana. The acquisition of horses made the previously poor plains tribes wealthy, for they became inspired buffalo hunters. It also made them deadly enemies, for skills from the buffalo hunt transferred easily to warfare. A Comanche warrior could ride into battle by hooking a heel over a horse's neck, keeping the animal between himself and the enemy, shooting arrows from under its neck, and spinning away before an opponent could find a target. While white fighters were still tied to the musket, which took at least thirty seconds to load and was notoriously inaccurate, a Comanche brave could keep arrows in the air continuously—all sharp as scalpels—and shoot them with such force that they could go through a buffalo. Tribes like the Sioux and the Comanche, nomadic bands loosely connected by kinship, culture, and interest, held their land in an iron grip. By the 1850s, the Sioux and their allies the Arapaho and Cheyenne held the northern plains, while the Apache and Comanche tribes pushed constantly against their neighbors in the Southwest. As the powerful Sioux and Cheyenne spread southward and the Apache and Comanche spread northward toward overlapping territories in what is now Kansas, the tribes they overran—the Crow, for example, and the Pawnees—turned to white Americans as allies to hold off Indian intruders.[59]

One of Charles Goodnight's Comanche enemies in 1865 was Quanah, a famous warrior and brilliant fighter, still celebrated in popular lore for never losing a battle to the white man. The relationship of these two men symbolized the mixed history of warfare, cooperation, and cultural exchange between western Indians and eastern interlopers. Quanah's mother, the famous white Comanche Naudah (Someone Found), was born Cynthia Ann Parker, captured as a child, and adopted into the Comanche tribe. The wife of Nocona Comanche war chief Peta Nocona, with whom she had two sons and a daughter, Naudah gave her entire allegiance to her tribe. In 1861, Texas Rangers—including Charles Goodnight—attacked a Comanche encampment on the Pease River, recaptured Naudah and her infant daughter, held them as prisoners, and returned them to Naudah's white uncle. Held against her will by her white relatives, Naudah and her baby died, while Quanah, who was probably about nine years old, moved deeper into Comancheria, the "Staked Plains," that encompassed 250,000 square miles of plains and mountains in what are now the Texas and Oklahoma panhandles. Attaching himself to the Quahadi (Antelope) band of Comanches, Quanah was orphaned in his early teens and had to scrounge for food and clothing with his brother.[60]

Prewar skirmishes between border whites and Plains Indians had given way to full-scale war in the 1860s. In the Southwest, the Texas Rangers pushed south and west against Mexicans and Indians as the Comanches and their allies on the southern plains took advantage of the relative weakness of the Confederacy and the Union in the West to raid the wagon trains on the Santa Fe Trail that stretched from Missouri to Sante Fe, New Mexico. In 1864, the southern plains burst into full-blown war as wartime mining strikes made whites pour into Indian lands. On November 24, 1864, Union forces led by famous frontiersman Kit Carson attacked a Kiowa-Apache village on the Canadian River in the Texas panhandle. The Kiowas and Apaches retreated to "Adobe Walls," an abandoned trading post, where Kiowa and Comanche reinforcements met them. Carson claimed victory in the smoky confusion that followed as each side set fire to the grass and tried to ambush the other in the haze, but Comanches boasted that only Carson's howitzers saved his command.[61]

The violence on the northern plains was even worse. In 1855, a young American lieutenant sparked war with the Sioux when he killed a chief in retaliation for Indian butchery of a stray cow; the Cheyennes, Sioux allies, entered the war in 1857. This conflict simmered during the first years of the Civil War. Then, in 1862, starving Santee Sioux in Minnesota launched an attack on white settlements when an Indian agent refused to give them provisions they had been promised. The U.S. Army pushed into the plains to retaliate for the Santee Rebellion, enflaming the Sioux War and engaging thirty-three-year-old Hunkpapa Lakota Sioux Sitting Bull in 1863 in his first battle with American soldiers. Then, as the Union army drained troops to the eastern battlefronts at the same time that Indian raiding against emigrants increased, new white settlers in the western territories panicked. By 1864, the governor of Colorado Territory determined to strike decisively against the Indians he believed were retarding the development of Colorado and whom he feared would attack as soon as more troops left. He ordered an overeager colonel of the Colorado militia to attack a surrendering party of Cheyennes camped by federal order at Sand Creek, Colorado. On November 29, 1864, 700 drunken militiamen brutally slaughtered and then mutilated the bodies of 105 Cheyenne women and children and the 28 men who had not gone hunting with the rest of the braves. By early 1865, Sioux, Cheyenne, and Arapaho bands had avenged the Sand Creek Massacre by burning homes and stage stations and killing whites along the South Platte River.[62]

Americans wanted Indians out of their way, but it was not clear how that should be accomplished. Westerners hated the Indians and wanted them destroyed. In April 1865, under the headline "THE INDIANS MUST BE EXTERMINATED," the Nevada *Daily Territorial Enterprise* declared: "The prosperity of the State can not be retarded by these 'plumed riders of the desert.' They have thrown themselves in front of the advancing giant, and must be hurled from his path or crushed. They must be followed with fire and sword, until they are thoroughly convinced of the danger as well as the futility of making war upon the whites." Easterners, in contrast, were horrified by events like the Sand Creek Massacre. Congressmen demanded an investigation of "the condition of the Indian tribes and their treatment by the civil and military authorities of the United States." Popular anger was directed at the Indian agency system, whose infamous corruption seemed to inflame Indian troubles. Under this system, Indian agents appointed by the president were charged with caring for a tribe by spending its government allotment on the tribe's behalf. Indian agents were supposed to use these federal monies to buy needed supplies for their charges, and they had unchallenged authority to disburse the monies as they saw fit. But Indian agents were political hacks notorious for using tribal allotments to fund inflated contracts awarded to friends. Destitute tribes had little recourse when the agents charged with their care stole their money.[63]

After the Civil War, the West seemed to be a region of inexhaustible resources, where labor could easily realize profit from nature as soon as resistant Native Americans could be overcome. With the backing of western resources and the nationalization of the free labor ideal, a growing cadre of northern farmers, laborers, mid-level businessmen, and government officials (joined by some southern Americans who hoped to make the best of the postwar economy) were determined to make America the greatest nation on earth. "The powers of Europe may now recognize in the United States a colossal rival," wrote an optimistic New Southerner, "vast in territory, in population, and in ambition; enured to arms and to industry; a nation of soldiers, sailors, and workmen, ready for the sword or the scythe, fearing nothing which the world can offer in competition or in conflict." And what could stand in the way of such might? "The monarchies of Europe combined would present but a feeble barrier to the future advance of this now giant power!"[64]

With Lee's surrender, it seemed that America was on its way to fulfilling that promise. After leaving Appomattox Station, U. S. Grant went directly back to Washington with some of his staff to rearrange his armies and prepare for peace. By April 14, he was well enough through his work to visit his children at their school in New Jersey. Eager to see them and anxious to avoid the temperamental Mary Lincoln, Grant and his wife declined the invitation of President and Mrs. Lincoln to join them at Ford's Theater that night to see a production of *Our American Cousin.* Grant, the Union's great general, missed the terrible final blow of the war.

John Wilkes Booth's bullets exacerbated rifts not only between the North and South, but also between those who held different visions of the national government. "Sic Semper Tyrannus," Booth reportedly declared after he pulled the trigger; "Thus Always Tyrants"—Virginia's state motto as well as a reference to Brutus's assassination of Caesar after he had turned the Roman republic into a dictatorship. In contrast, the Republican *Harper's Weekly* blamed northern Democrats for inspiring Booth with their constant harping against the new powers of the national government. "Mr. Lincoln . . . has been denounced as a despot, as a usurper, as a man who arbitrarily annulled the Constitution, as a magistrate under whose administration all the securities of liberty, property, and even life, were deliberately disregarded and imperiled. . . . If there was a military despotism in this country, as was declared, he was the despot. If there were a tyranny, he was the tyrant. Is it surprising that somebody should have believed all this, that somebody should have said, if there is a tyranny it can not be very criminal to slay the tyrant?"[65]

Sorrowing over Lincoln's death, Grant succinctly summed up its terrible meaning for the nation's future. "I knew his goodness of heart, his generosity, his yielding disposition, his desire to have everybody happy, and above all his desire to see all the people of the United States enter again upon the full privileges of citizenship with equality among all. . . . I felt that reconstruction had been set back, no telling how far."[66]

CHAPTER TWO

1865–1867

The Future of Free Labor

The Union victory in the Civil War meant the nationalization of northerners' free labor worldview, but no one knew quite how to translate the northern ideal of free labor into a working economic and political reality. For Nat Love, working tobacco for his master in Tennessee, the end of the war didn't actually change much. "In common with other masters of those days," Love recalled, his master "did not tell us we were free. And instead of letting us go he made us work for him the same as before, but in all other respects he was kind. He moved our log cabin on a piece of ground on a hill owned by him, and in most respects things went on the same as before the war." Union soldiers were the first to try to explain to slaves like Love what free labor meant. They reduced freedom to the terms that mattered in the immediate postwar South. "You are now free," one soldier explained in 1865 to a group of former slaves, "but you must know that the only difference you can feel yet, between slavery and freedom, is that neither you nor your children can be bought or sold." "Shooting and whipping are done with," added another soldier. To these immediate concerns army officers and Republican politicians added the other important factor that lay at the heart of their free labor vision. "All you can earn is your own, you have the . . . right to be as rich as you can make yourselves by your own energy, industry, and economy."[1]

How could the South best be reconstructed into a free labor society? The answer to this question would depend on an even more fundamental one: Who should decide how to rebuild the South? In a republic, voters should elect representatives to handle this difficult question, of course, but who should be able to vote in the postwar nation? There was a vast difference between the American ideal of sober, thoughtful, and independent voters and the reality of elections. Voting in America had traditionally been a rough-and-tumble business, a man's affair where voters were often influenced by whiskey; polls were frequently in saloons. Individuals literally voted "the ticket," a ballot with the party's nominees printed on it and handed as a whole to an election official. The party organizations printed these ballots, often color-coding them both to guarantee that their semi-literate voters would not be duped into voting the wrong ticket and to be able to keep renegades from switching parties. There was no need for voters to check off specific individuals, and "splitting the ticket"—voting for some of a party's candidates but not others—was impossible. As a young girl in Minnesota on election days, Luna Kellie saw "drunken men going by whipping their horses and swearing as they never did any other day. And we children were not allowed to go downtown that day as there were [sic] so much danger of fights and drunken men driving teams and having runaways etc." Under what circumstances could this system create a vibrant, free labor American republic? Should everyone have a voice in government, or should the vote be limited by loyalty, wealth, race, or gender? These questions were not academic when, for the first time in American history, the use of millions of tax dollars and a newly strong national government were at the disposal of American voters. The question of the reconstruction of the nation was inseparable from the question of postwar suffrage.²

Southern white Democrats had very clear ideas about who should have a say in policy, ideas based on their prewar notions about the necessary hierarchy in a republican society and the need to limit government—especially the hated Yankee government—to protect white liberty and property. The man in charge of establishing free labor in the South, President Andrew Johnson, was keenly aware that the question of southern reconstruction would directly affect the American system of government; indeed, he was almost obsessed with this aspect of the problem. Historians still speculate about how Abraham Lincoln might have applied the principles of free labor, in which he believed so wholeheartedly, to the South after the war, but ultimately we can only wonder. The reality was that the mantle of the presidency had fallen on Johnson, a war Democrat from Tennessee whom Lincoln had brought onto the presidential ticket in 1864 to attract moderate Democrats to the standard of a new, national, Union party. Johnson staunchly believed in free labor, but as a racist absolutely committed to the idea of limited government, he had a vision of a new postwar society that differed dramatically from that of Republicans. Johnson had begun his fortunes as a tailor in Tennessee and had great affection for struggling white men who were trying to succeed, but he did not trust wealthy white southerners, African Americans, or Republicans. As the editor of *De Bow's Review*, published in New Orleans, reflected, Johnson was a Union man but a southerner at heart, and he "was indoctrinated in those political ideas that recognized, in a very liberal degree, the rights of the States; and did not, therefore, look with favor upon the Federal Government absorbing all the powers and privileges which, from the foundation of the republic, had been conceded to the States." True to his Democratic principles, Johnson believed that wartime Republicans had deliberately increased the power of the national government to cement their hold on it.[3]

For the first eight months after Appomattox, Johnson had a free hand in designing a plan for what he called "restoration" of the southern states to the Union. In that time, he worked hard to restore the prewar nation with changes that he believed would prevent southern aristocratic slaveholders from ever again breaking it up. The Thirty-eighth Congress had adjourned in March, shortly before Lincoln's death, and the Thirty-ninth Congress was not scheduled to reconvene until December. Johnson could have called it into special session if he wished—as Lincoln had called the Thirty-seventh Congress into special session during the crisis summer of 1861—but he declined to do this. He held tight to the belief that the South had been dragged out of the Union by a few hotheaded slaveholders and that, once the rebellion of men like Wade Hampton had been quenched, the loyal South could resume its former relation to the Union. Worried about the great powers Congress had assumed during the war, he was anxious to thwart what he considered the Republicans' revolutionary radicalism by returning small government Democrats to Congress as quickly as possible. He also knew that, as a Union Democrat from a seceding state, elevated to the presidency by an assassin's bullet, his political future was bleak unless he could steer a course between the northern Republican radicals like Carl Schurz, who wanted the government to guarantee black rights, and the radical white southern Democrats like Hampton, who wanted to revive the prewar southern way of life. If he could draw moderates of both sections to his standard by promising to create a postwar America of free labor opportunity for whites, overseen by a limited government, he could create a new, national, free labor party, much as Lincoln had wanted to (although on different terms than Lincoln's). He would have successfully restored the nation by steering between the two sets of extremists on whom many blamed the war and at the same time secured his own hold on national power.[4]

Immediately upon taking office, while armies were still in the field, Johnson signaled that he meant to break the South's aristocracy. The "government . . . is strong, not only to protect, but to punish," he told an audience; "Treason . . . is the blackest of crimes." A month later, only three days after General Kirby Smith's May 26 surrender of the Trans-Mississippi Army to General Edward R. S. Canby at New Orleans, Johnson's harsh tone disappeared. He announced a moderate plan for restoration of the South, granting amnesty to all Confederates who took an oath of allegiance to the United States, except for high-ranking officers and those who owned more than $20,000 of taxable property. ("It was the wealthy men in the South who [dragged?] the people into secession. . . . If it hadn't been for the men worth more than $20,000, there would have been no war," he snarled.) Those excepted from the proclamation could apply to Johnson himself for clemency, which he promised would "be liberally extended." It was. Over the summer Johnson pardoned 100 Confederates a day, eventually pardoning 13,500 southerners out of the 15,000 who applied. He also established provisional governments for the seven states that Lincoln had not organized and told provisional governors to organize conventions to restore their states to the Union. Delegates to the conventions were to be elected by all "loyal" citizens, including all former Confederates who had taken the oath of allegiance. The conventions were asked only to recognize the abolition of slavery, nullify state ordinances of secession, and repudiate the Confederate war debt. (This last requirement would force both southern states and the former Confederacy to default on debts they had contracted during the war and, by ruining their credit, should destroy future secessionists' ability to finance another rebellion.) This meant a virtual restoration of the South's prewar society, its body politic almost unchanged except for the skimming off of a few top leaders Johnson personally distrusted.[5]

White southerners like Wade Hampton and Charley Allston greeted even these limited changes with fury. The national government's disfranchisement of the South's leaders and the emancipation of former slaves convinced them that their antebellum suspicions about northerners were right. Their "free labor system" was a plan to use an increasingly strong national government to destroy white southern liberties safeguarded before the war by southern white monopoly over government and society. No longer a proud planter whose needs determined government policy, Elizabeth Allston's brother Charley, a former member of Hampton's cavalry, was not even a citizen in 1865. Recently returned from the army, he was forced to watch his mother and sister—those elegant antebellum symbols of planter society—negotiate with angry former slaves for the return of family property. "It was a very mortifying position for a man," Elizabeth Allston recalled, "being perfectly powerless, not having taken the oath, he was not even recognized as a citizen, and had no rights and would have no support from the law." For white southerners, it seemed that the very essence of republican government had been overturned. Propertied, educated white men could not vote and had no power over their government, while the downtrodden—poor, uneducated, and black—had been turned loose to participate in society with the national government's support.[6]

White southerners faced with chaos after the war quickly tried to reestablish their antebellum vision of a republican society with the propertied elite controlling an organic community. First, they sought to regain their property. "There rose a sullen murmur from the crowd" as her mother called for the keys to the locked plantation barn full of food stores, Elizabeth Allston recalled, "and a young man who had stood a little way off, balancing a sharp stone in his hand and aiming it at mamma from time to time, now came nearer and leaned on the wheel of the carriage." Her personal acquaintance with her former slaves enabled Allston's mother to retake control of her own plantation property within a day, but when she tried to do the same thing on her son's plantation, the former slaves armed themselves with "large, sharp, gleaming rice-field hoes," pitchforks, hickory sticks, and guns and warned they would kill any white person who came in the gate. The Allstons went to soldiers for support, and the U.S. Army, desperate to restore order and production to the South, backed them up. "So when we arrived, backed by soldiers, to take from them what they had collected of our belongings, they were much taken aback, and some of them were inclined to resist. However, we gathered up enough furniture and stuff to get along comfortably," Charley Allston remembered.[7]

Once the white landowners regained possession of their lands, Charley recalled, "Then came the agreements as to planting; what portion of the crop they should have in payment of their labor, and what portion we, the owners of the land, should have; here again the military had to be called in." Short of cash for wages—Mrs. Allston owned Chicora Wood plantation "but not an animal nor farm implement, no boats nor vehicles—just the land, with its dismantled dwelling-house"—landowners expected freedpeople to work in gangs under an overseer in exchange for food and clothing, much as they had done before the war.[8]

Assuming their former roles of leadership in southern society, landowners insisted they must reestablish production to prevent starvation and to stop crime in the South. There was much logic in this argument. Their economy was in such bad shape that many southerners were in danger of starvation. The fields were gone to weeds, draft animals dead, heirloom seeds lost. The army worm—the larvae of a common gray moth that gathers now under our porch lights—was attacking crops, marching in clumps through fields, destroying everything in its path. Some farm laborers had left the countryside to go to the cities to find rations; others refused to plant and work the fields on the terms landowners offered. Crime flourished on the rural roads of the South where a steady stream of impoverished white and black travelers rubbed elbows. Former Confederate soldiers were slowly making their way back to their homes after being mustered out of service in Virginia, North Carolina, or Louisiana. They were "worn, weary, gaunt, and hungry," Elizabeth Allston recalled. "They had lived days and days and fought on a handful of parched corn. Their shoes were worn out, their uniforms ragged; only their spirit was undimmed, and that made them suffer so in the sense of failure." Impoverished white refugees were also on the roads, trying to find food and shelter. Freedpeople were there, too, looking for family lost during slavery or headed toward cities looking for work or for the rations that would sustain them while the rural countryside starved. The collisions between these angry, hungry, and despairing people visited terror on parts of the South. Although white people feared black criminals, the black population bore the brunt of the crime wave. White gangs abused and intimidated freedpeople, torturing, raping, and killing those who ran afoul of them. As late as 1867, as he walked through the South, John Muir was repeatedly warned that "there were a good many people living like wild beasts on whatever they could steal, and that murders were sometimes committed for four or five dollars, and even less."[9]

But white southerners' argument of pressing need often simply justified violence against freedpeople, brutality designed to restore the prewar system of white dominance that whites believed safeguarded America's unique republic of freedom and equality. Encouraged by Johnson's leniency and threatened both by freed slaves and by the increasing grumbling of northern Republicans unhappy with Johnson's program, white southerners began to try to reestablish the racial and political boundaries of their prewar society by intimidating the black population back into subservience. Since white southerners believed that black people would not work without compulsion, efforts to reinstate a "proper system of labor" meant beating African Americans who refused to work on white employers' terms, or even shooting recalcitrant freedmen or raping their wives or daughters as an example to others. Employers often cheated working African Americans, refusing to pay fair wages and then physically intimidating anyone who complained.[10]

Determined to control their region, most white southerners attacked national government action on behalf of the freedmen as a Republican attempt to destroy the limited government on which American republicanism depended. In March 1865, Congress created the Bureau of Refugees, Freedmen and Abandoned Lands to help ex-slaves and white refugees survive the transition to peacetime. Freedmen's Bureau agents required employers and laborers to sign written contracts that specified work to be done and wages to be paid. They mediated disputes between southern whites and freedmen, who were forbidden to testify in local courts, deciding in favor of freedmen about 68 percent of the time. Freedmen's Bureau officers also rented abandoned lands to refugees loyal to the Union—loyal southerners would almost all be black, of course—for three years, with the option to buy. White southerners opposed this attempt to bring free labor to the South, railing that government power had expanded dangerously, reaching directly into their homes and dictating their relations with their black neighbors. Refusing to acknowledge the systematic economic oppression of African Americans, a writer for De Bow's Review insisted: "There is no greater propriety for a FREEDMEN'S BUREAU, now that the war is over, than there should be for a poor man's bureau or a rich man's bureau, or any other such institution. . . . Private enterprises must be left to regulate these things. . . . Now that the negro is free, he has received enough at the hands of the nation without expense to himself. No one disputes his freedom. He has no more right to a support than has the free laborer of Maine or Iowa, nor the right to dictate the terms of his employment." Southern whites saw the Freedmen's Bureau as part of a northern plot to expand the government to create an oligarchy of party officials funded by taxpayers' money. The Freedmen's Bureau, a columnist for De Bow's Review noted, required "the comfortable sum of nearly eleven millions of dollars . . . which was about the amount of the whole national revenue some thirty or forty years ago."[11]

When northern Republicans began to talk of enfranchising loyal freedmen to offset Johnson's wholesale pardons of Confederate leaders, southern whites saw a radical plan to control government. They became convinced that radicals in Congress would try to shove black suffrage down their throats and might even confiscate their lands and redistribute them to black constituents. In August 1865, a handwritten broadside lampooning the popular black news-paper the *New Orleans Black Republican* revealed white anxieties. The vi-ciously racist "Black Republican and Office-Holder's Journal" insisted that black Americans were determined to take political office in order to confiscate the wealth of their white neighbors or, failing that, planned to beg for charity rather than work. In this plan they received support from the military and the Republican Party, which believed any lie as long as it justified crushing south-ern whites. The paper began with "loyal nominations" for office, including caricatured former slave "Caesar Guss" for president and a slate of black senators and congressmen. An "advertisement" in the paper read that "Fred-menhaus & Lee, two eminent Communists from Germany, will instruct emancipated negroes in the rights of property," while "Amor J. Tax" was one of the "eminent Abolitionists" purportedly encouraging the murder of white ex-Confederates, and "de siety for equal diwision ob property, and a law agin marriage between two pussons of de same color," would meet in Boston, "next Tuesday." "Wanted immediately," another article read, "fifty Perjurers to attend trials by military commission. None but Abolitionists or colored gentlemen need apply. As the sole object in these courts is to convict, persons of inventive genius, who have no foolish scruples about honor or principle, may be sure of constant employment and ample remuneration. Apply to WAR POWER & Co., Washington, D.C."[12]

The constitutional conventions held under Johnson's plan during the summer and fall of 1865 proved the determination of white southerners to preserve the prewar society that they believed represented true American republicanism. Delegates to the conventions insisted first of all upon the importance of states' rights, refusing to acknowledge the power of the na-tional government. Some of the states declined to repudiate secession or the Confederate debt. Some of the conventions also opposed emancipation; Texas and Mississippi rejected the Thirteenth Amendment. In the elections held under the new constitutions, southerners returned a number of wartime leaders to political power. Confederate congressmen, generals, and state offi-cials were elected to the U.S. Congress; Georgia went so far as to elect Confederate Vice President Alexander H. Stephens to the U.S. Senate. It initially appeared that South Carolina had elected Wade Hampton as gover-nor. Since he was one of the few who had not been pardoned and thus probably could not hold office, his early lead slowed down enough to permit another man to overtake him.[13]

Trying to institutionalize the white power that had ordered society before the war, the provisional governments set about regaining control over the African Americans, many of whom were refusing to stay in the fields and were heading for towns and cities. Freedpeople were newly assertive. Although many retained old habits of deference, others actively insisted on equal rights. Black soldiers carried guns and wore uniforms; many freedmen not in uniform talked back to whites, refused to step off sidewalks into the street, and gathered when and where they chose. White southerners saw the new assertiveness not simply as a social issue but as a complete reworking of American democracy. If the bottom tier of the community could participate equally in society, what would become of government that had always been organized by a few elite individuals? Anxious white legislators passed the infamous "Black Codes," in an attempt to force freedpeople back into their prewar place as subservient workers. Some of the new codes bound freedmen to field labor in white-owned fields by prohibiting them from working outside of agriculture without a license or from buying farmland to work on their own, and by requiring that freedmen sign year-long contracts every January. In most southern states, "vagrant" freedmen—those unemployed—could be arrested and bound to white landowners.

For their part, freed slaves and northern Republicans had their own ideas about what a new, free, postwar America should mean, and they had no intention of permitting white southerners to replicate the traditional South. With their strong connection to the government, ex-slaves and Republicans were willing to use federal power to establish free labor in the South; they turned to it increasingly as southern whites withheld wages or hurt their black neighbors. While many former slaves rejected capitalism in favor of a more communal economy, others immediately adopted some of the economic goals of free laborers. Following to its logical conclusion the idea that labor created value and that workers were entitled to the fruits of their labor, former field hands wanted the land and possessions their work had paid for. ("The nigs had been told that everything would belong to them; that the government would punish the whites for the war, by taking their property and dividing it among the nigs, giving forty acres to each head of family, etc.," recalled Charley Allston scornfully.) They were not happy to see plantation owners returning from their wartime havens to repossess former holdings. If they could not get land, freedpeople were determined at least to have wages and control over their own hours, and to live in households with a bread-winning husband and a domestic wife and daughters who could be protected from white sexual predators. Nat Love's father "was a man of strong determination, not easily discouraged, and always pushing forward and upward, quick to learn things and slow to forget them, a keen observer and a loving husband and father," his son recalled. He refused to stay on the old plantation with other slaves, who "work[ed] for their masters in return for their keep."[14]

Love's father "decided to start out for himself," renting twenty acres of unimproved land from his former master and hammering out a range of different products to try to sustain his family. In addition to clearing, plowing, and harrowing the land, Love's father "would make brooms and mats from straw and chair bottoms from cane and reeds, in which my brother and I would help him, after he had taught us how," Love remembered. On Friday night, Love's father would carry their products a dozen miles to town to exchange for seeds and food. The family planted corn and vegetables for subsistence, along with tobacco as a cash crop. Love had the easy carriage and compact build of a natural athlete, but even as a grown man, he could recall the grinding exhaustion created by the overwhelming amount of work required to grow tobacco.[15]

The economic uplift required of free laborers was hard to come by in the postwar South. The Loves, like other southerners, found postwar agriculture a desperate business. Successful farming depended on increasing amounts of capital to invest in production, but the South's poverty put investment in farms out of reach for most farmers. Despite their best efforts, Love recalled, "Our crop the first year was not large and the most of it went to pay the rent and the following year proved a very hard one, and entailed considerable privation and suffering among the many ex-slaves, who had so recently been thrown on their own resources, without money or clothing or food." Nature itself seemed to conspire against small farmers, as heavy rains in spring 1866 hurt planting. The crops that did make it into the ground had little chance against the army worms, which arrived in time for the 1866 harvest. By 1867, food was so scarce in the South that northerners were organizing charity drives to prevent starvation.[16]

Systematic discrimination and abuse by white employers compounded freedpeople's economic troubles. In the struggle to survive, blacks and whites cheated each other, but whereas people like Love simply continued the pilfering that had been a regular part of slavery times, whites actively undermined the system of wage labor. Freedpeople's anger at dishonest employers was palpable, especially when the theft of food earned quick punishment by the law yet cheating black workers was often looked at as rather clever or funny. The young Love supplemented his family's production by taking a job with a neighboring planter. Within a week of starting, he recalled, "I made my first visit home, taking with me some potatoes, bacon, cornmeal, and some molasses, which I had rustled in various ways." Love quickly found himself in the same position as other illiterate freedpeople, though: cheated of his wages. He took a job with a "Mr. Brooks" who was to pay him three dollars for a month of work. Determined to buy a dress for his mother with his pay, Love was "continually asking Mr. Brooks if my month was not soon over. He would laugh and say, 'yes, soon.' But it seemed to me that was the longest month I ever knew. When at last the month was over he gave me fifty cents, claiming I had drawn my wages during the month." Love solved his problem himself. "I knew that was not so. I also knew I had a balance coming to me and told him so. But he denied it and the result was we had a fight. I hit him in the head with a rock and nearly killed him," Love recalled, "after which I felt better."[17]

Watching white ex-Confederates regaining control of the South infuriated black Unionists. They had risked their lives to support the winning side of the war; why should they be losing the peace? Northern Republican army leaders and newspaper editors preached to black southerners primarily about the economic aspects of their new status in American society and had faith that freedpeople would acquit themselves honorably by working hard as free men, but those just emerging from slavery recognized that they must have political rights in order to protect economic ones. In the face of Johnson's support for white southerners, they insisted upon their right to a voice in their own government and called for the government to address their needs. In July 1865, the National Republican Association of the City of New Orleans issued resolutions declaring first of all that "the power of the Government should be derived from the consent of the governed." Its members also advocated universal suffrage as "the only true basis of a republican form of government, where all are equal before the law." The association went on to lecture on political economy. It resolved "that intelligent labor is the true basis of national prosperity, that the working classes are entitled to all the benefits of humane and enlightened legislation, and that therefore we will advocate the enactment of such laws as will dignify and foster labor."[18]

Its prescription for these laws was not the same benevolent development that northerners had advocated during the war. The New Orleans association actively sought both government policing of industry and a redistribution of wealth in order to level the South's economic playing field. It wanted the government to "render it beyond the power of capitalists to deprive industry of its just reward." In addition, because it was "in the interest of the country to encourage agricultural pursuits," the group advocated "taxing uncultivated lands in such manner as will compel their improvement and cultivation," or what amounted to confiscation of land through taxation. Joined to this suggestion was the announcement that "We further advocate a distribution of the lands owned by the State into free homesteads to the heads of families for actual cultivation." Finally, they protested Lincoln's provisional governor of Louisiana, J. M. Wells, who governed under a new constitution limiting the vote to white men, as "subversive and destructive of the rights and liberties of the loyal people of this State."[19]

Most radical Republicans would not go so far as the New Orleans association, but they, too, saw an active role for a government defending black rights in postwar America. Reports of the southern situation horrified northerners. Like the powerful Republican politicians with whom he now associated, Carl Schurz had been thrilled at Johnson's apparent determination to destroy the antebellum oligarchical Slave Power. He worried that Johnson's May 29 proclamation of amnesty would restore the antebellum southern leaders to power, and peppered the president with advice about southern affairs. Eager to get rid of him, the president encouraged Schurz to tour the South to report on conditions there. After traveling through South Carolina, Georgia, Alabama, Mississippi, and Louisiana, Schurz concluded that the South's problems were caused not by ex-slaves, who were eager to work as long as they were fairly treated, but by white southerners who hated the idea of free labor and were planning to reinstate some kind of slavery as soon as the troops left. Johnson's policy of restoring the states to the Union as quickly as possible "is the worst that could be hit upon," Schurz thought, for all of southern society, not just the region's political relations to the federal government, must be reconstructed.[20] This could be done only by forcing disloyal whites out of power and giving the vote to the loyal freedmen, who might not have an education or property but whose interests were identical to those of the government—and, not incidentally, to the Republican Party. "Nothing is more foreign to my ways of thinking in political matters than a fondness for centralization or military government," Schurz insisted, but "the national government . . . [must] continue to control the development of the new social system in the late rebel States until . . . a final settlement of things upon a thorough free-labor basis." Back in Boston, Julia Ward Howe agreed with Schurz that black men must vote. "Legal right . . . secures universal liberty," she scribbled in her diary.[21]

Opponents, especially white southerners, tended to focus on radicals like Schurz and exaggerate their importance, but the radicals never held enough power to dictate national legislation. Schurz's proposed program of national power and black suffrage was too much for the vast majority of northerners, Republicans and moderate Democrats alike. These men—small farmers, artisans, and shopkeepers who had to work hard to support their families—were willing, even eager, to transform cheap slave labor into more expensive free labor that would not undercut their wages, but they had little interest in doing anything other than ending slavery and turning black men loose to make their own way in the world. Certainly they had no interest in sharing political power with the majority of the southern black population, uneducated and impoverished, newly freed from the stultifying world of slavery. Furthermore, they disliked the idea of an active government almost as much as they disliked African Americans. Johnson knew Schurz's account of southern affairs would condemn the president's approach to reconstruction, and to undercut Schurz's report Johnson sent U. S. Grant on his own tour of the South. Grant's report reflected moderate northern opinion. He agreed that the military must stay in the South "until such time as labor returns to its proper channel, and civil authority is fully established." But he also suggested that white southerners had, in fact, accepted the results of the war. In contrast to Schurz, Grant wrote that freedmen believed "that the lands of their former owners, will, at least in part, be divided among them" and that they had "the right to live without care or provision for the future." Grant did not mention black suffrage and concluded that freedmen must be advised "that by their own industry they must expect to live." In the ideal free labor society envisioned by moderate northern whites, all white men—and a few hardworking black men, if necessary—would be able to make their way up in the world without having to worry about competition from cheap slave labor or about high taxes that would reduce their income to support a strong government.[22]

Although most northerners disliked both government activism and African Americans, there was no way that they were going to let southern whites erase the results of the war. They had lost years of their lives, and perhaps limbs or nerves, to destroy the Slave Power. They had sacrificed sons, fathers, and friends in the war; had seen images of goblets made of soldiers' skulls engraved in *Harper's Weekly*; and had perhaps seen photographs of Anderson-ville prison camp, where starving prisoners drank from a sewage-filled stream and huddled for shelter in pits they dug in the ground. They were utterly determined that the men who commanded these atrocities not be permitted to retake control of the South. If they did, under Johnson's plan, their national power could be expected to increase dramatically after 1870, when a new census would count African Americans as whole persons rather than as three-fifths of a person, as slaves had been since the founding of the nation. As a result, the South would pick up a number of seats in the House of Representa-tives. On a more immediate level, by the end of the war, the heroism of black soldiers had convinced many previously hostile white northerners that black Americans deserved at least some rights. In April 1865, a drawing in *Harper's Weekly* showed two crippled Union soldiers, one black and one white, shaking hands. "Give me your hand, Comrade!" the caption read. "We have each lost a leg for the good cause; but, thank God, we never lost Heart." The drawing was titled "A MAN KNOWS A MAN." It simply seemed wrong to support Confeder-ates at the expense of Union veterans, no matter what their color.[23]

Throughout 1865 and 1866, Democrats and Republicans battled to define what exactly a free labor South would look like and what the government should do to establish it. At first, in the summer and fall of 1865, it didn't mat-ter what former slaves or Republicans thought, for, until Congress recon-vened, Johnson alone was in charge of reconstruction. With his southern heri-tage, Johnson shared with other white southern Democrats a horror of what they saw as the radicalism of freedmen and northern Republicans determined to replace traditional American republicanism with a large, Republican-dominated government that ran the country for the benefit of party members. In July 1865, the *National Intelligencer*, a staunchly pro-Johnson newspaper, applauded the president for breaking the southern aristocracy but warned that New England radicals were advancing their own oligarchy, weakening the states and imposing a rule that they themselves would never tolerate. "The only serious danger that now threatens the country comes from fanatics and ruthless party politicians," it declared. Determined to undercut a Republican reworking of the American government, Johnson winked at the virtual reim-position of slavery in the South and at white southern unwillingness to bow to the supremacy of the federal government. He insisted only that southern states repudiate their war debt, nullify their secession ordinances, and abolish legal slavery, convinced that these measures would be enough to destroy any remaining impetus for southern nationhood. By the end of 1865, every state but Texas had done as he requested.[24]

When Congress reconvened in December 1865, Johnson assured its members that restoration had been accomplished. All that remained was for Congress to readmit to good standing the newly elected southern senators and representatives waiting in Washington. Standing firm on the principle of limited government, Johnson insisted that prolonging the federal occupation of the South would be prohibitively expensive. Worse, it would increase the size of the federal government, creating a host of new jobs that would be filled by patronage and turn the government into a political machine. A true free labor system should reflect the interests of the workingman, not tax him to support a political party, Johnson lectured.[25]

Johnson was not alone in his belief that reconstruction was effectively over and that, while it would have been better if southern whites had not come down quite so hard on the freedpeople, it was time to move on. A major stumbling block to southern reconstruction was a lack of capital, and without security, investors would not send their money south. Johnson's careful protection of private property relieved investors in the southern economy, and his leniency promised to pacify white leaders, who should in turn rein in local violence. In late 1865, a London financial circular noted that American securities were strong in international markets, because "the conciliatory nature of President Johnson's speech to the delegates from the Southern States, appears to have inspired general confidence in the speedy and cordial reunion of the North and South." The press continued to report other reasons to be hopeful about the South. In July, the *Richmond Times* reported that the tobacco market was strong, and a new national bank opened in Savannah. In January 1866, the newly resumed *De Bow's Review* noted that the reopening of the New Orleans School of Medicine was "evidence of the return of peace."[26]

Republicans in Congress were not convinced. Incensed at the idea of the return of unrepentant southerners to Congress, northern congressmen rejected Johnson's plan for restoration out of hand and refused to seat the southern congressional delegations waiting at Washington boardinghouses, whiling away their time marveling at the wartime changes that had made the sleepy country town a bustling city. But rejecting Johnson's ideas was easier than coming up with new ones to rebuild the devastated South, protect African Americans, foster the loyalty of southern whites, and keep the loyalty of northerners who feared an increasingly powerful government. Ideally,

America's new free labor society should consist of hardworking, economically independent, and loyal voters with enough education to understand their own interests. They would elect representatives who would legislate for the good of a society of like-minded hardworking, loyal individuals. In reality, though, the educated, propertied men in the South were disloyal, and the staunchly loyal men were poor, uneducated, and black. Somehow, congressmen had to find a way to reform a republican government out of conditions the founding fathers had never foreseen.

Shortly after reconvening in December 1865, Congress appointed nine congressmen and six senators to a Joint Committee on Reconstruction to hammer out a plan. Although prominent radicals sat on this committee, moderates dominated. As these men tried to construct a permanent settlement, Congress worked on establishing fair play in the South. It used federal power, but as sparingly as possible. After watching white vigilantes attack freedmen and seeing the new southern legislatures refuse to permit African Americans to sit on juries, Congress decided in February 1866 to expand the Freedmen's Bureau, extending federal protection to African Americans and federal jurisdiction over courts in areas where freedmen could not participate equally with whites in the justice system. In the same bill, they provided for federal funding of freedmen's schools and asylums, as well as for black land ownership. They also passed a civil rights bill that formally declared black Americans citizens entitled to all the rights of citizenship, enabling them to make and enforce contracts, sue, testify in court, own property, and bear the same "punishment, pains, and penalties" as white men regardless of "any law, statute, ordinance, regulation, or custom, to the contrary." This law not only destroyed states' abilities to enact Black Codes, it also undermined state power by establishing federal authority over civil rights cases in the South.

This attempt by Congress to take over reconstruction ran smack into President Johnson, who was not about to let Congress strengthen its hold on the government. He saw in the fight over reconstruction a struggle over the very existence of America and believed, as southern and northern Democrats charged, that radical congressmen hoped to dominate government permanently. He vetoed both the new Freedmen's Bureau and the civil rights bills, deliberately depicting the reconstruction fight as a struggle between competing theories of government. His vetoes argued that the Freedmen's Bureau bill was unconstitutional, aimed at establishing a military government over the South, one that would require a large, expensive system of patronage. The proposed expansion of the bureau and federal protection of civil rights would create an unprecedented welfare system, paid for by tax dollars, with African Americans receiving special rights no other Americans enjoyed, he argued. Rather than permitting freedpeople to become free workers like all other Americans, it would "transfer the entire care, support, and control of 4,000,000 emancipated slaves to agents, overseers, or taskmasters, who, appointed at Washington, are to be located in every county and parish throughout the United States containing freedmen and refugees. Such a system would inevitably tend to a concentration of power in the Executive which would enable him, if so disposed to control the action of this numerous class and use them for the attainment of his own political ends." Four million African Americans "have just emerged from slavery into freedom. Can it reasonably be supposed that they possess the requisite qualifications to entitle them to all the privileges and immunities of citizens of the United States," he asked in astonishment. Johnson then threw down the gauntlet: Congress could not legislate with eleven states still unrepresented, he announced. Thus, he implied, future congressional legislation would not be valid until southern representatives were admitted to its deliberations. The battle over America's political system had become the primary fight of reconstruction.[27]

In spring 1866, Congress announced its own plan of reconstruction, which relied on the national government to protect African Americans and to prevent the restoration of the South's prewar aristocracy. In April, the Joint Committee on Reconstruction devised a plan that was more radical than Johnson's but much more moderate than what the radicals wanted. The committee proposed a new amendment to the Constitution declaring that black people were citizens entitled to the "privileges and immunities" of all American citizens, and that state law could neither take their "life, liberty, or property, without due process of law" nor "deny to any person . . . the equal protection of the laws." The Fourteenth Amendment prohibited from holding office any person who had sworn to protect the U.S. Constitution before the war and then joined the Confederacy. (This meant that most of the new state officers elected under Johnson's plan were ineligible for their jobs.) To answer concerns that the 1870 census would increase white southerners' power unless African Americans had a political voice, it tried to push southern states toward black suffrage by warning that a state's congressional representation would be reduced if black men were kept from voting. (The formula for this reduction was unworkable and this part of the amendment has never been used.) Congress passed the Fourteenth Amendment in mid-June 1866 and sent it off to the states for ratification. Congress also passed a weakened Freedmen's Bureau bill and the civil rights bill over Johnson's vetoes.

Southern whites were outraged at Congress's terms of reconstruction, incredulous that the prominent southern leaders who had always run public affairs—men like Wade Hampton—were barred from office while the vote was suggested for former slaves. In April, white police officers in Memphis tried to assert the supremacy of both whites over blacks and state authority over federal authority by forcing black federal soldiers off a sidewalk. With the tacit approval of white Memphis officials (the mayor was too drunk to function, observers later noted), white mobs turned with fury on the black civilian population, burning three black churches, fifty black homes, and eight schools—five of which belonged to the U.S. government—and destroyed about $100,000 worth of property. They killed about 30 African Americans and wounded 50 others. Then, when Louisiana Unionists convened in late July 1866 to try to revise the 1864 constitution to include black suffrage and to disfranchise the ex-Confederates who had just taken control of the state legislature, rioting whites killed 37 black and 3 white delegates and wounded 136 more. Angry southern whites sang "I'm a Good Old Rebel":

I hate your spangled banner,
Your great republic, too,
And I hate your Freedmen's Bureau,
In uniforms of blue.
I hate your Constitution,
Your eagle and its squall,
And a lying, thieving Yankee,
I hate the worst of all.

Three hundred thousand Yankees
Lie moldering in the dust—
We got three hundred thousand
Before you conquered us.
They died of Southern fevers
And Southern steel and shot,
And I wish it was three million
Instead of what we got.[28]

White southerners denounced what they called "black domination," a term that joined traditional racism with southern Democratic anxiety about the loss of their political power to what they saw as a growing northern oligarchy. "The war," Hampton noted, "was prolific of monstrosities—new theories of Republican government—new versions of the Constitution—new and improved constructions of the divine precepts of the Holy Writ." Now, "to secure the freedom . . . of four millions of negroes at the South . . . eight millions of whites are made slaves!" With the issue of slavery now moot—for few had any illusions it could be entirely reimposed—radical white southerners began to redefine the war, arguing that it was fought not over slavery but to protect the states from northern radicals who were intent on unleashing a federal juggernaut. In *De Bow's Review*, W. A. Carey explained that the war came when "the radical school of the North desired to indoctrinate new principles, to engraft them into our republican government, widen the Constitution, by implied doctrines, to meet the developments and rising demands that they believed our national life so absolutely required." They had done so during the war, and "their fell purpose" had created "concentrated, consolidated Despotism!" In an open letter to the president, Hampton demanded an end to this radical reworking of American government and insisted that Johnson restore the South to the Union "properly, harmoniously, honorably."[29]

Only a year before, northern Democrats had been struggling on battlefields to defeat the Confederacy, but now they agreed with Hampton that the Republicans must be stopped. Sunset Cox, who had moved to the Democratic stronghold of New York City, insisted that representatives from the southern states must be readmitted to Congress, or "there will be civil war more terrible and atrocious than that just ended." Johnson himself railed against Congress and stood firmly against the Fourteenth Amendment. The Republicans would be swept out of power in the 1866 congressional elections, he insisted, and when that happened, southern states could return to the Union under Johnson's plan. (Only Johnson's home state of Tennessee, controlled by the president's political enemies, pointedly ignored him, ratified the Fourteenth Amendment, and was readmitted to the Union.) Johnson's own sense of crisis made him go so far as to offer himself, Christlike, as a sacrifice to preserve true American limited government.[30]

The elections proved that white southerners had backed the wrong horse. Voters, it turned out, were less frightened by the growing Republican government than by Johnson Democrats and southerners who were trying to overturn the results of the war and reinstate the government of the antebellum South. (They were also mortified by Johnson's intemperate campaign speeches.) In the elections, voters backed Congress's plan to use the government to establish free labor in the South and gave Republicans more than two-thirds of the seats in Congress to make sure it happened. These election results meant that Republicans in the next Congress could pass legislation with or without Johnson's approval. Convening in December 1866, the second session of the Thirty-ninth Congress quickly pressed forward its own vision of reconstruction. In January, House radicals charged the Judiciary Committee with determining whether to start impeachment proceedings against Johnson, who might not have broken laws but who had undoubtedly used his public office to harm the nation. (Among other things, on his 1866 campaign tour Johnson had called for the hanging of several Republican congressmen.) The committee declined to charge him, but Congress had made it clear he was on notice. It agreed to convene the Fortieth Congress immediately after the adjournment of the Thirty-ninth so that Johnson would not have another free field for action during its usual recess. Then, on March 2, 1867, at the end of the final session of the Thirty-ninth Congress, members of the Senate replaced the conservative president pro tem with Benjamin F. Wade, a leading radical from Ohio.[31]

Overshadowing these important challenges to Johnson and the Democrats was the breathtaking new centerpiece of congressional reconstruction: the Military Reconstruction Act, a law designed to broaden the southern voting base and keep white southerners from reestablishing their antebellum world. Passed on March 2, 1867, this landmark piece of legislation placed the federal government firmly in control of southern reconstruction and formally changed the definition of who would have a say in American government. It gave African American men the right to vote so that they might help to establish a free labor society in the South. It divided the ten unreconstructed states into five military districts overseen by military commanders and demanded that the southern states write new constitutions. All men—black as well as white—could vote for delegates to the constitutional conventions, except for any Confederates who were prohibited from holding office under the terms of the Fourteenth Amendment. Once elected, the new constitutional conventions were required to establish new state governments that guaranteed black suffrage and ratified the Fourteenth Amendment. When these requirements were met, southern states could apply to Congress for readmission to the Union. To guarantee that Johnson could not undermine the Military Reconstruction Act in his role as the commander in chief of the army, Congress passed the Command of the Army Act, which required that Johnson issue all military orders through the general of the army, U. S. Grant, who had sided with Congress against Johnson. To keep the president from purging his cabinet of Republicans appointed by Lincoln, Congress also passed the Tenure of Office Act, a piece of legislation of highly questionable legality requiring Senate approval for the removal of any government official who had been appointed with the advice and consent of the Senate. With these steps, a staunchly Republican Congress put the national government in charge of protecting free labor. Determined that white southern elites would not determine the nation's future, Congress had decided that for a voter, education, property, and even race mattered less than a belief in free labor and support for the government.[32]

Congress's plan didn't rebuild a harmonious South, for most white southerners wanted less government interference in the region and most black southerners wanted more. Fully recognizing that the Military Reconstruction Act was designed to destroy traditional southern society, state officials in the South simply refused to start enrolling voters. Congress had to pass three more reconstruction acts to get the process of framing new southern state governments under way, and ultimately it had to put the army in charge of voter registration. Once registration began, many white voters refused to sign up for what they considered an illegal, rigged election overseen by a military dictatorship. Taking another approach, Wade Hampton resolved to direct African Americans to support small government. In a speech shortly after the passage of the Military Reconstruction Act, he encouraged blacks to vote with southern whites. Hampton wrote privately to John Mullaly, editor of *New York Metropolitan Record*, "It seems to me that but one hope is left to us and that is to direct the Negro vote. . . . We are appealing to the enlightened sense and the justice of mankind. We come forward and say, we accept the decision rendered against us, we acknowledge the freedom of the negro and we are willing to have one law for him and for us."[33]

The attempts of a few white southerners like Hampton to court black voters made northern Republicans rejoice that their plan of reconstruction was working, for once whites were competing for black votes, the safety of black southerners seemed assured. Politicians anxious for votes would guarantee black suffrage while defending black rights, and African Americans would insist on education so they could adequately understand their interests. The flip side of this, however, was that Republicans quickly began to worry that the Democrats would attract black voters. In summer 1867, Republican politicians set out to gather southern freedpeople into Republican organizations. They established Union League clubs, which were intended to channel existing black political activism into support for free labor ideals and thus to garner votes for the Republican Party. Important northern Republican politicians supported the Union League with money as well as speeches, and the Republican Congress also provided financial support to southern Republican newspapers through printing contracts for government notices, thus making sure the impoverished southern Republicans had a voice. Northern politicians and southern white Republicans worked to pull freedmen into the Union League to support the Republican ticket.[34]

Quickly realizing that they needed local organizers on the ground, northerners chose as leaders those African Americans who seemed to embrace the Republican free labor vision. Upwardly mobile African Americans, who were usually light skinned, biracial, sometimes educated, and often free before the war, echoed northern politicians and called for self-help, education, and thrift. Representatives of the "intelligent mass of the colored population" who made up the 1866 Georgia Freedmen's Convention, for example, declared, "we discountenance vagrancy and pauperism among our people, and . . . will make it our especial business to aid every one to obtain employment and encourage them to earn a competency by honest labor and judicious economy." These leaders were visible and vocal, and to northerners they often seemed to be representative of their race. But in reality they were a small minority of the free population. In North Carolina in 1870, for example, only 6.7 percent of all African Americans held land, and those listed in the census as "mulatto" were four times more likely to own land as those described as "black."[35]

The majority of freedmen, unskilled, uneducated, impoverished, and darker skinned than those African Americans who were managing to advance in the postwar South, had a much more radical vision of southern society than Republicans had expected. Nat Love explained why. He had grown up surrounded by plantations where "thousands of slaves . . . [garnered] the dollars that kept up the so-called aristocracy of the South, and many of the proud old families owe their standing and wealth to the toil and sweat of the black man's brow," he mused. "Wealth was created, commerce carried on, cities built, and the new world well started on the career that has led to its present greatness and standing in the world of nations. . . . All this was accomplished by the sweat of the black man's brow."[36]

People with experiences similar to Love's had a hard time believing that there was economic harmony in American society which would enable everyone to rise together. For them, freedom had simply replaced the master-slave relationship with one of employer-employee. When employers cheated them out of wages, tried to force them into the same gang labor system slaves had endured, and continued to inflict corporal punishment, they saw an inherent struggle between labor and capital rather than economic harmony. Ignoring the Union League's cheerful program of economic uplift through hard work, they called for the government to back them against their traditional enemies, who were hampering their economic success at every turn. Radical freedmen agitated for land confiscation, squatted on planters' lands, and stopped work or struck until their demands were met. Strikes and associated riots swept through southern towns, and hostile newspapers reported them widely. Freedmen also demanded that state governments fund social welfare programs through taxation. They gathered around prominent black political leaders from within their communities to demand land confiscation and radical economic policies to enable them to get on their feet. "I want [property owners] taxed until they put these lands back where they belong, into the hands of those who worked for them," former hotel slave W. Beverly Nash told a political rally of freedpeople. Previously owned by Wade Hampton's cousin, William C. Preston, Nash might have envisioned the extensive lands of the Hampton family when he thundered, "You toiled for them, you labored for them, and were sold to pay for them, and you ought to have them."[37]

White southerners greeted such black political meetings with loathing, their traditional racism combining with their fear of a voting underclass to make them viciously attack black political activism. As a small girl in 1867, former slave Ida B. Wells of Holly Springs, Mississippi, knew that politics was a dangerous business for her carpenter father "by the anxious way my mother walked the floor at night when my father was out to a political meeting." Racist white southerners saw black political gatherings as another attempt by northern radicals to destroy the South. An article entitled "Army of the Republic," reprinted in the *Houston Weekly Telegraph* from the *Clinton (La.) Register*, illustrated the military image of black politicians: "A mounted squad of [these colored radical Republican armed forces], some twenty-five or more in number, rode into town, all armed with guns and revolvers." They took possession of "a school house . . . throwing out pickets to prevent the intrusion of none but those who could give the password." Derogatorily, the reporter wrote that the freedmen were discussing either "the coming election or . . . the rites and mysteries of Voodooism."[38]

The yellow fever epidemic of summer and fall 1867 encouraged white southerners to believe that black political activity was killing whites. "I attribute the sickness of my family, in great measure, to the filth of a lot of negroes" who were meeting regularly at a neighboring house, a man from Navasota, Texas, complained in September 1867. A neighbor had rented his home to African Americans. "They made this their headquarters for the most degraded negroes about town, and made night hideous with their revels and debauch, disturbing the peace and quiet of the sick and dying in the neighborhood. A physician, with whom we consulted, pronounced the filth created by these negroes, sufficient to engender the most loathsome disease." The white man fretted that "unprotected citizens [were thrown] on the mercy of a depraved negro population, that are watching their opportunity to steal, being too lazy and thriftless to work."[39]

Southern Democrats were convinced that black suffrage meant the utter destruction of the American republic. When his attempts to convince former slaves to let elite whites direct their voting failed, Wade Hampton joined a November meeting of white South Carolinians protesting the upcoming election in which the propertied, educated men were disfranchised, putting the lowest element of society in control of the government. The meeting declared: "in the name of citizenship under the Constitution . . . in the name of our Anglo-Saxon race and blood . . . we protest against these Reconstruction Acts as destructive to . . . the greatness and grandeur of our common future."[40]

White southern attacks on black suffrage tied racism to political tradition. Southern opponents of black suffrage had a well-articulated political theory that meshed easily with the ideas of northern Democrats like Sunset Cox. Republican radicals had changed the very nature of American government, gathering more and more power into their own hands, Democrats argued. Republicans had passed the Thirteenth Amendment, which placed the federal government above the state governments for the first time in American history. They were using the army to occupy the southern states, where they had established military government. They were inflaming northern voters with stories of abused freedpeople to trick them into supporting their unconstitutional grab for power. Worse, when white southerners protested Republican trampling of the Constitution, the Republicans used the protests as an excuse to destroy even more liberties. They had established the Freedmen's Bureau, a federal agency that intruded into the very households of southern whites and favored freedmen. In order to destroy utterly the southern state governments, they had enfranchised uneducated men they knew would vote for them, and to make absolutely certain of their success, they used federal money to launch southern Republican newspapers to get more votes. When Johnson had tried to halt their mad course, they had tried to get rid of him. In September 1867, the *National Intelligencer* put together the pieces of a conspiracy long suspected by Democrats: "All these matters constitute one grand revolutionary movement, looking to the deposition of the President, confiscation, the subversion of the Government, and the creation of one exclusive Radical oligarchy, to be fed by the Treasury, which is to be the mainspring of the machine." This was most unfair, the paper concluded, for "never has a people shown a more prompt and universal acquiescence in the authority of the United States than the discomfited Confederates. . . . Never were exactions greater; never submission and Christian patience more complete."[41]

Few northern Republicans would have swallowed the claim that southern whites had shown complete submission and Christian patience. But many northerners weren't comfortable with activist freedpeople advocating what seemed to be class legislation either, for a new specter was rising on the American horizon. The racist justification of a desperately unequal society had not been very convincing to northerners before the war, but by 1867, southern complaints about people who wanted to harness government to their own interests resonated in the North, where workers had begun to organize on an unprecedented scale and to demand that government respond to their needs. Before Appomattox, most northerners had not given much thought to what free labor would mean in the North, focusing instead on the destruction of legal slavery and the spread of a free labor system below the Mason-Dixon Line. One thing on which they did agree, though, was that the triumph of free labor should mean prosperity for everyone, and after a brief recession at the end of the war, the nation's economy was indeed booming. Deepening capital reserves, immigration, new technologies, and extraordinary inventions made industry thrive in new national and international markets. Businesses were growing and consolidating as railroads and the telegraph enabled managers to handle larger markets, and the resulting economies of scale made wholesale prices drop steadily even as unemployment was low. At the same time, word of the money to be made in the West in agriculture, hunting, mining, or cattle had spread east quickly, and western towns were springing up overnight. In 1866, *De Bow's Review* reported a population of more than half a million people living west of the Mississippi, with another half a million in California. As the transcontinental railroads hammered west, the numbers climbed.[42]

With the victorious end of a war for free labor and with the economy strong, it seemed as though America should be a paradise for anyone willing to work. Instead, many wage laborers worried that something had gone wrong during the war, something that unbalanced the stability of the free labor economy and threatened to capsize it altogether by creating extremes of wealth and poverty in the nation. Business was certainly thriving and creating jobs, but business owners were pocketing profits that dwarfed the paychecks of their workers. At the same time, wartime legislation designed to be evenhanded ended up benefiting the wealthy. Tariffs protected agriculture, but since Americans were exporting grain, this was moot. Manufacturers enjoyed protection for their products while laborers paid higher prices than they would have without Republican tariffs. The payment of the interest on war bonds also exacerbated workers' sense that the rich were receiving unfair benefits. During the war, the Republican Congress had authorized the issue of bonds to raise money. To make the bonds salable, most were payable in gold, as was their interest, with money raised by manufacturing taxes that fell on everyone alike, workers as well as employers. As gold got more valuable and greenbacks inflated—meaning that it took more than a dollar in greenbacks to buy a dollar of gold—many began to call for repaying war bonds not in gold but in depreciated currency, insisting that taxpayers should not be bled dry for rich bondholders.

Immediately after the war, workers began to organize to restore the world of free enterprise and prosperity for which they had fought. Trade unions struck for higher wages and fewer hours and joined with labor reform organizations to try to defend the free labor dream. Arguing that new business practices crushed individual workers, labor groups advocated an eight-hour day, temperance, and any other reform they believed would return the nation to a true free labor system and restore equality between workers and employers. Increasingly, these groups denied that laborers and employers were working their way up together in America. Pointing to the tariffs that nurtured business by keeping consumer prices high, they charged that government economic policies were serving businessmen. Economic conflicts occurred naturally in society, they argued in an echo of the rhetoric of labor organizers before the war, and it was government's responsibility to adjust them fairly.

For those who believed that economic harmony was a hallmark of America's free labor system, the problem with this vision of a competitive society was twofold. First, the idea of the nation as an arena of class conflict struck profoundly at traditional beliefs about America's place in the world. Those who held the traditional free labor worldview believed that this system worked first because God was benevolent and had provided for Americans with a vast continent stocked with a treasure of natural resources. In the largest sense, denying that all men could use their labor to make these resources valuable and thus give rise to economic security denied both God's goodness and America's status as His favored nation. Second, the demands of disaffected workers for the newly powerful government to intervene in the economy in ways that bolstered the position of a particular group would destroy the harmonious economy that underlay America's free labor society. The traditional free labor worldview demanded that government protect property and treat everyone equally; wartime Republicans had carefully designed their economic legislation on this basis, protecting agriculture as well as industry to nurture all aspects of the economy. If the government began to broker between different factions—by reducing work hours, fixing wages, or taxing one group to provide services for another—it would privilege some at the expense of others. The wealthy would take their capital to other countries where property was better protected, and good workers would stop working as hard, knowing they would not keep the fruits of their labor. Bad workers could revel in their laziness and dissipation, knowing that they could live with little effort. From its favored status as God's chosen land, America would fall to the depths of human misery.

In August 1866, more than 60,000 people from various reform and labor groups came together in the first national congress of the National Labor Union (NLU), launching a nationwide movement that called for government intervention in the economy on behalf of workingmen. Delegates condemned "wage slavery" and advocated a restoration of individual self-sufficiency. "The Address of the National Labor Congress to the Workingmen of the United States," produced after the meeting, called for workers to pressure Congress to enact an eight-hour day and declared "that any system, social or political, which tends to keep the masses in ignorance, whether by unjust or oppressive laws, or by over-manual labor, is injurious alike to the interests of the state and the individual." The NLU called for workers to organize, an end to monopolies, and cooperation with black workers, even if the idea was unpalatable. "The interests of labor are one; . . . there is but one dividing line—that which separates mankind into two great classes, the class that labors and the class that lives by others' labor." It called for the establishment of a workers' political party. At the 1867 convention of the National Labor Union, one labor leader introduced a resolution asking Congress for $25 million to establish the eight-hour day, to send workers West, "and for the general benefit of laborers, without distinction of sex, color, or locality."[43]

To the dismay of those who believed that America's free labor system depended on economic harmony preserved by evenhanded government, important politicians supported those workers demanding beneficial government activism. Democrats traditionally represented organized labor, and the interests of postwar workers fit well with the Democrats' postwar ideas. Both resented the rise of wealthy industrialists, disliked black workingmen, and hated taxes. A few radical Republicans also extended their belief in free labor to include the need for laborers to be protected as a special interest. The most dramatic proponent of such an idea was none other than the president pro tem of the Senate, Benjamin Franklin Wade. In an 1867 speech in Kansas, Wade, a rough, brash man who had once worked as a cattle drover and a day laborer, told the audience that the theme of postwar America was the struggle between labor and capital. "Property is not equally divided, and a more equal distribution of capital must be wrought out," he said.[44]

Wade did not speak for the majority of his party, most of whom were horrified that a man of such ideas could hold such a powerful Senate position. Conservative and moderate Republicans, as well as wealthy Democrats, worried that class organization threatened a harmonious economy and feared those workers who increasingly defined themselves as a group with different needs than the general population. *Harper's Weekly* put a brave face on Wade's speech, calmly commenting that he had only identified "what every student and observer of modern civilization very well knows, that the capital and labor question is one of the most vital subjects." But the *New York Times* growled that Wade "assails the whole industrial and business fabric of the country. . . . [He] springs from the domain of American republicanism to the region of French socialism."[45]

For those committed to developing a harmonious free labor society, other frightening developments loomed on the horizon. Wage laborers were not the only ones wondering what the triumph of the northern vision of free labor meant for them. Like other northern women, Julia Ward Howe had found freedom during the war to work and speak outside her home, but her husband, famous reformer Samuel Gridley Howe, strongly opposed his wife's expanding public life and demanded she stay at home managing the household. She often flouted his demands, reflecting that "the internal necessity conquer[s] the external" but suffered terribly for her daring. After a bitter fight on their twenty-second wedding anniversary in April 1865, Howe was torn between her societal role as a wife and her responsibility to herself. "He attacked me with the utmost vehemence and temper . . . I feel utterly paralyzed and brought to a stand-still—know not how to live and work any further," she lamented. For Howe and many other women, the enfranchisement of African American men on the principle that all people should have a say in the government in order to protect themselves automatically raised the questions of women's rights. "The Civil War came to an end, leaving the slave not only emancipated, but endowed with the full dignity of citizenship," she pointed out. "The women of the North had greatly helped to open the door which admitted him to freedom and its safeguard, the ballot. Was this door to be shut in their face?"[46]

Faced with these challenges to their vision of America's political economy, northern Republicans reiterated their powerful belief in America's harmonious system, in which every man had the right to the fruits of his labor. In their election rhetoric in summer 1867, they portrayed most southern African Americans as hardworking, thrifty, good citizens, although they, too, worried about black radicalism, especially when it looked like such radicalism might be infecting disaffected white workers as well. The Republican *Philadelphia Inquirer* reported that in Louisiana, "the colored man standeth forth in his dignity as a freeman, a citizen, a voter. And so doeth the 'white trash.'" The *New York Times* worried about land confiscation, advanced, as suffrage had been, with the argument that it was necessary for black equality. "It is not easy to see where it will stop. Why, if forty acres of land are essential to freedom, are not men to work it also essential? Why is land more essential than horses, or railroad stock or an investment in Government bonds?" It had a different prescription for black success: "Habits of industry and thrift—the faculty of taking care of themselves, of thinking and acting for themselves—are their first necessities." While Democrats insisted that Republicans were trying to cement a permanent voting base, Republicans held firm to their free labor ideas, that every man could work his way up, self-sufficient and independent of government support.[47]

Starting a trend that would continue throughout the rest of the century, in the 1867 elections, voters endorsed the free labor vision of economic harmony and rejected the idea of government aid to specific groups. In the South, new voters replaced traditional leaders with southern white Unionists, mostly upcountry farmers and small merchants, professionals, and artisans who had not previously held political office. About one-sixth of the delegates were

"THE FIRST VOTE."—DRAWN BY A. R. WAUD.—[SEE NEXT PAGE.]

Figure 2. Emphasizing the postwar Republican view that freedmen would make good citizens, Thomas Nast portrayed a worker, a businessman, and a soldier as representative black voters in this cartoon from *Harper's Weekly*, November 16, 1867. Courtesy *HarpWeek*.

young, well-educated white northern emigrants who had moved South after the war, and whose professional skills enabled them to draft key parts of the new constitutions. Although white southern Democrats denigrated the "black conventions" they claimed were dominated by field hands, in fact African Americans were underrepresented. Black delegates were a majority of the South Carolina and Louisiana conventions but made up only about 40 percent of the Florida delegation. In Alabama, Georgia, Mississippi, and Virginia, African Americans held about 20 percent of the seats, while in Arkansas, North Carolina, and Texas, about 10 percent of the delegates were black. Few of these delegates were field hands or common laborers; most were ministers, artisans, teachers, or farmers, and only a handful—freeborn and educated—were major actors in their conventions.[48]

In the North, too, voters emphasized moderation and backed away from the radicalism of the past year, registering their dislike primarily of black suffrage, which had been put on the ballot in most northern states. Their votes against Republican suffrage policies indicated their distrust of presidential impeachment, civil rights legislation, and land redistribution. In Ohio, voters replaced Republicans in the legislature with Democrats, guaranteeing that radical Benjamin F. Wade would not be reelected to the Senate in 1868 (for senators were still chosen by the legislature in the nineteenth century). Massachusetts Republican Nathaniel P. Banks thought that the election was "a crusher for the wild men," and prominent Republican James G. Blaine wrote to a colleague that the election results were "good discipline in many ways," for if they had carried "everything with a whirl in '67 . . . knaves . . . would control our National Convention and give us a nomination with which defeat would be inevitable *if not desirable.*"[49]

But while moderate Republicans were relieved that the delegates to the new southern state constitutional conventions were not illiterate radicals and that radicalism had been curbed in the North, too, southern Democrats took a different lesson from the 1867 elections. They saw antebellum southern leaders replaced by the white Unionists they detested, northern emigrants they loathed, and, even worse, African Americans, at a time when northerners refused to let blacks vote in their own region. Republicans congratulated themselves on the sense and moderation of reconstruction. Democrats—especially southern Democrats—saw an illegitimate government of ex-slaves forced upon them by Yankee emperors.

The relation of the government to the spread of free labor was more straightforward in the West, where there was no traditional American system of government to overturn. In Texas, circling his favorite black horse around a herd of milling cattle, Charles Goodnight wasn't theorizing about free labor, he was trying to stay alive. The war had almost ruined Goodnight. His cattle were gone; Texas was rife with stock theft and crime; his hearing was ruined in a bout with the measles that had swept through Confederate ranks, making him unable to hear the tell-tale sound of a rattlesnake; and Union military officers in the South treated former Confederates like dirt. "It looked like everything worth living for was gone," Goodnight recalled. "The entire country was depressed—there was no hope. We could not see what the Re-constructionists would do, nor how long they would hold out." Unionists who had fled from Confederate Texans were back, and now, with federal authorities on their side, they were neither willing to be intimidated nor above stealing the cattle of their former enemies. The *New Orleans Picayune* worried about conditions in Texas after the Confederate troops had disbanded, leaving no authority behind them. "The whole State has been invested by jay-hawkers of the worst description, who take both public and private property alike," it warned.[50]

Goodnight had joined other cowmen in "working the round-up" after the Civil War, gathering the cattle that ran loose through the state. Like the rest of Texas cowmen, Goodnight suffered from a depressed cattle market after the war. By 1865, a fattened beeve could be purchased in Texas for $4. In a booming northern city like Chicago, the same beeve would sell for between $30 and $40. Goodnight figured that anyone who rounded up cheap cattle and got them safely to a northern market stood to make a fortune. He concluded that he had to move his cattle out of the state and up to the Indian agencies and army posts in Colorado, where beef was needed to feed starving reservation Indians and army troops. By September 1865, he had recovered a herd of 2,000 and was preparing in September to move it north to market when Indians ran it off.[51]

In spring 1866, Goodnight joined forces with cattleman Oliver Loving, with whom he had fought as a Texas Ranger. Together they gathered a crew of fourteen cowhands and set off toward New Mexico en route to Colorado, braving drought-parched land, storms, Indians, and deadly rivers. Their desperate venture set the terms of the postwar cattle drive. Their cowboys included poor southerners at loose ends after the war who could ride and shoot, and who had nothing but the clothes on their backs. There were white men on the crew, including a guerilla dismissed from Confederate service for mental instability, and also former slave Bose Ikard, who began his cattle career as Loving's trail driver and who became over time such a close friend to Good-night that the white man later reflected that he trusted Ikard "farther than any living man. He was my detective, banker, and everything else in Colorado, New Mexico, and the other wild country I was in." Ikard's position on the crew reflected the general rule that one-third of western cowhands were men of color.[52] Fittingly for the first cattle drive of the western cattle industry, their route along the Pecos River blazed the way for cattlemen after them and became famous as the Goodnight-Loving Trail. Goodnight and Loving had planned to take their cattle up to Colorado but found a ready market in New Mexico, where the army bought Goodnight's entire herd for eight cents a pound to distribute to reservation Indians. Goodnight headed back to Texas with $12,000 in gold packed on his mule. The cattle rush was on.[53]

As Teddy Blue Abbott, a Texas cowboy from 1871 to 1889, remembered: "In 1866, the first Texas herds crossed the Red River. In 1867 the town of Abilene was founded at the end of the Kansas Pacific Railroad and that was when the trail really started. From that time on, big drives were made every year, and the cowboy was born." The cowboy's life was harsh, but it quickly got a romantic image. Cowboys often went for days without sleep, especially in the first two weeks of the drive when the cattle were liable to stampede. Goodnight recalled: "The men slept on the ground with their horses staked nearby. Sometimes the demands were so urgent that our boots were not taken off for an entire week. Nerves became so tense that it was a standing rule that no man was to be touched by another when asleep until after he had been spoken to. The man who suddenly aroused a sleeper was liable to be shot, as all were thoroughly armed and understood the instant use of a revolver and rifle." Cowboys, working in extremes of heat and cold, were constantly in danger of death under the hooves of stampeding cattle, in rivers, or in battles with hostile Indians. Their pay was low. They "lived on straight beef . . . they had no tents, no tarps, and damned few slickers," Teddy Blue explained. "They never kicked, because those boys was raised under just the same conditions as there was on the trail—corn meal and bacon for grub, dirt floors in the houses, and no luxuries."[54]

In 1867, a popular book admitted that the cowboys' work was "both disagreeable and fatiguing, in addition to which there is considerable risk from vicious cattle. . . . There is also much exposure to the heat of the noonday sun, and the damp, chilly midnight winds that blow fresh over the extensive prairies." Nonetheless, the book's author continued: "This wild life has also its attractions and exciting pleasures, especially for the young and adventurous; as it is not devoid of risk, and affords to the aspiring mind of youth an opportunity of a display of courage and prowess that is not found in any other department of rural life. The young men that follow this 'Cow Boy' life, notwithstanding its hardships and exposures, generally become attached to it. For a camp life, they live well, carrying out with them plenty of coffee and sugar, hard bread . . . bacon, etc., and when on a 'hunt,' never want for fresh meat as the unbranded yearlings afford a plenty of the most delicious. . . . Deer, prairie-hens or grouse, and other game being also plenty, they

In My Fighting Clothes

Figure 3: In 1869, ex-slave Nat Love turned his back on the struggling southern economy and headed west to try his hand as a cowboy. He was not the only impoverished freedman to look for opportunity in the West, about one-third of cowboys were men of color. Courtesy of Harvard College Library.

fare, sumptuously." Teddy Blue agreed. Most stories of the trail "are entirely accurate as to facts," he commented in his old age, "but they are not told right. . . . [They] told all about stampedes and swimming rivers and what a terrible time we had, but they never put in any of the fun, and fun was at least half of it." We were "the most independent class of people on earth."[55]

Goodnight and Loving weren't the only men trying to make a free labor dream come true in the West. Buffalo hunters came to the plains with the railroad crews that began to cut through Kansas during the Civil War and quickly discovered that the animals were valuable and easy to find, if dangerous to confront without a steady hand and a good gun. In 1867, twenty-one-year-old William F. Cody began hunting buffalo to feed the men building the Kansas Pacific Railroad, the first stage of the great rail line to the Pacific. Cody had been a horse wrangler, a prospector, and a Pony Express rider before acting as a Union scout against the Comanche and Kiowa during the Civil War. He claimed to have killed 4,280 buffalo on the plains of Kansas in eighteen months. While "Buffalo Bill," as he became known, killed animals to feed the railroad crews, other buffalo hunters sent the hides east on the railroads to become cheap leather for machine belts and straps.[56]

Miners, too, found wealth in the western hills. Montana's *Helena Herald* reported that "Mr. Bateman took from Dam No. 12 a clean nugget valued at $158," while the *Salt Lake Vidette* noted "that a gang of Chinamen working near Kankaka flat, California, found a chunk of gold weighing forty-five pounds" and that "many large pieces of gold were found in the vicinity of Salt Lake." Newspapers like the *Houston Weekly Telegraph* reprinted this news for their impoverished readers, and despite the fact that mining was a game for businessmen, it was no wonder that *De Bow's Review* announced that "the rapid growth and precious productions of the newly opened regions of the upper Mississippi demand the attention of our readers." Recording the value of the minerals from Montana as between sixteen and twenty million dollars in the past few years, it listed the most productive mines there and the best ways to extract gold. By 1868, famous humorist Artemus Ward treated mining seriously when he described the West for an English audience. "Virginia City—in the bright new state of Nevada," he told them, was "in the heart of the famous Washoe silver regions—the mines of which annually produce over twenty-five millions of solid silver. This silver is melted into solid bricks—of about the size of ordinary house bricks—and carted off to San Francisco with mules. The roads often swarm with these silver waggons [*sic*]."[57]

White and black adventurers crowding into the plains met hostile Indians prepared to defend their territory. Goodnight and Loving skirted the southern edge of Comancheria as they took their cattle west. Angry at incursions and the death of the bison at the hands of the buffalo hunters, Comanche warriors attacked the whites crossing their territory. In 1867, Goodnight's partner Loving incautiously decided to ride ahead of the main herd to be sure to reach Santa Fe in time to bid for government meat contracts. Riding straight into a band of Comanches, Loving caught a bullet in the wrist. He managed to escape and make his way back to Fort Sumner, but the amputation of his arm came too late. He died of gangrene three weeks later. "I regret to have to be laid away in a foreign country," he told his partner, so Goodnight and his men packed Loving's body in a tin coffin filled with charcoal and took him back to Texas.[58]

For Indians, America's free labor economy meant either assimilation or death. Men like Quanah in the Southwest and Sitting Bull in the Northwest fought against the American free labor ideal, trying to hold their communal lands and economy against those who would divide it up for individual opportunity. "I do not wish to be shut up in a corral," explained Sitting Bull, who was widely known as generous, unassuming, and wise. "It is bad for young men to be fed by an agent. It makes them lazy and drunken. All agency Indians I have seen were worthless. They are neither red warriors nor white farmers. They are neither wolf nor dog." Indians' refusal to adopt a white economy justified for easterners their determination to take tribal lands, both to develop the resources there and to force Indians into "civilization." In 1868, the commissioner of Indian affairs told Congress that white settlement would destroy game and compel Indians to turn to farming to survive. This had worked with the Cherokees, he claimed. "Agriculture and stock-breeding brought with them the important idea of individual rights or of personal property, and the notion of fixed local habitations, of sale and barter, profit and loss," important concepts for American free workers that made little sense to the communal economies of native tribes. Sitting Bull pointedly noted, "The white man knows how to make everything, but he does not know how to distribute it." The Fourteenth Amendment excluded "Indians not taxed" from the rights and privileges of citizenship in part to guarantee that citizens owed loyalty only to the United States and in part to protect state laws prohibiting the sale of guns and alcohol to hostile Indians. This exclusion, though, meant that tribal Indians had no way to protect their lands. Not citizens, they could not defend their rights in court.[59]

The U.S. government had a strong interest in promoting eastern settlement of the West. Not only would increased production mean higher tax revenues to pay off the Civil War debt, but also the newly powerful nation had every intention of becoming—as a congressman said during the war—the greatest nation on earth. With the end of the conflict, the way seemed clear for America to expand across the continent, and even the globe. "Stand clear there, all airth and ocean!" Uncle Sam announced to the world in a May 1865 *Harper's Weekly* cartoon. Holding an American flag that stretched west past Indians to a steamship on the far western horizon of the Pacific Ocean, he continued: "My hands are free now, and I'm goin' to hyst a flag so big it'll cover most o' the land and a good bit o' the seal." The government had encouraged miners to go into the Far West to find gold during the war; with the conflict over, it began organizing major government surveys of the region to clear the way for settlement by easterners. The first two expeditions set off in 1867, with Clarence King investigating the fortieth parallel that runs through Colorado, Utah, and Nevada, and Dr. Ferdinand V. Hayden conducting a geological survey of Nebraska and Wyoming.[60]

So determined was Congress to settle the West that, during the war, it had pledged land and the backing of the federal Treasury to anyone willing to build a railroad across the plains and mountains to the West Coast. Eastern railroads built before the Civil War had followed settlement, coming when communities wanted a rail line to markets and railroad companies calculated that there was enough business to make a railroad a paying proposition. The western railroads, in contrast, anticipated settlement and offered no immediate business for the company building them. Because the construction of railroads was frightfully expensive—requiring costly grading, bridges, rails, rolling stock, and crew before the line could carry an ounce of freight—even the most adventuresome entrepreneurs would undertake only the short lines guaranteed enough business to turn a quick profit. The lines through unpopulated areas, the very lines that Republicans hoped would develop the country by bringing settlers in and resources out, could never be built by private capital alone. Anxious to spread settlers west and to link the markets of China and the Orient with East Coast factories, Congress in 1862 offered free land to any entrepreneur willing to build a railroad line across the country, land that could be sold to finance the cost of construction. When this offer proved insufficient to make railroad bonds salable, Congress two years later guaranteed that the government would pay interest on the railroad bonds if the companies themselves could not. With this seed money and guarantee, the transcontinental railroad project took off in 1864, and by 1865 the road was plowing into the plains.[61]

Once there, workers and the buffalo hunters who fed them ran into a new problem requiring government aid. Attacks from hostile Indians meant army protection or the abandonment of the project. The Indian Wars increased the government presence in the West as Congress poured in troops to protect white and black railroad workers and settlers. In 1867, Major General Winfield Scott Hancock testified that all of the Plains Indians were hostile. The *Houston Weekly Telegraph* reported: "He avers that the Indians are more hostile this year than formerly, and says he has never known any period when the war was . . . conducted with so much spirit and malignity. . . . The Indians are now carrying on the war with all the new improvements. They have field glasses. . . . They come up like a regiment of cavalry, and appear like a regular regiment." He estimated the warriors at around 400 Cheyennes, around 400 Arrapahoes [*sic*], around 400 to 500 Apaches, and over-estimated the Camanches [*sic*] at around 3,000. At its peak in 1867, the U.S. Army had 57,000 troops stationed in the West.[62]

The U.S. government also negotiated treaties with the Indians to bring them as close as deemed possible to an "American" way of life. In October 1867, the Treaty of Medicine Lodge—a name that encompassed three treaties signed near Medicine Lodge, Kansas, from October 21 to October 28—was a dramatic solution to the Indian wars on the southern plains. By the terms of the Medicine Lodge agreement, the Kiowa, Comanche, Apache, Cheyenne, and Arapaho Indians exchanged their claims to 90 million acres of their traditional lands for confirmation of their title to around 3 million acres in what is now Oklahoma. For their cooperation, the government promised to build a number of public buildings, including a schoolhouse, and to provide a doctor, farmer, blacksmith, carpenter, miller, engineer, and teachers. They also agreed to provide the Indians with clothing. In exchange for these benefits, the Indians promised to leave railroad construction crews alone and pledged that they would "not attack any persons at home, nor traveling." They would stop storming military posts and agreed neither to "capture or carry off from the settlements white women or children" nor to "kill nor scalp white men nor attempt to do them harm." On the northern plains, the Treaty of Fort Laramie in May 1868 gave the Sioux the Black Hills reservation in the Dakotas forever, with terms similar to the Treaty of Medicine Lodge the previous year.[63]

The treaties calmed the trouble on the plains but did not solve it. Although 5,000 Native Americans attended the Medicine Lodge meeting and the white press made much of it, the tribes were divided about the treaty even before some of their representatives signed it. While the eastern bands of

Comanches accepted the treaty, Quanah Quahadas wanted no part of it and never considered ending their opposition to white encroachment. Like many others, they recognized that the control of Indian agents over the tribes was fatal, and they preferred to trust their lives to their own skill as hunters. To this conviction Quanah himself likely added a burning desire to overcome the taint of his white blood by proving himself a leading hunter and warrior. The Comanches were not the only holdouts. Farther south, on the border with Mexico, inexperienced army officers had abused Chiricahua Apaches and sparked a war almost a decade before, and continuing hostilities were fueling more fury. In the north, some of the Sioux's fiercest fighters—including Sitting Bull—signed the Treaty of Fort Laramie but intended that whites would keep their bargain or pay for their transgressions. Within a year, the Northern Pacific railroad crews were encroaching on Sioux land, and by 1871, 2,000 Indian warriors led by Sitting Bull were riding to war to turn back a Northern Pacific surveying party. "If they come shooting," Sitting Bull and his friend Crazy Horse told their warriors, "shoot back."[64]

By 1868, free labor America appeared to its adherents to be within reach, although it seemed threatened in the East by those who sought to commandeer government for their own ends and in the West by those Indians who attacked those trying to bring a free labor economy west. It was imperative for America's free labor world that all Americans support the idea of a shared harmony of interest, that all believed they were working their way up together. If one group or another began to demand government action on its own behalf, the free labor system would fall apart as privileging one group would necessitate discriminating against another, thus destroying economic harmony. Nowhere was the government's responsibility for defending the free labor vision clearer than in the West, where without government money, the army, and government surveyors, easterners hoping to use their labor to turn natural resources into something valuable would almost certainly lose their lives to arrows, nature, or starvation. How to establish a national free labor society remained the most important question of the day, but by 1868, it was compounded by the growing evidence that not all Americans subscribed to the idea of economic harmony, which was the vital underpinning of the free labor ideal.

CHAPTER THREE

1868–1871

Conflicting Visions

Sustaining free labor, it seemed, depended on a growing national government, but a strong government could be dangerous if it were hijacked by those who would use its power against others. By 1868, those who believed that radical African Americans would disrupt the system. Compounding their fears were wage earners who were organizing to demand legislation establishing shorter hours and better working conditions. Cigar maker Samuel Gompers was a barrel-chested man with heavy features, dark hair, and a walrus mustache who tended toward fat and waddled when he walked, looking every inch the part of a labor organizer. But anyone who misjudged Gompers as a slow-witted worker was in for a rude awakening, for inside his heavy frame was one of the sharpest minds of his era. Gompers was among those who were unconvinced that America's political economy guaranteed that employers and employees working together in economic harmony would climb upward together.

The world of many postwar workers was rapidly changing from the antebellum ideal of self-sufficiency to a precarious life of dependency on low-paying seasonal jobs. Their reality demanded amelioration, but their demands directly challenged the idea that government should not support one segment of society over another. To many workers who viewed the different economic interests in America as naturally in conflict, the call for government to adjust those differences seemed appropriate. Gompers later recorded his introduction to wage labor: "For the first year and a half after we came to New York I worked with my father at home," he recalled. "Father paid a deposit for materials and worked at his bench at home instead of in a shop." When he was between sixteen and seventeen, Gompers became a journeyman at M. Stachelberg's on Pearl Street. "There was much unrest in the shop," he remembered. "The men were discontented. They asked me to present to the employer their grievances and the new conditions they wanted." Stachelberg sneered at Gompers, saying he should "be ashamed to be representing men old enough to be my father," but Gompers retorted "that the men were entitled to have whoever they chose. When Stachelberg found that I couldn't be intimidated, he tried to bribe me. He sought me out in conversation, offered to treat me to beer, and to do everything to alienate me from the men." Gompers stuck by his fellow workers, though, "and finally succeeded in winning the case."[1]

Most northern Americans, along with some upwardly mobile southerners, could not conceive of the inequalities of industrial labor. Still overwhelmingly rural and enjoying the postwar economy, they believed that America's free labor society was indeed creating universal prosperity as everyone worked their way up together. Immediately after the war there had been a brief recession, but by the end of 1867, the nation was booming. Ulysses S. Grant caught the heady optimism of the postwar economy for those it was serving. He thanked God for the nation's benefits: "a territory unsurpassed in fertility, of an area equal to the abundant support of 500,000,000 people, and abounding in every variety of useful mineral in quantity sufficient to supply the world for generations; with a variety of climate adapted to the production of every species of earth's riches and suited to the habits, tastes, and requirements of every living thing. . . . Harmony is being rapidly restored within our own borders. Manufactures hitherto unknown in our country are springing up in all sections, producing a degree of national independence unequaled by that of any other power." The emphasis of the free labor vision on economic expansion fit perfectly into the aims of entrepreneurs poised to develop their industries across the new, national markets. Republicans had created sweeping tariffs during the war, and Grant reflected happily that these tariffs made manufacturing boom and would soon free America from imports. Factories were spreading across the country, he said, employing hundreds of thousands of people.[2]

The nation's first big businesses were the railroads. As they grew after the war, they transformed the economy. Trade that had previously traveled north and south along coasts and rivers now went east and west on railroads.

Immigrants flowed into the nation to work in the industries that fed the roads—like Carnegie's iron factories—as well as to make the goods that would travel on them. Financiers poured into railroads and other new businesses money they had made during the war by investing in bonds and in the wartime businesses that supplied the armies. New fields for enterprise meant new fields for inventors, who registered for 13,762 patents from September 1868 to September 1869 alone (compared to an average of slightly more than 5,000 a year for the seventy years from 1790 to 1860). From 1860 to 1890, the U.S. Patent Office issued more than half a million patents. New inventions meant new companies. By 1867, for example, Andrew Carnegie had invested in the Pullman Palace Car Company (organized by George Pullman) to make sleeping cars for trains. No longer did a trip from Chicago to New York mean dozing uncomfortably on wooden seats for three nights as the low-slung cars jerked noisily over the rough tracks. The trip got easier—and safer—still after 1868, when inventors developed air brakes. Easterners went west on the railroads, too, and were streaming into western states and territories. In the years between 1860 and 1870, Minnesota's non-Indian population jumped from 172,443 to 439,706; Nebraska's from 28,842 to 122,993; Kansas's from 107,206 to 394,377; Nevada's from 6,857 to 42,491; California's from 397,994 to 560,223. Territories unorganized in 1860 also showed big numbers on the 1870 census. Montana had 20,594 non-Indians; Colorado, 39,864; Dakota, 14,181; Idaho, slightly more at 14,998; and Wyoming, not separated from Dakota until 1868, had 9,118. Railroads and the companies that supplied them were the most visible big businesses immediately after the war.[3]

The new economy needed unskilled labor, but it also needed clerical workers, bankers, and managers. Typists learned to use the new typewriters, invented in 1867 and quickly accepted in business once their inventors found a better system for producing the print than soaking hair ribbons in ink. These white-collar workers lived in bustling cities and towns. After 1871, urban residents could ride to work on the cable streetcar; if they lived on a coast, they could see the four-masted schooners that carried grain, guano, and other goods around the world dominating harbors bustling with smaller ships. After the 1865 invention of the compression ice machine, they could have cold food even in the summer, transforming ice cream from a rare luxury to a commodity sold by street vendors. In 1869, the first synthetic celluloid, a precursor to our ubiquitous plastic, meant that women's clothing could have bright buttons in fanciful shapes: leaves, blackberries, and flowers. If men were daring, they could try one of the newfangled big-wheeled bicycles, whose height and narrow tires made them susceptible to accidents but which gave even a man of average income a range of daily travel previously unimaginable. Most dramatic, perhaps, was the construction of Brooklyn Bridge, begun in 1870. New Yorkers watched the marvel of human engineering take shape on the banks of the East River and wondered what American technology and labor could not accomplish.

It was not just men who blossomed in the fertile ground of the postwar nation. This progressive American society nurtured the energy women had found during the war. In February 1868, Julia Ward Howe and her friends in the Boston area agreed "to hire . . . parlors . . . in some convenient locality, and to furnish and keep them open for the convenience of ladies residing in the city and its suburbs." The New England Woman's Club began as a place for women to study and improve their minds. Quickly it became "an organized social centre for united thought and action," Howe's daughter recalled. Southern women, too, found new roles after the war as the need for money drove previously elite white women into the workforce. Forced to teach in the school her mother opened, Elizabeth Allston found her new job changed her life. Previously prone to depression and guilt over living as a social butterfly, she wrote of her teaching, "every second of my time is occupied, and oh, I am so happy!" Exchanging the stultifying life of a southern plantation belle for the excitement of busy Charleston and work she loved, she saw nothing to regret. "My mind is so eager for knowledge . . . it springs forward so to meet things," she recorded in her diary in 1869, "If only I had a man's education . . ."

As the economic boom combined with the loss of young men in the war, more and more colleges opened their doors to women like Allston. In Illinois, Jane Addams, the daughter of the man Lincoln had fondly called "my dear Double-D'd Addams," graduated from Rockford Seminary in 1881 and was awarded one of the college's first BA degrees in 1884. In school she developed life-long friendships with other young women determined "to do noble and true things." By 1870, girls made up the majority of high school graduates. Fewer than 2 percent of college-age Americans went to college; women made up 21 percent of that group.[4]

One of America's most famous children's books captured the postwar changes in women's attitudes. In October 1868, the Roberts Brothers Boston publishing house printed 2,000 copies of Louisa May Alcott's *Little Women, or, Meg, Jo, Beth and Amy*, the enduring story of four genteelly poor girls coming of age in the postwar years. The girls read books and spoke their minds, and only one of them led the life of an undereducated antebellum homebody. Josephine—who preferred her name be shortened to the masculine "Jo"—was a writer; Meg, a governess who dreamed of acting; Amy, a schoolgirl who aspired to paint. Beth, the one March girl who could not envision a career outside of her parents' home, wasted away and died young of an unspecified illness (although even she was involved enough in the world to drop hand-knit mittens out of her sickroom window for passing children). In their new public roles, the March girls were careful to improve the world around them, ministering to the poor, nurturing the motherless boy next door, writing uplifting stories for mass consumption. The book rocketed to popularity. The first printing disappeared within the month, and by the end of 1869, another 30,000 copies were in the hands of young readers. "I am the only girl in college who wasn't brought up on 'Little Women,'" an orphan commented in a turn-of-the-century novel. "I haven't told anybody, though (that *would* stamp me as queer)."[5]

Opportunities seemed to be everywhere for young Americans in the vibrant postwar world, and their newly strong nation seemed poised to dominate the international stage. Angry at Europe for its lukewarm support of the Union and confident that wartime economic legislation would permit America to become the greatest country on earth, northern businessmen and government officials worked to consolidate the nation's economic and political power. So confident about American growth was Secretary of State William Henry Seward that he arranged to buy the territory of Alaska from Russia in 1867, largely because he hoped to force the valuable ports of western Canada to fall into American hands. Although the purchase was ridiculed at home as "Seward's Icebox" and "Seward's Folly," the threat of American expansion into Canada was strong enough to make British officials permit the organization of the dominion of Canada for protection against the country's aggressive southern neighbor. England's fear of America was proof, indeed, that the nation was a force to be reckoned with. By 1868, expansionists confidently predicted that Hawaii would soon be American, and in order to enable American business to grow internationally, in 1870, Congress approved the Burlingame Treaty that opened the huge markets of China to American business. The world seemed to be at America's feet.[6]

For all the good news about American life, though, those thriving in the new economy had cause to worry that not everyone believed in the American system that seemed to be promoting such prosperity, that some hoped to succeed by using government power to stack the economic deck in their own favor. For starters, something was wrong in the South. Northerners clung to the idea that the South would soon start producing an enormously valuable cotton crop, but it stubbornly refused to do so and northerners could not understand why. The reality was that southern cotton could not recover the ground lost during the war: heirloom seeds had been lost, fields overgrown with weeds, levees broken. American production was down, and Egypt and India had taken over the international cotton market previously dominated by the South. The region was struggling with its labor system, too. There was no clear formula for employing labor, so ex-slaves and poor whites determined to be paid up front had to hash out terms for employment with cash-poor landowners who favored the system of gang labor that had prevailed during slavery. Sometimes people worked for wages—generally during harvest or planting, when extra hands were needed—but more often southern laborers farmed as tenants on rented land or worked their employer's land on shares. Sharecropping meant that farmers pledged a portion of their crop to the landowner in exchange for the use of land and sometimes tools. Although this system was a solution to the region's lack of cash and the farmers' desire for autonomy, it locked the region into a reliance on cotton—a crop that could easily be turned into cash—at a time when the cotton market was softening.[7]

Underestimating the importance of economic obstacles to the South's recovery, observers blamed the region's malaise on southerners. Northern Republicans like Carl Schurz had believed that, once free, African Americans would work hard, earn property, and rise quickly to become independent farmers. When white southerners cheated them out of wages and hampered their ability to fit into a free labor system, northerners had given African Americans the vote to protect themselves, gambling that blacks would automatically defend the principles of hard work and harmonious economic development Republicans held so dear. In winter 1868, the delegates to the new southern state constitutional conventions organized under the Military Reconstruction Act rewrote their state constitutions to take southern governments out of the hands of the small circle of white aristocrats—people like the Allstons and the Hamptons—who had controlled them before the war and who were threatening to regain their ascendancy. The new constitutions called for universal manhood suffrage and the popular election of judges and officials, and they removed property qualifications for office-holding and jury service. They also guaranteed black political and civil rights, abolished whipping as a criminal punishment, and ended imprisonment for debt. At the same time, the delegates expanded the duties of the states to their citizens,

Figure 4. While observers focused on the needs of freedmen for economic protection, women and children also worked, usually for much lower wages than men. Politicians who insisted that black men must be able to vote to protect their economic rights only rarely made the same argument about women. Keystone-Mast Collection, UCR/California Museum of Photography, University of California at Riverside.

establishing state-funded schools, orphan asylums, insane asylums, and, occasionally, poor relief. Supporters of the congressional plan of reconstruction blamed the South's continuing poverty on prominent white southerners who refused to let free African Americans and poor whites rebuild the South and who would not work themselves. Increasingly, congressmen used the government to keep angry white southerners from hampering those actually working to restore the South.[8]

White southerners tied to their old ideas of political economy had another explanation for the the region's postwar troubles. Spinning out the logic of their antebellum social structure to conclude that if given political power, workers would automatically attack employers, they insisted that freedpeople had no intention of working. Invoking the new southern state constitutions, they argued that the newly enfranchised African Americans were revolutionaries intent on confiscating the region's wealth and property. Black political power was proof of a Republican conspiracy to destroy the American republic, they insisted. Black suffrage had been forced on the white South with bayonets to create a Republican majority that would cement the Republicans' stranglehold on the government. White southerners hammered on the inaccurate idea that the convention delegates were non-property-holding, illiterate ex-slaves and attacked them as freeloaders hijacking the government. This was not American republican government but its opposite: the attempt of powerful politicians to maintain power through a corrupt voting base while eliminating all potential opponents from the polls. According to the *Atlanta Constitution*: "The government of the United States is either one of limited powers or it is not. . . . If limited in the exercise of its power, it is a Republic; if absolute, it is a Despotism. If the former, the people are the rulers; if the latter, then Congress, or any other branch, individual or a few, arrogating themselves to be. . . . The great danger of our government has always been from the encroachments of Federal power on our State and domestic institutions." Dramatically, in South Carolina, Wade Hampton declared bankruptcy at a time when Beverly Nash, an ex-slave formerly owned by his cousin, took Hampton's old seat in the legislature as a senator from Richland County.[9]

The political implications of the southern struggle splashed over into national politics. President Johnson agreed with white southern Democrats that Republican congressmen were attempting to monopolize a growing government, and he decided to challenge them by flouting the legally tenuous Tenure of Office Act. After months of sparring with Secretary of War Edwin M. Stanton, a Lincoln appointee who was deliberately working against him, Johnson tried to throw him out of office. "I think I do not exaggerate," wrote Carl Schurz, "in saying that an overwhelming majority of the loyal Union men North and South saw in President Johnson a traitor bent on turning over the National Government to the rebels again, and ardently wished to see him utterly stripped of power, not so much for what he had done, but for what . . . they thought, he was capable of doing and likely to do." Stanton had initially acquiesced when Johnson replaced him in December 1867 but, backed by Republicans, he returned to the War Department and refused to leave, eating and sleeping in the building from December 14, 1867, until May 26, 1868, to demonstrate that Johnson could not remove him. In late February 1868, the House voted to impeach Johnson on eleven charges. He had violated the Tenure of Office Act by firing Stanton, representatives charged, and he also had tried "to bring into disgrace, ridicule, hatred, contempt and reproach the Congress of the United States." The House supported these charges with specific examples of his "intemperate, inflammatory, and scandalous harangues . . . loud threats and bitter menaces" against Congress and the laws.[10]

The angry struggle between Johnson and Congress combined with the continued military occupation of the South to make moderate Americans nervous that republican government was being undermined. If the Senate convicted Johnson, his replacement would be the president pro tem of the Senate, leading radical Benjamin F. Wade, infamous for his statement that wealth must be better distributed between labor and capital. At the same time, southerners charged that soldiers on duty in the South added terror to the tactics of northern radicals. The *Atlanta Constitution* reported that four soldiers from an Alabama garrison had dragged a southern man out of bed, with two holding him under arrest while the other two of them robbed his home of "$500 in money and other valuables." That same military was registering voters who were overwhelmingly Republican and black. As southern African Americans registered to vote, hostile observers made much of black radicals' call for land redistribution, welfare legislation, and educational aid. Even sympathetic moderates worried that black voters were toying dangerously with the idea of enlisting government power to control a world of class conflict.[11]

Northerners began to shrink back from the apparent radicalism of Republican congressmen, who seemed to be changing the proper nature of American government. From March through May, the Senate conducted Johnson's impeachment trial. On May 16, thirty-five Senators voted for conviction and nineteen—twelve Democrats and seven Republicans—voted for acquittal, leaving prosecutors one vote short of the two-thirds majority necessary for conviction; a second vote ten days later also came up a vote short. Democrats supported Johnson's stand against Republican expansion of the government. So, too, did many Republicans, who hated Johnson but cringed at the idea of Wade in the White House.[12]

Northerners were also nervous about the continued military occupation of the South, paid for with tax money, which seemed to guarantee voters for the Republican Party. Pressure from disgruntled northern constituents made congressmen agree to readmit to the Union southern states that had ratified the Fourteenth Amendment to the Constitution, although they continued to worry that southern whites would turn on freedpeople as soon as civil government was restored. On June 22–25, 1868, Congress passed the Omnibus Act, readmitting Alabama, Arkansas, Florida, Georgia, Louisiana, North Carolina, and South Carolina, leaving out only Mississippi, Texas, and Virginia, which had not approved new constitutions. Thanks to the votes of the newly readmitted states, the following month, on July 28, the Fourteenth Amendment was added to the Constitution of the United States. After readmission, white Democrats in the Georgia legislature illustrated the necessity for federal protection of African Americans by immediately expelling their black colleagues, claiming that the Georgia constitution made them ineligible to hold office. It was clear that the white Georgians were counting on a Democratic president in 1868 to support their actions.

The 1868 election indicated that questions about the nature of America's political economy and its government had become intertwined during the previous three years. These questions proved to be the central issues in the election. Democrats insisted that the election was about the Republicans' corrupt seizure of the government, thanks to votes obtained both from freedmen—characterized by Democrats as poor, lazy, and ignorant—and from rich businessmen in exchange for government largesse. The Democrats charged that, far from protecting free laborers, the Republicans were creating class struggle in America, impoverishing workers in order to build an oligarchy by catering to southern freedmen. As they placed themselves "upon the Constitution as the foundation and limitation of the powers of the government, and the guarantee of the liberties of the citizen," the Democrats reflected the anger and bitterness of white southerners.[13]

Although prominent white southerners could not vote in the upcoming election, they were not barred from participating in politics. Along with powerful ex-Confederates James Chesnut, Robert Barnwell Rhett, and Nathan Bedford Forrest, among others, Wade Hampton served as a delegate to the National Democratic Convention, which convened on July 4. Appointed to the Committee on Resolutions, his voice was clear in the platform. It accused the Republicans of establishing a military despotism, stripping the president of his constitutional power, and doubling the national debt solely to maintain the army, navy, and patronage jobs necessary to "secure negro supremacy." To repair the damage, the convention demanded that all southern states be readmitted to the Union, southerners be offered universal amnesty, and states alone determine voting rights. On this latter point it positively snarled. The founding fathers had put the determination of suffrage into the hands of the states, it noted; giving the national government control over suffrage would create "an unqualified despotism." In language suggested by Hampton, the platform declared "the reconstruction acts so-called, of Congress, as such an usurpation, and unconstitutional, revolutionary, and void." If the Republicans were reelected, the Democrats concluded, Americans would be "a subjected and conquered people, amid the ruins of liberty and the scattered fragments of the Constitution."[14]

The Democratic platform rejected the idea that all Americans shared the same interests, endorsing instead the idea of class competition. It declared sympathy "with the workingmen of the United States in their efforts to protect the rights and interests of the laboring classes of the country." It called for repaying the national debt in currency rather than gold and demanded the taxation of bonds, although it straddled the tariff question, claiming both that it should be for revenue only and that it should "best promote and encourage the great industrial interests of the country." Even the aristocratic Hampton in his convention speech of July 9 reiterated that the Democrats stood with the common men of all sections against the Republicans who were harnessing the government to the rich. He reminded listeners that he had met the Democratic vice presidential candidate Frank Blair, who had been Sherman's lieutenant on his March to the Sea, "on more than one field," then declared that he and "the soldiers of the South cordially, heartily and cheerfully, accept the right hand of friendship that is extended to them." Thanking Andrew Johnson for "resisting the aggressions of Congress upon the Constitutional rights of the States and the people," the Democrats nominated a ticket of New York's former governor Horatio Seymour and former Union general Francis P. Blair, Jr. Carl Schurz noted that the Democratic platform "stopped but little short of advocating violence to accomplish the annulment of the

Reconstruction laws adopted by Congress, and it demanded the payment of a large part of the national debt in depreciated greenbacks."[15]

In the election summer of 1868, Democrats repeatedly hammered home the idea that Republican policies meant that "the manufacturers, speculators, and money-dealers grow rich, and the industrious poor are still further impoverished." Taxes to maintain an army in the South and the officeholders to support it cost more than $300 million a year. Thanks to the Republicans, Democrats snarled, "the poor whites of the country are to be taxed—bled of all their little earnings—in order to fatten the vagabondish negroes." Incendiary Associated Press items from Democratic reporters in the South seemed to support this version of events, telling northern readers, for example, of an event in which freedmen tried "to overawe the citizens and kill the leading Democrats of the town and vicinity," although in reality this particular riot killed seventy-five to one hundred African Americans and only wounded five whites.[16]

For Republicans, the election was about the survival of the free labor system based on economic harmony for which the North had fought. Meeting in Chicago in May, they nominated popular moderates—U. S. Grant for president and Speaker of the House Schuyler Colfax of Indiana as his running mate. Insisting that there was no class conflict in America and that all hardworking Americans were climbing upward together, they emphasized America's founding principle of republican equality. Their platform resolved to make "the great principles laid down in the immortal Declaration of Independence . . . a living reality on every inch of American soil." Military protection for African Americans was imperative, they argued, not to guarantee a Republican constituency, but because it was "the duty of the Government to sustain . . . [the new southern] constitutions securing equal civil and political rights to all . . . and to prevent the people of [the South] from . . . a state of anarchy." Congress's guarantee of black suffrage in the South "was demanded by every consideration of public safety, of gratitude, and of justice," it noted. According to the Republicans, the problem was not congressional Republicans but Johnson, who had "persistently and corruptly resisted, by every means in his power, every proper attempt at the reconstruction of the States lately in rebellion." The growing popular concern over Republican manipulation of the voting base was clear, though. In 1867, Carl Schurz had moved his family to St. Louis, where he edited the Republican *Westliche Post*; in Missouri he found former Unionists and Confederates struggling for control of state government. Trying to undercut the accusation that Republicans were deliberately keeping Democrats from the polls, Schurz wrote a plank in the party platform calling for "the removal of the disqualifications and restrictions imposed upon the late rebels in the same measure as the spirit of disloyalty will die out, and as may be consistent with the safety of the loyal people."[17]

The Republicans reiterated the economic harmony of the American system, meeting head-on the money problem that was agitating society by 1868. They explained that Democrats were wrong to talk of wealthy bondholders because "the bondholders, as a class, are mechanics, laborers, salaried officers, and tradesmen, rather than rich men and capitalists." A bondholder who had lent money to the government during its time of need was neither a "designing speculator who had taken advantage of our necessities to make usurious investments" nor "trying to suck the blood of our people," Schurz recorded. It would be "a national crime" to renege on promises to pay bonds in gold, for that would destroy America's harmonious economy by making the demands of one class overrule justice to all. Wealthy men would invest their money overseas rather than at home, business would be "prostrated," and the economy would collapse. The editors of *Harper's Weekly* made the connection between Democratic arguments and the Confederacy and suggested that repudiation was part of the lasting Confederate effort to destroy the Union. The *Chicago Tribune* insisted that the conflict was between "right and wrong . . . good and evil."[18]

During the campaign, Republicans insisted that their free labor vision was the true American ideal. Emphasizing their own humble backgrounds, they claimed to be the true party of the average man, "the friends of the poor without respect to race or color," unlike the Democratic followers of elitist southern white leaders. They favored protecting African Americans not to create a voting base, but to enable good black workers to enter the free labor economy. And their plan was working, they maintained. Congress permitted the disbanding of the Freedmen's Bureau in July because of freedmen's "good behavior, thrift, eagerness and aptness to learn," which had made them advance at a "simply marvelous" rate. Ex-slaves "do not expect to control Southern politics," a campaigning Republican congressman insisted, and could never do so. Rather, they were model free laborers, eager to get an education and to work for wages. The government could not help them any more than it already had: "Everything now depends upon the freedmen themselves—upon their perseverance, their patience, and, above all, upon their intellectual and moral progress."[19]

Northern Democrats continued to hammer on the idea of Republican domination of the government and fleecing of the common man, but their voices were drowned in the summer of 1868 by the actions of southern Democrats. Determined to prevent the ratification of the new constitutions, angry white southerners intimidated black voters and their white supporters. Growing out of the postwar white gangs that had terrorized freedpeople, the Ku Klux Klan (KKK) was first organized in Tennessee by former Confederate general Nathan Bedford Forrest, who was infamous for ordering black prisoners of war killed at the battle of Fort Pillow. In 1868, the KKK was formally organized to incite southern white pride and to destroy black political participation. "This is an institution of chivalry, humanity, mercy, and patriotism," the Ku Klux Klan Organization and Principles stated, "to protect the weak, the innocent, and the defenseless from the indignities, wrongs, and outrages of the lawless, the violent, and the brutal." It was designed "to protect and defend the Constitution of the United States" and "to aid and assist in the execution of all constitutional laws, and to protect the people from unlawful seizure and from trial, except by their peers in conformity to the laws of the land." Candidates for admission to the order had to deny membership in "the Radical Republican Party"; oppose "Negro equality both social and political"; and favor "a white man's government," "the reenfranchisement and emancipation of the white men of the South, and the restitution of the Southern people to all their rights, alike proprietary, civil, and political." They must also favor "a government of equitable laws instead of a government of violence and oppression." Those offered membership in the Ku Klux Klan defended their ideas of right and justice by terrorizing black voters, ultimately murdering more than a thousand black and white southern Republicans, including a congressman, before the election of 1868.[20]

The 1868 election revealed that although Americans were unwilling to jeopardize the results of the war, they were also uncomfortable with a growing government that seemed monopolized by a particular party with a special agenda. Grant's election "was a foregone conclusion," Schurz later remembered, but at the time it was not so clear. Capitalizing on fears that a Democratic victory would erase the results of the war, the popular Union general won handily in the Electoral College but had a popular majority of less than 400,000 out of 5,715,000 votes. In part, this close vote reflected the Democratic terrorism that had kept southern Republicans from the polls, but it also showed a developing uneasiness with the government activism necessary to maintain Republican reconstruction. The results of the election were not at all an endorsement of radicalism. Small government spokesman Democrat Sunset Cox reentered the House of Representatives, this time from New York. Also revealing was the immediate acquiescence in the election results by southern Democratic leaders like Wade Hampton, who announced in early November that they would support the elected Republican officials in their states, clearly expecting influence in their administrations. Northern Republicans greeted these demonstrations with enthusiasm, predicting that with Grant's election, a reasonable end to reconstruction was at hand, one that safeguarded a free labor system in the South without destroying America's republican government by developing an activist government that worked on behalf of a particular group.[21]

The growing popular uneasiness with a Republican machine was reflected in Carl Schurz's election to the Senate. When Charles Drake, the leader of Missouri's Republican Party, tried to dictate the election of a lackey to be his colleague in the U.S. Senate, Schurz and others who thought like him opposed the Republican leader's machine style of politics. Schurz's friends persuaded him to challenge Drake's candidate. Incensed at the upstarts, Drake launched bitter attacks on Schurz and his German-American supporters. (Schurz, who could be devastating with a pen, later commented, "I do not know to what religious denomination he belonged, but he made the impression as if no religion would be satisfactory to him that did not provide for a well-kept hell fire to roast sinners and heretics.") Schurz won the seat easily, probably by comparing the war record of Missouri's German-Americans to that of Drake, who had declined to fight. Portraying his victory as that of an honest government David against a dictatorial party Goliath, Schurz remembered proudly that "my whole election expenses amounted only to my board bill at the hotel," and he was elected "absolutely unencumbered by any promise of patronage or any other favor." Schurz was a dedicated Republican, but by 1870 he had begun to echo the Democratic critique of his party.[22]

The Republican victory of 1868 granted a respite to those who believed in the traditional free labor worldview, but they continued to worry about Americans who seemed to reject hard work and the idea of economic harmony, hoping instead for government aid. Angry Democrats made much of the fact that the votes of 70,000 freedmen in the South spelled the difference between electing Grant and choosing Seymour, although they kept quiet about the Democratic violence that kept thousands of Grant supporters away from the polls. The political jockeying of southern freedpeople made many

Americans nervous, but their actions in many ways seemed to echo those of some northern workers who threatened traditional free labor values. In 1865 and 1866, a number of workers had organized into reform and labor organizations designed to recover the free labor dream from the increasing pressures of industrialization. By 1868, though, postwar industrial growth prompted more and more workers to perceive themselves as a permanent class of wage earners. In a world where they moved frequently from one unskilled job to another, always at the mercy of poor wages and unemployment, they increasingly recognized their inability to accumulate enough money to become self-sufficient. The world of industry after the war was changing rapidly from the bucolic one adherents of free labor still imagined. Large urban factories had different rhythms than smaller rural enterprises. "It was frequently necessary to hunt a new job," Samuel Gompers recalled of 1869. "This necessity was due to fluctuations in the industry, at that time anything but stable; to lockouts, then much more common than strikes; and to resistance to wage reductions which recurred regularly with the changing seasons."[23]

Perhaps the most important of these changes was that the large scale of industry increasingly separated workers from their employers. In antebellum rural America, it was not unusual for a worker and an employer to greet each other on the street by name, live in similar housing, dress in the same sort of clothing, and attend the same church. Indeed, in the 1840s, apprentices commonly lived in their employer's home. Workers could earn enough money to support a family. The postwar world was different. Although agricultural workers outnumbered industrial workers until 1880, a shift was under way. Growing businesses like the railroads required huge numbers of workers, a management staff that operated from distant locations, and extensive work sites. Workplaces became larger, with staff and management divorced from the men and women on the shop floors. Wages dropped and hours increased. Immigrants banded together in the cheap districts of growing industrial cities; native-born workers lived in nearby, slightly more upscale working-class neighborhoods. By 1866, more than just miles separated Carnegie's elegant home in the leafy Pittsburgh suburb of Homewood from his workers' haunts in the sooty inner city. In 1867, when Carnegie moved to New York City to negotiate the international bond market, that distance had become insurmountable. By the 1880s, workers at Carnegie's mills were stoking the brutally hot furnaces twelve hours a day, seven days a week, for less than $2 a day while multimillionaire Carnegie mused that hard work guaranteed success.[24]

No longer could industrial wage laborers believe that they shared the same interests as their employers, that they were all working their way up together. Decades later, Terence V. Powderly recalled the event that he inaccurately claimed had launched his career as one of the nineteenth century's most popular labor organizers. The eleventh of twelve children born to Irish Catholic immigrants who settled in the mining region of Pennsylvania, the self-educated Powderly was working as a machinist at the Pennsylvania Coal Company in Dunmore, Pennsylvania, in September 1869 when a mine explosion in nearby Avondale killed 179 miners. Three days later, Powderly visited Avondale, where he heard a labor organizer call for justice. This "was the first man I had ever heard make a speech on the labor question," Powderly recalled. "I was just a boy then, but as I looked at [him] standing on the desolate hillside at Avondale, with his back toward a moss grown rock the grim, silent witness to that awful tragedy of ignorance, indifference, thoughtlessness, and greed . . . I caught inspiration from his words and realized that there was something more to win through labor than dollars and cents for self. . . . [He] gave expression to a great thought . . . when he said: 'You can do nothing to win these dead back to life, but you can help me to win fair treatment and justice for living men who risk life and health in their daily toil.'"25

Back in Dunmore, and later in Scranton, Powderly tried unsuccessfully to find "a union or brotherhood among [the] men. . . . One could read the papers of that day from one end of the year to the other, and if they found any reference to a labor organization it was one of abuse, ridicule, or scorn. No one connected with organized labor dared to allow his name to appear publicly as a member. The blacklist would be employed and idleness, poverty, destitution, and perhaps death would be the reward of open identification with a labor union in that era." Without formal education, Powderly "feared a communication from me might not make a good impression," so he had a friend write to the president of the Machinists and Blacksmiths International Union headquartered in Cleveland, Ohio, for information on organizing a local chapter. Shortly, an organizer came to establish the Scranton "Subordinate Union No. 2 of Pennsylvania." Powderly was "not permitted to join because I was not old enough," he later remembered. When finally admitted in 1871, he was promptly elected secretary and then president, "though I had never, up to that time, mustered up courage enough to make a motion." Significantly, in his recollection of these events, Powderly played down the fact that in 1869 he was an enthusiastic machinist who loved his job but had been laid off a month before the Avondale disaster, when a miners' strike forced his company to cut back. Moving to Scranton, Powderly found work repairing engines for the Delaware, Lackawanna, and Western Railroad through the good offices of William Scranton himself—nephew of the city's founder—who took a liking to Powderly and became his mentor. Scrawling "Onward and Upward" in his diary twice at the end of 1870, Powderly worked hard to rise. One of his biographers concluded that he joined the machinists union in 1871 largely because it had a life insurance plan.[26]

When Powderly later placed his conversion to labor activism in 1869, he identified himself with those who, by the end of the 1860s, were increasingly inclined toward organization to correct the growing imbalance between wage laborers and employers. In December 1869, a secret labor fraternity, the Knights of Labor, organized in Philadelphia. Unlike trade unions, which organized around a specific type of work, the Knights of Labor accepted as members all men who worked for a living, pointedly excluding bankers, lawyers, doctors, and liquor dealers. The Knights were composed of loosely affiliated local organizations that recruited secretly from the ranks of labor, demanding that members swear only to believe in God, obey His law by "gaining your bread by the sweat of your brow," and be bound "to secrecy, obedience, and mutual assistance." Once admitted, a new recruit was welcomed with a speech explaining that the organization was "dedicated to the service of God, by serving humanity." Since open organizations had failed, the Knights of Labor used secrecy to protect themselves from persecution as they sought fair wages and conditions. They noted that capitalists had organized into large businesses, crushing "the manly hopes of labor and tram-pl[ing] poor humanity in the dust." The Knights wanted to "create a healthy public opinion on the subject of labor (the only creator of values or capital), and the justice of its receiving a just, full share of the values or capital it has created." Although he embraced their cause later than his memoirs suggested, the extraordinary charisma of the slight, gentle-eyed, mustachioed, bespectacled Powderly, who looked more like a college professor than a leader of "the horny-fisted sons of toil," made him the leading spokesman for the labor reform cause.[27]

In 1869, the men who created reform organizations primarily wanted to defend their own version of free labor—safe conditions, reasonable hours, fair wages—against avaricious employers, but they frightened those from across the economic spectrum who endorsed the idea of economic harmony. People who identified themselves as members of a working class seemed alien to those who did not, for increasingly they dressed, spoke, spent free time, and voted differently than those Americans—from beginning workers to established businessmen—who still believed anyone could rise to economic success through hard work alone. Organizing workers explicitly attacked the growing idea that postwar liberty meant only the freedom of individuals to enter into contracts. Forced to take grueling work that paid pennies, they recognized that wage laborers' "liberty of contract" could not be free when they were desperate for work to stave off starvation, and they called for government intervention in the economy to bolster workers' position.

In the postwar world, the perceived political danger posed by laborers who believed in economic conflict was compounded by a number of social factors that made industrial workers seem alien to American values. After the Civil War, immigrants poured into the nation thanks in part to the Contract Labor Law passed by Congress during the war to enable impoverished Europeans to borrow money to pay their passage to America. About 300,000 new immigrant laborers arrived almost every year from 1865 to 1871. With their traditional clothes, languages, and cultures, they seemed alien to native-born Americans. Immigrants who managed to move to farms often formed their own enclaves that replicated old-world patterns, but their insularity made them easier to ignore than the urban workers, both immigrant and native-born, who took pride in their working-class culture. In New York City's Five Points district, gangs like the Bowery Boys swaggered in the streets, drank in saloons, bet on bare-knuckle boxing, or went to inexpensive theaters with working girls who flaunted their independence from their fathers. Workers wore cheap, bright clothing and spoke their own slang, and many entertained no illusions that they would rise unaided in American society.[28]

Working girls added their own element of sexual danger to the working classes in America. They dated men without their parents' approval, for one thing. After they had "drifted along all summer," sixteen-year-old cigar worker Sophia Julian married Samuel Gompers "without consultation or announcement of plans" on January 28, 1867. After their visit to Brooklyn City Hall, Gompers recalled, "We went to a cheap restaurant and got a bite to eat as our wedding supper, and went to the theater to see the play 'La Poveretta' or 'Under the Snow.'" Girls like Sophia were beyond parental control; they kept their meager income for gaudy clothing and trashy novels. A female reformer noted in disgust that the working girls in a paper box factory read escapist romances like *Little Rosebud's Lovers*, a bloodcurdling tale of a beautiful girl hounded to her grave by cruel lovers. When the reformer tried to convince them to read *Little Women* instead, the working girls scoffed. "That's no story—that's just everyday happenings. I don't see what's the use putting things like that in books. . . . I suppose farmer folks likes them kind of stories. . . . They ain't used to the same styles of anything that us city folks are." Working girls had no use for stories of virtue and hard work, marriage and children. They wanted riches, lovers, and excitement to help them forget their monotonous, dirty jobs.[29]

Even their living conditions associated urban industrial workers with frightening images for native-born, rural Americans. The growing postwar cities were places of excitement and opportunity, but also of filth and disease. In the country, garbage could be thrown away outside where it would decompose or be eaten by scavenging animals, and single-family outhouses were treated often with lime, which discouraged bugs, kept down smells, and happened to disinfect as well. In the city, these same practices were deadly. Germ theory was unknown in the 1860s and 1870s, which meant, among other things, that garbage lay in the streets to rot, attracting disease-carrying flies and rats. Worse, people crowded into poor districts either threw their slops into the street or shared outhouses with the people around them, and overflowing privies spilled into water and public areas. New York City had a population of 1.2 million people in 1880, a number that would rise to over 1.5 million within a decade. After the development of steel frame construction in the early 1880s, tenements grew higher and more people were crowded into even less space. By the 1890s, every acre of New York City's Lower East Side held almost 1,000 people. Aside from the complications of human life, what could be done with dead animals in such crowded conditions? An epidemic that struck New York City's horses in July 1871 was a catastrophe indeed, for not only were valuable horses dying within a day of taking ill, but also there were too many horse carcasses in the city to be carted away. Dead horses in New York City in July were no joke.[30]

For those lucky enough to live outside of this atmosphere, it seemed a miasma of contagion, adding the stigma of illness to those inside it. The nineteenth century was a dangerous era, to be sure. People died in childbirth, in accidents, of cold, of infections (the discovery of penicillin was a generation away). But in the crowded cities, yellow fever, cholera, typhoid, and tuberculosis took an appalling toll, especially on children. Urban childhood death rates were twice as high as those in rural areas, and for parents it was devastating to hold a child too sick to cry any longer, helplessly knowing it was doomed, then look around at a home full of other children and wonder how many of them would soon show symptoms of the same deadly illness. In 1882, more than half the children born in Chicago would die before they turned five, and in 1890, almost a quarter of all urban children born that year would die within a year. With poor city districts suffering death rates of up to 25 per-cent, according to one horrified observer, the association of urban life with deadly disease made it a place to be feared.[31]

Urban workers frightened those who did not identify with them not only by their dress, culture, and living conditions, but also because they appeared to reject the free labor principle of economic harmony. While free labor advocates looked at the marvel of the Brooklyn Bridge and insisted that everyone in America shared the same interest in creating such a wonder of progress, unskilled workers knew what conditions were like in the project's pressurized underwater concrete caissons where workers dug out the riverbed and risked the bends for $2.25 a day. Unlike the prosperous Americans who feared them, they were not individualists accumulating capital for their own success as they joined America's upwardly mobile economy. They seemed to reject the idea of economic harmony between themselves and their employ-ers; sometimes they rejected it explicitly. "Who is the prop and support of the land," asked a popular drinking song, "is it the rich man . . . or the . . . hard working man":

> The poor man is happy when he has got work,
> If the rich man would only them give
> A fair day's pay for a hard day's work,
> And their motto "to live and let live."
> But the rich strives more for to rob the poor,
> Starves and takes from a man what he earns,
> But if they could boast that they rule the roost,
> Why the poor they would treat like slaves.[32]

Some explicitly drew upon European radicalism to call for a different ethic from that of the emerging world of postwar capitalism. More simply recog-nized that the free labor dream could never be theirs without some basic protections to level the playing field for labor and capital. Increasingly they engaged in collective action to force employers to grant higher wages and better working conditions. They advocated government regulation of those conditions and supported politicians who promised legislation to make gov-ernment responsive to workers' needs. As they did so, Americans who be-lieved in success solely through hard work interpreted them as disaffected, lazy louts who wanted government handouts.[33]

Labor organization took on frightening proportions in the early 1870s in the minds of those who endorsed the idea of economic harmony. By that

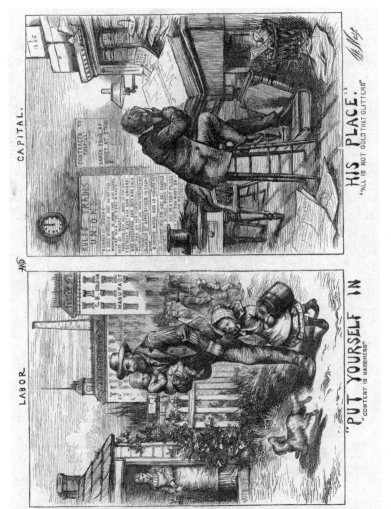

Figure 5. In this cartoon from March 4, 1871, *Harper's Weekly* tried to calm the growing tension between workers and employers by comparing the trials of a businessman with an idealized picture of the simple pleasures of a worker's life. Courtesy *HarpWeek*.

time, the National Labor Union boasted more than half a million members, and its leaders had concluded that workers could no longer hope for justice from regular political parties. Instead, they must organize politically as workers to achieve their ends. Labor parties had begun to organize in states like Massachusetts, New York, and Nebraska, and in July 1871, the National Labor Union issued a call for a convention to meet in October 1871 in Columbus, Ohio, to form the Labor Reform Party and nominate candidates for office. Americans who held tight to the vision of economic harmony protected by an evenhanded government began to fear that laborers could swing an election—as southern African American voters had done in 1868—handing government power to any demagogue who promised them special interest legislation.[34]

Dramatic developments in 1871 both internationally and at home made many Americans especially nervous about the effect of laborers in politics. In

March 1871, in the chaotic aftermath of the Franco-Prussian War, French Communards had taken control of Paris. In the three months they held it, Americans watched in horror as what they perceived as a labor-controlled government seemed to attack civilization, confiscating property; burning homes, businesses, and public buildings; and killing politicians and even priests. Their doctrines turned the world upside down, as innocent-seeming women became viragos bent on destruction, lobbing incendiary devices into cellars to burn down homes. News bulletins from Paris arrived in America daily over the new transatlantic cable, and Americans, used to sensational stories after their own terrible war, followed developments closely. Republican and Democratic newspapers both agreed that the Communards' "political economy consists essentially in the dispossession . . . of the present holders of capital, and in assigning the coin, instruments of labor and land, to associations of workmen." Their actions revealed their belief in the "communistic idea 'that property is robbery.'"35

Some Americans feared that the Commune was a forerunner to a revolution in America. They noted that the headquarters of the International Workingmen's Association had moved to New York in 1867, where it was led by a lieutenant of Karl Marx. When Chicago went up in flames in October 1871—coincidentally the same month labor organizers had planned to launch a new political party, although they had put it off—some blamed the Great Fire on communists. Even those unwilling to see a deliberate plot in the conflagration blamed the fire on stupid immigrants careless about fire in the city's poorly constructed wooden tenements. Mrs. O'Leary and her cow were a colorful legend, but one that illuminated the class and ethnic animosities of 1871. Reformer Charles Loring Brace wrote, "In the judgment of one who has been familiar with our 'dangerous classes' for twenty years, there are just the same explosive social elements beneath the surface of New York as of Paris." *Scribner's Monthly* warned readers that "*the interference of ignorant labor with politics is dangerous to society.*" "Possibly the very extravagances and horrible crimes of the Parisian Communists will, for some years, weaken the influence of the working classes in all countries," the *New York Times* predicted. "The great 'middle-class,' which now governs the world, will everywhere be terrified at these terrible outburst[s] and absurd[ities], they will hold a strong rein on the lower."36

As the *New York Times* indicated, the image of Paris under siege by a frenzied mob translated all too well into situations closer to home. Trouble began in the South. The Fifteenth Amendment, ratified in February 1870, gave all black men the right to vote and thus protect themselves from persecution from whites. It was hailed across the North, by both Republicans and Democrats, as the end of reconstruction. At last the black American had been "merged politically with the rest of the people," wrote the Republican *Chicago Tribune*. "Hereafter he has to run the race of life, dependent, like all others, upon his own energy, ability, and worth." The Democratic *New York World* agreed. The freedman had been "raised as high as he can be put by any action other than his own." When Georgia rejoined the Union (again) on July 15, 1870, "it was all over,—the war, reconstruction, the consideration of the old questions," recalled Republican politician-turned-novelist Albion W. Tourgée. "Now all was peace and harmony. The South must take care of itself now. The nation had done its part; it had freed the slaves, given them the ballot, opened the courts to them, and put them in the way of self-protection and self-assertion. The 'root-hog-or-die' policy . . . became generally prevalent." The nation heaved a sigh of relief."[37]

But for those primed to see them, there were signs that African Americans and their radical supporters wanted not equality for African Americans, but superiority. Skeptics were wary when, just two months after the ratification of the Fifteenth Amendment, Massachusetts Senator Charles Sumner introduced in the Senate a new civil rights bill that would empower the federal government to enforce equal rights in juries, public transportation, hotels, schools, churches, theaters, and public cemeteries. The Fourteenth and Fifteenth Amendments could not guarantee these rights, and the idea that hard work and upward mobility would place blacks and whites on the same level was not panning out. Blacks were routinely kept off southern juries, sent to smoking cars on trains, refused from hotels, and offered schools far inferior to those white students attended. Mississippi Sheriff John M. Brown explained: "Education amounts to nothing, good behavior counts for nothing, even money cannot buy for a colored man or woman decent treatment and the comforts that white people claim and can obtain." Once *this* bill passed, Sumner told the Senate with grating pomposity, "I [will] know of nothing further to be done in the way of legislation for the security of equal rights in this Republic." The Committee on the Judiciary quietly ignored the bill, but six months later Sumner announced he would press for its passage.[38]

Northerners from both parties as well as white southerners vociferously opposed Sumner's efforts. Unable to see how poverty was combining with traditional racism to create systematic discrimination against African Americans in the postwar South, they made much of freedpeople who were succeeding, noting, for example, that Mississippi ex-slaves who had been "penniless" in 1865 owned more than $200,000 worth of property in 1870, and that "the blacks never worked harder or better under slavery than they do now." African Americans were already equal, they argued; any more action on their behalf would give them privileges other Americans did not share. The Republican *Chicago Tribune* reiterated that southern prosperity was the key to advancing black rights. "He now has all that law can confer, viz.: equality of legal rights, together with the ballot and the right to hold office. The rest depends on opinion and custom, which are principally controlled by pecuniary interest. If the free black laborer develops into the successful cotton-raiser, his wages will form the measure of his growing freedom, and it will not be many years before he will be found owning his plantation, directing heavy operations in capital, and employing many hands. The road to the negro's social equality lies through his capacity for work and his ability to give direction to the labor of others." The Democratic *New York World* warned that "through terrible blood-spilling and with many a weary tug and groan it has been brought to pass that Cuff is given 'a white man's chance.'" Now Sumner was imperiling that opportunity by "loading it down with social equality imposed by law."[39]

While the civil rights bill languished, from South Carolina came apparent evidence that some African Americans were indeed rejecting hard work and self-denial and planned instead to use the government for their own benefit. Since the drafting of the new constitutions white southerners had insisted that the new southern governments were designed to redistribute wealth, and in 1871, they argued that events in South Carolina proved their point. In order to fund the rebuilding of the state, South Carolina's postwar legislature had levied taxes on landed property, rather than placing it on the personal property owned primarily by professionals, bankers, and merchants, which had borne the brunt of taxation before the war. This meant that landowners confronted new, much higher taxes at a time when their income was at an all-time low. At the same time, South Carolina's legislature used state funds to buy land for resale to settlers—usually freedmen—at low prices and funded new schools, hospitals, and other public services. All of these changes addressed the post-war needs of the state, whose black population had received no services at all before the war, of course, but landowners were irate. Since a majority of South Carolina's elected officials were African American between 1867 and 1876, the legislature's actions bolstered white charges of class warfare.[40] White South Carolinians inaccurately portrayed the legislature as one of poor, lazy, ignorant field hands determined to plunder the wealth of the whites in order to give jobs and services to blacks. Although this image grossly misrepresented the members of the South Carolina legislature, white southerners believed it wholeheartedly. When the legislature passed a new tax law in 1870, a British observer reported from Charleston that, with wealthy white South Carolinians disfranchised, "a proletariat Parliament has been constituted, the like of which could not be produced under the widest suffrage in any part of the world save in some of these Southern States." In March 1871, the Charleston Chamber of Commerce met to protest the new tax and called for a taxpayers' convention to meet in Columbia on May 9. The delegates to the convention represented South Carolina's white elite.[41]

Southern white charges that the reconstruction governments were catering to poor blacks played into the hands of northern Republicans who were disillusioned by President Grant's cronyism and heavy-handed attempt to annex Santo Domingo. They realized they could use the southern situation to alarm northerners already nervous about the expansion of the government and, possibly, pry Grant out of the White House. Squirrely little Horace Greeley, the powerful editor of the radical *New York Daily Tribune*, sent a reporter to cover the taxpayers' convention. His first article appeared on May 1, 1871.

Entitled "Political Problems in South Carolina," the article drew a portrait of the state that reflected the southern white fear of government by the lower classes. Echoing angry whites, the reporter described South Carolina as a "typical Southern state" victimized by disaffected black workers who believed in class conflict and were using the government to promote their own interests. South Carolina's population was mostly "negroes, who as a class, are ignorant, superstitious, semi-barbarians," he wrote. "They are extremely indolent, and will make no exertion beyond what is necessary to obtain food enough to satisfy their hunger. . . . Upon these people not only political rights have been conferred, but they have absolute political supremacy." Lazy freedmen elected to office demagogues—African Americans or white carpet-baggers—who promised to redistribute to them the wealth of the state's hard workers by increasing taxes. In 1870, "the rate of taxation was largely increased over that of the previous years, and the property-owners honestly believed that they were robbed to support the extravagance of the 'Nigger Government,' which they so cordially hated." A few days later, the *New York Daily Tribune* lamented that "the most intelligent, the influential, the educated, the really useful men of the South, deprived of all political power, . . . [are] taxed and swindled by a horde of rascally foreign adventurers, and by the ignorant class, which only yesterday hoed the fields and served in the kitchen."[42]

While white southerners were especially sensitive to the corruption of government by the poorer classes, northerners had their own examples of such corruption close at hand to make them nervous about the situation in South Carolina, as portrayed by the *New York Daily Tribune.* In July 1871, the *New York Times* launched an exposé of Democratic machine politician William Marcy Tweed. "Boss" Tweed's machine seemed a perfect example of the corruption of government at the hands of lazy laborers looking for a handout: it courted immigrant workers, who voted the Democratic ticket in exchange for the jobs and protection political bosses could provide. While providing valuable services for poor immigrants, who otherwise would find themselves at the mercy of employers and unscrupulous landlords, the bosses also plundered the city treasury for the funds to provide the lucrative contracts that cemented businessmen's loyalty to their machines and thus gave them a slate of available jobs for their poor constituents. "I can always get a job for a deservin' man," one Tweed politician boasted. "I make it a point to keep on the track of jobs, and it seldom happens that I don't have a few up my sleeve ready for use. I know every big employer in the district and in the whole city, for that matter, and they ain't in the habit of sayin' no to me when I ask them for a job."[43]

The exposé of the Tweed Ring emphasized the machine's corruption of politics and plunder of the public money. Cartoonist Thomas Nast made his career on his devastating pictures of Tweed as a vulture fattening on the public treasury. Nast used Tweed to represent the corruption of government by a mass of poor—usually caricatured Irish immigrant—voters and the machine politicians who manipulated them, portraying Tweed leaning triumphantly on a ballot box boasting of his ability to manufacture a majority. Nast unerringly identified the misuse of taxes as an issue close to the hearts of most Americans. In May 1871, *Scribner's Monthly* reported that people were restless under the taxes required in part by the war debt and in part because of "the growth of expenditure—national, state, and local—for new objects." Although much of the expenditure promoted national development and increased wealth, "large expenditures of public money, even for the best objects, ... breed carelessness, if not corruption, in those through whose hands they pass—evils more threatening to the country than any other to which it is now exposed." The *Chicago Tribune* maintained that New York and South Carolina both suffered under corrupt governments elected by vicious constiuencies. "New York is abandoned by her property-owners to the rule of one set of adventurous carpet-baggers and vagabonds. . . . South Carolina is ruled by carpet-baggers and irresponsible non-property-holders for other reasons."[44]

By fall 1871, disaffected northern laborers seemed to be growing stronger as observers and workers both lumped a wide range of labor protesters together. Cigarmaker Samuel Gompers was active in the local cigarmakers' union and a variety of other reform and fraternal organizations in the 1860s, but an unsuccessful 1869 strike against mechanization convinced him that it was useless to call for a general reform of society. Instead he turned his focus to specific improvements in the lives of workers. In 1871, the eight-hour movement "aroused intense enthusiasm," the determined man with the handlebar moustache recalled. The *New York Times* had complained in 1867 that the eight-hour day was the trick by which communists meant "to get the first wedge of their theory introduced into our industrial system by statutory enactment," and the 1871 movement only hardened that perception. In early September, unions and the New York branch of the International Workingmen's Association held a parade of about 25,000 people to promote the eight-hour day. But the march backfired by associating a mild reform with extreme radicalism. Gompers remembered that watchers paid most attention to "a group of negro workers" and to members of the International carrying "the red flag and a banner with the French slogan, 'Liberty, Equality and Fraternity.'" When Victoria Woodhull, a woman's suffrage advocate, and her sister, Tenny C. Claflin, both prominent in the radical branch of the New York International, issued a circular calling for "free-love, anarchy, and every extreme doctrine that appealed to their speculative fancy," labor's "enemies rejoiced and hastened to profit. The daily papers utilized the opportunity for a campaign of ridicule and calumny. They classified all labor purposes as Communism," Gompers lamented.[45]

Even in Massachusetts, a Republican stronghold, laborers seemed to threaten to take power. That fall, former Union general Benjamin F. Butler rallied workers in a coalition that almost ousted old guard Republicans from office. A sometime Democrat, Republican, and now labor candidate (he liked power in any form), Butler was famous as a spoilsman who used patronage and promises of government influence to any constituency willing to back him. He sought the Republican nomination for governor of Massachusetts at the head of a prolabor organization. Panicked mainstream Republicans held onto power, but no one dismissed the importance of Butler's threat. E. L. Godkin, editor of the influential *Nation*, wrote that Butler's "organization of such a commune as America would now supply.... came dangerously near to success."[46]

Americans who believed in the nation's harmonious free labor society feared disaffected workers because they could gang together to elect politicians who would support them with jobs, political offices, or benefits paid for by taxes on hardworking Americans. They had illustrations of this at home, it seemed, as freedmen in South Carolina and immigrants in New York City organized to take over government and run it for their own benefit. Indeed, it was beginning to seem as if a dangerously large number of Americans had begun to regard the government as the source of personal benefits. Not only freedmen and workers, but even women called for access to the American government so they could shape its policies according to their needs. The rhetoric of black freedom and equal suffrage fueled a growing push for women's suffrage. In 1867, women's activists fought hard to get women's suffrage included in New York's new state constitution. When they were unsuccessful, in 1869, Susan B. Anthony and Elizabeth Cady Stanton formed the radical National Woman Suffrage Association to agitate for the vote and to strike at legal inequality between the sexes. Then, in 1869, Wyoming included women's suffrage in its territorial constitution and enfranchised about a thousand women. The next year, Utah's territorial legislature allowed more than 17,000 women to go to the polls. Hopeful reformers expected that these women would provide the votes to outlaw polygamy, thus destroying one of the evils that still plagued the American state. Instead, they voted overwhelmingly in favor of it, powerfully illustrating to disappointed observers the potential of the vote to corrupt American society.

Those adhering to America's traditional free labor ideals began to coalesce as they anxiously rejected the idea of special interests controlling government, insisting that America was a land of economic harmony and individual enterprise. They defined themselves by identifying their opponents: "hardworking Americans" from all walks of life denigrated strikers and workers' organizations and attacked the corruption of lazy African Americans in southern governments, the Tweed Ring, and labor agitators. Beginning to articulate what an ideal American government should look like, they reviled the corruption of government by the manipulation of uneducated voters with promises or threats. As they did so, they revised the previously inclusive idea that all could earn a living in America.

In 1868, Horatio Alger's popular story *Ragged Dick* reformulated the original free labor dream by suggesting that not all Americans could succeed. This triumphant rags-to-riches story was full of characters who were not succeeding in the city because they were either lazy, wasteful, or immoral. Most notable as an anti-hero was the obviously Irish boy Micky Maguire, a "stout, red-haired, freckled-faced" gang leader from Five Points who despised anyone who tried to improve himself. "If he had been fifteen years older, and had a trifle more education," Alger wrote, "he would have interested himself in politics, and been prominent at ward meetings, and a terror to respectable voters on election day." As a street boy, he took out his spite on his superior, Dick, by throwing rocks at him, trying to beat him up, and eventually stealing a set of ragged clothing the upwardly mobile Dick no longer needed. Alger indicated that Mickey Maguire and his kind would never succeed in America until they got rid of the idea that gang organization and political demands would replace hard work.[47]

In contrast to Micky and other ne'er-do-wells was Dick Hunter, the handsome young hero who began the story as an impoverished fourteen-year-old bootblack, dressed in rags and sleeping in a wooden box on the street. Dick was poor and dirty, occasionally swore, smoked cigars, and even gambled. But he "was above doing anything mean or dishonorable. He would not steal, or cheat, or impose upon younger boys, but was frank and straightforward, manly and self-reliant." Industrious and energetic, he hoped to "learn business, and grow up 'spectable." When prosperous businessmen assured him that he could rise if he worked hard and continued to be "strictly honorable in all his dealings," he determined to get an education, go to church, and save his money. In little more than a year, Dick—by then known as Richard—was off the streets, educated, and a clerk in the counting room of a warehouse. "He is Ragged Dick no longer," preached Alger. "He has taken a step upward, and is determined to mount still higher." Micky Maguire and his gang had closed themselves off from the free labor dream, but it was still viable for the self-reliant Richard Hunters of the world. This ideal American got a portrait in 1871 when Thomas Eakins painted *Max Schmitt in a Single Scull*, an image of an intelligent city man engaged in the "thinking man's sport" on the Schuylkill River in Philadelphia, pitting his own strength and wits against the new urban landscape.[48]

Carl Schurz became the political voice of Americans concerned about the domination of government by special interests. As a new senator in March 1869, he took the floor of the Senate to condemn the government's spoils system, and that same year Grant forced him into a dramatic stand against machine politics when the president's ill-advised plan to annex Santo Domingo—the Dominican Republic—stirred up a political hornet's nest. Grant tended to run the government as he had run his military staff, requiring party loyalty and considering disagreement a personal affront. In 1869, he authorized his personal secretary to negotiate the annexation of the island nation, whose minerals, timber, fruit, sugar, and coffee made it a potentially rich prize. The treaty surprised and angered the unconsulted cabinet, which agreed to it only under extreme pressure. The Senate proved less tractable, resenting Grant's personal appeals for such an irregular proceeding and interpreting the scheme as proof that Grant was carrying machine politics too far. Unpopular with white citizens who wanted no part of trying to integrate another body of black people into their political system, the treaty failed to pass the Senate, although many Republicans eventually bowed to the president's demands. (Schurz was not one of them.) Grant, though, was unwilling to let the issue drop.[49]

Grant's pressure for passage of the Santo Domingo treaty combined with peculiar conditions in Missouri in 1870 to give a new political form to the growing dislike of machine government. Missouri had suffered terribly during the war. The only state north of the Missouri Compromise Line where slavery had been legal, it had been torn apart in the antebellum years by the hatred between proslavery and free labor forces. During the Civil War, the state's Confederate and Union sympathizers undertook such devastating guerilla warfare that in 1863 the Union army actually evacuated three counties of the state bordering Kansas in an effort to flush out the southern-sympathizing Quantrill's Raiders. Missourians' quite personal hostility toward each other did not evaporate with peace. (Indeed, violence there was so bad that J. G. McCoy turned Abilene, Kansas, into a railroad depot in 1867 in part to enable cattle drivers to get their beeves to a rail head without having to encounter Missouri gangs.) Determined to keep southern sympathizers from power, Republicans placed strong restrictions on former Confederate supporters in the new state constitution of 1865, preventing them from voting and from practicing a number of professions. This kept Confederates out of government and positions of authority and also guaranteed that the state was controlled exclusively by Republicans. Missourians quickly grew restive at such dominance, especially after the former Confederate states had been readmitted to the Union.[50]

Schurz had no love for the Missouri Republican machine that had written the 1865 constitution and opposed his election to the Senate. In 1870, he joined Democrats and moderate Republicans in the state to demand the voting limitations be removed. When regular Republicans ignored him at the 1870 state convention, he bolted it and, together with Missouri Senator B. Gratz Brown, organized a new convention that called for the immediate end to political disabilities and nominated Brown for governor. "In leaving that body we carried the honor, the good faith, the true principles, and the true banner of the Republican party with us," Schurz declared. Furious regular Republicans read Schurz out of the party. President Grant, still smarting from Schurz's opposition to the Santo Domingo treaty, publicly accused him of trying to turn the government over to Democrats. The president made it clear that Republicans must toe the party line; his followers dismissed Brown supporters from government positions. Grant's attempt to enforce party discipline probably helped Schurz, for in the election a coalition of the Missouri bolters and Democrats ousted the regular Republicans.[51]

After the election, in a long and heartfelt speech to his Senate colleagues, Schurz explained that the Missouri bolters had been motivated by their conviction that party Republicans were controlled by special interests trying to take over the government. In Missouri, he claimed, the passions of the war were over. Everyone was obeying the laws and working to bring prosperity to the state. The only remaining reminder of the war keeping passions alive was that "thousands and thousands of citizens . . . [were] . . . cut off . . . from all the political rights of citizenship while they were fulfilling its duties and bearing its burdens." When right-thinking Republicans tried to restore them the franchise, party politicians refused because they wanted "to monopolize the local offices." "We found inveterate prejudice and unscrupulous greed arrayed against . . . fidelity to sacred pledges and sound statesmanship," Schurz complained. "Call such a system what you will, but call it not republican government."

Schurz produced a devastating document that illustrated the means by which the party held on to power. The document demanded 1 percent of the "gross receipts of your office" from officeholders to raise money to attack Brown's candidacy in Missouri. The Republican state committee that issued the assessment claimed to be acting on behalf of "our friends at Washington, where it is confidently expected that those who receive the benefits of Federal appointments will support the machinery that sustains the party which gives them pecuniary benefit and honor." The party's needs were great, it said, and "delay or neglect will rightly be construed into unfriendliness to the Administration," a thinly veiled threat of dismissal from government jobs. Schurz then produced a letter requesting the resignation of an honored public official because he was supporting Brown for governor. This was wrong, Schurz insisted. The fundamental principle of government, he declared, was not to enrich a political oligarchy but "to guaranty the largest possible liberty, and, at the same time, the greatest security of individual rights to all in our political and social organization."

Schurz's actions reflected Missouri's peculiar political situation, but they had repercussions across society. The development of a worldview attractive to moderates of both parties, based on keeping government out of the hands of special interests, began almost immediately to limit arguments that called for government to enforce equality. Growing distrust of the Republican administration bled Republican attempts to protect African Americans in the South. When it appeared that white southerners would answer the Fifteenth Amendment by attacking any active black Republicans, congressmen responded with the Ku Klux Klan Act of 1871, which permitted the president to declare martial law in nine South Carolina counties to break the Klan. But unwillingness to allow white vigilante groups did not mean an advocacy of active government support for black advancement. Indeed, the Ku Klux Klan Act itself began to swing moderates toward the Democratic belief that Republicans were deliberately using the government to strengthen their hold on power. Grant declared martial law in South Carolina in mid-October, and 168 people were arrested immediately before fall elections there. Placing the U.S. military at the polls protected black voters, but it also undoubtedly stifled opposition to the Republican government. Grant assured Americans that the outrages that made such drastic action necessary would be revealed during the hearings of the congressional Committee to Investigate Southern Outrages (popularly known as the Ku Klux Klan hearings), but opponents noted that those who testified before the committee were paid a dollar a day for their testimony—higher wages than unskilled workers could make in the fields—giving them a financial incentive to tell the Republicans what they wanted to hear. Carl Schurz, for one, did not approve of the Ku Klux Klan law. When pressed to vote for it he declared: "I stand in the Republican party as an independent man." He went on to declare that he was not a partisan Republican, but that he was a "liberal Republican." Of himself and those like him, he said: "We desire peace and good will to all men. We desire the removal of political restrictions and the maintenance of local self-government to the utmost extent compatible with the Constitution as it is. We desire the questions connected with the Civil War to be disposed of forever, to make room as soon as possible for the new problems of the present and the future."[52]

The attempt to keep special interests out of government also changed the direction of women's activism after the war. Women's activists who argued that suffrage was an absolute human right to be enforced by government found themselves under attack. "A Veteran Observer" in the *New York Times* ridiculed Elizabeth Cady Stanton and her argument that women had "a natural right" to suffrage. The only natural rights, he claimed, were admirably listed in the Declaration of Independence, the right to life, liberty, and the pursuit of happiness. "The authors of the Declaration of Independence never dreamed of any natural right to vote," he claimed. It did not help women's activists that Benjamin F. Wade supported women's suffrage in his Kansas speech, insisting—according to an unhappy observer—that "*radicalism upon this and all other questions was righteousness, while conservatism was hypocrisy and cowardice.*" Wade's advocacy reinforced the idea that women's call for suffrage was another attempt to harness the government to yet another special interest group.[53]

The dislike of special interests offered another avenue for women to promote their rights, though. Some argued that, unlike disaffected workers and African Americans, most women shared with their husbands the desire to keep government out of the hands of factions. Men who refused to accept women's suffrage as a natural right rallied to it as an opportunity to clean up government. The same "Veteran Observer" who ridiculed Cady Stanton confessed that he supported women's suffrage but "on grounds . . . very different from those announced by some of its advocates." As long as the nation had admitted "ignorant foreigners and negroes" to the ballot, it should also admit women. They would undoubtedly handle it as well or better than the degraded men recently admitted. A Republican politician in the South agreed. "It is a lamentable fact . . . that rum and demagogues exert a great influence over the elections in this country, and it is certainly high time that we took the ballot out of the grog shop and the hands of corrupt men, and made it pure and respectable."[54]

Women trying to expand their roles after the war took a new avenue to their goal, one more in line with the growing emphases on the traditional independent man with a family and good government free of special interests. Before the war, Julia Ward Howe had found the idea of women's suffrage "repugnant," but her wartime activities and growing disgust with her husband's determination to keep her quiet changed her mind. An 1868 suffrage meeting run by older moderates converted her to the cause. She was elected president of the newly formed New England Woman Suffrage Association in 1868 and helped to issue its call the following year for a national organization.

In November 1869, representatives from twenty-one states met in Cleveland to form the American Women's Suffrage Association, deliberately keeping their efforts separate from the more radical association formed by Stanton and Anthony a few months earlier. Most dramatically, they differed with the National Woman Suffrage Association by insisting that men as well as women should have prominent positions in the organization; theirs was a humanist, not a feminist, organization, Howe's daughter later recalled. "We . . . are not a frantic, shrieking mob," Howe once told suffrage advocates. "We are not contemners of marriage, nor neglecters of home and offspring. We are individually allowed to be men and women of sound intellect, of reputable life, having the same stake and interest in the well-being of the community that others have. . . . We have had, or hope to have, our holy fireside, our joyful cradle, our decent bank account. Why should any consider us as the enemies of society, we who have everything to gain by its good government?"[55]

Women who continued to exercise their womanly roles could press for advances more acceptably than those who advocated women's rights on the principle of human equality. By 1870, it seemed to Howe that women were finally coming into their own. She looked at the terrible costs of the Civil War and at the current struggle raging between France and Prussia and became convinced that women must band together to stop human warfare. She issued a call for a women's antiwar conference, condemning men for resorting to armed conflict and insisting that "women need no longer be made a party to proceedings which fill the globe with grief and horror. Despite the assumptions of physical force, the mother has a sacred and command-ing word to say to the sons who owe their life to her suffering." She called on women to "Arise!" and to demand that "our husbands shall not come to us, reeking with carnage, for caresses and applause. Our sons shall not be taken from us to unlearn all that we have been able to teach them of charity, mercy, and patience." In France, another woman had issued a similar call, and *Harper's Weekly* commented that this conjunction showed "that the influence of women is ceasing to be a passive emotion, and . . . is moving them toward an equal voice, as they have an equally vital interest, in the conduct of human affairs." When Howe's world congress failed to take off, she enshrined her ideas in a "Mother's Day," to be held every spring, when women and children could come together to promote peace.[56]

In 1870, Howe was one of a number of editors for *The Woman's Journal*, a weekly paper from "the friends of Woman Suffrage who wish to keep the issue as clear from entangling alliances with other reforms and the endless host of individual whims and vagaries," according to *Harper's Weekly*. "*The Woman's Journal* is a fair and attractive paper in appearance; while the variety and spirit of its articles, and the dignity, self-respect, good-humor, and earnestness of its tone, will show how profoundly mistaken are those who suppose that folly and extravagance are necessarily characteristic of the discussion of the question." *Harper's Weekly* encouraged readers to subscribe to the journal. Even the best-selling *Little Women* ultimately emphasized women's power within a traditional framework. While Meg, Amy, and Jo had dreamed of professions outside their homes—Meg as an actress, Amy as an artist, Jo as a writer—they settled down with husbands and children, changing the world as mothers rather than as independent professional women.[57]

The idea that the family of the ideal American individualist must be protected from special interests fed an attack on the practice of abortion, organized to guard women from those who seemed to be evil butchers killing children and often women themselves. The Republican *New York Times* launched an attack on "malpractice" in August 1871, insisting that the Democratic Tweed Ring in charge of New York City government refused to stop the widespread practice because the uneducated, criminal "doctors" who performed abortions supported Tweed Ring politicians and bought tens of thousands of dollars in advertising in Democratic newspapers. The *New York Times* printed a sordid exposé of fetuses rotting in the cellars of "malpractitioners" in August 1871, and less than a week later the story of the editor's dreams appeared (rather too opportunely) when a New York City railroad porter noticed a stench coming from a trunk waiting to be sent to Chicago. Opening it, he found a mass of lovely blond hair covering the frail body of twenty-five-year-old Alice Augusta Bowlsby. Evidence suggested that she had tried to procure an abortion from Jacob Rosenzweig, and when she died, he panicked, packed her body in the trunk, and tried to get rid of it. This scenario provided a perfect illustration of the vulnerability of the family and of women to quacks who could not be arrested because they supported the Tweed politicians who, in turn, refused to shut down their evil dens. The corruption of the political system quite literally seemed to threaten the lives of mainstream Americans.[58]

The search for a world uncorrupted by special interests also affected the way easterners looked at the West. In their romantic view, the West was a world where unlimited resources were free for the taking by unfettered individuals, a pristine world untouched by the corrupt struggles of eastern government. There were cattle in the West, and gold and silver, and apparently endless herds of buffalo. In the years after the Civil War, the West grew dramatically. Wyoming Territory organized in 1868, and people began to flood into Texas and Dakota. In 1868, a popular magazine outlined the value of Portland, Oregon, and concluded "if any young person who reads this is casting about for a place where a fair stock of sense, industry, and good habits will, within certain limits, pay certainly and well in any honest calling, let him or her take passage at once for Portland." Nat Love recalled how the West offered economic freedom and excitement. At fifteen, he had had enough of picking nuts and berries to support his family: "I wanted to see more of the world and as I began to realize there was so much more of the world than what I had seen, the desire to go grew on me from day to day." On February 10, 1869, he left his home near Nashville, Tennessee, and "struck out for Kansas, of which I had heard something . . . [and believed] it was a good place in which to seek employment. It was in the west, and it was the great west I wanted to see." In Dodge City, Kansas, Love fell in with a cattle outfit of about fifteen men from the panhandle of Texas "who had just come up with a herd of cattle and having delivered them they were prepared to return. There were several colored cow boys among them, and good ones, too." Love signed on for $30 a month, and with "a new saddle, bridle and spurs, chaps, a pair of blankets and a fine 45 Colt revolver," he started life as a cowboy, noting that "the wild cow boy, prancing horses of which I was very fond, and the wild life generally, all had their attractions for me." Love was right that there was money to be made in cattle, but it was rarely made by cowboys. By 1870, Charles Goodnight was worth $72,000 (part of which he gave to the Loving estate). In 1871, he cleared a net profit of $17,000. He started ranching in Colorado, forty miles from Trinidad, "where I lived for a time and enjoyed the reputation of being the largest farmer in eastern Colorado," he later boasted.[59]

Although the West seemed a land of individualism, the government was hardly uninterested in the region; if anything it became more involved as easterners moved in. President Grant realized that white settlement would sweep over the West, but he had traveled extensively there as a young army officer before the war and sympathized with the plight of the Indians. In his inaugural address in March 1869, he endorsed "any course toward them which tends to their civilization and ultimate citizenship." Nine months later, in December 1869, in his first message to Congress, he noted that the government's management of Indians "has been a subject of embarrassment and expense, and has been attended with continuous robberies, murders, and wars." His experience on the frontier made him aware that whites were not blameless for the troubles no matter what western settlers claimed. He determined to try his hand at improving relations by replacing Indian agents and superintendents with Quaker missionaries—famous for pacifism and "strict integrity and fair dealings"—and army officers. Unlike civilian Indian agents, army officers held their jobs for life and had a personal interest in living in harmony with the Indians. Also, the government supervised their job performance. Grant refused to contemplate the systematic "extinction of a race" and called instead for "placing all the Indians on large reservations, as rapidly as it can be done, and giving them absolute protection there. As soon as they are fitted for it they should be induced to take their lands in severalty and to set up Territorial governments for their own protection." For Grant, the destruction of Indian culture was the only possible chance tribes had to survive. He wanted to bring Indians under the free labor umbrella to prevent their extermination.[60]

While westerners depended on the government to survey the land, finance the railroads, and manage hostile Indians, Texans like Goodnight and the buffalo hunters had fought the Indians and the western environment on their own—organized as rangers or simply fighting for land and cattle—and believed they had won the land by themselves. One Texan recalled that he had joined the army to fight Comanches but found government service was degrading as well as useless. "The first three months that we were out the government furnished us rations; our bread was hardtack, full of worms, weevil, and spiders; we killed our own meat. The next three months our rations got misplaced and we did not have a bit of bread for twenty-two days." Indian fighters often went a step further and believed that, when the government got involved, it only caused trouble. Indians were often more dangerous on reservations than off them, for when there were supplies on a reservation, the young braves could rest and feed themselves and their ponies. When government supplies did not come through, they turned to raiding neighboring whites. If the government provided what it promised, the Indians would stay on the reservations, westerners reasoned. If it provided nothing, warriors would starve. Either way, Indians would be less trouble than they were in the halfway system the government supported. Goodnight felt sorry for "the poor devils" who "did not get half of what the Government appropriated" for them but hated their depredations on his own holdings. "The Navajos used to slip away from the reservation, come down to our ranch . . . and eat up our horses, which they preferred to beef," he recalled. "The dirty buggers ate up my own saddle-horse one time—a cracker-jack—while there were plenty of cattle all around him." Westerners had little use for the federal government.[61]

Southerners took this dislike a step further and despised the federal government as an instrument of their enemies, the northeastern Republicans. They liked to believe that the West was a land free of government intervention. "Presently the vast empire of the West, and all the vast empire which is growing on the Pacific, will speak to us in words of comfort, and we and they will go on to control this country and New England will have no voice in it, except whining. Any man in a reasonable degree of health will live long enough to find out this fact," insisted southern newspapers. Men like Charles Goodnight grew to hate government agents in the West, who usually offered contracts and protection to those known to be loyal during the war rather than to those with Confederate histories. So angry was Goodnight at Union men by 1867 that he assumed the Fort Sumner surgeon put off amputating his partner Loving's festering arm solely "because we were rebels." When Goodnight threatened to kill him, the doctor operated, and later told Goodnight that, as a new immigrant, "I don't know a thing about your rebel government," but he had been afraid that anesthesia would kill the weakened Loving. When "I found I'd either have to kill you, operate on him, or be killed. . . . I decided I'd just take my chances on the old gentleman," he explained. Goodnight and other cattlemen also resented the army's apparent unwillingness to stop Indian cattle thieves like Quanah's Quahada Comanches, who stole Texas cattle and traded them in New Mexico.[62]

Increasingly convinced that the Republican federal government meant a despotism of party members, southern Democrats looked to the West as the only place in the nation where liberty survived. "As civilization advances liberty recedes," an author in *De Bow's Review* noted, "because laws become more complex and numerous, public opinion more stringent and dictatorial, religion and morality more dominant and restrictive, fashion more exacting in its requirements, human wants and luxuries more numerous, and the labor needed to supply them greater. Hence it will even be found that in large cities, the great centres and foci of civilization, there is least of liberty. Not only the laws of the State and of the Union, but the corporate laws, more restrictive than either, curtail men's liberties in such cities."[63]

For other Americans, the West offered a new national culture distanced from the tensions between the North and South. Epic paintings like Albert

Figure 6. Albert Bierstadt caught the sublime image of the West in his 1868 painting, *Among the Sierra Nevada, California.* His idyllic West had no sectional strife, no government, no people; it was a beautiful wilderness full of opportunity. Smithsonian American Art Museum, Washington, D.C./Art Resource, N.Y.

Bierstadt's 1868 *The Sierra Nevada in California* depicted an America without any sectional strife and, in fact, without any of the causes of that strife—no people, no politicians, no agriculture, no businesses. But Bierstadt's portrait of the West was not simply an absence of conflict. It portrayed a sublime spirituality that showed the West as majestic and edenic. In *The Sierra Nevada in California,* warm light from heaven falls into a pristine valley of water and wildlife, asking the viewer to imagine America as God's own land. That Bierstadt's trip West had been funded by the Union Pacific Railroad pointedly illustrates the divorce between this romantic image and reality.

Northerner John Muir refined the idea of the romantic West as growing cities and factories added value to the untouched land that previously had seemed simply to be a source of raw materials. Although farming was regarded as the heart of the nation, the reality of farm life was anything but romantic. Muir, whose family immigrated to America from Scotland when he was a boy, recalled the daily grind of work on his father's western wheat farm. "In those early days, long before the great labor-saving machines came to our help," he remembered, "almost everything connected with wheat-raising abounded in trying work,—cradling in the long, sweaty dog-days, raking and binding, stacking, thrashing,—and it often seemed to me that our fierce, over-industrious way of getting the grain from the ground was too closely connected with grave-digging." He fantasized about nature as a place free from industry, where man could reach his spiritual potential rather than digging his own grave. By the end of the war, Muir had come to believe that botany revealed "glorious traces of the thoughts of God, and leading on and on into the infinite cosmos." He had begun to take excursions around the virgin forests of the Great Lakes, where he was "able to wander many a long, wild mile, free as the winds in the glorious forests and bogs, gathering plants and feeding on God's abounding, inexhaustible spiritual beauty bread." An eye injury convinced him to abandon his new profession of carriage making for his love of nature. In August 1867, a lean man whose strong features, wild hair, and long beard have become emblematic of outdoorsmen, he walked from Indiana to Florida, then traveled on to Cuba, examining plants and animals and immersing himself in the natural world around him. Finally he set out for the West. Contrasted to an increasingly industrial East, Muir's American West was rural and pristine by definition, despite the growth of cities like San Francisco, whose population was almost 150,000 in 1870.[64]

In July 1868, the *Overland Monthly*, whose masthead declared it was "devoted to the development of the country," started publication in San Francisco. It began with the premise that modern city life destroyed men. "There is a wearisome sameness in this human current which is shot through the narrow grooves of the great city," it explained. "What inspiration does one get from this human concussion? Are there any sparks of divine fire struck . . . into a man by it?" "The apparent tendency of modern civilization," it said, "is to repress and prevent the growth of individual extremes and produce only the more average man. The city is the great promoter and centre of this civilization." Western reality was a network of towns and small cities that drew resources from the land around them, but the western image would be of a rural land, the antithesis of confused, corrupt, city life.[65]

The magazine's prescription for rejuvenation was to "turn . . . away from all familiar sights and sounds, all the jarring, creaking, and abrasion of city life" and to go on vacation to the West, where a man could live "without a sight of the sheriff, the doctor, or the undertaker." "The opening vista in the redwood forest where the path is flecked with tremulous shadows and gleams of sunlight, will lead near enough to Paradise, provided one . . . never blasphemes against nature by enquiring the price of stocks." The California woods were full of rabbits, wild doves, trout, and so on, the article explained, and "the quail is so wonderfully prolific here that it would overrun the country, destroying vineyards and grain fields without limit," if predators did not keep them in check.[66]

Indeed, the West offered a spiritual rejuvenation to those worn down by the daily grind of eastern tedium. A poem in *Overland Monthly* described it:

> O foolish wisdom sought in books!
> O aimless fret of household tasks!
> O chains that bind the hand and mind—
> A fuller life my spirit asks.
>
> . . . . . .
>
> For Eden's life within me stirs,
> And scorns the shackles that I wear.
> The man-life grand: pure soul, strong hand,
> The limb of steel the heart of air!
>
> . . . . . .
>
> So I, from out these toils, wherein
> The Eden-faith grows stained and dim,
> Would walk, a child, through Nature's wild,
> And hear His voice and answer Him.[67]

At the end of the Civil War, northerners dreamed of their free labor vision spreading across the nation and transforming the backward South into a realm of small farmers, prosperous and educated, whose votes supported a small government that developed the national economy for the good of everyone. By 1871, this dream had begun to turn frightening as freedpeople, workers, and activist women argued that the nation's economy was not, in fact, a harmonious organism where all rose together, but that there was a conflict in society between the haves and the have-nots. Calling on government to level the playing field between these groups, they seemed to threaten the very essence of America. Opposing their activism, a growing number of Americans began to define themselves as standing for values of hard work and independence and worried that government power might fall into the wrong hands. The government must not be influenced by factions promoting their own interests, they believed. Southerners and westerners who hated the domineering Republican government bolstered this view as they developed an antigovernment rhetoric that ignored the importance of government investment in and oversight of their regions. Their rhetoric created an image of an ideal, pristine West where individuals lived in a world unfettered by government or special interests, and where one could live as God had intended. In a world of terrible turmoil, this developing image attracted those Americans who stood to lose if government began to privilege groups shunted aside in the postwar nation.

CHAPTER FOUR

1872

A New Middle Ground

By 1872, the strains of reconstruction were approaching a crisis. The extension of suffrage to an undereducated population at the very time that new tax laws supported a newly active government raised the specter of a bloated government supporting a population of lazy ne'er-do-wells, despite the fact that in 1872 the Treasury ran a surplus of $94 million and spent only $270 million, of which less than 36 percent of the grand total—$130 million—came from taxes. (In today's dollars, that translates to a surplus of $1.4 billion, expenditures of $4 billion, and a little less than $2 billion in taxes.) For those discouraged by the continuing chaos in the South, or angry at the tendency of Republican administrators to award valuable government contracts to wartime Unionists, or furious that they could not vote while their former slaves could, or worried about the growing ties of business and the administration, it seemed that parasites were keeping the Republicans in power so they could live off government money.[1]

Since B. Gratz Brown's victory in Missouri in 1870, Carl Schurz had been wondering if a national coalition could carry the principles of clean government divorced from special interests into a national election. On September 30, 1871, he wrote to his friend Charles Sumner to commiserate about the evils of Grant's administration. "The organization of the Republican party is almost entirely in the hands of the office-holders and ruled by selfish interest. . . . I shall not support [Grant]. Neither shall I support the Democrats. Far from it. But I think,—in fact I firmly believe,— . . . we shall have a third movement on foot strong enough to beat both him and the Democrats. I have commenced already to organize it, and when the time comes, I think it will be ready for action. . . . A very large number of Southerners, especially young men who have become disgusted with their old leaders . . . are sincerely willing to uphold the new order of things *in every direction*, if they are generously treated. . . . This will be a power fit to absorb the best elements of both parties,—and there is the prospect of beating the Democrats on one side and the personal-government-men on the other side." In 1872, people who shared Schurz's vision came together to define a new middle ground for America.[2]

The national political movement to stop the "corruption" of American government began in Missouri, where the tensions between former Confederates and Republicans were still white hot. On January 24, 1872, a mass meeting of "liberal Republicans" in Schurz's model came together at Jefferson City, Missouri, to try to reform the American government. They insisted that the Republican Party must offer amnesty to Confederates, guarantee equal suffrage for all, reform the civil service, and fix the tariff laws so that they did not promote the interests of manufacturers at the expense of consumers. Those at the meeting invited all like-minded Republicans to gather in a national convention at Cincinnati on May 1. Planning to force the Republican Party to dump Grant and fasten on a presidential candidate not beholden to special interests, most reformers hoped to pressure the Republican Party to change from within rather than to bolt the party altogether. If it did so, men like Schurz trusted, Democrats would gradually drift over to it and abandon the outmoded conservative wing of the Democratic Party. Together, moderate Republicans and Democrats would reform an ideal American government that scorned special interests and benefited everyone.[3]

Few congressmen dared to speak up against the president, but a number of Republican newspaper editors jumped onto the reform bandwagon. Critically, Horace Greeley at the *New York Daily Tribune* had lost faith in President Grant and was looking to injure him enough to make him lose the nomination. Grant was most vulnerable in the area of his southern Republican governments, which had increased taxes fourfold since 1860 to pay for new services and which had incurred $132 million in debt since 1865. Democrats had been portraying the southern governments as black mobs confiscating wealth from whites. Determined to press this sensitive issue, Greeley harped on the corruption of southern governments during January and February, and he sent James S. Pike, an embittered and racist former radical from Maine, south to collect more ammunition.[4]

Pike went willingly, stopping first in South Carolina, where he made it a point to interview Wade Hampton. The general's description of southern politics became the driving voice of Pike's powerful reports. In March, Greeley printed "A State in Ruins," Pike's exposé of South Carolina politics based on his interviews with Hampton and other men with financial interests in the state. The article harked back to the taxpayers' complaints of the previous year—that lazy freedmen were trying to confiscate wealth through taxation. Prominent writer J. W. De Forest picked up this argument and voiced it even more powerfully than Pike in his viciously racist short story about a newly elected black legislator, "The Colored Member," published in *The Galaxy* in March. In that story, the government said to "unworthy" slaves: "You never struck a blow for your liberty, and nevertheless you shall have it. You are as ignorant, as heavy-brained, and as morally degraded as the vulgarest peasant of the oldest despotism of Europe; nevertheless you shall be a citizen of a great and proud republic, which depends for its strength and honor upon the intelligence and virtue of its citizens. You never governed even yourself, and have not the slightest knowledge of statesmanship, nor a conception of right or wrong in politics; nevertheless I constitute you an elector, with the possibility of being a juror, a dignitary in the commonwealth, an executor of justice, and a lawgiver." Then the government left the freedman to the evil demagogue, who promised him that if he would "run for office and support my little bill . . . you shall have more money than you can get by hoeing."[5]

By mid-April, it was clear to the reformers that Grant would win the Republican nomination, and, indeed, putting someone else on the ticket would antagonize those hundreds of thousands of former Union soldiers who looked to him as their greatest chief. In disgust, Greeley wrote: "The Federal office-holders have called their Convention to meet at Philadelphia in June." The reformers had little choice but to try to nominate their own leader and hope to pull reform Democrats in their wake. Their hopes rose when, in April, leading Democratic newspapers advocated supporting the anti-Grant Republicans.[6]

In May, disgruntled Republicans led by Schurz joined with "New Departure" Democrats to organize the Liberal Republican Party, in an attempt to recapture the liberal dream of individual responsibility and independence within the political strictures of the postwar era. The New Departure Democrats were anxious to distance themselves from the unreconstructed southern Democrats who still railed against the reconstruction amendments and insisted that black Americans had no rights a white man was bound to respect. For their part, unhappy Republicans wanted to turn back the government from the patronage-spewing behemoth it appeared to have become. They envisioned a nation where individuals could truly participate in economic and political freedom and rise—or sink—to whatever level their determination and ability dictated. On May 1, the liberals assembled at Cincinnati with Schurz as the "leader and master mind of this great movement." The Missouri delegation—including Schurz's young protégé, newspaperman Joseph Pulitzer—was determined to see B. Gratz Brown as its presidential candidate. Elected permanent chairman of the convention, Schurz delivered a keynote address that tried to hold the reformers true to their mission and above petty politics. "We want the overthrow of a pernicious system; we want the eradication of flagrant abuses; we want the infusion of a loftier spirit into our political organism; we want a Government which the best people of this country will be proud of," he thundered.[7]

The Liberal Republican platform defined a new middle ground in American republicanism, a compromise between the original northern free labor vision and the southern ideas of proper government. It began by asserting, "We recognize the equality of all men before the law, and hold that it is the duty of Government . . . to mete out equal and exact justice to all, of whatever nativity, race, color, or persuasion, religious or political." It pledged the Liberal Republicans to the integrity of the Union, to "emancipation and enfranchisement," and it held the Thirteenth, Fourteenth, and Fifteenth Amendments to the Constitution inviolable. It then demanded "the immediate and absolute removal of all disabilities" imposed on ex-Confederates, claiming that "universal amnesty will result in complete pacification in all sections of the country."[8]

The platform echoed southern Democrats by endorsing small government as safer for a republic than a large federal government. Although the practical basis for southern Democrats' insistence on small government was their determination to control their black neighbors, they claimed a principled opposition to government growth. As with the Democrats, the heart of Liberal Republican complaints about large government was corruption. The platform called for civil service reform: "The civil service of the government has become a mere instrument of partisan tyranny and personal ambition, and an object of selfish greed." It also insisted that the military power must be subordinated to civil authority in the South. And, in a final thrust against Grant, it required that "no President shall be a candidate for re-election."[9]

By taking the northern emphasis on free labor and the southern emphasis on small government, the Liberal Republicans hoped they were offering a world that blocked the influence of special interests. On the one hand, they pushed back against those workers and African Americans demanding government support. The platform endorsed federal taxation to pay the expenses of an "economically administered" government, but it specified that taxes should not "unnecessarily interfere with the industry of the people." The Liberal Republicans denounced calls for paying the debt in greenbacks and called for a speedy return to specie payment. On the other hand, they did not side with business either, opposing land grants to railroads and other corporations to protect the public domain for individual settlers. The convention was not keen on activist women. It rejected the petition of Mrs. Laura DeForce Gordon to be a delegate from California, then hissed her into silence when she attempted to protest from the floor.[10]

Liberal Republicans believed they were embracing principles that would attract all who truly had the best interests of the country at heart. Inherent in their opposition to special interests was a refusal to accept the idea that systematic racial, economic, gender, or social inequalities made it harder for some Americans to climb the economic ladder. Anyone who complained of such systematic discrimination, they implied, was not, as they put it, a "patriotic citizen." This was a serious charge indeed, for "patriotic citizens" in this era supported the Union whereas unpatriotic ones were disloyal. This construction not only attacked those groups calling for federal protection of equality, but it also implied that southern whites who threatened voters and industrialists who turned private guards against strikers were only trying to return the nation to its true political economy. "For the promotion and success of the . . . vital principles" they had outlined in their platform, they invited to their standard "all patriotic citizens, without regard to previous affiliations."[11]

Stalwart Republicans combated the Liberal Republican movement by insisting they were developing the country for everyone. They had won the war, freed the slaves, created equal citizenship, established universal suffrage (for men), and launched "a wise and humane policy toward the Indians." To answer accusations that they were deliberately keeping Democrats from the polls, the Republican congress passed an amnesty act that restored all but about five hundred prominent ex-Confederates to full citizenship. Although Republicans agreed that there should be no "further grants of the public lands to corporations and monopolies," preferring homestead settlement, they also endorsed a tariff to "promote the industries, prosperity, and growth of the whole country," condemned repudiation, and called for retiring the popular greenbacks in favor of a specie-backed currency. They nodded to those women who were agitating for the suffrage, declaring, "The Republican party is mindful [that] the honest demand of any class of citizens for additional rights should be treated with respectful consideration." In general, though, they relied on Americans' fear of southern Democrats and optimism about the nation to carry Grant back to the White House.[12]

It was easy in 1872 for many Americans to believe that the United States under Republican government was indeed becoming the greatest nation on earth, as party members had promised it would. Upwardly mobile Americans enjoyed the benefits of an economy that needed a growing cadre of middle managers and white-collar professionals. They had well-paying jobs, time for leisure activities, money to buy the new products increasingly available, and a growing popular literature that lionized their own values of domesticity. The benefits of the new economy were apparent, especially in the cities. Bananas, a rare and "delicious tropical fruit," were available on eastern street corners. In 1872, the *Manufacturer and Builder* published the plans for a "cheap country cottage," a spacious four-bedroom house that could be built in the towns around New York City for around $3,000. New Yorkers could come in from the suburbs to look proudly at the new Metropolitan Museum of Art, which opened its doors in 1872 with more than 170 paintings worth about $140,000. In San Francisco officials laid the cornerstone for a new city hall, which was not only large and beautiful, but supposedly fireproof and secure against earthquakes. For younger Americans, there were new, cheaply produced toys —leaping horses, velocipedes, swings, sleds, and skates—as well as children's magazines. Even bad news carried a silver lining of better things to come. A smallpox outbreak claimed many lives in 1872, but widespread systematized vaccination prevented the epidemic from spreading as it might have. *Harper's Weekly* emphasized the enormous progress in America when it informed its readers that "480 tons of coal, with an engine and hoisting machine, would have raised every stone of the Great Pyramid to position. It should be remembered that the Great Pyramid weighs 12,760,000,000 tons, and, according to Herodotus, it took the labor of 100,000 men twenty years to build it." Those in the country had increasing access to new products, too, when, in 1872, Chicago's Aaron Montgomery Ward offered to sell directly to farmers without middlemen, promising up to 40 percent savings for those who ordered from his list of offerings.[13]

Throughout 1872, growing attention to the West helped to reinforce ideas of America as a beneficent land where anyone willing to work could succeed. By 1872, the image of the American West as a land of opportunity and excitement was so ubiquitous that Mark Twain could poke fun at it in *Roughing It*. The very first paragraph of the book told of Twain's envy of his brother, headed for Nevada: "Pretty soon he would be . . . away on the great plains and deserts, and among the mountains of the Far West, and would see buffaloes and Indians, and prairie dogs, and antelopes, and have all kinds of adventures, and may be get hanged or scalped, and have ever such a fine time, and write home and tell us all about it, and be a hero." Twain barely mentioned the bison in his book, but he certainly could have said more about them. The buffalo hunt peaked in 1872; in the next two years settlers and sportsmen would tag animals for food and sport while hide hunters would kill about 4,374,000 buffalo and Indians about 1,215,000.[14]

Even with all this good news, those who believed in the traditional vision of the American economy continued to be nervous about pressure from those rejecting the idea of economic harmony. African Americans, workers, and prominent women's suffragists all seemed to believe that there were natural conflicts in society and that the government must privilege their particular interests over those of the rest of the community. The 1872 election would be the first national election in which black voters participated, and in the 1872 campaign, Democrats and Liberal Republicans portrayed freedpeople as working with northern carpetbaggers in southern states to redistribute wealth. Trying to weaken Grant by attacking the southern Republican governments, newspapers and magazines like Horace Greeley's *New York Daily Tribune*, the *Cincinnati Commercial*, the *Chicago Tribune*, the *New York Evening Post*, and the *Nation* complained that freedmen were failing as free laborers. Rather than saving to buy land, they wasted their money "in drink, tobacco, balls, gaming, and other dissipation," according to Greeley. In turn, most African Americans condemned the Liberal Republican movement as an express ticket for the Democrats to regain power. In declaring themselves strongly for Grant, they solidified their opponents' belief that they stood firmly behind the spoilsmanship of the popularly discredited southern Republican governments. Black leader Frederick Douglass's famous dictum—"The Republican party is the ship and all else is the sea"—seemed to illustrate the attachment of black voters to the Republican Party solely for the benefits it promised, rather than on principle.[15]

Workers, too, seemed to be more and more determined to use the state as an arena to effect changes in the economy that would benefit them. Postwar workers often faced unemployment during slack times, especially during the winter, and February and March 1872 were so bad in New York City that the International Workingmen's Association called for city authorities to take action. When unemployed workers, organized by the International and waving red flags, rallied in Tompkins Square on March 14, newspapers reported that New York had its own Commune. Workers were also assuming a political voice nationally. On February 22, 1872, the National Labor Convention nominated its own presidential and vice presidential candidates at Columbus, Ohio, and adopted a platform declaring "that it is a duty to establish a just standard of distribution of capital and labor."[16]

Suffragists also demanded unprecedented government power to assure that women's needs were adequately addressed. "Having petitioned State legislatures to change the statutes that robbed her of her children, wages, and property, she demanded that the Constitutions—State and National—be so amended as to give her a voice in the laws, a choice in the rulers, and protection in the exercise of her rights as a citizen of the United States," Elizabeth Cady Stanton recalled. But female voting seemed to threaten traditional American society, *Harper's Weekly* dryly noted that Mormon women in Utah had voted for a Mormon governor in addition to approving the proposed Utah constitution, whereas Gentile men had abstained from participating in the election. Women had been included in new Wyoming and Utah Territorial constitutions, but other states did not follow their lead. In the face of their failure to get women's suffrage adopted in New York, women like Susan B. Anthony decided to test the proposition that the Fourteenth Amendment enfranchised them through the privileges and immunities clause. Leading up to the 1872 election, activist women across the nation attempted to register to vote.[17]

Those who adhered to the idea of a harmonious economy based on all working their way up together worried about the destruction of that system not only at the hands of labor agitators and southern reconstruction governments, but also at the hands of big businessmen. Their growing disillusionment with men like Andrew Carnegie convinced them that the Republican Party was the tool of business, just as Democrats charged. At the end of the war, these men had seemed like national benefactors. Although some Democratic leaders and a few workingmen's organizations complained about the low wages, dangerous conditions, and long hours in the factories springing up across the country, most Americans looked toward successful industrialists as role models.

In the 1860s, wealthy businessmen often seemed more loyal to the nation than the workers who opposed them. Carnegie was a staunch Republican, so loyal to the government during the war that he risked his career by standing up to a Democratic supervisor who had maligned Lincoln. He spent the war years supervising and repairing Union telegraph lines. Other businessmen supported the government by buying bonds and even by providing the Treasury with gold in the early days of the conflict when a lack of funds threatened the survival of the Union. Carl Schurz recalled that his close friend Jay Cooke, the great financier of the Civil War, had "rendered valuable service to the country during the Civil War, and I do not think anybody grudged him the fortune he gathered at the same time for himself." In contrast to these public-spirited capitalists, organized workers had been tainted by the 1863 New York City draft riots and the wartime strikes that were popularly portrayed as treasonous for the damage they did to the Union cause.[18]

During the war, admiring Americans fit men like Carnegie into their antebellum vision of an economy in which every worker could one day become an employer, if only he worked and saved. Businessmen supported the government because, like all Americans, they shared its interests and had a personal stake in making sure it stayed healthy. Ironically, though, as wartime congressmen tried to develop this bucolic model of the national economy, they hastened its destruction. Believing that the government should encourage American economic development because such growth benefited everyone, Republican congressmen designed wartime tariffs and taxes to protect American business from foreign competition, and their plans worked. Northern industry expanded dramatically. Those with the cash to invest in new enterprises made huge profits. Carnegie skillfully rode this wave of business expansion. In 1861, at twenty-six years old, Carnegie was superintendent of the Pennsylvania Railroad's western division. His annual salary was a princely $2,400 at a time when a common soldier made $13 per month, but it was only a fraction of his income. By 1863, Carnegie's investments in new businesses paid him almost $40,000. In the postwar years he found himself a staunch defender of tariffs, convinced that they encouraged the manufacturing that both developed the country and made him rich.[19]

Not everyone approved of the huge fortunes to be made in the new economy. Democrats made much of the fact that consumers bore the burden of taxes and tariffs as businessmen raised prices to cover higher expenses at the same time that tariffs choked off cheaper foreign competition. By 1864, Democrats and even some Republicans—primarily those who represented western constituencies—charged that businessmen and financiers were making personal fortunes off the war. They called for increased taxation on wealthy Americans. "New England manufacturers are getting richer every day," Sunset Cox snarled in 1864, "richer and richer and richer. . . . They are . . . becoming the owners of this country. . . . They are getting all the protection of the Government." A Republican Congress desperate to find money had cautiously developed a 3 percent income tax in 1861. Many congressmen hesitated to continue the tax, but ultimately they not only kept it but increased it in response to growing hostility to the wealthy. By 1864, Congress established an income tax of 10 percent for incomes over $10,000. While opponents of the tax objected to the "inequality" of the tax, claiming that it was "no less than a confiscation of property, because one man happens to have a little more money than another," proponents stated that "it is just, right, and proper that those having a large amount of income shall pay a larger amount of tax."[20]

Although he was not from New England, Carnegie was just the sort of man Cox was railing against. In 1863, Carnegie had begun to invest in the iron industry that was booming in Pittsburgh during the war, and in 1865, he merged his ill-performing mill with that of a neighboring concern. The newly formed Union Iron Mills Company was capitalized at $500,000. The Union Iron Mills sold its product at a discount to another new Carnegie concern, the Keystone Bridge Company, capitalized at $300,000 in April 1865 and formed to build iron bridges "for railways, canals, common roads, streets, etc., etc." Keystone's working capital came from J. Edgar Thompson and Thomas A. Scott, the president and vice president of the Pennsylvania Railroad, Carnegie's good friends, former employers, and, most likely, customers.[21]

Like other postwar entrepreneurs, Carnegie operated in national rather than local markets. Competition drove him and his partners to try to control their production and marketing as thoroughly as they could. They began to expand production vertically and horizontally. Vertical integration meant that a manufacturer would try to incorporate into his system as many of the steps necessary for production as possible, from gathering the raw materials to marketing the final product. By 1870, a Carnegie interest was smelting its own pig iron; on October 24, 1874, the "Lucy" furnace smelted more than one hundred tons of iron ore. Carnegie integrated forward as well as backward, investing in railroads and joining young carpenter George Pullman in creating the Pullman Palace Car Company to make railroad sleeping cars. The need to cut costs also led Carnegie and his partners to invest heavily in knowledge, hiring trained engineers and trying out the promising innovations that made their product constantly cheaper and better.[22]

While vertical integration solved the problems of supply and marketing, it did not answer the problem of cutthroat competition in expanding industries after the war. To protect their share of the market and expand, businessmen integrated horizontally, merging with similar businesses to make larger and more powerful firms. Carnegie and his associates swept three companies together from 1863 to 1865 and would continue to grow, even attempting to gain control of the Union Pacific in 1871. This tendency ran across the spectrum of industrial production, and it made consumers worry. Railroads seemed the biggest culprits. Laying about 33,000 miles of track between 1868 and 1873 required that the many different companies work together to raise vast sums of money, hire huge numbers of workers, and promote legislation that gave them land and kept production cheap. In January 1872, an Ohio man wrote to his governor, Rutherford B. Hayes, noting that "railroads and other corporations are not only a great power in the State, but will, unless curbed, become 'The State.'" They were acting "not exactly with concert but identity of interest gives unity to their actions; and in Ohio and Pennsylvania especially, have the invidious reachings of these grasping corporations become dangerous."[23]

Such extensive operations demanded large pools of capital, weeding out all but the wealthiest operators. The ability of postwar businessmen to raise money came largely from the changing definition of the corporation during the war. Before the mid-nineteenth century, a company interested in incorporating had to prove to a state legislature that it was performing a function that directly promoted the public good. During the Civil War, this definition shifted. A corporation still had to perform a public function but was no longer bound by the moral imperatives imposed on early corporations. This enabled more and more businesses to incorporate. Incorporation meant that they could sell stock, which represented a share of the business, on the open market to raise money. Reorganized in 1869 to try to weed out fraudulent businesses, the New York Stock Exchange became an increasingly powerful tool in the economy, bringing together individuals with money and businesses seeking to expand. By 1870, it was annually handling more than $22 billion in sales; on February 25, 1871, more than seven hundred thousand shares changed hands in a few hours. While antebellum companies were funded with the capital of the owners themselves, corporations' money came from share-holders who invested a portion of their capital in the enterprise. Corporations could survive the death of individual investors and changes in directors, becoming independent entities very different from antebellum partnerships or individual proprietorships.[24]

Large corporations increased the distance between workers and employers. Like those of other entrepreneurs, Carnegie's bustling factories required new organization, huge workforces, and whole cadres of managers, clerks, and engineers who reported to Carnegie. Middle managers divorced workers from the industrialists at the head of the operation, who no longer had personal contact with their workers. In 1867, when iron puddlers in Pittsburgh struck to protest wage reductions, employers organized a pool to import new workers from Europe to keep their factories running. The unemployed puddlers felt little camaraderie with capitalists like Carnegie. Carnegie himself reflected that, in the modern industrial world, "we assemble thousands of operatives in the factory, and in the mine, of whom the employer can know little or nothing, and to whom he is little better than a myth.... Rigid castes are formed, and, as usual, mutual ignorance breeds mutual mistrust." In January 1872, the *Overland Monthly* ran the story of a man who had tried to get an audience with the head of "a corporation more powerful than a handful of States." This illusive being, whom he irreverently called "the soul of the corporation," was less accessible "to common men [than] a Congressman, or the President of the Great Republic." "Day by day, week by week, month by month," he waited like "an insignificant insect" to be allowed an audience with "the soul of the corporation," leaving him—and his reader—wondering if, indeed, the corporation had a "soul" at all.[25]

The image of benevolent capitalists had been crumbling gradually after the war, driven primarily by popular distrust of the rapidly consolidating railroads, but in 1872 dramatic developments changed the public image of postwar businessmen from benefactors to parasites. On January 6, 1872, Edward D. Stokes shot prominent railroad baron James Fisk, Jr., on the stairs of New York's Grand Central Hotel. Jim Fisk was a rich man-about-town, famous for his unscrupulousness, generosity, lavish displays of wealth, and beautiful mistress. News of the shooting raced through the streets of the city. When Fisk died the next day, crowds gathered outside the hotel. The story became a national sensation. Ned Stokes and Fisk had been friends but had fallen out when Fisk's beloved but manipulative "Josie" fell into the arms of the handsome Stokes.[26]

Fisk's murder threw open the sordid story of the Erie Ring, the business venture that had transformed Fisk from relative obscurity into a financial power. The Erie Railroad had been embroiled in factional fights among its principals—Daniel Drew, Cornelius Vanderbilt, Jay Gould, and Jim Fisk—since at least 1866. By 1868, Gould and Fisk had control of the enterprise. They raised money by selling stock in England and protected their interests at home by working with William Marcy Tweed and Peter B. Sweeny, "the two most prominent leaders of that notorious ring which controls the proletariat [sic] of New York city and governs the politics of the State." Thus, revealed an exposé, the Erie Ring and the Tammany Ring were "brought together in close political and financial union. . . . This formidable combination . . . wielded the influence of a great corporation with a capital of $100,000,000; it controlled the politics of the first city of the New World; it sent its representatives to the Senate of the State, and numbered among its agents the Judges of the courts. Compact, disciplined, and reckless, it knew its own power and would not scruple to use it."[27]

Fisk had shown his determination to enrich himself at the expense of the people in September 1869, when he and Gould had tried to make a fortune by cornering the gold market. Using President Grant's unsavory brother-in-law to prevent the government from selling its gold reserves, they forced the price of gold up to 162—more than $30 higher than it had been six months before—making their own holdings increasingly valuable. Because expensive gold meant cheap paper money, their efforts created sudden and dangerously high inflation, threatening the livelihood of anyone who received wages or conducted business in greenbacks. It also encouraged other financiers to try their luck in the gold market. Finally aware that his brother-in-law was part of a gargantuan financial scheme, Grant ordered the Treasury to sell $4 million in gold, thus popping the speculators' bubble and ruining those unlucky gamblers with bad timing. Fisk's and Gould's plan failed, but "Black Friday" convinced average Americans that the profiteers were out to ruin their country-men by obscure financial manipulations solely to make more and more money.

Sensational books about the Fisk murder rolled off the presses, redefining industrialists as their pages fed simmering popular anger at the antics of men like Fisk and Gould. One hasty story painted Fisk as a representative postwar financier, "coarse, noisy, boastful, ignorant," who had "swindled the government" during the Civil War, saddling the American people with taxes that would take years to "free themselves from." From a background as "a sharp Yankee peddler," Fisk had risen rapidly to "the head of a gigantic corporation, . . . able, by an hour's effort, to . . . gather into his clutches a score of millions of other people's property, impoverish a thousand wealthy men, or derange the values and the traffic of a vast empire." Fisk and Gould were "all that is dark and deceitful" and held "irresponsible authority," although they "belonged to a low and degraded moral and social type." The book concluded that "a bold, bad man has come to a stop in his career [sic] by the hand of an assassin, and the honest people of New York, and of the entire country, will breathe more freely now that he has gone."[28]

National focus on these unsavory railroad kings brought attention to their enormous salaries and the scandalous ways they spent them. "Into . . . the spectacles, the military regiments, the Long Branch parades, the steamboats, the brass bands, and the long array of bedizened harlots whom he supported, went the earnings of the Erie road," complained the author of a sensational book about Fisk. Complaints tainted even reputable businessmen; in March 1872, *Harper's Weekly* noted that Andrew Carnegie's mentor and good friend, railroad magnate Thomas A. Scott, had the highest salary in the United States, making $150,000 a year as the head of "several great corporations." A popular history of Washington, D.C., lamented that Pennsylvania Avenue would never be as grand as its designers intended because "the Gradgrind politicians of to-day have voted to dump down a railroad 'depot' in its very centre, because Mr. Thomas Scott wants it, and because they have free railroad passes, and a few other little perquisites in their pockets."[29] Legislation in favor of Erie had come from Tweed's men in the New York legislature, and the association with Tweed quickly made Erie fair game for reformers. The *New York Times*—fervently and angrily anti-Tweed—harped on the connection between Tweed and Erie, making it a point to note that Tweed "furtively" came to view Fisk's body in the hotel room to pay his last respects to his friend.[30]

Fisk was a flamboyant example of a profiteering businessman, but he was also emblematic of larger trends in industry. More respectable businessmen like Carnegie were also making fortunes, taking the free labor principles of production and protection of private property toward economies of scale and unbridled profit-making. By 1872, business was showing signs of overexpansion. Those who could manage it began to try to eliminate competition by forcing smaller enterprises out of business. Although virtually all businesses were trying to consolidate through pools or elimination of competition, the practice was associated most strongly with John D. Rockefeller, a pioneer in the oil business, who was destroying his rivals in the Pennsylvania oil industry.

JUSTICE ON THE RAIL—THE RAILROAD (RING) SMASH UP.

Figure 7. Once Justice had destroyed the corrupt railroad barons, Thomas Nast's 1872 cartoon suggested, the "track" would be "clear" for the development of the country. Courtesy *HarpWeek*.

Popular feeling about the public spirit of businessmen was not helped by the way Congress decided to raise money. The Republican congresses that imposed the nation's first income tax during the Civil War were very uneasy about this "inquisitorial" tax because they did not want energetic capitalists to move to other countries where their wealth would be safer. Republicans insisted that the income tax was solely a war measure. To guarantee that it would not become a permanent feature of American life, in the same law that imposed the tax they provided for its automatic expiration in 1870, which was later extended to 1872. In a revenue bill of that year, congressmen in favor of protecting business concluded to fund the operations of the government through continued high tariffs rather than an extension of the progressive income tax. This meant that the money to repay the debt—held largely by the wealthier members of society—would come from regressive tariffs and liquor and tobacco taxes collected primarily from average workers. There was little agitation for the continuation of the tax, but the fact that Congress turned automatically to a revenue system that benefited the wealthy to the detriment of the poor indicated the general sense that Congress worked for business.[31]

The Erie scandal and the growing sense that business was taking over government fueled the Liberal Republican campaign. If only Liberal Republicans could tie a dramatic scandal directly to the Republican Party itself, they could hammer home the idea that stalwart Republicans were destroying the nation by catering to African Americans and selling out to business. Schurz had tried to implicate Grant in War Department scandals but had succeeded only in weakening his own credibility. Then, in September 1872, Liberal Republicans found the goods. The *New York Sun* broke the story that a number of important Republican congressmen as well as the current vice president, Schuyler Colfax, had been bribed by railroad men constructing the Union Pacific Railroad. Greeley's *New York Daily Tribune* instantly picked up the cry.[32]

The story of the Credit Mobilier scandal was complicated. During the war, Congress had permitted the Union Pacific Railroad Company to issue bonds up to a certain amount per mile of railroad constructed to finance the construction of the road. Congressmen had not required open bidding or acceptance of the lowest bids for construction. Directors of the Union Pacific organized their own construction company, the Credit Mobilier, which was the only bidder for the railroad's business and, of course, won the contracts to build the road. The Credit Mobilier bids were only slightly below the upper limit of the bonds per mile allowed by law, enabling the Union Pacific, in turn, to raise the maximum amount of money allowed by Congress through bond sales, even though actual construction cost much less. These grossly inflated bids enabled the owners of the Credit Mobilier—the same men who ran the Union Pacific—to pocket huge sums of money. In 1872, the *Sun* charged that four years earlier prominent Republican politician Oakes Ames had distributed Credit Mobilier stock to congressmen in exchange for a positive legislation on behalf of the company, in which he had a controlling interest.[33]

When the story first appeared, stalwart Republicans angrily denied that congressmen had been bribed. Colfax immediately defended his honesty, declaring, "Bribing me to support Pacific Railroad interests is just as incredible as that I should need to be bribed to vote the Republican ticket." Republican newspapers charged Greeley and the Liberal Republicans with "prevarication," "slanders," and "utter falsity." But, in fact, the railroads had always worked hand-in-glove with government. The western promoters of a transcontinental railroad had deliberately made stolid Republican Leland Stanford the president of their concern during his 1861 campaign for the California governorship. "A good deal depends upon the election of Stanford," their leader wrote, "for the prestige of electing a Republican ticket will go a great way toward getting us what we want." The overlap of business and government had grown naturally from the belief that economic growth benefited everyone in a harmonious system and had been an established part of American life since at least the beginning of the nineteenth century. Some of the key Republican players in the scandal seemed honestly surprised that anyone would have seen any misconduct in the affair. By 1872, though, the expansion of the government and the growing power of business made many Americans suspicious about such connections, especially when the Democrats harped constantly that Republicans were deliberately using public resources to ensure their own reelection. Despite congressmen's protests, most Americans were primed to believe that the railroad men had been bribing Republican congressmen and, knowing that the railroads had received valuable grants of public land, felt that something must be wrong.[34]

An investigation of the Credit Mobilier scandal revealed that Ames had sold stock to a number of congressmen for significantly less than its value, earning them hundreds of dollars of dividends per share—a total of up to $33 million, according to some. One of the weaknesses in proving that this money had bought favorable legislation was that Ames insisted there had been no

1872

Figure 8. Photographed in 1872 after extensive additions and renovations, Leland Stanford's grand California home illustrated the great wealth of postwar railroad men. Courtesy Stanford University Archives.

significant legislation in favor of the Union Pacific since 1864. The investigation eventually went deep enough to answer this point, revealing that congressmen supporting the 1864 transcontinental railroad bill that gave land to the Union Pacific Railroad had been offered stock in the Union Pacific Railroad Company. Promises of stock did not appear to sway their votes, for those involved were staunch advocates of government development of the railroads, but a railroad notebook with congressmen's names in it next to amounts of promised stock looked pretty damning.[35]

Even those who could not follow the twists and turns in the trail of Credit Mobilier and Union Pacific Railroad affairs could see that railroad officials had tried to buy congressional goodwill and might well have succeeded. Then, too, the scandal uncovered the complicated relation between the Union Pacific and the Credit Mobilier construction company. Technically, the Credit Mobilier scheme broke no laws—for Congress had not specified that the road must be built as economically as possible—but the men behind the scheme clearly were not building the road with the needs of the public in the forefront of their minds.

In this atmosphere Mark Twain and Charles Dudley Warner wrote *The Gilded Age: A Tale of Today*, a biting satire of the greed and speculative mindset of the day. At the heart of the novel were two grandiose schemes that looked much like the Credit Mobilier scandal and the Freedmen's Bureau. In the book, unprincipled speculators bribed congressmen to fund a railroad (which then sold bonds to raise far more money than needed to build the road) and to purchase a vast tract of worthless land in Tennessee for millions of dollars to build a school for freedpeople. "A Congressional appropriation costs money," a knowing railroad man in the novel told a naïve youth who wondered what happened to a $200,000 appropriation. "Just reflect," the man told him:

A majority of the House Committee, say $10,000 apiece—$40,000; a majority of the Senate Committee, the same each—say $40,000; a little extra to one or two chairmen of one or two such committees, say $10,000 each—$20,000; and there's $100,000 of the money gone, to begin with. Then, seven male lobbyists, at $3,000 each—$21,000; one female lobbyist, $10,000; a high moral Congressman or Senator here and there—the high moral ones cost more, because they give tone to a measure—say ten of these at $3,000 each, is $30,000; then a lot of small-fry country members who won't vote for anything whatever without pay—say twenty at $500 apiece, is $10,000; a lot of dinners to members—say $10,000 altogether; . . . and then comes your printed documents . . . printing bills are destruction itself. Ours, so far amount to—let me see—10; 52; 22; 13;—and then there's 11; 14; 33—well, never mind the details, the total in clean numbers foots up $118,254.42 thus far![36]

Twain and Warner did not stop their excoriation of modern society with the railroads. They made thinly veiled references to Tweed as "the great and good Wm. M. Weed . . . who had stolen $20,000,000 from the city and was a man so envied, so honored, indeed, that when the sheriff went to his office to arrest him as a felon, that sheriff blushed and apologized." They hit upon Jim Fisk with a reference to men who would give a mistress "a railroad or an opera house, or whatever she wanted—at least they'd promise" and with a dramatic shooting on the steps of a New York City hotel. They made fun of the modern girl's deluded belief that she wanted an education and a career rather than a husband; they lampooned suffragists when a woman who had murdered her faithless lover decided to "turn to that final resort of the disappointed of her sex, the lecture platform." They were devastating about criminal justice, attacking William Howe and Abe Hummel, the lawyers who defended Joseph Rosenzweig in his trial for the murder of Alice Augusta Bowlsby, by mimicking them with the novel's Mr. Braham and Mr. Quiggle, whose ridiculous defense of a killer and manipulation of the ignorant jury enables a "devil" to walk free after committing a brazen, premeditated murder. At the end of their jumbled exposé of American life, Twain and Warner permitted only Philip Sterling, a man who had worked hard in his chosen profession and lived within his means, to succeed. After Sterling rises to prominence, a young speculator who finds he has nothing after years of hoping for undeserved riches by manipulating legislators concludes to "begin my life over again, and begin it and end it with good solid work."[37]

In his preface to the London edition of the novel, Twain claimed that the book was designed to illuminate America's "all-pervading speculativeness" and "the shameful corruption which lately crept into our politics, and in a handful of years has spread until the pollution has affected some portion of every State and Territory in the Union." He applauded the arrest of Tweed and his judicial henchmen and called for the "straightforward and honest" men "to attend to the politics of the country personally and put only their very best men into positions of trust and authority."[38]

Twain's determination to prod the "best men" into political responsibility came from his disappointment in the result of the 1872 election. Much to the chagrin of true reformers in the Liberal Republican movement, political machinations gave the party's nomination to the erratic and comical editor Horace Greeley, famous primarily for his vicious attacks on southern Democrats. This was hardly the way to create a new unity between right thinking men in both parties. The "Straight-out" Democrats held a national convention in September and nominated candidates, but when both declined the nomination, Democrats had little choice in the election. Many simply refused to vote at all.[39]

Although Greeley's nomination guaranteed that the movement would not elect a president (even Schurz tried to wash his hands of the new candidate), the Liberal Republican campaign of 1872 created a truce between a body of Democrats and Republicans across the nation that dominated the rest of the nineteenth century. That truce depended first on the self-assurance of upwardly mobile Americans that the nation was, in fact, progressing and that anyone who tried could succeed. It also depended on the fear that those who refused to work hard might take over the government and use it to redistribute the wealth earned by hard workers, and on the related fear that corporate leaders would demand legislation to promote their own interests at the expense of all. If this happened, then America's unique free labor world of economic harmony would fall apart. Once the government began favoring one group in society over another, different interests would be forced to compete for resources, and the free ability to rise would end.

In the 1872 presidential campaign, Liberal Republicans used growing anxiety about special interests to bridge the gulf between Democrats and Republicans that had carried over from the war. Those with Democratic antecedents argued that Republicans were deliberately increasing the size of the government to provide party members with jobs and beneficial legislation, and that the party stayed in power by catering to ignorant black voters to whom politicians promised jobs. Picking up the argument of southerners like Wade Hampton that African Americans' and workers' calls for government aid were thinly disguised class warfare, Democrats in the new coalition argued that the taxes necessary to pay for government jobs crushed the average taxpayer while they benefited either lazy nonproducers or the extremely wealthy. With a number of prominent black rights activists in their midst—including Carl Schurz and Charles Sumner—the Liberal Republicans who hailed from the Republican Party emphasized the attempts of disaffected workers and corporate giants to corrupt the government more than they attacked southern black voters. The editor of the *Chicago Tribune* complained that "those who style themselves 'the working classes'" needed to be taught "a few sound truths of political economy." "Now that their representatives are becoming more and more prominent in politics, their lack of knowledge is painfully evident." The *New York Daily Tribune* claimed that laborers were hinting that "if the wrongs of the American laborers are not righted," they would "resort to the revolutionary violence of the Paris Commune." Together, the Republicans and Democrats in the movement created a picture of an American republic of independent, self-sufficient Americans endangered from both above and below by those who demanded government favoritism.[40]

Most Republicans remained true to Grant, recognizing that, no matter how much they might sympathize with the principles of the Liberal Republicans, a Liberal Republican victory would essentially hand the government over to the Democrats. (Wade Hampton agreed that the Liberal Republican movement was "our only hope to defeat Grant.") Insisting upon a straight Republican ticket, they defended the southern Republican governments as examples of true free labor systems. The South was producing more cotton than ever, a correspondent to the *Cincinnati Daily Gazette* inaccurately insisted. "The negroes have done their part, and they have done it with no disposition to assume anything on account of their political privileges." While Liberal Republicans and Democrats attacked black officeholders, Republicans presented them as examples of good Americans, rising through hard work. A Republican profile of Samuel Peters, a black congressional candidate from Louisiana, noted that he was "cashier of the Freedmen's Bank at Shreveport, where he is much respected for his integrity and modesty of deportment." Born into poverty, "he worked as a field laborer, studying at night and morning, saving his earnings until garnering enough to go to school for a term." Teaching to earn money and uplift his race, he later went to college before moving into banking. *Harper's Weekly* used Peters to attack squarely the idea of black Americans as freeloaders. "He has fairly fought his way, and fairly won the respectable position in the community which he occupies."[41]

But even stalwart Republicans knew they had to combat the growing image that the party worked for special interests. Increasingly, stalwarts threw out tentative lines of reconciliation with Democrats. In February, *Harper's Weekly* ran a long biography of Sunset Cox, now a Democratic congressman from New York, describing him as "a ready, graceful, self-possessed, vigorous debater, so mingling argument with wit, and sarcasm with good humor, as always to command attention and respect. He is a high personal favorite with members, irrespective of party, and is ever on the alert to serve his constituents, regardless of politics." It also lauded him—rather disingenuously—for being above party.[42]

The conjunction of a western exploring trip and popular anger at railroad barons like Fisk also helped to spread the Liberal Republican idea of reconciliation by continuing to develop the image of the West as a place where northerners and southerners met on common ground in the spiritual heart of the nation. In August 1870, an exploring expedition had headed West from Fort Ellis, Montana, toward the Yellowstone River. By October the men had reached the Yellowstone, where they "pitched their camp amid magnificent scenery," according to their widely reprinted reports. "They found abundance of game and trout, hot springs of five or six different kinds . . . and basaltic columns of enormous size, that . . . suggested some mighty effort at human architecture." The huge waterfall they found "must be in form, color and surroundings one of the most glorious objects on the American Continent." Indeed, the editor of the *New York Times* thought the record of their discoveries "reads like the realization of a child's fairy tale." On the strength of the expedition's reports, the secretary of the interior sent out an official surveying team under Ferdinand V. Hayden to chart the Yellowstone region. With him went the son of Illinois Congressman John A. Logan, the son of Massachusetts Congressman Henry L. Dawes, a photographer, and famous fine artist Thomas Moran. Artist Albert Bierstadt had also been invited but could not make the trip.[43]

By 1872, the very corruption that plagued the East appeared to threaten this fairy-tale land. Within a year of the expedition's entry into Yellowstone, the Northern Pacific Railroad was surveying the region with an eye to laying track to bring in tourists and business. Indeed, Jay Cooke of the Northern Pacific had arranged for Moran to travel with the Hayden expedition. *Scribner's Monthly* gave the surveyors' report of Yellowstone top billing in its issues of May and June 1871 in an article with illustrations by Moran, promising that the Northern Pacific would soon enable tourists to come to the great natural wonder of the continent. But once private interests took possession of the land—either by buying it or by inducing employees to preempt it under the Homestead Act—they could charge tourists whatever they wished to see the wonderful sights of Yellowstone. In part, Northern Pacific money had encouraged the exploration of the region, but by 1872 its interest no longer sounded benevolent.[44]

Many Americans were starting to wonder if the West was just another place to make money. Grant had vetoed an attempt to stop the bison slaughter in 1870, but the idea that the West was not simply a source of raw materials was gaining popularity. The West's spiritual importance was gaining adherents. By 1872, John Muir had added to the idea of western wealth in his articles extolling the spiritual virtues of the western landscape. Arriving in San Francisco in 1868, he headed out to the Yosemite Valley to find wilderness. After working first as a sheep herder and then in a sawmill, Muir fell in love with the Sierra Nevada. Ralph Waldo Emerson tried to entice Muir back east to share his love of nature with the world, but Muir chose instead to preach from where he was. Muir's minute and poetic descriptions of the natural beauty in the West's mountains, glaciers, and even floods insisted that this was a place divorced from eastern government and money-making. "Visions like these do not remain with us as . . . flat shadows cast upon our minds, to brighten, at times, when touched by association or will, and fade again from our view, like landscapes in the gloaming," he admonished readers. "They saturate every fibre of the body and soul, dwelling in us and with us, like holy spirits, through all of our after-deaths and after-lives."[45]

Americans increasingly angry at big businessmen turned to the federal government to guarantee that Yellowstone would not become simply another corporate enterprise. After presenting a detailed description of the region in an article for *Scribner's Monthly* in early 1872, Hayden concluded: "We have been able in this article to do little more than to allude to a few of the wonderful physical phenomena of this marvelous valley. . . . The intelligent American will one day point on the map to this remarkable district with the conscious pride that it has not its parallel on the face of the globe." He called for Congress to pass a law setting Yellowstone apart as a public park. On December 18, 1871, Senator Samuel Pomeroy of Kansas and Delegate William H. Clagett of Montana Territory obliged by introducing into the Senate and House of Representatives bills to protect the Yellowstone area from private interests. The measure would make Yellowstone a public park, protect it in a natural state, and provide against "wanton destruction of the fish and game . . . their capture or destruction for the purposes of merchandise or profit."[46]

Supporters defended the plan to create Yellowstone National Park as a blow against the vultures of big business. Setting apart the land would not hurt real producers, they argued, since the land was not suitable for farming, stock raising, or mining. The Yellowstone Valley had a sparkling climate, wonderful views, and hot springs "adorned with decorations more beautiful than human art ever conceived," the House Committee on Public Lands reported. It warned, though, that "persons are now waiting for the spring . . . to enter in and take possession of these remarkable curiosities, to make merchandise of these bountiful specimens, to fence in these rare wonders so as to charge visitors a fee, as is now done at Niagara Falls, for the sight of that which ought to be as free as the air or water." Yellowstone would be a famous resort, the report noted, and if not protected immediately, "the vandals who are now waiting to enter into this wonderland will, in a single season, despoil, beyond recovery, these remarkable curiosities which have required all the cunning skill of nature thousands of years to prepare."[47]

Saving Yellowstone for the people was the government's responsibility. The *New York Times* declared that should the region be made a national park, from which business "should be strictly shut out, it will remain a place which we can proudly show to the benighted European as a proof of what nature—under a republican form of government—can accomplish in the great West." On March 1, 1872, Grant signed the bill making Yellowstone a national park, and Congress took on responsibility for the West gladly. Underlining its interest and commitment to the park, Congress paid $10,000 for Thomas Moran's painting *The Grand Canyon of the Yellowstone* to hang at the top of the grand staircase in the Senate wing of the Capitol.[48]

The establishment of Yellowstone National Park reflected the new accord in American politics. The Liberal Republican *Nation* approved of the general principle of congressional action to protect natural lands. Also voting in favor of establishing the park was Sunset Cox, ardent opponent of government activism. Despite his general distrust of government activity, he was willing to promote government ownership of Yellowstone, probably in part because of his determination to thwart a business monopoly on the region, but also because of his great enthusiasm for the West as the heart of America. The West, it seemed, was where American individuals could flourish, and it was the government's responsibility to defend it.[49]

Despite the importance of the government's role in the West, the western experience was increasingly portrayed as the realm of individuals. The popular attraction of the West was apparent immediately after the war. Prominent political and business leaders traveled to the plains to hunt, and the completion of the Union Pacific Railroad in 1869 meant highly publicized trips by rail across the country. In 1868, General Philip Sheridan had made William F. Cody the chief scout for the Fifth Cavalry, and self-promoter Buffalo Bill saw the money to be made in selling the West to easterners. By 1869, the romantic image of the westerner moved east thanks to newspaperman E. Z. C. Judson, known as Ned Buntline, who made Buffalo Bill the hero of cheap novels and a popular play which occasionally starred Cody himself. In December 1869, the *New York Weekly* began a new serial novel by Buntline, "the greatest of all living romance writers." *Buffalo Bill: The King of Border Men* promised to be wild, thrilling, humorous, romantic and pathetic; "it is life as it is, and not as it is fancied by those who have hunted in cities and fought their battles in drawing-rooms." Buffalo Bill, the advertisement in *Harper's Weekly* read, "is known, especially among our army officers, as the BEST HORSEMAN, THE BEST-INFORMED GUIDE, AND THE GREATEST HUNTER of the present day." He was also "the handsomest man . . . on the Plains . . . an Apollo in the saddle."[50]

By 1871 Cody was actively promoting himself as a western hero, cultivating his looks and stories of his heroism. This paid off, and on April 26, 1872, Congress awarded Cody the Congressional Medal of Honor for gallantry. He was the logical person for Sheridan to assign as a guide for Grand Duke Alexis of Russia and a party of other notables on a western hunt, and an account of that trip by W. E. Webb embellished Buntline's picture of Cody, calling him "athletic and shrewd . . . with sinews of iron and eye ever on the alert, clad in a suit of buckskin," even as he poked fun at the popular vision of a western scout as "an eagle-eyed giant, with a horse which obeys his whistle" and which "is usually occupied by a rescued maiden." Cody cultivated his growing fame, popularizing the individualist image of the American West as he created himself as a western hero. In 1872, he acted as himself in a play, "Scouts of the Prairie," and the image took hold. That year, *Harper's Weekly* ran a number of pictures of western scouts, suggesting that the man in buckskin spying out hostile Indians was a true American westerner. This, it appeared, was the ideal individual. Ironically, it seemed that the government must protect him from big businessmen.[51]

The presidential election of 1872 was freighted with importance. It was a critical event in American history when growing fears of those who seemed to reject a free labor ideal produced an enduring realignment in American politics and reoriented the political debates of the era. On one hand, Liberal Republicans worried about labor agitation and southern reconstruction governments, which seemed to them to be controlled by the lazy poor who wanted wealth distribution. On the other hand, they worried about wealthy businessmen who seemed to be manipulating government to carve up the economy for their own benefit, destroying competition and stealing from other men their chance to rise. Standing firm on the idea that America's unique political economy meant that all who worked could rise, and that all Americans shared a harmony of interest so that all would rise together, they opposed anyone who argued that natural conflicts in society demanded government adjustment.

In the election, Republican candidate U. S. Grant retained the presidency, but the Liberal Republican platform defined a new alliance in American politics for the rest of the century and began the reconciliation of North and South around the idea of individualism. In this increasingly mainstream vision, individual men could rise on their own, so long as government refused to pander to the interests of industrialists or disaffected workers. Critically, this new vision did not include activist women but rather placed women firmly in the home of an individualistic man. Domestic imagery and antiabortion agitation reinforced its domestic ideals. Together, the men and women who embraced this worldview made up a new "middle class," distinguished not by their income but by their determination to hold what they believed was an evenhanded government steady from the demands of those at the top as well as those at the bottom of society. Curiously, though, in the same year these Americans came together to insist that the government must not cater to special interests, they expanded its activities to the protection of the West, a land that—with the help of men like Buffalo Bill—seemed to be a world of unfettered individualism open to those who embraced the mainstream vision. The government had begun to protect American individualism.

1873–1880

Years of Unrest

Almost as soon as the coalition of Liberal Republicans and Democrats, forged during the election of 1872, presented their new mainstream vision of America, they worried that special interests were attacking their ideals of citizenship and government. From the time of the Panic of 1873 to the economic recovery at the end of the decade, they faced example after example of government under siege as the economically threatened insisted that systematic inequalities in society simply had to be addressed. When a serious recession pinched everyone, the tension between the view of government as impartial and the call for government activism rose until, eventually, it boiled over. For most Americans, the 1870s were a time of profound crisis; it seemed that the American republic, the last great hope of the world for human self-government, was in grave danger.

Feeding the sense of crisis in the 1870s were disaffected westerners who added their voices to those seeking government support. Farmers had gone west in the great optimism of the postwar years, convinced that they, too, could succeed if only they tried hard enough. Luna Kellie recounted the events that took her from Minnesota in 1875. Her mother had been given railroad pamphlets "telling of the glories of Nebraska and how there were homesteads to be taken within 4 miles of the State Capital and the University." She urged her husband to go. When he "very sensibly told her he had absolutely nothing to start on except one team and wagon . . . she still urged him to put our household goods in the wagon and start out before all the homesteads close to the Capitol were taken." Fourteen years old, Luna dreamed of the western paradise described by the railroads and had "a vague idea . . . that they were doing a noble work to let poor people know there was such a grand haven they could reach." But conditions in the 1870s meant that for farmers like Luna Kellie's father—as well as for freedpeople, activist women, and many wage laborers and businessmen—success would be elusive. Frustrated and angry, these people rejected the idea of economic harmony and looked to the government to redress what must, they believed, be something wrong in society.[1]

Financial instability grew into a full-fledged panic in 1873, heightening the tensions that cut through society. In the great optimism of the postwar years, railroad directors had speculated in unprofitable construction, industrialists had overexpanded their operations, and farmers had increased their production to unprecedented levels. By late spring 1873, the postwar bubble was popping. "As a New York workman in 1873, I first watched the crisis and depression of what we now call the business cycle," wrote Samuel Gompers. "During the summer of that year we heard rumors of pending financial troubles." Employers dismissed workers and cut wages at a time when the country was absorbing the more than a million new immigrants who had arrived during the past three years. Jay Cooke, the man who had handled U.S. Treasury bonds during the war, had involved his powerful banking company heavily in the Northern Pacific Railroad Company (hence his interest in securing an artist for Hayden's Yellowstone expedition to drum up popular enthusiasm for a railroad to the area), and on September 18 he announced bankruptcy. "The crash came in September when the Jay Cooke Company and Fiske and Hatch announced failure. The scenes downtown were wild on that rainy day," Gompers recalled. Other banks, overextended in railroad securities, followed Cooke, precipitating a downward spiral in prices and employment.[2]

The South had stubbornly refused to prosper even before the panic knocked the bottom out of the economy. Well into the 1870s, poverty, racial struggles, and disease conspired to keep the region unsettled. The economy could not seem to recover from the war. American cotton could not regain a dominant share of the international market and after 1875, when cotton production reached prewar levels, overproduction across the cotton countries kept prices low. Recurring epidemics of yellow fever swept the South, causing full-blown epidemics in 1873 and 1878 that not only unsettled trade and created unemployment but also left destitute widows and orphans dependent on charity. The poverty of the region exacerbated the South's racial troubles. The army had brought Ku Klux Klan outbreaks in South Carolina under control by 1873, but black fears and white animosity remained high until at least 1880.[3]

Heightening northern frustration at the South's continuing poverty was the growing perception that African Americans wanted to be supported by the government rather than by working. In spring 1873, supporters of Louisiana's discredited Republican administration refused to give way to new claimants of government posts and holed up in the Colfax courthouse. The resulting clash with white opponents who charged the courthouse left eighty to one hundred of the black and white Republicans dead. The popular press defended the attackers, describing the situation as proof that Republicans wanted control at all costs and were preserving their power by promising government largesse to black voters. At the same time, African Americans were advocating government aid to education and demanding civil rights legislation to end discrimination, a request that most white Americans thought was unconstitutional. When the Freedmen's Bank, mismanaged by its white officers, collapsed in 1874, black investors demanded that the government refund their lost deposits. The government had, after all, created the bank and strongly encouraged freedpeople to use it. Their position was sensible, but the many white Americans who had also lost money in the panic found it outrageous since they had no similar hope of government refunds. Then, to honor the recently deceased Charles Sumner, Congress passed the Civil Rights Act of 1875, despite its unpopularity in the nation at large. It appeared to nervous observers that black Americans wanted special treatment at the hands of the government. "Is it not time for the colored race to stop playing baby?" the *Chicago Tribune* demanded. "Let them obtain social equality as every other man, woman, and child in this world obtain it,—by showing themselves in their lives the social equals of those with whom they wish to consort. If they do this, year by year the prejudices will pass away." But if they relied on the Civil Rights Act, "that prejudice will grow deeper and more bitter."[4]

Of even more concern to the adherents of the mainstream worldview were people who increasingly identified themselves as permanent members of a working class and agitated more and more stridently for better wages and conditions. Even at their peak in 1886, unions never organized more than one-third of all American wage laborers, but their strength in the 1870s seemed to be growing. By 1873, there were twenty-six national unions, led by railway workers, molders, and shoemakers. More than 300,000 workers belonged to these national organizations. (There were so many workers in

Reno, Nevada, that tailor Jacob Davis decided to apply for a patent on the denim "waist overalls" he made, riveted at pressure points and sewn with orange thread to match the rivets. He asked San Francisco dry goods merchant Levi Strauss to provide the money for the patent application, which they received on May 20, 1873. Within a year they sold over 20,000 pairs, and about twenty years later they gave their popular pants the number 501.) As the panic closed factories, workers across the country increasingly demanded that government help them survive the crisis. With unemployment high by fall 1873, ward meetings in New York City called for public works projects, "maintenance or money for . . . the needy while out of work," and an end to evictions for the unemployed unable to keep up with their rent. In December, a mass meeting at Cooper Union appointed what it called "a Committee of Safety"—taking the name from the French Revolution. "Many street meetings followed to burn into the hearts of all tragic demonstrations of human need. The unemployed filled the city's streets and squares. . . . Those in authority did not rest comfortably. The press began hinting at the 'Commune,'" Samuel Gompers remembered.5

Trouble erupted in New York City in January 1874. Unions had planned a mass demonstration in Tompkins Square on January 13. As Gompers recalled, "The daily press . . . made the city feel that Communists were in control and that they were on the verge of a revolutionary uprising." On that morning, the park was packed. Around 10:30, the police attacked a group of workers marching into the park, using their deadly nightsticks. "Shortly afterwards," Gompers remembered, "the mounted police charged the crowd . . . riding them down and attacking men, women, and children without discrimination. It was an orgy of brutality. I was caught in the crowd on the street and barely saved my head from being cracked by jumping down a cellarway. The attacks of police kept up all day long. . . . Mounted police and guards . . . repeatedly charged down crowded avenues and streets. A reign of terror gripped that section of the city. They justified their policy by the charge that Communism was rearing its head."6

Businessmen were not meeting the financial crisis with confident faith in the nation's political economy, either. In order to combat volatile shifts in the economy that threatened them with bankruptcy, powerful businessmen continued to consolidate their enterprises. They began to form "pools" to control prices by agreeing to carve up markets. Andrew Carnegie later recalled that the idea for pools had come from his days as a messenger boy. Permitted to collect an extra ten cents for messages "delivered beyond a certain limit," the

THE EMANCIPATION OF LABOR AND THE HONEST WORKING-PEOPLE.—[See next Page.]

Figure 9. In this Thomas Nast cartoon of February 7, 1874, Death is hidden under respectable clothing as he invites a workingman and his family to join a "communist" mob destroying the city. Courtesy of Harvard College Library.

boys fought over the fair distribution of "dime messages." To restore harmony, Carnegie proposed that the boys "pool" their money "and divide the cash equally at the end of each week." Carnegie insisted that the boys' plan was intended only to restore "peace and good-humor" and not to "create artificial prices," but the same could not be said about the pools of the 1870s. In business pools, the idea was the same as that of the boys, but these informal business arrangements were designed precisely to reduce competition and fix prices.[7]

Industrialists also continued to influence legislation to their benefit. Not only did they support tariffs, but they also pushed hard for monetary policies that would benefit established businesses. When Congress authorized increasing the greenbacks in circulation to $400 million in April 1874 to combat the financial stringency caused by the panic, Grant vetoed the bill. Congress then changed course, capping the number of greenbacks in circulation at $382 million. In January 1875, it passed the Specie Resumption Act, which called for the resumption of specie payments by January 1, 1879, and reduced circulating greenbacks to $300 million. Just as the nation's workers, farmers, and new entrepreneurs cried out for money, Congress reduced the money supply in the name of business security.

The corrupt ties between business and the Republican government were dramatically illustrated in the mid-1870s. Shortly after the passage of the Specie Resumption Act, the Whiskey Ring Scandal broke, and unlike the Crédit Mobilier affair, it could be traced directly to the White House, making it look as though big business was deliberately buying influence in an increasingly corrupt administration. In the scandal, revenue officials in patronage positions joined with distillers in major cities across the country to defraud the government of taxes. After the *St. Louis Democrat* broke the story, the secretary of the Treasury launched a secret investigation. The scandal grew and grew, implicating distillers, those who stored whiskey, liquor dealers, and, finally, government officials charged with collecting taxes on the liquor. It quickly became clear that liquor interests across the nation were cheating the government and were paying off appointed officials to maintain the fraud. Eventually 238 people were indicted in the scandal, including General Orville E. Babcock, Grant's private secretary, who escaped conviction only because the president stepped in to vouch for Babcock's honesty. The very best spin that could be put on this fraud was that businessmen were trying to pad the profits from their business. But many Americans saw the Whiskey Ring as another step in the corruption of the government. They believed that the purpose of the Whiskey Ring was to funnel money to the Republican Party to enable it to stay in power.[8]

Strong from their wartime experiences and buoyed by the Republican Party's acknowledgment of their quest for greater rights, women were also expanding their claims on the government. In 1869, Myra Bradwell passed the entrance tests for admission to the Illinois bar but was rejected by the Illinois Supreme Court because she was married and therefore not a free agent. Taking the case to the U.S. Supreme Court, her lawyer argued that the Fourteenth Amendment's privileges and immunities clause guaranteed her the right to choose a profession, since "it is one of the privileges and immunities of women as citizens to engage in any and every profession, occupation or employment in civil life." Other women insisted they had the right to vote, using as justification the same clause of the Fourteenth Amendment, arguing that suffrage was a privilege of citizenship. In the presidential election of 1872, suffragists like Susan B. Anthony tried to break the gender barrier at the polls. Convicted of voting—a fascinating concept—the angry Anthony delivered speeches across New York, declaring that "this government is not a democracy. It is not a republic. It is an odious aristocracy; a hateful oligarchy of sex; the most hateful aristocracy ever established on the face of the globe." While Anthony suggested that she could tolerate a world where "the rich govern the poor . . . [or] where the educated govern the ignorant, or even . . . where the Saxon rules the African," she railed against a system that placed "father, brothers, husband, sons . . . over the mother and sisters, the wife and daughters, of every household." In Missouri, the president of the Woman Suffrage Association, Virginia Minor, sued the registrar of the St. Louis polls for refusing to let her register to vote in 1872. Her case, too, went to the Supreme Court.[9]

On July 4, 1876, at Philadelphia's Centennial Exhibition, members of the National Woman Suffrage Association, including Susan B. Anthony and Elizabeth Cady Stanton, distributed copies of a "Declaration of Rights for Women." "May not our hearts, in unison with all, swell with pride at our great achievements as a people; our free speech, free press, free schools, free church, and the rapid progress we have made in material wealth, trade, commerce and the inventive arts?" they asked. "We do rejoice . . . yet we cannot forget, even in this glad hour, that while all men of every race, and clime, and condition, have been invested with the full rights of citizenship under our hospitable flag, all women still suffer the degradation of disfranchisement." They carefully specified: "We ask of our rulers, at this hour, no special privileges, no special legislation. We ask justice, we ask equality, we ask that all the civil and political rights that belong to citizens of the United States, be guaranteed to us and our daughters forever."[10]

Western farmers and miners joined in the chorus of Americans seeking legislation to protect their interests. Easterners had moved west during and after the war to cash in on the agricultural boom. Republican political economists insisted that agriculture was the heart of America's free labor society and farmers the primary—and most important—part of the American economic pyramid. Farming was the most basic way to turn natural resources into a valuable product. During the war, Congress had put this idea into practice with the Homestead Act and the Pacific Railroad Acts; in June 1866, it had expanded this idea with the Southern Homestead Act. In the West, the 1873 Timber Act, offering land grants for those who planted trees on the prairie, illustrated the continuing hope for western settlement on free labor principles, but actual settlement of the prairies was not feasible until two years later when barbed wire became widely available for fencing. People like Luna Kellie's mother bought into the idea of the primacy of farming. A move west meant her family's economic security, but it also showed confidence that her way of life was central to the new American dream. The reality of the western environment and the true nature of the national economy, though, quickly made their hopes fade. Feeling cheated, they demanded that the promise of the free labor dream be fulfilled.[11]

Those constructing the railroads were eager to sell the lands Congress granted to them in order to raise the money to fund construction. They advertised western lands as the "BEST FARMING LANDS in the WORLD," painting a rosy picture of the fortunes to be made on the prairies. Luna Kellie's mother certainly believed that her family's fortunes could be made on a western farm, even though they were so poor that bankruptcy would take Luna's father's horse and wagon by 1872. Luna's father refused to move until poverty and his wife's death made him willing to try his chances in Nebraska. By then, Luna Kellie was married, and she and her husband J. T. decided to follow him west in 1875. "We had youth and *hope* which means happiness and we worked ourselves harder than slaves were ever worked to be able to fulfill our hopes." "Oh the farm of our dreams was fair to behold and gave a good living and would enable us to bring up a large family in plenty. That was all we asked of life," she remembered.[12]

In reality, many western farmers were isolated, living in squalor and poverty exacerbated by the extreme weather and environmental conditions of the prairies. In 1875, Kellie, by then a married nineteen-year-old woman with five-month-old son, Willie, took the train to Nebraska to settle in while her husband stayed in Missouri to earn enough money to start homesteading. Frightened when her father did not meet her at Grand Island—especially when she learned that the railroad towns were full of refugees from an Indian uprising—she hired a man to take her as far as Hastings. On the way, "we saw a team and lumber wagon coming the horses old and poor but good travellers and the man so haggard and poor we almost passed him but he pulled up and it was Father." He had been seventy miles away from Grand Island when he received word Luna would arrive later that day. "It almost broke my heart to see my father look so old and poor and worried besides being so poorly clad," Luna recalled.[13]

Not only her father, but also the West seemed poor in comparison to what Luna had dreamed of: "There had been some rain and Hastings seemed to be in a mudhole no sidewalks and altogether the worst looking little town I had ever seen." The prairie was no better. As they traveled under a scorching sun, Luna's heart sank. The prairie grasses had been burned, and no trees or bushes broke the sere landscape. She could see a few sod houses, but these structures, made of blocks of prairie stacked together, "sickened" her. She had imagined sod houses to be "nice and green and grassy" rather than "a dirty looking thing," she told her father. "Well," he retorted, "It's dirty because it's made of dirt." Luna finished the trip with a blinding headache from the sun, terrified as the wagon dipped through ditches as it traveled along what passed for a road.[14]

"Nothing around seemed good to me," Luna later recalled. She was happy to see her family but "heartsick" at their "wretched circumstances." It took her some time to realize that her own family was better off than many of its neighbors. Luna's family lived not in a soddy but in a dugout—a cave hollowed from the side of a bank. But while most people had only one room in their dugout, they had two, as well as a nearby cave for storage. Even better in terms of comfort was that, unlike most settlers, Luna's father had managed to construct a roof that was thick enough not to leak, no small benefit as rain usually turned a dugout into a muddy hole. Luna did not realize at the time how lucky she was (although a move to worse accommodations enlightened her). Other homesteading women complained of the centipedes and snakes that fell from the roofs of the dugouts; the lack of light and ventilation; and the dirt that could not be kept from clothes, bedding, and even food.[15]

Figure 10. Soddy houses like this one in Oklahoma were a striking contrast to the mansions of the nation's wealthy. This is a relatively nice soddy, with a glass window and wooden shingles, but since families usually displayed their worldly goods for the camera, it is notable that this family could muster only a single chair. Research Division of the Oklahoma Historical Society, Oklahoma City, Oklahoma.

Ironically, the West's economic problems came from the same drive for development that had sparked the push west during the Civil War. Farmers had taken to heart the drive for economic expansion. From 1866 to 1875, they planted 40 million acres of land in corn, 22 million in wheat, 11 million in oats, 9 million in cotton, and 20 million in hay. Farmers worked their growing fields with new technologies. The McCormick reaper had been invaluable for keeping production high during the war; other inventions and techniques followed rapidly, and by 1870 farmers had invested $271 million in farm implements and machinery and used 321 tons of commercial fertilizer. No longer did farmers rely on their fathers' farming techniques; after 1877 they used a spring tooth harrow whose independently attached teeth smoothed fields efficiently by vibrating, rarely broke, and caused little lost time when they did break because they could be replaced easily. Spring tooth harrows quickly took over the market, as did twine binders, introduced the next year, which enabled farmers to turn the backbreaking work of tying sheaves of grain over to machines. Centrifugal cream separators, invented in 1879, skimmed the cream off milk in minutes, ending the days of pouring fresh milk into milk pans, leaving it undisturbed for twenty-four hours to let the cream rise, and skimming off the cream for butter and cheese. All that was left of this traditional folkway were the idioms that had grown up around it: "mean as second skimmings" and "skimmed milk."[16]

The health of the western economy was affected by national monetary policies. When Republicans created national bank notes during the war, they had intended to spread them equally over the nation as business grew. The plan was to expand the bank notes into the South and West at the same time the Treasury removed the inflationary wartime greenbacks from circulation, gradually shifting the nation from a reliance on unsecured paper greenbacks to the paper national bank notes that were secured by bonds redeemable in gold. This was a good theory, but since the national bank notes were tied to the ability of local financiers to put up the money for the bonds that were required to secure the notes, they did not spread to the South and West very quickly. Wise national policy would have either waited for underdeveloped regions to raise the necessary money or provided for the expansion of currency as the South and West could support it. Instead, immediately after the war, a comptroller of the currency swept up in the postwar northern boom gave northern bankers the bulk of the national bank notes. By 1874, New York and Massachusetts had close to $60 million apiece in bank notes, while all of the former Confederate states together had only about $30 million. The South fared better than the West, though; in 1874, Kansas had $1.5 million in national bank notes; Nebraska less than $1 million, Dakota less than $50,000. Nevada had less than $10,000 in bank notes. All of the western states together —from wealthy Ohio at $23 million to Washington with none—had less than $80 million in national bank notes.[17]

Western settlers just starting out had to borrow from easterners, and as production climbed both nationally and internationally, the wholesale prices of farm products declined. Overextended westerners struggled under debt they couldn't repay. "If anyone needed money to buy seed or grains or anything which was needed to farm with the town was full of money lenders the most of whom took 10 times the needful security and as a great favor procured your money 'from a friend in the east' at never less than 2 come 10," a two-year loan at 10 percent interest. "It meant that to borrow a hundred dollars for seed or harvest hands or anything you gave a mortgage on everything you had and all your future prospects for $100 at 10% interest. Then if it was to run 6 months 3% a month or $18 was kept back. The note was made for 100 and 10% interest but you only got 82 dollars. This was the business that started a number of soon wealthy families and they were known as 3 come 10ers," Luna Kellie recalled bitterly.[18]

This cash-poor economy was fragile. The completion of the transcontinental railroad, which was supposed to make California the hub of commerce with the Orient, precipitated a crisis in the West. Instead of propelling Californians to riches, it opened western markets to national and even international competition, driving down prices. California slid into a recession in 1870, and the plains were not far behind. The Panic of 1873 devastated western settlers. Goodnight recalled: "In the panic of '73 I saw my property to the amount of $100,000 suddenly swept away, leaving me nothing in the way of working capital save a herd of 1,800 head of cattle. With this small remnant of my former capital I determined to again return to the pursuits of my earlier life, fully determined if possible to retrieve my losses in the same manner that my first start in life had been gained." Urban Californians blamed the recession on the Chinese laborers who had come to America to build the western railroads and who migrated to western cities after the completion of the transcontinental railroad. Rural farmers had no such obvious scapegoats.[19]

The 1874 arrival of a grasshopper plague that stretched from the Dakotas to Texas highlighted the difficulties of trying to carve a farm out of the western environment. Luna Kellie had thought it would be interesting to see a cloud of grasshoppers, but when they landed on her farm, she was quickly disillusioned. The hoppers came down like snow, so thick it was impossible to step without squashing them. They ate everything green—grass, crops, even green stripes in clothing. Following the stems of garden plants down into the ground, they ate beets, carrots, and onions, leaving only holes. They came into houses under doors, in milk pails, and on clothing; they had to be swept—or even shoveled—out. In her memoirs of her childhood, Laura Ingalls Wilder told of her family's encounters with hunger, outlaws, Indians, blizzards, and wild animals, but the thing that almost broke her mother was the grasshoppers. Wilder recalled lying in bed during a grasshopper storm, listening to "whirring and snipping and chewing" while she imagined feeling "claws crawling on her." When the insects finally went, they left behind them egg cases, sometimes one hundred per square foot, promising that the next year's crops were doomed, too.[20]

The renewal of Indian wars distressed western farmers and miners even further. By 1873, the buffalo hunters had almost cleaned out the bison, and, made desperate by destruction of the animals that supported them, Indian warriors were skirmishing with whites in the plains. At daybreak on June 27, 1874, Quanah helped lead around three hundred Comanche, Kiowa, and Cheyenne warriors in an attack on twenty-eight buffalo hunters at the Adobe Walls trading post just north of the Canadian River in the Texas panhandle. With their powerful weapons, the professional hunters drove off the attackers, killing more than ten and wounding many others. Quanah took a bullet in the shoulder when his horse was shot from under him. For the next year, the Red River War raged as Indians raided white settlements, cattle outfits, and buffalo hunters, and army troops and white settlers hunted down the Indians. Trouble had erupted farther south, too. On the border with Mexico, the Apache War had calmed briefly when Apache leader Cochise surrendered to the U.S. Army in 1871, but he later escaped to prevent his tribe from being sent to a reservation in New Mexico. In 1872, the Apaches agreed to move to a Chiricahua reservation in Arizona, but when forced onto a barren reservation in Arizona after Cochise died in 1874, angry and desperate Apaches led by the warrior Geronimo went back on the warpath to defend their traditional way of life.[21]

The upper plains had burst into trouble again as early as 1871, when the Northern Pacific Railroad ignored the Treaty of Fort Laramie and began moving workers across Sioux land. After his men had killed forty soldiers in battle in September 1872, Sitting Bull warned the army's commanding officer to go east "or he would give him plenty of fight." ("The white soldiers do not know how to fight," Sitting Bull boasted. "They are not lively enough. They stand still and run straight; it is easy to shoot them.") Worried officers estimated that 15,000 to 20,000 hostile braves threatened eastern incursions into the Yellowstone Valley. Then, in 1875, an army expedition led by George A. Custer confirmed reports of gold in the Black Hills, the land the Sioux had come to consider their sacred ancestral homeland. Prospectors pouring into the mining regions sparked the Great Sioux War that lasted until 1877. For western settlers, the amount of trouble on their doorstep was unfathomable. There must be something wrong, they thought, someone interfering with the natural order of things.[22]

Farmers were unable to understand why the economy was increasingly controlled by businessmen and why the harder farmers worked, the more they fell behind, especially since Republican ideology held that agriculture was the heart of the economy and that hard work would create capital. Their anger turned first on the railroads, which had painted such a rosy picture of western life, monopolized transportation of crops, and seemed to be controlling the government. "The minute you crossed the Missouri River your fate both soul and body was in their hands," Luna Kellie remembered bitterly. "What you should eat and drink, what you should wear, everything was in their hands and they robbed us of all we produced except enough to keep body and soul together and many many times not that as too many of the early settlers filled early graves on account of being ill nourished and ill clad while the wealth they produced was being coldly calculated as paying so much per head." When they lost their homestead, she and J. T. "realized . . . we had left not only our youth but most of our hope there. . . . We realized that the best 7 years of our lives had been given to enrich the B. & M. R[ailroad]. That they had cleared annually more from our toil than had been wrung in old times from the colored slaves." Records showed that the railroad was clearing $2 million a month, she sighed. If only they had been content with $1 million, she continued, "we would not only [have] been enabled to keep our place and thousands more like us but would have been enabled to live in comfort and out of debt." Charles Goodnight, too, was angry at the railroads, but for a different reason. He bemoaned that they had ruined his early monopolies on beef and farm products.[23]

Even worse, in some ways, was that the government seemed to be actively working against western settlers by protecting some Indians on reservations while their hostile compatriots attacked farmers, cattlemen, traders, and miners. By 1874, a government agent sent to analyze the condition of Indians from the Rocky Mountains to California concluded that all of the Indians his commission visited "fully appreciate the hopelessness of contending against the Government of the United States and the tide of civilization. . . . Their power is entirely broken." This was not convincing to cattlemen who knew that Quanah's Comanches were stealing steers to sell to Mexican traders, or to settlers hearing reports of Geronimo's clever slipperiness and of Sitting Bull's calm belligerence. One frustrated Texas cowman armed a gang and repossessed 10,000 head of cattle along the Goodnight-Loving Trail, cattle that he insisted had been stolen, publishing manifestos to the government as he went about how it could stop the trade if it tried. Settlers looking to the army for protection against hostile Indians were no more confident than the cattlemen; in 1877, the army repeatedly lost to Chief Joseph's Nez Perce warriors, who were trying simply to retreat to safety. When Goodnight later recalled this period on the plains, he made it a point to credit the end of Indian depredations not to the army, for which he had absolutely no use, but to the buffalo hunters. Northwest Texas, he said, had been "practically opened up for settlement by that fearless body of men, the buffalo hunters, who by killing out the buffalo stopped forever the terror of the settlers and the cattlemen, the depredating tribes of plains Indians who had for centuries roamed and fought over this fair and productive part of Texas."[24]

Their anger at the railroads and the government gradually drew farmers into politics. Immediately after the war, Oliver H. Kelley of Minnesota and six of his colleagues from the Department of Agriculture concluded to start a secret organization, the Patrons of Husbandry, to combat the isolation of farm life and give farmers access to information about new agricultural techniques, and to organize farmers against railroad monopolies. Rejecting the idea that all Americans shared economic interests, members of the old Granges ignored their organization's prohibition on political involvement and organized to advocate measures that would defend farmers. In 1873, a Missouri correspondent to the *New York Times* explained: "While in Boston and New-York and Philadelphia corn is a commodity that always commands high rates and a ready market, in the [West] it is sold for a pittance, if by begging it finds a sale at all, or is burned for fuel, or lies scattered and wasted upon the ground from which it was coaxed after much weary labor. . . . It takes two bushels of . . . corn—and last winter it took four—to get one to market." The Granges grew dramatically in the 1870s. A picnic at Mount Pleasant, Iowa, in June 1873 drew 10,000 Grangers; the movement quickly took root in the South. By August 1873 there were more than 5,000 Granges in the nation. Iowa had almost 1,800; Illinois and Missouri over 500 Granges each; Indiana, Kansas, Minnesota, Nebraska between 275 and 400 each. Granges in the southern states were in the double digits. Of the New England and Atlantic states, only Pennsylvania had more than 10 Granges, and it boasted only 11. The movement centered in the West and South.[25]

Taking their cue from businessmen, Grangers called for cooperation to fix prices and limit supplies, storing grain in warehouses until prices rose. They picked up national concerns that the government was working for business and called for government to respond to their needs instead. "The theory of our Government is that the people should govern, and that office-holders should be their servants," one Granger declared. "These . . . days we are nourishing a set of office-seekers and office-holders. When they once get the offices . . . they will then give . . . attention to the agents of monopolies, men whose pockets are well filled with money, who want special legislation to replenish their own coffers. . . . We propose to drop these politicians." Blaming railroads and grain elevator operators for taking the profits of the farmers' labor, they called for government support and state laws that regulated the storage, sale, and transportation of crops. By 1875, 800,000 farmers had joined the Grange and were demanding that midwestern legislatures regulate the rates charged by "middlemen"—the railroads and grain elevator operators who stood between the producers and their markets. In 1875, after legal challenges destroyed attempts to force railroads to adhere to an established schedule of rates, the Illinois legislature passed a law setting the rates that Illinois grain elevator operators could charge grain producers, setting the precedent for government regulation of business.[26]

During the 1870s, farmers' anger at railroad monopolies turned to a preoccupation with money. By mid-1875, when Granger laws had begun to answer their concerns about freight rates, a new series of events convinced them that Congress was ruinously manipulating the money supply to aid businessmen. Not only did Congress refuse to issue more greenbacks, but it also destroyed inflationary silver currency. Until 1873, silver could be legally coined into money—at a ratio of sixteen ounces of silver to one ounce of gold—but after gold discoveries in the antebellum years increased the supply of gold (and thus reduced its price), silver was so expensive that it was rarely, if ever, coined. After the Civil War, though, silver production climbed, threatening inflation and making businessmen nervous. In a routine revision of American money in 1873, congressmen left silver out of the new coinage act, right before dramatic silver strikes in Nevada, Colorado, and Utah precipitated a drop in the price of silver. The Comstock Lode in Virginia City, for example, produced $300 million in gold and silver in twenty years. If the old law had been in place, silver coined at the old ratio would have been significantly cheaper than gold and would relax the money supply. To angry farmers—and silver miners—the Coinage Act of 1873 became "the Crime of 1873," perpetrated by a "gold conspiracy."[27]

In the 1873 and 1874, a number of western antimonopoly and reform parties managed to win the election of three U.S. senators and three congressmen, the Wisconsin governor, the Minnesota state treasurer, and forty-one antimonopoly representatives in California. Sharing with eastern laborers a conviction that greenbacks would solve many of their problems, farmers launched their own political party in 1875, the Greenback Party, whose platform called for the inflationary expansion of the currency to combat declining farm prices. "The Republican organization was controlled by the monetary interests of the country," an Indiana Greenbacker explained, and it was time "to crush out and remove all the impediments that lay in the path of the workingmen of the United States." Organizers agreed it was time for "a new political organization of the people, by the people, and for the people, to restrain the aggressions of combined capital upon the rights and interests of the masses, to reduce taxation, correct abuses, and to purify all departments of the Government." They called for inflationary greenbacks to replace the national currency backed by specie and agreed to field their own candidates in the next year's presidential campaign. For the rest of the century, the money question would be the symbol of the division between those who wanted the government to broker between different interests in society and those who maintained that America was a land of economic harmony whose government must not fall into the hands of special interests.[28]

For those who were making it in America, the demands of disaffected farmers, miners, wage laborers, African Americans, suffragists, and industrialists seemed to be the complaints of those looking for government aid. The prosperity of the war years had been widespread, and mainstream ideology said it would remain so as long as the government was evenhanded in its development of the economy. The idea of structural economic or racial or gender inequalities made little sense to people who still thought of the world in small town terms. To those who did not identify themselves with these struggling groups, it seemed as if prosperity was in reach for all who wanted it, especially as the burgeoning economy brought dramatic technological advances into economically stable homes. Upwardly mobile Americans enjoyed the benefits of the expanding economy. They had more money than ever before, more time to spend it, and more to spend it on. The growing cities had theaters, fancy restaurants, paved streets, public transportation, and a wide variety of new products for sale. In 1876, Alexander Graham Bell perfected the telephone, and after President Rutherford B. Hayes had one installed in the White House, they spread rapidly to urban areas. Middle-class Americans could send the newfangled postcards that had been introduced to America in 1873 (but which, at three cents apiece, were out of Luna Kellie's reach when she desperately wanted to wish her grandmother a happy birthday). In

1874, the first exhibition of Impressionist paintings was organized in France, and although these revolutionary paintings would not come to America until the famous 1913 Armory Show in New York City, their inventiveness electrified American painter Mary Cassatt, who saw them in Paris. In 1879, Thomas Edison invented the carbon filament lamp—the electric light—and by 1880 he had set up a manufacturing plant in Menlo Park, New Jersey, to make enough lights to illuminate the whole country. "On October 21, our world may have entered a new age," mused the *New York Weekly Herald.* "Thomas Edison, in his working laboratory, has produced the first lamp to be lit by an electric current, now known by the term, 'the Incandescent Lamp.'" "The advantages of the electric light over that produced by the ordinary means of illumination are its intense brightness, greater steadiness, cheapness of production, and the ease with which it is managed." The actual construction of the Brooklyn Bridge, a symbol of the progress of the age, began in 1878; Carnegie got the contract to provide steel for it.[29]

Newspapers emphasizing the mainstream vision contrasted dire images of lazy African Americans wanting government jobs with hopeful stories of prospering African Americans and farmers. Downplaying the recent activities of the Ku Klux Klan, they suggested that right-thinking southern whites were encouraging their black neighbors' success. In 1873, the *New York Times* reported that an examination of twenty-one Texas counties showed that black Texans there owned "taxable property, mostly real estate, valued at $2,076,000." Emancipated in abject poverty, freedmen had "quickly acquired habits of forethought and thrift, and were mastered by a desire to become rooted as proprietors in the soil to which they had been attached as slaves." The *Philadelphia Inquirer* noted the speeches of two prominent white Louisiana politicians declaring that southern whites and blacks had "a common country, common interests" and that whites had a duty to guarantee equal rights. The *San Francisco Daily Alta California* maintained in August 1873 that, even in South Carolina—where the Ku Klux Klan had recently been forced underground—"the public rights of the freedman, as secured to him by the Constitution . . . are frankly acknowledged by all classes and citizens."[30]

News like the 1873 silver strike in Nevada, Custer's 1875 report of gold in the Black Hills, and the continuing drama of cowboys and the establishment of Dodge City, Kansas, in 1875 kept the dream of mining and farming in the West alive for easterners. In 1875, miners poured into the Black Hills, into towns like Deadwood, South Dakota. In 1876, the Black Hills produced almost $2 million in gold, and the author of *The Pacific Tourist*, which described the West for easterners, recorded that most of the gold came from near Deadwood. "On Deadwood Creek," he explained, "the average to the miners on each claim was $300 to $700 per day." By 1876, an average of 800 miners a week were coming to the Deadwood mines—so many that Nat Love's crew received an order to move 3,000 three-year-old steers from Texas up to Deadwood, one of the largest orders they had ever had. (A town full of miners also attracted gamblers, and that brought Wild Bill Hickok to the poker table where he met his death, holding the two aces and two eights that became known as a "dead man's hand.") For anyone "dissatisfied with mining, still there is room for thousands of farms and peaceful homes," *The Pacific Tourist* continued in blithe ignorance of the reality of dry farming on the plains. "The agricultural value of the [Black] Hills is beyond all words of expression. The valleys have been found to be surpassingly fertile, the rainfall regular and constant." South Dakota, according to one explorer, was "the richest country" in the West. It had "excellent timber in the greatest abundance; as fine pasturage as I ever saw; rich black loam soil; splendid water; showers every few days; no disagreeable winds; a delicious, bracing atmosphere to either work or rest in; a splendid diversity of hill and valley; prairie and timber forest; a landscape of which the eye never tires."[31]

Although hostile Native American warriors challenged the miners in the Deadwood district and swept across the plains, terrorizing the western settlers whose incursions were destroying their tribes, a government agent reflected eastern perceptions when he concluded in 1874 that Indians were rapidly coming to a mainstream model of self-sufficiency. To induce them to work, he wrote, "no able-bodied Indian should be either fed or clothed except in payment for labor." They should be required to make their own clothing and to live in houses. Tents, which could be moved easily, encouraged them "to continue their nomadic life." In fact, the destruction of the buffalo meant that the middle-class vision was indeed infiltrating the plains tribes, including even the remaining hostile Comanches. A bad drought in 1874 decreased the forage for warriors' ponies. Then, in September of that year, Colonel Ranald Mackenzie cornered in Palo Duro Canyon in the Texas panhandle a large band of Comanches who were, according to Charles Goodnight, leading the trade with Mexicans in stolen cattle. The men escaped, but they had to leave behind their ponies, and Mackenzie, determined not to let the famous horse stealers recapture them, shot more than 1,000 of the animals. This carnage proved Mackenzie's determination; it shocked Indians for its wholesale slaughter of a sacred animal, and it shocked whites because horses were so

combined the prominent public act of conducting services at the Newport, Rhode Island, Unitarian Church with a traditional sermon. "Her text was taken from the story of the Pharisee who thanked God that he was not as other men were," reported *Harper's Weekly*. "In her view, neither as a nation nor as individuals can Americans properly thank God after this fashion. We should rather, in view of His great gifts and mercies, feel ourselves overcome with penitence, like the publican, and cry, 'God be merciful to America, a sinner.'" Women making strides in education also emphasized their modesty and mainstream propriety. On February 22, 1879, a committee of ladies issued a circular announcing that certain Harvard professors would teach "properly qualified young women who desire to pursue advanced courses of study." A participant later recalled that the women who signed the circular were chosen partly because they supported higher education for women and partly because "they were in no way exponents of extreme views either on education or the woman question in general." More radical women would have roused the opposition of "the more conservative element of the Harvard corporation," which would have killed the experiment. With moderate women advancing the plan, Harvard leaders did not complain. The women took this as "a tacit approval of the undertaking," an organizer recalled. "On the other hand," she added, "the Annex management was always careful to ask no favors of Harvard."[34]

Americans enjoying the benefits of the new economy turned vehemently against those they perceived as threats to American progress, those who seemed to want to turn the government into an agency for redistributing tax dollars into their own grasping hands. Former Liberal Republicans, downcast at Grant's victory and angered by the premature death of Greeley, who had run himself into the ground during the campaign and died immediately after it ended, deliberately fed this perception as they continued to try to discredit the stalwart Republicans. Harping on the image of disaffected workers controlling government for their own ends, they stayed on common ground with Democrats by attacking black voters in the South. The Liberal Republican *Nation* reported that at least one prominent southern black stalwart Republican politician "has literally nothing under him but Federal bayonets and an injunction."[35]

In January 1873, the new editor of the *New York Tribune*, Whitelaw Reid, sent disillusioned former radical Republican James S. Pike back to the South to investigate conditions there. Harking back to the traditional southern idea of government by an educated, established elite, his reports provided a blueprint for future attacks on African American and organized workers' participation in government. Although Pike wrote that he "was moved to visit S. Carolina from the extraordinary circumstances of its political condition," he clearly intended for his discoveries to discredit the stalwart Republican government there. Pike's articles, which ran in the *Tribune* in March and April, echoed his 1872 exposé of South Carolina politics and garnered so much attention that he reprinted them as a book in December 1873. Its title, *The Prostrate State: South Carolina under Negro Government*, summed up his viciously slanted vision of South Carolina. In his investigations, he had carefully excised positive references to African Americans and had sought his information from white planters, most notably from Wade Hampton.[36]

Hampton's influence on Pike was obvious. In his reports Pike began by informing readers that in South Carolina, society had been turned upside down. "The wealth, the intelligence, the culture, the wisdom of the State," "men of weight and standing in the communities they represent" no longer controlled the government. Instead, the legislature was run by "the most ignorant democracy that mankind ever saw, invested with the functions of government." Misrepresenting the professional and educated African American legislators, Pike described black lawmakers as stereotypically ignorant and degraded field hands. They wore "coarse and dirty garments of the field; the stub-jacket and slouch hats of soiling labor." Representatives of wealthy Charleston were "swamp negroes." Pike reprinted in his book the report of the 1871 South Carolina Taxpayers' Convention, charging that "they who lay the taxes do not pay them, and that they who are to pay them have no voice in the laying of them." He also quoted a convention speaker who insisted that African Americans had been given "the privilege, by law, of plundering the property-holders of the State, now almost bankrupt, by reason of the burden of taxation under which they labor." South Carolina was "an elysium for an agriculturalist," with cheap land that grew profitable cotton with only "easy and enticing" labor, according to Pike, but it was "prostrated" by African Americans who wanted wealth without work. Twice Pike quoted a white man's report that Senator Beverly Nash had attracted voters by insisting: "The reformers complain of taxes being too high. I tell you that they are not high enough. I want them taxed until they put these lands back where they belong, into the hands of those who worked for them. You toiled for them, you labored for them, and were sold to pay for them, and you ought to have them."[37]

As mainstream opinion turned against blacks who were caricatured as wanting government benefits without work, Americans opposed the growth of national government power to protect African Americans from the widespread discrimination they faced. In the complicated 1873 Slaughterhouse Cases, the Supreme Court limited the federal government's power to defend civil rights when it decided that the Fourteenth Amendment protected only the rights of federal citizenship but could not prevent a state from curtailing other individual rights. Then, in 1875, the passage of the Civil Rights Act brought down the wrath of opponents, who howled that African Americans who used the law to challenge their exclusion from public places were not protesting a real disability, but rather were the degraded tools of designing politicians. Even the staunchly Republican *Boston Evening Transcript* reported that black agitators were "instigated by evil and designing white men," explaining that "there is, . . . and always will be, a class of low, designing politicians, who by appealing to the prejudices and jealousies of the negroes will use their political power in opposition to any measure designed to give the whites ascendancy." Ignoring that fifteen years after emancipation 70 percent of the black population remained uneducated, mainstream Americans pointed out the bill's integration of schools would destroy the South's nascent educational system, which had already brought literacy to about 30 percent of the black population by 1880. When the bill passed, the *New York Times* concluded that northern African Americans were "quiet, inoffensive people who live for and to themselves, and have no desire to intrude where they are not welcome." In the South, though, "there are many colored men and women who delight in 'scenes' and cheap notoriety." It was this sort of person, the "negro politician, . . . the ignorant field hand, who, by his very brutality has forced his way into, and disgraces, public positions of honor and trust—men . . . who have no feeling and no sensibility," who would "take every opportunity of inflicting petty annoyances upon their former masters."[38]

While mainstream Americans turned against what they perceived as grasping African Americans, they also came down on white laborers who seemed to want something for nothing. Newspapers portrayed all striking workers as communists and rabble-rousers, regardless of their goals, and advocated their suppression. "The Tompkins Square outrage was followed by a period of extreme repression," Samuel Gompers recalled. "Private indoor meetings were invaded and summarily ended by the ejection of those present. The police frustrated several meetings held to protest against police brutality and in defense of the right of free assemblage for a lawful purpose." That repression seemed justified in the face of labor agitation in the Pennsylvania coal mining districts, where laborers, organized as "Molly Maguires," terrorized those who refused to join their union. Popular reports suggested that the tactics of the Mollies were like those of the Ku Klux Klan; they organized secretly, sent notes with coffins sketched on them warning holdouts to leave town or join, attacked bosses and scabs, elected friends to office, and controlled the government. The unrest in the coal fields and a trial of the prominent leaders of the Mollies kept the strife in the public eye from about 1873 to 1875, making labor organizers look like criminals repressing the hard workers who refused to join them.[39]

Farmers, too, it seemed, were either making it on their own or were at fault for their own failure. Western farmers had good markets and fair prices for wheat, corn, pork, beef, and mutton, the *New York Times* reported, and groceries and dry goods were cheap. "As a class we do not believe they have been unthrifty," wrote the *New York Times*, "but if any of them are insolvent debtors they have only themselves to thank for it. We believe that the predominant opinion in the West among men of sound judgment and integrity, as distinguished from the bankrupts, demagogues, communists, spendthrifts, and speculators, is as decidedly opposed to inflation as it is at the East. . . . A great party cannot be built up in this country by brainless denunciation of the 'creditor class' and 'money power.'" The *Chicago Tribune* tied organized farmers to striking laborers, condemning "the spirit of Grangerism, Workingmanism, Communism, Grievanceism, or by whatever name the present fever among those who assume to themselves the title of 'the industrial and producing classes.'"[40]

Fears about challenges to the mainstream vision created a backlash against women who were using the broad vision of human rights embodied in the Fourteenth Amendment to argue for gender equality. In 1873, the Supreme Court handed down the *Bradwell v. Illinois* decision, in which Justice Joseph P. Bradley carefully articulated a domestic role for women in post–Civil War America. There was "a wide difference in the respective spheres and destinies of man and woman," he wrote, with men as "woman's protector" and timid and delicate women firmly in "the domestic sphere." Translating the idea of economic harmony into gender relations, he continued: "The harmony, not to say identity, of interests and views which . . . should belong to the family institution, is repugnant to the idea of a woman adopting a distinct and independent career from that of her husband." "The paramount destiny and mission of woman are to fulfill the noble and benign offices of wife and mother," he concluded. Virginia Minor fared no better. In *Minor v. Happersett*, handed down in 1874, the Supreme Court decided that women were citizens, but citizenship did not automatically include the privilege of suffrage.[41]

Indeed, congressional legislation reinforced the idea that women must be protected from the vices that flourished on the streets of cities like New York, and which municipal governments would not curb because the wrongdoers kept the corrupt officials in power. Thinking, no doubt, of cases like that of the murdered Alice Augusta Bowlsby, they pressured women to conform to a domestic role as wives and mothers. In 1873, Congress passed an "Act for the Suppression of Trade in, and Circulation of Obscene Literature and Articles of Immoral Use." This law, known as the Comstock Law after New York reformer Anthony Comstock, who crusaded against sexual vice, prohibited the sale or distribution not only of pornography, but also of birth control information and products. Birth control literature, advocates claimed, is "quite as disgusting and demoralizing as are the professedly obscene publications which are sold less openly." Indeed, "their obscenity is their only salable quality," and those who sold it were "more guilty than the venders of undisguised obscenity, since the latter are content to seek their customers among men and boys, while the latter strive to sully and ruin the pure souls of innocent girls." Heavy penalties for breaking the law—including hard labor for six months to five years for each offense—put even the era's primitive birth control out of the reach of most women.[42]

The elections of the mid-1870s showed the triumph of pressure for government to reject special interest legislation. It was no accident that Thomas Nast drew his famous and enduring cartoon of the Republican Party as an elephant in 1874. The Republican Party had presided over the booming prosperity of the early 1870s, but it had also nurtured the railroads, sponsored the freedpeople, and now bore the blame for the recession, which many blamed on the hard-money policy that served business. In response to fears that African American and business interests were dictating the policies of a growing Republican government, the Republicans lost seventy-seven congressional seats, turning the House over to the Democrats. S. S. Cox, the unrelenting voice of small government, was reelected with a more than 10,000 majority, the biggest in the House, and New Yorkers also voted for amendments to the state constitution that would stop election bribery. In Cox's mind, Republican calls for a civil rights bill had given the election to the Democrats. The question was not that a man should not be "ashamed to sleep in a tavern, or go to a theatre, or be buried in a grave-yard with his colored brother." It was, to him, a question of "the function of the Federal Government." For their part, mainstream Republicans celebrated the rebuke to corrupt politicians. "Corruptionists who made their way into power in the Republican party have been almost entirely spewed out by the people," the *Cincinnati Daily Gazette* reflected happily.[43]

Designed to illustrate American hope and progress to both the nation and the world, the Centennial Exhibition of 1876 painted a picture of the mainstream vision of America. International fairs were popular after England's Crystal Palace in 1851; this would be America's chance to show its strength to the world. Held in Philadelphia to conjure up images of America's Declaration of Independence, the "International Exhibition of Arts, Manufactures and Products of the Soil and Mine" opened on May 10, 1876, hosted thirty-seven nations, and drew nearly nine million visitors. Americans should celebrate the anniversary of the Declaration of Independence, read the text of the official guidebook, "by such demonstrations . . . as . . . become a nation so rapidly risen from struggling infancy to a position of power and prosperity, as at once to command the respect of all Governments and the admiration of the world." The president opened the exhibition, starting the huge Corliss Engine "with his own hand." The fair covered 236 acres, with seventeen entrances, 5 principal buildings and 150 other buildings. Admission was fifty cents, and visitors could take a narrow-gauge steam railway around the grounds, stopping at a soda-water fountain for refreshment at ten cents a glass.[44]

The dramatic glass and steel Main Exhibition Hall, the largest building in the world at the time and built with iron and steel bought from Carnegie's plants, covered more than twenty acres and showcased international manufactures of household goods and scientific instruments. The most popular exhibit was the Corliss Engine in Machinery Hall, which provided steam power to the displays ranged over the hall's fourteen acres. The state exhibitions were small houses, and states were prohibited from making any political or "offensive" reference to the Civil War. The United States Government Building, one of the largest and most important of the buildings on the site, was designed to "illustrate the functions and administrative facilities of the Government in time of peace, and its resources as a war power, and thereby serve to demonstrate the nature of our institutions and their adaptations to the wants of the people." In the government building visitors saw exhibits of natural resources—animals, fish, minerals—as well as of western Indians, whose tepees were open for the inspection of eastern visitors. Women were denied permission to exhibit separately in the main hall, so they took their needlework and inventions to the Women's Pavilion. Determined to show themselves as independent and progressive but not radical, the female exhibitors refused to identify themselves with the woman suffrage movement and ignored the July 4 protest by Susan B. Anthony and her followers.[45]

To this celebration, though, came symbolic evidence that the triumph of the American system was not assured. Nat Love's trip north to South Dakota had been troubled by rumors of an impending battle between the army and Indians trying to defend their territory; at the end of June an army scout had ordered the cowboys back to camp, safe from the hands of hostile Indians. Love heard before easterners about what became known as the Battle of the Little Bighorn. During the week of July 4, 1876—ironically the official centennial of the nation—news reached the East of the annihilation of Custer and his men at the hands of the Sioux under medicine man Sitting Bull and war chief Crazy Horse. Always eager for glory, Custer had pressed his men forward of the bulk of the army, forcing them in late June toward what he believed would be an easy victory against an unprepared Indian village on the Greasy Grass River in Montana Territory. Instead, Custer's 260 exhausted men attacked a well-rested encampment of 1,500 Sioux and Cheyenne warriors who were so astonished at the attack they assumed the soldiers were drunk. "We want no white men here," Sitting Bull insisted. "The Black Hills belong to me. If the whites try to take them, I will fight." The warriors easily defeated the American soldiers, leaving as witnesses only the Crow and Arikara scouts who had led Custer to the Greasy Grass and now carried the tale of his defeat back to the main army. "I feel sorry that too many were killed on each side," reflected Sitting Bull, "but when Indians must fight, they must." The news of the "disaster" was "so terrible and ghastly . . . that at first . . . it was considered incredible," recalled *Harper's Weekly*.[46]

Against this backdrop, the election of 1876 became a test of the government. Was it really a force to promote the free labor system and economic growth that benefited everyone, or was it a tool of special interests that used the state to advance their own interests at the expense of others? In the North and South both, those challenging the Republican administration called for clean government, by which they meant an organization uncorrupted by special interests. Wrapped in the call for clean government, though, was often a generous measure of racism or anti-immigrant sentiment, which meant that white supremacists and nativists often justified their aims by insisting they were after "reform." In the South, reform meant an all-out push to overthrow the Republican state governments. In the North, it meant a reform of the Republican machine. But although some northern Democrats were anxious to throw out the Republicans altogether, northern reform Republicans did not want to risk handing government over to a Democratic government that, as the Democratic Tweed Ring had, might cater to poor immigrants. The Greenback Party wanted its own sort of reform that reinforced the idea of class conflict in America. Calling for a government responsive to the needs of farmers rather than to businessmen, Greenbackers nominated their own presidential and vice presidential candidates.[47]

At the national level, Democrats had the easy job in this election. They simply had to reiterate the middle ground of the Liberal Republicans and capitalize on Republican corruption to attract moderates of both parties. And this they did well. Their platform rejected southern separatism and embraced the reconstruction amendments. It calmly announced a belief in "the equality of all citizens before just laws of their own enactment," a seemingly uncontroversial statement that appeared to support black rights but that also endorsed opposition to tax assessments that benefited African Americans. The Democrats went on to explain. The real issue of the day was not the old chestnuts of the war but rather the need to reform the federal government. The Union must be "saved from a corrupt centralism which, after inflicting upon ten States the rapacity of carpet-bag tyrannies, has honeycombed the offices of the Federal Government itself with incapacity, waste and fraud; infected States and municipalities with the contagion of misrule, and locked fast the prosperity of an industrious people in the paralysis of hard times." They called for lower tariffs, which currently enriched the few at the expense of the many, and lower taxes, which had risen from $60 million in gold in 1860 to $450 million in currency in 1870, from less than $5 to more than $18 per head. Increasing governmental expenses must be curbed and a "rigorous frugality," observed. Blaming the Republicans for squandering 200 million acres of land on the railroads alone, the Democratic platform demanded a stop to this "profligate waste." The Democrats demanded civil service reform and insisted that it could come only by throwing the Republicans out of power.[48]

The Republicans had little to offer voters other than their destruction of slavery and defense of "government of the people by the people and for the people." They fell back on the Declaration of Independence, claiming that they alone had tried to bring to fruition the idea that all men are created equal. Obliquely defending federal protection of black voting and calling upon the egalitarian idea that all Americans could rise, Republicans maintained that the government must secure to "every American citizen complete liberty and exact equality in the exercise of all civil, political, and public rights." They recognized the elite tradition behind Democratic rhetoric and, accusing Democrats of trying to oppress the southern black vote, charged that the party was "the same in character and spirit as when it sympathized with treason."[49]

To answer Democratic accusations of corruption, the Republicans promised to "hold all public officers to a rigid responsibility" but insisted that the party in power must be able to control nominations to offices where "harmony and vigor of administration require its policy to be represented," that is, that the president must be allowed to put his cronies into office. They defended their tariffs, opposed further land grants to corporations, and advocated homesteading. Turning to the issue of women's rights, the Republican platform applauded "the substantial advances recently made toward the establishment of equal rights for women" through changes "in the laws which concern the personal and property relations of wives, mothers, and widows, and by the appointment and election of women to the superintendence of education, charities, and other public trusts." It promised to give "respectful consideration to "the honest demands of this class of citizens for additional rights, privileges, and immunities." Notably, even Republicans did not support absolute equality for women, but rather the admission of wives, mothers, and widows into positions where they could advance their traditional roles of charity and education.

For president, the Democrats nominated the popular New Yorker Samuel J. Tilden, famous as the reformer who busted the Tweed Ring. Running under the banner of reform, Tilden gathered the support of disaffected Republicans disgusted by the growing Republican machine and southern Democrats who liked anyone who wanted to end the military presence in the South. Republicans nominated Ohio governor Rutherford B. Hayes, a moderate party politician and Union veteran, thus emphasizing their moderation but making it clear that they intended to defend black voters in the South.[50]

The themes of the 1876 election played out in South Carolina, where "reform" Democrats set out to purge African Americans from government. They drafted Wade Hampton as their candidate, and he ran a powerful campaign for governor against the Republican incumbent, Daniel H. Chamberlain, insisting that the Republicans were plundering the state's property holders to distribute jobs to their poor black constituents.[51] Hampton's campaign echoed the Mississippi Plan of 1875, when armed Democrats kept Republican voters from the Mississippi polls with threats and violence. In South Carolina, Hampton marshaled an army of loyal "red shirts," men who followed him out of their devotion to white supremacy, to reform, or to him personally. Elizabeth Pringle's brother lionized his former military commander for "redeeming" the state from the "degradation" "when its legislative halls were given up to the riotous caricature of State government by the carpetbaggers and Negroes, who disported themselves as officials of the State of South Carolina." For all this high-minded language, Hampton's campaign drew to it ex-Confederate soldiers who made no secret of their hatred for black political power and held deliberately intimidating "rifle club" meetings—complete with target practice—on the outskirts of Republican political rallies. Hampton's campaign was not purely one of white supremacy, though, for the economic language of his "reform" rhetoric drew enough African American followers to make him request federal protection for them from their hostile Republican neighbors, a political ploy to be sure, but contemporary accounts from a few prominent black followers supported his complaints.[52]

In the election, both Hampton and Chamberlain claimed success. Republicans vociferously insisted that Democrats had kept black voters away from the polls with violence; Democrats claimed that the Republicans relied on fraud for success, refusing to count Democratic ballots. Chamberlain was inaugurated, but Hampton's men refused to resign the field, charging Republicans with fraud. A recount of the votes included the ballots from two counties previously undercounted, and the state supreme court declared Hampton the victor. But Chamberlain's men still held the statehouse, where they were protected by federal troops.[53]

The problems in South Carolina—and Florida and Louisiana—had vital national importance. Tilden had won the popular vote with a 250,000 majority, but both Republicans and Democrats claimed victory in the Electoral College. The presidency depended on the returns from Oregon, and from South Carolina, Florida, and Louisiana, the only southern states that still had Republican governments. Charging Democrats with violence that prevented a Republican majority from voting, Republican canvassing boards in the South gave their states' electoral victories to Hayes. In Oregon, a Democratic governor violated state law to replace a Republican elector with a Democrat. Congress appointed a fifteen-member commission to arbitrate the disputes, and by a straight party vote of 8-7, they ruled that Hayes had won all four of the disputed states and thus the presidency. Recognizing his own tenuous hold on legitimacy, Hayes bowed to Democratic pressures in South Carolina and withdrew the federal troops defending the Chamberlain government from around the South Carolina statehouse. Wade Hampton was inaugurated governor in April 1877.[54]

This deference to southern Democrats was not sufficient to assuage mainstream fears of special interests dominating government. The election of Hayes under such conditions only reinforced the conviction that stalwart Republicans would stop at nothing to retain power. Years later, S. S. Cox still fumed that "the Republican party . . . stole another term of power." Cox was not alone in his fury. One newspaperman recalled that, for a time, the "anger of the majority" seemed to threaten a new civil war.[55]

After the election, pressure on the mainstream vision continued to mount as an increasingly wide spectrum of Americans demanded that the government choose sides in America's economic struggles. Growing labor agitation led to the 1877 Great Railroad Strike, which united workers nationally and terrified those who did not identify with a labor interest. In July, the Baltimore and Ohio Railroad cut wages 20 percent, sparking a strike in West Virginia. The strike spread across the nation, shutting down most of the nation's railroads, leaving 100 dead, and destroying $10 million in property. As Samuel Gompers recalled "the railroad strike of 1877 was the tocsin that sounded a ringing message of hope to us all." Allan Pinkerton, who ran the infamous Pinkerton Detective Agency that specialized in strikebreaking, reflected that the strike revealed "that we have among us a pernicious communistic spirit which is demoralizing workmen, continually creating a deeper and more intense antagonism between labor and capital, and so embittering naturally restless elements against the better elements of society, that it must be crushed out completely, or we shall be compelled to submit to greater excesses and more overwhelming disasters in the near future." Anxious Americans wondered if the strike was "the beginning of a great civil war in this country, between labor and capital."[56]

On July 26, the Amalgamated Trades and Labor Union held a mass meeting in New York City. In the blazing heat, the meeting resolved "that it is the imperative duty of all workingmen to organize in trade unions and to . . . aid in the establishment of a national federation of trades, so that combined capital can be successfully resisted and overcome." In January 1878, the Knights of Labor adopted a new constitution whose preamble denounced the aggression of wealth against "the toiling masses" and called for the organization of all industries, increasing wages, reducing hours, and making sure workers received a greater share of "the benefits, privileges and emoluments of the world." They demanded that the government establish a bureau of labor and statistics, abrogate all laws that did not bear equally upon capital and labor, and adopt health and safety measures for workers. They wanted equal pay for equal work for both sexes, an eight-hour day, greenbacks, and an end to child labor.[57]

In 1878, it appeared that the disaffected in society were gaining political power. That February, T. V. Powderly was elected mayor of Scranton, Pennsylvania, at the head of a Greenback Labor Party, despite opponents' insistence that the party represented the same sort of "communism" that had taken over Paris. Elsewhere in the 1878 elections, the Greenback Labor Party polled more than a million votes and elected fourteen congressmen. Their votes changed the complexion of Congress and made the inflationary forces powerful enough to force Congress to pass the Bland Allison Act of 1878. This law ordered the secretary of the Treasury to buy between $2 and $4 million of silver monthly at the market price and convert these purchases into standard dollars. This fell far short of the desires of greenbackers, who wanted free and unlimited coinage of silver at the old ratio of 16:1, but it illustrated the growing power of cheap money advocates in the government. In 1879, Powderly took over the Knights of Labor to organize skilled workers, uniting an elected office with workers' organization in the same charismatic figure.[58]

A workingman's party in California symbolized for many what would happen if the disaffected were permitted to take charge of government. In San Francisco, Dennis Kearney had begun his career not as a labor agitator but as a drayman anxious to get the city government to fix the potholes that made it hard for his carts to negotiate the streets. Angry when city leaders ignored him, he began to agitate against them and soon became the spokesman for laborers opposed to wealthy employers. By 1877, he was elected secretary to the newly formed Workingman's Party, which fulminated against Chinese immigrants and those who employed them. In 1878, the secret platform of the Workingman's Party demanded life imprisonment for malfeasance in office, the end of land monopoly, an eight-hour workday, and the end of Chinese labor. In 1879, California voters approved a new constitution drafted by members of the Workingman's Party and attacking Chinese rights. That year, Kearney's candidate, Isaac S. Kalloch, was elected mayor of San Francisco after an opponent shot and wounded him. Newspapers across the country reported the San Francisco Board of Supervisors' condemnation of

Kalloch; he had "tried to engender a wicked and brutal feeling among the poor against the rich inciting them to lawlessness . . . he has advised them to be in readiness for bloodshed and violence." His own son took this advice to heart in 1880, killing the opposition editor of the *San Francisco Chronicle*, the man who had shot Kalloch during the campaign. Young Kalloch was acquitted on the grounds that he had acted in self-defense, although he had emptied six rounds into his victim after seeking him out in the man's own office. For opponents of the Workingman's Party, Kalloch's acquittal simply confirmed that Workingman's Party thugs had taken over the city's courts and perverted them, permitting Workingman's Party criminals to walk free. By 1880, California workers were strong enough to force presidential aspirants to endorse the exclusion of the Chinese from America, an extraordinary policy that replaced the belief that labor created value with the idea that labor was a commodity in a world of economic conflict. Mainstream Americans watched Kearney's career with horror.[59]

The publication of Henry George's best-selling *Progress and Poverty* in 1879 revealed that distrust of the American system of individualism was not limited to an underclass of wage laborers. George was a newspaper editor from San Francisco who had lost his job at the *Post* after bitterly attacking the state's railroad interests and monopolies. He supported the Liberal Republicans in 1872 and Tilden in 1876, guaranteeing himself a job in the city government. "The association of poverty with progress is the great enigma of our times," he mused in *Progress and Poverty*. How would a person a hundred years earlier perceive the events of 1879, he asked. If he saw

the steamship taking the place of the sailing vessel, the railway train of the waggon, the reaping machine of the scythe, the threshing machine of the flail; could he have heard the throb of the engines that in obedience to human will, and for the satisfaction of human desire, exert a power greater than that of all the men and all the beasts of burden of the earth combined; could he have seen the forest tree transformed into finished lumber—into doors, sashes, blinds, boxes or barrels, with hardly the touch of a human hand; the great workshops where boots and shoes are turned out from improved facilities of exchange and communication—sheep killed in Australia eaten fresh in England, and the order given by the London banker in the afternoon executed in San Francisco in the morning of the same day; could he have conceived of the hundred thousand improvements which these only suggest, what would he have inferred as to the social condition of mankind?[60]

An observer from the past would have assumed that these new forces were elevating society, eliminating poverty, easing labor. From prosperity would come moral elevation: "Youth no longer stunted and starved; age no longer harried by avarice; the man with the muck-rake drinking in the glory of the stars! . . . How could there be the vice, the crime, the ignorance, the brutality, that spring from poverty and the fear of poverty, exist where poverty had vanished?" But somehow, in reality the opposite was happening. Truly, "the association of poverty with progress is the great enigma of our times." George could not attribute industrial problems to particular political policies, pointing out that soft money and low tariff policies seemed to produce no less poverty than hard money and high tariffs. Standing armies were not the heart of the problem either, for poverty seemed to thrive in both the North and the South. Progress itself must somehow be at fault, George decided, and his solution for the equalization of wealth in America harked back to traditional American values.

"Land is the habitation of man," George reminded Americans, "the storehouse upon which he must draw for all his needs, the material to which his labour must be applied for the supply of all his desires; for even the products of the sea cannot be taken, the light of the sun enjoyed, or any of the forces of nature utilized, without the use of land or its products." The true problem of progress was the monopoly of land, and the ability of landowners to charge rents for the use of land made valuable by the inevitable increasing population in a prosperous nation. Living in California, George had seen firsthand the financial payoff for those lucky enough to have well-located land. With no effort on his part, a man who happened to own property in a place that society in general decided was valuable—say, on Fifth Avenue, in New York City—could become a millionaire overnight, while a man who had settled in rural Colorado had no such advantage. The only solution to this inequality was the common ownership of land, which George believed could be achieved by placing a single tax on it.

This simplistic solution to the problems of industrial America was strikingly similar to the one advocated by radical African Americans immediately after the war, but whereas radical freedmen found few supporters outside of their community, George drew great enthusiasm. His emphasis on land reform first drew Irish workers, who advocated Irish land reform, then workers more generally. In 1883, Powderly invited him to become a member of the Knights of Labor, and in 1886 he used George's photograph in a Knights of

Labor poster honoring American producers. George's tax plan was moderate compared to the Kearneyites (whom George hated), and it attracted not only workers but also reformers generally, whose hatred of big businessmen and horror at the poverty around them made them join the growing call for a government that brokered between special interests. Single-tax clubs began to form across the country, and George's popularity soared. Before long, people were playing a popular board game inspired by the single-tax movement; the idea of the game was to buy up property and hold it, charging other players rent when they landed on your "monopoly."[61]

It seemed that organization of the disaffected had just begun. Farmers started organizing into "Farmers' Alliances" to promote their political influence. Luna Kellie's husband joined an Alliance in his neighborhood; its organizer knew, she later speculated, "that if the farmers once got organized and discussing their situation they would eventually find they had to resort to politics to get any needed reform." Hundreds of delegates from the new Alliances, old Granges, and antimonopoly clubs gathered in Chicago in April 1880 to call for government regulation of the railroads. The railroads were "a virtual monopoly . . . defiant of all existing law . . . oppressive alike to the producer and consumer, corrupting to our politics, a hindrance to free and impartial legislation, and a menace to the very safety of our republican institutions." "The government must bring them under control, and politicians who did not heed the farmers' wishes were warned that they would lose voters.[62]

In 1880, farmers and laborers organized into the Greenback Labor Party nominated their own presidential ticket. Echoing Henry George, they noted that increased production and labor-saving machinery had neither eased the work of laborers nor shortened working hours. Claiming that few workers were rising into comfort and independence, they blamed monopolists and the rich for controlling a strong government and deliberately keeping workers weak. In a convention that included Kearney as well as forty-four delegates from the Socialist Labor Party, they demanded the end to national banks and the increase in greenbacks, unlimited coinage of silver, labor legislation, regulation of business, a graduated income tax, and "a Government of the people, by the people, and for the people, instead of a Government of the bondholder, by the bondholder, and for the bondholder," "Slashing at Republican rhetoric against southern Democrats, they denounced "every attempt to stir up sectional strife as an effort to conceal monstrous crimes against the people." Their presidential nominee, General James B. Weaver, called for "a full ballot, a fair count, and equal rights for all classes, for the laboring man in the Northern factories, mines, and workshops, and for the struggling poor, both black and white, in the cotton fields of the South."[63]

Americans dedicated to the idea of economic harmony and evenhanded government reacted to this "political orgie" with horror. It was a meeting of "every one that was in distress, and every one that was in debt, and every one that was discontented." It was a gathering of Grangers, Socialists, women suffragists, and all malcontents. The *New York Times* pointed out in astonishment that "while denouncing a 'strong Government,' the Greenback-Labor Party demand[s] that Congress shall take charge of all railroad and steamship lines, abolish private land-holdings, regulate industrial establishments, and do a great many other things which the strongest advocate of a strong Government has not yet dared to approve. . . . These midsummer madmen ask that . . . Congress . . . shall regulate everything, abolish debt and evidences of debt, and be a species of special providence to every person who proves himself incapable of taking care of himself."[64]

It was high time to divorce government from special interests, they thought, and that effort began in the administration itself, where Hayes's promise not to seek a second term made him willing to forgo packing official positions with his own men. Hayes worked hard to mollify those who had opposed his election. He appointed a southerner to his cabinet as postmaster general—a key office for patronage distribution—and withdrew most of the remaining troops from the South. At the same time, though, he refused to bow to southern efforts to control national policy, repeatedly vetoing Democratic riders to appropriations bills despite the government's dire need of money. Anxious to assure Democrats that he would not feed a Republican machine, Hayes appointed Carl Schurz to his cabinet as secretary of the interior, a position that had at its disposal many patronage posts, including those in the hugely lucrative Indian agencies. This was a politic thing to do not only to mollify Schurz's supporters, but also because Charles Henry Dana at the *New York Sun* had sent Schurz's protégé Joseph Pulitzer to Washington to cover the election controversy, giving him leave to say what he liked. Pulitzer and Dana were bitter that Hayes got the presidential chair through obviously political machinations, and keeping around the friend of such a powerful newspapermen was a wise move on Hayes's part. Schurz probably influenced Hayes to issue his order of June 22, 1877, that "no officer should be required or permitted to take part in the management of political organizations, caucuses, conventions or election campaigns," and that "no assessments for political purposes on offers or subordinates should be allowed."[65]

Congressmen angry at the outcome of the 1876 election insisted that the apparatus of government must be separated from the interests of a particular party. In 1878, they passed the Posse Comitatus Act prohibiting the deployment of the army to enforce the laws, except under a very few circumstances. The president could still use the military to put down domestic insurrections, for example, but it could no longer oversee southern elections. This law also reduced the ability of employers to call on the army to put down strikers, as it had done during the 1877 railroad strike. As it reduced the ability of the army to protect black rights in the South, the Posse Comitatus Act terribly weakened the ability of the army to protect reservation Indians from white criminals. Under the act, local government was supposed to prosecute local crime, but white sheriffs refused to hunt down people who stole from Indians. Those trying to separate the government from special interests with the Posse Comitatus Act made the equality of blacks and Indians dependent on the goodwill of their white neighbors.[66]

While divorcing the government from special interests was important, it was also becoming clear that it might be necessary to use the government actively to disseminate the individualist vision. After Custer's defeat, Buffalo Bill, increasingly the symbol of the individualistic West, went back to work for the government as an army scout. Nat Love unconsciously noted the paradoxical dependence of the image of individualism on the reality of army protection when he remembered July 4, 1876. On that day, he claimed, he was nicknamed "Deadwood Dick" by the people of Deadwood, "after I had proven myself worthy to carry it, and after I had defeated all comers in riding, roping, and shooting" in an impromptu rodeo of cowboys around Deadwood for a purse of $200. But when word reached these brave, individualistic western cowboys of Custer's defeat, individualism stopped dead. Love recalled: "the indignation and sorrow was universal . . . but we could do nothing . . . as they Indians were out in such strong force. There was nothing to do but let Uncle Sam revenge the loss of the General and his brave command."[67]

Pursued by the army, Sioux leader Spotted Tail and about 1,500 warriors surrendered in April 1877, but Sitting Bull and his followers fled to Canada, across "the medicine line" that ended U.S. government jurisdiction. After Chief Joseph of the Nez Perce surrendered, the government appointed a commission to talk with Sitting Bull about peace. On October 17, he and other chiefs "declined, with scorn, the proposals for a peace made by the commission, and the latter retired; whereupon the British authorities there gave Sitting Bull notice that if he attempted to cross the border with hostile intentions he would not only have the Americans but the British as his enemies," according to an observer. Determined to break the power of free Indians once and for all, opponents of Grant's "peace policy" demanded that Indian Affairs be transferred from the Interior Department to the War Department.[68]

In fall and winter 1877, a joint committee of Congress tried to determine if, indeed, Indians could ever be brought into the American mainstream. Should they be treated solely as hostiles under the auspices of the War Department, or could they be turned into productive farmers under the management of the Interior Department? On December 6, Carl Schurz testified in favor of continuing the policy of trying to domesticate the Indians. He called for teaching them to farm and graze animals and for providing them with education. Congress agreed with Schurz in February 1878, leaving the Interior Department in control of the Indians. From then on, Schurz was a staunch advocate of measures that would enable them to join mainstream life, advocating, among other things, their admission to Hampton Institute in Virginia—a school established for freedpeople after the war—for an education. His last report as secretary of the interior, delivered in 1880, declared that his policies had been highly successful and that the Indians were on their way to civilization. Anyone, it seemed, could learn to be a good American, if only the government put some muscle into it.[69]

The election of 1880 was an exercise in moderation for the major parties, rallying to a common middle ground. The Republicans called for civil service reform, continuing the protective tariffs that helped business (although they bowed to pressure from workers to call for the restriction of Chinese immigration), and veterans' pensions. The Democrats countered with a platform that was virtually identical to that of the Republicans, except that they called for a tariff for revenue only rather than to develop national productivity. Hayes had pledged not to run for a second term, leaving the field wide open. The warring branches of the machine Republicans—the Stalwarts and the Half-Breeds—destroyed the chances of Grant and Blaine, their respective candidates, and Republicans turned instead to a dark horse, Ohio's James A. Garfield, who was not identified with machine Republicans. The Stalwarts, in turn, were appeased with the vice presidential nominee, Chester A. Arthur of New York City, a popular man-about-town closely associated with the

Republican machine patronage system in New York City. The Democrats nominated a Civil War general, Winfield Scott Hancock, and party regular William H. English, promising that they would provide small, honest government and attacking the Republicans for stealing the previous election. With little to separate the candidates, the Republicans campaigned heavily on their war record, while the Democrats attacked Republican corruption. In November, Garfield took the White House, but his plurality was less than 10,000 out of the more than 9 million votes cast. Greenback Labor candidate Weaver polled only 308,578 votes. For all the talk of radicalism and visibility of strikers and agrarian agitators, the national mandate, it seemed, was for a government that did not appear to respond to special interests but instead represented an America of upwardly mobile individuals in a harmonious economy that lifted all together.[70]

The panic and depression years of the 1870s had threatened to tear the country apart as various groups demanded government intervention in the economy to level the economic playing field. Trying to elect political leaders more sympathetic to their interests, these special interests—from workers and farmers to wealthy monopolists—terrified their opponents by raising the fear that special interests were taking over the government. Those fears only mounted when the 1876 election seemed to prove that the Republicans would stop at nothing to maintain their hold on the government, using what opponents viciously characterized as ignorant African American voters to maintain an empire that served business while average Americans suffered in the depression. The subsequent success of farmer and labor politicians increased the sense that America was on the verge of being buffeted between special interest groups at the top and bottom of society, while "the great middle" worked hard to pay the taxes that supported the demanding voters. If this came to pass, American government would be permanently corrupted, and America's great experiment in republican government destroyed. Surely, it seemed, in acting for the entire American people, the government must work to spread and defend the idea of mainstream individualism.

CHAPTER SIX

1881–1885

Years of Consolidation

For his part, twenty-one-year-old Theodore Roosevelt was as concerned as anyone could be about America's control by special interests. As a child he had watched Lincoln's funeral procession from his grandfather's New York City home, and in 1880, only fifteen years later, the world for which Lincoln had laid down his life seemed to be falling apart. In New York City, children were working rather than attending school, laboring men were at their jobs as many as sixteen hours a day, and drunkenness, prostitution, and vice spread across the city as the stringent budgets of the post-Tweed years meant fewer competent law enforcement officials. Four years at Harvard had convinced Roosevelt that something had to be done to return the nation to its traditional values. After his college graduation, Roosevelt joined the Republican Party, which was, he found, an elite club that disdained the voters who kept it in power. He entered Columbia Law School but quickly became more interested in changing the law than in interpreting it. In November 1881, Roosevelt became the youngest man ever elected to the New York State Assembly.[1]

Roosevelt was nominated by Republicans disgusted with machine politics, and he vowed that he would be "owned by no man, and that he would go to Albany untrammeled and unpledged, and in a position to vote independently." In the legislature, he faced "problems of honesty and decency and of legislative and administrative efficiency," Roosevelt recalled. Allying himself with men he carefully described as upstanding, average, and politically independent, Roosevelt set out to combat what he saw as the hijacking of government by special interests. "We were no respecters of persons," he later claimed. "Where our vision was developed to a degree that enabled us to see crookedness, we opposed it whether in great or small. . . . The only kinds of courage and honesty which are permanently useful to good institutions anywhere are those shown by men who decide all cases with impartial justice on grounds of conduct and not on grounds of class." Caught between disadvantaged groups advocating special interest legislation and increasingly dominant big businessmen like Andrew Carnegie, Americans who supported the mainstream vision fought back to defend the self-sufficient man. As he steered a course between the interests of workers and businessmen, Roosevelt embodied their values.[2]

For people like Theodore Roosevelt, the rapid changes in the nation brought tremendous benefits. By 1880, electric lights were "permanent fixtures in shops, halls, stores, and in streets and squares," *Scribner's Monthly* noted. Electricity lit up dramatic new public buildings—Philadelphia's international exhibition of electricity was lit with almost 6,000 electric lights and had a central fountain illuminated with colored lights that made the water fall "in a perpetual shower of jewels." Chicago's Dearborn Station, completed in 1885, cost $450,000, covered almost as much ground as Grand Central in New York, and was "admirable." Public buildings from the original Smithsonian Institution to Harvard's Memorial Church were fashioned after the Second Empire style from France with its blocky upper stories and fancy carving. In homes from New York City to San Francisco to Vinalhaven, Maine, this translated into the wonderfully ugly mansard roof, which offered contemporary elegance as well as a usable top floor. Carnegie's steel was now perfected, and in 1885, Louis Sullivan's Home Insurance Building in Chicago became the world's first skyscraper, its nine stories held up not by walls, but by a steel frame supporting the building's weight. Private homes were also showpieces, for this was the era of the Victorian houses that graced urban landscapes from Julia Ward Howe's Boston to Carl Schurz's St. Louis, where elaborate iron filigree decoration showed the proximity of iron manufacturing centers. Even in the countryside, new styles of housing crept into traditional towns.[3]

Andrew Carnegie illustrated the glory of his new life to the Scottish town of Dunfermline, from which his family had emigrated, impoverished. He must have thought back on his grim past as an immigrant child laborer as he drove his mother into town in a coach-and-four, fulfilling a promise he had made as a boy that at the time must have seemed as unobtainable as the stars. The town that was so important to him as a child appeared small and dingy after his experiences in America, and the difference reinforced his profound faith in business. New industries and economies of scale meant that "to-day the world obtains commodities of excellent quality at prices which even the preceding generation would have deemed incredible. . . . The poor enjoy what the rich could not before afford. What were luxuries have become the necessities of life. The laborer has now more comforts than the farmer had a few generations ago. The farmer has more luxuries than the landlord had, and is more richly clad and better housed. The landlord has books and pictures rarer and appointments more artistic than the king could then obtain."[4]

For people like Carnegie, America offered unprecedented opportunities. The lives of upwardly mobile families had changed dramatically since the antebellum years. Increasingly, the men in such families worked as clerks or managers in the city's growing businesses and industries. By 1870, out of a national population of 38.5 million, more than 1 million men worked in trade, finance or real estate, education, or other professional services. Another 100,000 worked for the government. Skilled workers, too, benefited from wages that were double those of their unskilled colleagues. For professional men these numbers only increased. By 1900, out of a national population of almost 76 million, 4 million men worked in white-collar jobs and another 300,000 in government. But in a reflection of the increasing mechanization of industry and the decreasing power of skilled laborers, after 1880 the government stopped tracking skilled labor and unskilled labor separately.[5]

Larger paychecks and white-collar work enabled more men to buy their own homes. They also had the cash to buy toys, books like *Five Little Peppers and How They Grew* (1880) and *Uncle Remus*, and magazines for their children, and they were able to turn increasing amounts of money over to their wives for buying clothes and decorating their homes. Their daughters were devoted to "lawn tennis," which had its own national association by 1880, and they spent money in fashionable soda fountains, where they could take refuge from the hot summer streets to sip soda water mixed with ice cream. Their sons rode bicycles and, by 1886, were drinking Moxie and would soon switch to Coca Cola. Their homes had refrigerators cooled by blocks of ice and possibly even newfangled indoor plumbing, including a water closet and bathtub installed in what had been an unused bedroom. A number of servants helped the household run efficiently, and technology, in turn, helped them. Cleaning a carpet used to mean pulling it up, dragging it outside, pounding the dirt out of it as it hung on a line, taking it back inside, and tacking it down again. In 1876, the new carpet sweeper was most welcome to those who had

had to "pull up carpet tacks, all around the edges of miles of carpet," as one little boy complained.⁶

When the dirt of the city hemmed in affluent Americans, they could head over to the green expanse of a baseball diamond and watch the increasingly popular teams compete: the Cincinnati Red Stockings, the Kansas City Cowboys, the Pittsburgh Alleghenys, the Washington Senators, the Detroit Wolverines, the Chicago Cubs, the New York Mutuals, and the Boston Braves. On summer vacation, prosperous families could leave the city altogether, with New Yorkers and southerners visiting fashionable watering holes like Saratoga, New York, or traveling to Europe; Boston families "rusticating" on the coast of Maine; and Chicagoans in summer cottages on Wisconsin's Lake Geneva. Indeed, with so many farmers moving west, it was increasingly easy for the affluent to have a summer home in the Northeast. One such rusticator from Boston commented of his summer home in western Massachusetts: "My constant wonder is that hundreds who must leave the city in the summer do not do as I have done. It means ten times the comfort for about one-half the expense of boarding in your trunks. And New England is dotted all over with homesteads going to decay, which can be purchased for a song, and made habitable and even charming for a few hundred dollars.... With what satisfaction we read that the mercury in New York yesterday stood at 103 [degrees] Fahrenheit!"⁷

No longer bound to sentimental novels or books of moral instruction, Americans now read books that spoke to their own lives. Lew Wallace's wildly popular *Ben-Hur* (1880) told the story of how one individual held firm to his convictions in the face of overwhelming government persecution. Novels by William Dean Howells dissected the modern world, and books like *The Rise of Silas Lapham* (1885) urged readers to uphold middle-class morality in the face of modernization. Most powerfully, in 1885, men like Roosevelt could sit in an armchair before a coal heater and read U. S. Grant's *Memoirs*. These enormously popular volumes emphasized the power of a single individual in American life and recalled Americans to the free labor vision of hard work and economic harmony that Grant carefully assigned to common people in both the North and South. His direct and powerful language gave readers the sense of immediacy, action, and the nation's greatness. "It is probably well that we had the war when we did," he concluded. "We are better off now than we would have been without it, and have made more rapid progress than we otherwise should have made.... Then, too, our republican institutions were regarded as experiments up to the breaking out of the rebellion, and monarchical Europe generally believed that our republic was a rope of sand that would part the moment the slightest strain was brought upon it. Now it has shown itself capable of dealing with one of the greatest wars that was ever made, and our people have proven themselves to be the most formidable in war of any nationality."[8]

Holidays and celebrations took on a new elegance in this age. When Roosevelt's sister Corinne married in April 1882, she didn't have the quiet home ceremony of her parents' generation. For her, the church was specially decorated with plants, and she wore a satin bridal dress with point lace, diamonds, a train, and with a dress front "heavily trimmed with beads of pearl and bordered with a deep pearl fringe." Eight ushers stood near eight brides-maids, all of whom carried bouquets of lilacs, roses, and forget-me-nots. A reception at her family's home featured a band, an elegant supper, and "floral decorations . . . on a scale of magnificence seldom surpassed on such occasions." By 1885, Thanksgiving had become a major holiday, and in New York, buyers could choose their turkeys from the shops in Washington Market. If they were not interested in turkeys, they could find something else to their liking: "Ducks and geese and chickens are piled in mounds on the zinc-covered counters, and the carcasses of fallen deer hang from the hooks, while banks of green-topped celery and rosy-cheeked apples lend color to the scene. Small tradesmen fill up the spaces between the regular market stalls with appetizing stores of hares, rabbits, and other small game, and big butchers in iron-starched white or checked aprons move around like jolly warders at a fair. At the street corners outside of the market little rosy-cheeked girls, and old women whose cheeks are no longer rosy, sit behind huge baskets of oranges and apples."[9]

Nothing illustrated more clearly the hopes of the American middle class in the early 1880s than the changes in Christmas. "The holiday season this year will be peculiarly pleasant," reported an article in *Harper's New Monthly Magazine* in 1880, "because the long prostration of industry is ended, and business everywhere revives. The good-will of the season will be even more cheerful and cordial, and the wish of a happy New-Year will have the charm of sincere expectation." From Prussia by way of England, the tradition of Christmas trees came to postwar America as Americans emulated the trees brought to the British court by Prince Albert, Queen Victoria's husband. On the branches of these novel trees, people tied gifts for each other. Beginning in 1885, federal workers were given a day off on Christmas so they could enjoy the holiday with their families. Mainstream families had focused increasingly on children after the war, and by the 1880s, children's birthdays were marked with cakes and later with parties designed to give youngsters their own entertainment. This focus on children was apparent in Thomas Nast's 1881 image of fat, jolly St. Nicholas, who brings toys to happy, healthy children and who still stands as the American version of Santa Claus. But Nast's early Santa Claus had one important feature that he has shed over the years. In the 1880s, Santa carried over his arm a belt with a broad buckle bearing the prominent letters "U.S." In the 1880s, prosperity had a distinctly American cast.[10]

Because the families that lived in urban areas made up the primary audience for the new, popular magazines like the *Century* and *Harper's New Monthly Magazine*, their culture and desires had a disproportionate effect on popular culture. Their lives as depicted in these magazines were something poorer workers and farmers dreamed about, and after 1872, the advent of the mail-order catalogue meant rural customers could purchase some of the items that represented affluence to them rather than being limited to the wares of local sellers. For new bride Laura Ingalls Wilder in South Dakota, for example, that meant a set of china that came all the way from Montgomery Ward in Chicago. Thomas Nast's jolly Santa Claus spoke volumes to people like Luna and J. T. Kellie, who hoped they, too, could have security, if only they worked hard enough. In the early 1880s, good crops and rising prices encouraged farmers in the Northwest to believe that the prosperity they saw in the East could also be theirs. The Farmers' Alliances—popular only a year or two earlier—were almost dead by 1884. Many workers, too, identified with the prosperous vision of America. Worker organization continued to rise, but at its peak in 1886 no more than one-third of wage laborers were members of unions. This was, in part, because unskilled workers were constantly on the move, looking for new jobs. It probably also reflected the fact that white workers in America enjoyed enough upward mobility to convince them that they, too, could rise on their own. In the late nineteenth century, about a quarter of all white men who began as manual laborers would rise to a white-collar job during their careers, while only about one out of every six men slid the other way. The numbers were even more dramatic between generations. The son of a family at the lowest rungs of society was more likely to rise to a white-collar job than not, whereas the one out of six of those who did not could expect to rise to the position of a skilled worker. Middle-class sons did not fall at nearly the same rate as others rose, either; most could expect to stay at the same level as their fathers. These numbers were dramatically different for people of color, but for white Americans, it seemed the American system worked.[11]

MERRY OLD SANTA CLAUS.

Figure 11. In Thomas Nast's iconographic 1881 image, Santa carried a "U.S." belt and brought an armful of toys to middle-class children. Courtesy *HarpWeek*.

The great triumphs of the postwar era were triumphs for all Americans together, boosters insisted. Certainly workers had it rough, but no worse than soldiers during the Civil War, who had endured disease, hunger, dirt, privation, and death for a great good. When the Brooklyn Bridge opened on May 24, 1883, the *Brooklyn Eagle* reported that the triumphant celebration was "confined to no class or body of the populace. It was a holiday for high and low, rich and poor; it was, in fact, the People's Day." The minister blessing the occasion noted, "All things—wealth, industry, energy, skill, genius—come of Thee; and when we consecrate their triumphs unto Thee, we give Thee but Thine own." Another speaker reminded the crowd that the engineers were not alone responsible for this great achievement. "The record would not be complete without reference to the unnamed men by whose unflinching courage in the depths of the caissons, and upon the suspended wires, the work was carried on amid storms, and accidents, and dangers, sufficient to appall the stoutest heart. To them we can only render the tribute which history accords to those who fight as privates in the battles of freedom, with all the more devotion and patriotism because their names will never be known by the world whose benefactors they are."12

To rising Americans it seemed as if the system worked for everyone and faced threats only from those who had no intention of working and planned to use the government to redistribute wealth to them. Tensions mounted between those who believed that hard work alone could guarantee success and those who knew that collective action was imperative to guarantee a level economic playing field. In July 1881, Americans nervous about special interests in government were handed a dramatic illustration of special interests' potential to destroy the government when a disappointed office seeker put a bullet in President Garfield's back as he stood at a platform in the Washington train station. "I am a Stalwart, and now Arthur is president!" the assassin announced. The attack was a direct product of the special interest system. Garfield was a Republican moderate who had been trying to undercut the party's image as a haven for spoilsmen by awarding patronage posts to applicants from a number of different factions. Vice President Chester A. Arthur, however, was the epitome of a machine politician who devoted his days to finding jobs for his political supporters. Garfield's deluded assailant shot the president because he wanted a government job.

Through the long hot summer Americans contemplated the dangers of special interests in government as Garfield lingered between life and death.

Garfield's death from infection in September spurred the creation of civil service legislation to curb the abuses of patronage. In 1883, Congress passed the Civil Service (or Pendleton) Act, which required that certain federal jobs be filled on a merit basis, determined by competitive exams overseen by a bipartisan civil service commission. The new law covered only about 10 percent of all federal jobs, but it allowed future presidents to expand the list of jobs protected from patronage. This they did—usually upon leaving office, to protect the supporters they left behind—and gradually the number of jobs covered by civil service requirements grew. That reform was the order of the day was clear from Arthur's course as president; he shocked machine Republicans by resisting their pressure and acting independently in hopes of being reelected on his own hook.[13]

Those who adhered to the mainstream vision of economic harmony increasingly felt the need to protect that harmony from those who would use the government for their own gain. In 1882, the Chinese Restriction Act powerfully illustrated that many workers no longer believed that the nation was a land of potential prosperity in which anyone could rise. This law—the first explicitly preventing a specific group of voluntary working-class immigrants from entering the nation—codified the idea that the economy was not, in fact, a harmonious system in which all rose together but that there were different, competing interests in society. Old-time Republicans fought such a vision of competing laborers exploited by capitalists, but ultimately they had to concede to the demands of western mobs who argued that the Chinese laborers undercut wages. When Republican politicians afraid of alienating workers signed onto the restriction act, *Harper's Weekly* reported its disgust at their willingness to prohibit "the voluntary immigration of free skilled laborers into the country, and . . . to renounce the claim that America welcomes every honest comer." Mainstream easterners condemned the murder of twenty-eight Chinese miners by a mob of white workers at Rock Springs, Wyoming, in 1885.[14]

In 1883, Yale political and social scientist William Graham Sumner, one of America's most prominent Social Darwinists, dubbed the average American "The Forgotten Man" in his manifesto *What Social Classes Owe to Each Other*. "The Forgotten Man works and votes—generally he prays—but his chief business in life is to pay. His name never gets into the newspapers except when he marries or dies. He is an obscure man. He may grumble sometimes to his wife, but he does not [drink heavily], and he does not talk politics at the tavern. . . . The Forgotten Man is not a pauper. It belongs to his character to save something. Hence he is a capitalist, though never a great one." The Forgotten Man was the true productive backbone of America, Sumner insisted, reflecting the economy that made hard work bring prosperity. This system offered "chances of happiness indescribably in excess of what former generations have possessed," but it offered "no such guarantees as were once possessed by some, that they should in no case suffer." Look, he demanded, at ex-slaves. They had lost security, "care, medicine, and support" when they gained their freedom and "now work and hold their own products, and are assured of nothing but what they earn." "Individual black men may seem worse off," he wrote, but "will any one say that the black men have not gained?"

Ignoring the dramatically increasing economic power of middle-class Americans, Sumner argued that the Forgotten Man was endangered by those advocating "the paternal theory of government." By this theory, "humanitarians, philanthropists, and reformers" tried to make "the industrious and the prudent" responsible for "the negligent, shiftless, inefficient, silly, and imprudent." It had become "quite disreputable to be respectable, quite dishonest to own property, quite unjust to go one's own way and earn one's own living." "Misguided "social doctors" were denigrating the self-made man and promising to the shiftless man government aid—funded by the prosperous— "to give him what the other had to work for." This was a grave error, Sumner warned. Reworking the idea that America's economy would provide a living to anyone if only he worked hard and avoided labor organizations, Sumner argued not only that those unwilling to work should fail, but also that trying to help them would destroy the nation.[15]

But it was not only the poor who seemed to threaten the mainstream vision in the 1880s. Sumner hated tariffs even more than charity, arguing that no part of American society more corrupted the political economy than taking wealth from all to redistribute to a particular group. The informal pools and horizontal integration of the early 1870s had never been very stable, for it was terribly hard to enforce cooperation among producers. As soon as prices had been fixed at an artificially high price, one or another opportunistic businessman couldn't resist dropping his prices and underselling his competitors for a quick profit. Once one business dropped its prices, the rest had to follow suit, and the benefits of the pool were gone. In the volatile years of the 1870s, businesses suffered, and their owners looked for some way to bring stability—and higher profits—to their industries. In 1879, they found a way. Not surprisingly, it was a lawyer for the devious J. D. Rockefeller who came up with the idea of a "trust." In this legal entity, the owners of a corporation put their shares of the business into a "trust" managed by a board of directors who were empowered to "hold, control, and manage" all of the trust's property. This meant rapid consolidation of industries and consequent control of markets and prices.[16]

The great middle got a powerful voice against businessmen in 1883. Coming east at Carl Schurz's behest, Joseph Pulitzer bought the New York World from Jay Gould in 1883, promising that, instead of catering to monopolists, his newspaper would "be truly democratic— . . . expose all fraud and sham, fight all public evils and abuses—that will serve and battle for the people with earnest sincerity." Within a week he announced that the World would stand against monopolists, calling for taxes on luxuries, inheritances, large incomes, monopolies, and corporate privileges, and for the punishment of corrupt voters, officeholders, and employers who coerced employees to vote for certain candidates. His new style caused consternation among wealthy New Yorkers, prompting a newspaperman years later to recall the "anathema [called] down upon the head of Joseph Pulitzer when he came bounding into New York from the breezy West." But a Philadelphia man who bought the first edition of Pulitzer's World later remembered that he "saw at a glance that the emancipation of the newspapers of this country had commenced, . . . that great wrongs were to be righted; that light was to be let in where darkness covered it."[17]

Pulitzer identified what he called "true democracy" as the guiding force of his paper and of the age. "True democracy," he wrote, "recognizes the millionaire and the railroad magnate as just as good as any other man and as fully entitled to protection for his property under the law. But true democracy will not sanction the swallowing up of liberty by property any more than the swallowing up of property by communism." Although he and Theodore Roosevelt rarely saw eye to eye on specific issues, their vision of government was strikingly similar. Roosevelt later recalled that his early years in the legislature were characterized by his friendship with countryman Billy O'Neill, who was "of different antecedents, ancestry, and surroundings" than Roosevelt. Roosevelt came from the wealthiest ward of the biggest city in America, and O'Neill kept a country store in the backwoods, but the two men stood together "in all the important things. . . . He abhorred demagogy just as he abhorred corruption. He had thought much on political problems; he admired Alexander Hamilton as much as I did, being a strong believer in a powerful National government; and we both of us differed from Alexander

Hamilton in being stout adherents of Abraham Lincoln's views wherever the rights of the people were concerned."[18]

Just as Pulitzer's journalistic course had, Roosevelt's course in the legislature quickly caught the public's attention. Mainstream New Yorkers liked him almost as much as political bosses hated him. The end of the recession of the 1870s reduced the economic pressure that had fueled labor protests, and Americans adhering to a vision of economic harmony gradually reasserted their values. At the end of his first term in office thirty-one of Roosevelt's friends, "irrespective of their political sentiments," took him to dinner at Delmonico's to thank him for "defending the rights of the people." Characteristically, Roosevelt declared that politics was not the property of either the very poor or the very rich, but that "fearless and honest men are wanted [in the Legislature] without respect to their position in society" and that "all voters, without distinction of class, should unite" to send such men to the legislature. "Pluck, honesty, and private morality must be carried into public life," Roosevelt insisted.[19]

As mainstream Americans defended the idea of individual hard work to achieve success, they tried to apply this principle to those over whom they had the most control. By 1884, General George Crook was able to tell the graduates at West Point—many of whom could expect to serve in the West—that the Indians "should be encouraged to work and save. The man who works and saves is fast leaving savagery behind him." Indeed, he concluded, "It is not impossible that, with a fair and square system of dealing with him, the American Indian would make a better citizen than many who neglect the duties and abuse the privileges of that proud title." Even the Apaches, including Geronimo's Chiracahuas, he later reported, are "hard at work trying to make a crop." This meant that "the Apache is kept from idleness, and is made a producer. No sermon that was ever preached on the dignity of labor could imprint upon the savage mind the impression received when he sees that work means money, and that the exact measure of his industry is to be found in his pocket-book. . . . An enlightened self-interest begins to dawn, and to teach him that intemperance and industry can not exist in the same camp." As long as they were not fleeced by "a gang of sharks thinly disguised as Indian agents," they were tractable.[20]

Sitting Bull, for his part, articulated the frustration of those who faced insuperable obstacles to participating in the mainstream vision. He and his people had tried to make a home in Canada, but lack of food forced them to surrender to the U.S. Army in 1881. Sitting Bull was held as a prisoner for two years before being permitted to settle on the Standing Rock Reservation in the Dakotas. Called before a Senate committee in 1883 to testify about the condition of Indian tribes in Montana and the Dakotas, he punctuated his fury at his tribe's loss of land, starvation, and lack of means of support with references to white ideals. "You white men advise us to follow your ways, and therefore I talk as I do," he said. "We want cattle to butcher. . . . That is the way you live and we want to live the same way. . . . If we get the things we want our children will be raised like the white children." Sitting Bull charged the senators with their own professions of goodwill and promises of help for Indians: "It is your own doing that I am here [on the reservation]," he said. "You sent me here and advised me to live as you do, and it is not right for me to live in poverty. I asked the Great Father for hogs, male and female, and for male and female sheep for my children to raise from. I did not leave out anything in the way of animals that the white men have; I asked for every one of them. I want you to tell the Great Father to send me some agricultural implements, so that I will not be obliged to work bare-handed." Meanwhile, a writer for the *Boston Globe* complacently noted that Indians were "gradually becoming exterminated because they will not adopt our methods of living."[21]

Unlike Sitting Bull, who with his people struggled to adapt to a changing mode of life, Quanah Parker found a way to follow the mainstream vision. Cattlemen were always looking for fresh grass for their herds and had been quietly drifting their cattle onto reservation lands since the mid-1870s. This was illegal but impossible to police, especially after the passage of the Posse Comitatus Act weakened federal authority for enforcing domestic laws. Until 1881, Quanah joined other leaders in standing firmly against white incursions on tribal land, citing rights guaranteed to the Indians at the Treaty of Medicine Lodge. The droughts of the 1880s increased pressure to run cattle on Indian lands, and Quanah used the inevitable for his tribe's and his own profit. Initially demanding cattle as informal payment for crossing their lands, Quanah and his band endorsed official leasing of Indian lands by 1883. In that year, Harrold & Ikard, a company running 60,000 cattle, presented 300 head of cattle and regular payments to Quanah and three others of his band in exchange for their influence with the tribe, whose approval was necessary for any leasing deal. Although other cattlemen had similar arrangements with other leaders, the group supported by Quanah ultimately won rights to graze cattle on more than 600,000 acres.[22]

Like others using the mainstream vision to garner government support, by 1884, Quanah had learned how to play to the idea of individualism. He defended leasing to the American authorities by arguing, "We are poor and in our present condition are unable to use these lands ourselves, and, we hope by these means to . . . secure the money with which to stock our lands, and . . . enable us to become self-supporting," but the deal also brought him a minimum of $35 a month and 500 cattle, as well as continued presents from cattlemen anxious to retain his goodwill and authority over those opposed to leasing. Fittingly, during the complicated lease negotiations, Quanah began to insist that his name be recorded with its white surname, Parker. "Quanah was a good fellow," recalled a white settler who surveyed the lease lands for cattlemen. "When he was out in this country he was a blanket Indian, but when he came here he always wore white men's clothes."[23]

By 1885, Quanah had become the head of the Comanches—an unprecedented role produced by the need for concerted Indian action—and in February 1885, he traveled to Washington to lobby Secretary of the Interior Henry M. Teller to support his leasing deals. Now prosperous, he built a farm and house, hired white farmhands, and had fathered a number of children by several wives. Deliberately courting Indian agents, he assured them that he "follow[ed] the white man's path." By 1890, he had 350 acres of land as well as a huge grazing range, at least 425 cattle, 200 hogs, 160 horses, 3 wagons, and 1 buggy. Astonishingly, he had become friends with his old enemy Charles Goodnight, who gave him "a good Durham bull" to improve his cattle. In an 1886 book about his mother, the author wrote approvingly: "Quanah speaks English, is considerably advanced in civilization, and owns a ranch with considerable livestock and a small farm; wears a citizen's suit and conforms to the customs of civilization—withal a fine-looking and dignified son of the plains."[24]

Encouraged by Indians like Quanah who seemed to be accepting their values, middle-class Americans also insisted that black Americans fit in. Many believed that race issues were being solved through the political splits and reform movements in the South that were forcing third parties to work to attract black votes, as well as through increasing black education and black businesses. So long as black voters were considered solidly Republican, Democrats would suppress their votes, but once they began switching parties, all southerners had an interest in protecting their votes. By 1880, Independent movements had organized in South Carolina, Georgia, and Arkansas. Independent movements in the South were vital in the 1880s; during that decade, Independents and Republicans polled at least 40 percent of the vote in seven

Figure 12. In this carefully staged photograph, Quanah deliberately blended his white and Indian heritages to indicate his acceptance of white ways. A portrait of his mother, Naudah, sits prominently to the right. Research Division of the Oklahoma Historical Society, Oklahoma City, Oklahoma.

202

states, challenging the idea of a solid Democratic South. Desperate for support of any color, Independents always called for "a free and fair vote" to attract African American voters. Northerners perceived Wade Hampton's governorship as moderate and noted with approval that southern Democrats in Virginia were nervous that angry black Republicans might join the Independents to defeat the Democrats. Desperate to mollify the delegates to a Republican convention, Virginia delegates desegregated the local hotels and restaurants. "A large number of stanch Democrats, men and women, who were present, went on with their dinners as if the scene was not an unusual one," the *New York Times* reported. Northern Democrats, too, had apparently begun to court the black vote, led by reformers like New York Governor Grover Cleveland, who broadened black appointments to office and desegregated the New York City police force. Independents and Democratic reformers seemed to have a color-blind dedication to the principle of hard work and economic harmony.[25]

A prominent rising black population encouraged the image of black advancement. This group included prosperous farmers, merchants, and professionals and was personified by Booker T. Washington. It emphasized its belief in general economic development and encouraged the idea that the race problem would be solved through individual black advancement. Born into slavery, the brilliant, biracial Washington managed to get a rudimentary education and work his way through Hampton Institute in Virginia, where his mentor, General S. C. Armstrong, recognized his potential. When Secretary of the Interior Carl Schurz conceived of educating Indian youths at Hampton, Armstrong hired Washington to teach them. He acquitted himself so well that when Armstrong was asked to provide a teacher for a new school being organized for local African Americans in Tuskegee, Alabama, he recommended Washington rather than the white man the school's founders expected.

Arriving in Tuskegee in June 1881, Washington found no school buildings but plenty of eager students. He set about creating a traditional Republican free labor education for African Americans, one that would teach them the skills necessary to start at the bottom rung of the ladder of economic prosperity. He later recalled that many whites in the Tuskegee area disliked the idea of educating African Americans, for they believed that "education" for them meant only teaching them to refuse to work. "The white people who questioned the wisdom of starting this new school had in their minds pictures of what was called an educated Negro," Washington explained, "with a high hat, imitation gold eye-glasses, a showy walking-stick, kid gloves, fancy boots, and what not—in a word, a man who was determined to live by his wits." The white image of an educated black man had merged with the popular minstrel show character of "Zip Coon," who was, according to the antebellum song that created him, "a larned skoler, Sings possum up a gum tree an coony in a holler." By the 1880s, this character had become a barely educated freedman who disdained the fields and mines where his neighbors sweated, instead planning to vote himself economic and social benefits. Washington was determined to combat this degrading image.

Washington carefully constructed Tuskegee Institute to echo the individualist vision of the American mainstream and to override the negative image of the lazy black voter. He worked to ensure that both black and white leaders of the Tuskegee community backed the school, making it clear that his students would be prepared to work their way up in society rather than trying to jump straight into white-collar professions. He made it a point to teach his scholars the elements of mainstream culture as well as branches of knowledge. Helped by Olivia Davidson, a Massachusetts-trained teacher whom he later married, Washington taught his students, he remembered, "how to bathe; how to care for their teeth and clothing . . . what to eat, and how to eat it properly, and how to care for their rooms." On that foundation, the school taught students the basic tenet of the individualist work ethic. According to Washington, "we wanted to give them such a practical knowledge of some one industry, together with the spirit of industry, thrift, and economy, that they would be sure of knowing how to make a living after they had left us." Knowing that most of their students were from farming districts, "we wanted to be careful not to educate our students out of sympathy with agricultural life, so that they would be attracted from the country to the cities, and yield to the temptation of trying to live by their wits."[26]

Washington's plan made Tuskegee popular with local whites and his fame began to spread, but he was by no means the only African American talking about economic success through hard work. Upwardly mobile professional African Americans embraced the same values as their white counterparts. In North Carolina, the number of black-owned, credit-rated firms quadrupled between 1880 and 1905, and black professionals were increasingly visible in the 1880s, especially as they moved out of the South and into northern cities after the election of 1876 made them nervous about southern politics. Members of this upwardly mobile portion of the black community tended to hold themselves apart from the lower levels of black society, organizing their own clubs, worshiping in their own churches, publishing their own newspapers, and taking their own stand in politics. By 1880, prosperous, light-skinned African Americans formed their own "black aristocracy" that associated with white society in the North and South in terms that approached equality. Echoing their white peers, upwardly mobile black men and women warned that a man's failure was almost always due to "neglect and even contempt of an honest business"; that "nothing can be accomplished, by waiting for somebody to do something for you. . . . The wisest plan is to get to work yourself"; and that "the negro problem is to be solved by the negro himself in his cultivation of intelligence, virtue, wealth, and good understanding." In his pathbreaking 1882 *History of the Negro Race in America*, black historian George Washington Williams contrasted a thriving community of prosperous black citizens with poor freedmen who, Williams suggested, should not participate in politics until they had bought land and acquired an education.[27]

In the South, tenant farming increased during the 1880s, but at the same time industry continued to develop and land ownership became more widespread. Hopeful observers of the New South paid more attention to the good news than to the bad. By the 1880s, new railroads were snaking through the South, bringing trade into the region. The roads carried products from 161 cotton mills operating in 1880; that number continued to climb until by 1900 there were 400. Fertilizers and new farming techniques increased the production of cotton to feed the mills; by 1875, production ran at about 4.5 million bales and equaled the best prewar years. The tobacco industry also boomed after 1880, as new technologies perfected the production of cigarettes. In order to stiffen the soft packs of the cigarettes, tobacco companies inserted baseball cards into them. The cards helped to turn cigarettes into a new fad while linking the South to the popular mainstream sport. Finally, the region seemed to be shedding the devastation of the postwar slump. Although increasingly mechanized farming pushed small producers into tenancy or wage labor, observers of the South insisted that "any Southern planter, white or black, with brains and industry, may own his land . . . after a few years." "The Yankees ought to be satisfied," a southerner told a northern visitor at the beginning of the decade, for "every live man at the South is trying with all his might to be a Yankee."[28]

In 1883, the Supreme Court codified a belief in personal advancement and fervent dislike of laws establishing black equality when it handed down the Civil Rights Cases. In this series of five decisions concerning cases from Tennessee, New York, Kansas, Missouri, and California, the Court overturned the Civil Rights Act of 1875, arguing that the law was unconstitutional because federal authority could overrule only state institutional discrimination, not the actions of private individuals. Americans of all political persuasions greeted the decision with enthusiasm, Republicans because it helped to erase the image of the party as catering to the black vote; Democrats because that same loosening of black ties to the Republicans gave them an opportunity to court black voters. Members of both parties cheered that it meant that African Americans would receive no special treatment from the government. Using the example of Jews excluded from Hilton's Hotel at Saratoga, newspapers argued that hotel, saloon, and boardinghouse managers could admit whomever they wished. It was "foolish" of Hilton to exclude Jews, read an article in the *Hartford Weekly Times*, "but no one questioned his right. No person, black or white, male or female, has a right to force himself or herself upon the premises and the bed and board of the owner of a hotel or a saloon." The Republican *Philadelphia Daily Evening Bulletin* summed up reaction to the decision, approving the return of black men to the ranks of all Americans. "Further advancement depends chiefly upon themselves, on their earnest pursuit of education, on their progress in morality and religion, on their thoughtful exercise of their duties as citizens, on their persistent practice of industry," it said. "They have it in their power to secure for themselves, by their own conduct, more really important 'rights' than can be given to them by any formal legislation of Congress."[29]

A dislike of the Civil Rights Act did not necessarily mean a blanket disregard for black rights. The Supreme Court still offered protection to black men trying to assert their right to suffrage; in 1884, reviewing what were known as the Ku Klux Klan cases, the Supreme Court in *Ex parte Yarbrough* determined that Congress could punish as a crime private interference with an individual's right to vote. More important to many African Americans on a daily basis was popular support for those African Americans who seemed to embrace the mainstream vision. Republican and Democratic newspapers celebrated successful black men like "Mr. John F. Cook, a colored man of character, who deservedly enjoys the respect of this entire community, who has held and administered with marked ability for years the responsible office of Collector of Taxes for the District of Columbia," and who did not approve of civil rights laws because he believed whites accorded fair treatment to African Americans who worked hard. "If all men of his race were like Mr. Cook there would never be any trouble on this subject," concluded the Republican *Philadelphia Daily Evening Bulletin*. The Democratic *San Francisco*

Examiner agreed, insisting that in San Francisco "there are . . . many intelligent and educated men and women of African descent," printing an interview with the Reverend Alexander Walters, who asserted that "in the West . . . race prejudice has died out." Even Wade Hampton, who had been elected to the Senate in 1879 (and who had mellowed considerably after losing a leg in a hunting accident the same day he was elected), declared unequivocally that black suffrage was permanently established.30

But middle-class Americans disliked African Americans like Ida B. Wells, who in 1884 insisted on her right to travel in the ladies railroad car for which she had bought a ticket rather than in the smoking car. When the conductor tried to drag her out of her seat, she recalled that "the moment he caught hold of my arm I fastened my teeth in the back of his hand. I had braced my feet against the seat in front and was holding to the back, and as he had already been badly bitten he didn't try it again by himself." With two other men he dragged her off the train; Wells sued the railroad. She later denied knowing that her actions were pathbreaking, but she must have known that hers was the first case in which a black southerner had challenged discrimination since the 1883 repeal of the Civil Rights Act. She won her case and $500 damages with the help of a white lawyer and a circuit court judge who had been a Union soldier, but lost on appeal. The appeals court reflected popular dislike of deliberate agitation for civil rights, concluding, "We think it is evident that the purpose of the defendant . . . was to harass with a view to this suit, and that her persistence was not in good faith to obtain a comfortable seat for the short ride."31

Americans committed to the idea of general economic harmony also had little patience with bellyaching farmers in the South or West. In the South, small farmers were increasingly squeezed off their land by large producers; western farmers faced that problem and also rising freight rates. Increases in freight rates in Nebraska nurtured the first state Alliance of farmers, which met and adopted a constitution in January 1881 and spread within a year and a half to Kansas, Iowa, Wisconsin, Illinois, Minnesota, and Michigan, as well as to New York and Texas. By October 1882, the third annual meeting of the Alliance reported 2,000 Alliances with a total membership of 100,000 farmers. But cheerful observers of southern agriculture had little patience with suffering farmers, reporting, for example, that "all the intelligent men . . . believe that the whole of Southern Virginia, and especially its tidewater portions, has within the last few years entered upon an era of greater prosperity than it has ever known, [and] this prosperity affects all classes, and had few serious drawbacks." In the West, Luna Kellie blamed the railroads for the death of her child and wanted the government to intervene in support of farmers, while in the East an article in *The Century* scolded that complaining farmers had brought their troubles on themselves by overspending their income. "The chances for a young man of average pluck and energy are unquestionably much better in the West than in the East," agreed the *Boston Globe.* "He shares the advantages of being among the first to open a fresh storehouse of natural wealth."[32]

Mainstream Americans could not accept that poor wages, dangerous working conditions, racism, lack of capital, or environmental disasters could keep hardworking individuals from success. Instead, they tried to force organized workers, agitating African Americans, Indians, and disaffected farmers to adopt an individualist vision. But even more troublesome for those insisting on economic harmony in America were business interests. Special interests from the poor end of the economic spectrum could influence politics by marshalling votes, but wealthy businessmen could use cash, which politicians needed to keep poor constituents happy. Men like Leland Stanford unabashedly poured money into politicians' pockets in order, as he put it, to keep "the noisy and demagogic element" from injuring railroad interests. In early 1884, the *New York Times* charged that sixteen senators "owe their election entirely to the indirect use of money and the exercise of corporate power and influence," and "the last Presidential election was determined by the use of money." The *Chicago Tribune* charged, "Behind every one of half of the portly and well-dressed members of the Senate can be seen the outlines of some corporation interested in getting or preventing legislation, or of some syndicate that has invaluable contracts or patents to defend or push." *Harper's Weekly* condemned "the rapidly increasing part which money plays in our elections and our government." By 1888, the U.S. Treasury ran an annual surplus of almost $120 million; the tariffs that protected business were so high that they brought in significantly more than the government used. To those nervous about the influence of business in government, this seemed proof positive that tariffs were not being used for anything but to enable robber barons to control the economy.[33]

Those tariffs were a godsend to Carnegie, who in 1880 had decided to expand his productions yet again. On April 1, 1881, he incorporated his iron companies, steel works, and coke plants as Carnegie Brothers & Company, Limited, with a capitalization of $5 million. Carnegie held more stock than the other six partners combined. In 1881, Carnegie opened his Pittsburgh

Bessemer Steel Company, employing 400 men and boys and covering sixty acres in Homestead, Pennsylvania; by 1885, 50,000 men and boys worked at the iron and steel furnaces and mills in the area around Pittsburgh, where they produced $102 million worth of iron and steel. Business was booming and growing increasingly powerful in American life. In California, Leland Stanford was determined to keep angry state legislators from hampering national corporations—Granger laws were "pure communism," he charged. He challenged a local effort to tax his Southern Pacific Railroad by hiring Republican Congressman Roscoe Conkling to argue that the authors of the Fourteenth Amendment designed that cornerstone of individual liberty not to protect individuals, but to protect corporations. Although the court did not rule on this dramatic (and ridiculous) assertion about the intent of the framers, they agreed with Conkling that the Fourteenth Amendment did protect corporations from state legislation.[34]

By 1883, corporations determined what people ate, what they wore, how they got to work, how they illuminated their homes. They even determined the time. Frustrated by the difficulties of creating time schedules when each town operated on its own local time, railroads developed standard railroad time. On Sunday, November 18, at 9:00 a.m., major cities in the nation switched to railroad time. This change made sense for the nation's increasingly professional citizens, but the change was not universally popular. "People . . . must eat, sleep and work . . . by railroad time," sighed a writer for the *Indianapolis Daily Sentinel*. "People will have to marry by railroad time. . . . Ministers will be required to preach by railroad time. . . . Banks will open and close by railroad time; notes will be paid or protested by railroad time." The influence of business in American life was frightening.[35]

In April 1884, fears that America was disintegrating because of the manipulation of government by special interests provoked a bloody riot in Cincinnati. The event that sparked the three days of rioting was the sentencing of William Berner for murdering his employer, stableman William Kirk. On December 24, 1883, Berner and fellow employee Joseph Palmer beat Kirk, strangled him, and tossed his body into the woods outside the city. On March 24, the jury convicted Berner not of murder, which carried a sentence of hanging, but of manslaughter. On March 28, he was sentenced to twenty years in prison.[36]

For the middle class in Cincinnati, and for those across the nation who closely followed the unfolding events in that city, Berner's trial proved that a government catering to special interests was a deadly peril. Cincinnati had been plagued by a high murder rate in the 1880s, and twenty-three accused murderers sat untried in the Cincinnati jail while the justice system slowly ground around to their cases. Cincinnati's citizens seethed in frustration at the government's inability to get rid of the criminals who threatened them. They charged that government inactivity resulted from officials' indebtedness to the ward politicians and lower-class voters they blamed for the murders. Cincinnati families watched the Berner trial suspiciously, determined that their will would be done.

On Friday, March 28, after the announcement of the sentencing, 8,000 of "the wisest and most prudent citizens" of the city, "well-known and respected citizens," met in the Music Hall to call for justice and a reform of the courts. Their meeting soon swept into the streets, becoming a mob of thousands that killed 56 and injured more than 200 over the next two days. The mob fought symbols of government authority, attacking the jail, police, and the few local militiamen willing to fire on them. On March 29, they burned the $700,000 courthouse to the ground. It took the state militia, armed with a Gatling gun capable of firing 600 rounds a minute, to quell the riot.[37]

Observers believed that the riot was sparked by an outpouring of frustration that the courts were controlled not by good Americans but by the criminal classes themselves through their control of government. As one writer reflected in the *Cincinnati Enquirer,* "So loosely had the law of Cincinnati been executed, and so long had a public sentiment like a raging volcano, been growing against this state of affairs, that when a self-confessed murderer was all but turned free to seek new victims, the best citizens of the Queen City could stand it no longer, but, like the lava from a volcano, swept everything before it, burning and carrying sorrow into many lives by cutting innocent lives short, in their endeavors to secure Berner, the murderer, and his brother murderers yet to be tried, and whom they feared would also be too leniently dealt with." The problem, *Harper's Weekly* explained, was that "intelligent citizens" had ceded politics to "venal politicians," who "dictate city charters and municipal legislation, and nominate candidates for office, including the lower and higher courts of law." Simply bemoaning universal suffrage or denouncing communism would not recover America, *Harper's Weekly* explained; laws must be stronger laws and their execution "swift and sure and solemn." If middle-class Americans were running government instead of the corrupt special interests currently in charge, eruptions of frustrated citizens like those in Cincinnati would not occur.[38]

Going into the campaign of 1884, both parties recognized the need to claim that they represented the American mainstream. The Democratic and

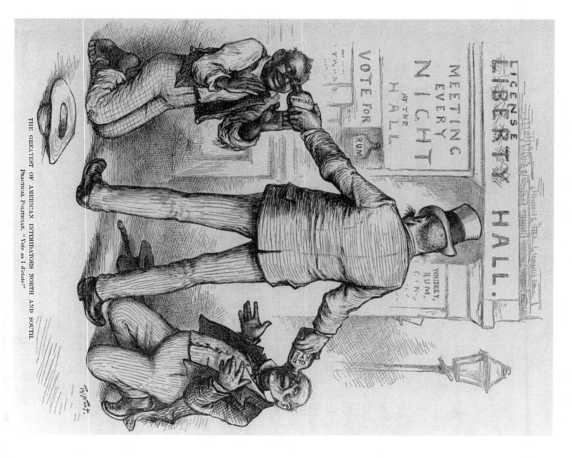

THE GREATEST OF AMERICAN INTIMIDATORS NORTH AND SOUTH.
PRACTICAL POLITICIAN. " Vote as I dictate!"

Figure 13. This November 7, 1885, *Harper's Weekly* cartoon was one of many in the 1880s that portrayed both African Americans and immigrants as tools of those who bought their loyalty with jobs or alcohol. In return for votes, reformers believed, politicians made sure that the justice system ignored crimes committed by their corrupt constituents. Courtesy of Harvard College Library.

Republican platforms had much in common. Both presented an idealized vision of the nation, asserting the equality of all men before the law, for example, calling it the duty of government "to mete out equal and exact justice to all citizens of whatever nativity, race, color, or persuasion—religious or political." Both called for "a free ballot and a fair count," code words for black suffrage, and argued for the preservation of state's rights within a federal system. Both defended judicious tariffs, taxes, and hard money, although each was vague about what any of these promises meant. Both called for the federal lands to be reserved for actual settlers, and both called for some sort of regulation of business—at least railroads—while endorsing the rights of property. Both supported soldiers' pensions. Both claimed to support laborers, although Democrats generally endorsed organized labor whereas Republicans, with their reputation of being the tools of business, had to add stronger language, supporting an eight-hour law, the Chinese Restriction Act, and the establishment of a National Bureau of Labor. The only point of contention between the policies outlined in the platforms was the role of government in the economy. Democrats insisted on a tariff for revenue only, while Republicans maintained that in order to promote productivity, tariffs must be made not only for revenue, but to "afford security to our diversified industries and protection to the rights and wages of the laborer; to the end that active and intelligent labor . . . may have its just reward."[39]

The Democratic platform identified Republican government as the tool of special interests. America had become a place where "Government, instead of being carried on for the general welfare, becomes an instrumentality for imposing heavy burdens on the many who are governed, for the benefit of the few who govern. Public servants thus become arbitrary rulers." The Republicans had become a party for enriching those who ran the country. Using the surplus to illustrate Republican corruption, Democrats complained that "crippling taxes" had produced an unprecedented surplus of more than $100 million, turning the government into a tax-gathering machine to redistribute wealth. The people had demanded a change in 1876 but were "defeated by a fraud which can never be forgotten, nor condoned." Then, in 1880, "the change demanded by the people was defeated by the lavish use of money contributed by unscrupulous contractors and shameless jobbers who had bargained for unlawful profits, or for high office." "The Republican party during its legal, its stolen, and its bought tenure of power, has steadily decayed in moral character and political capacity," it charged. While "it professes a preference for free institutions," it had "organized and tried to legalize a control of State elections by Federal troops." The Democrats promised to purify government, truly reflecting the will of the people.

Republicans countered by accusing the Democrats of fraud and violence to win elections, insisting that "the perpetuity of our institutions rests upon the maintenance of a free ballot, an honest count, and correct returns." They reminded voters that they supported the Civil Service Act and promised to continue to reform official life.

The election of 1884 became a referendum on the corruption of government by special interests. With both parties mouthing the same principles, the election came down to the candidates and what they represented. The Republican Party nominated two machine politicians: "Blaine, Blaine, James G. Blaine, the continental liar from the State of Maine," and John A. Logan of Illinois, a shady character who had taken control of the Grand Army of the Republic after the war to harness soldiers' votes to the Republican Party. Moderate Republicans greeted their nominations with dismay. The Republican Party "must plainly vindicate its claim to represent the moral intelligence and spirit of political reform and progress of the country," *Harper's Weekly* insisted. Under the Republicans, vast corporations had come to control politics, and rather than cleaning up Washington, party hacks had nominated for president one of the men most closely associated with corporate bribery. "The nomination . . . tends to identify the party with all that has most discredited it," *Harper's Weekly* sighed. "We are Republicans, but we are not slaves," the chairman of a meeting of Republicans in New Haven, Connecticut, announced when he protested party pressure to vote for Blaine. The party must, he declared, dedicate itself to "retrenchment, purity, and reform."[40]

As soon as the Republicans had made their nomination, independent Republicans hinted that the nomination of Democrat Grover Cleveland would win their votes. Cleveland had made a name for himself as a reform governor of New York, beating the Republican candidate by an astonishing 193,000 votes. "From what we have often said of his conduct as Governor," *Harper's Weekly* announced, "our readers will justly infer that it would give 'assurance of an honest, impartial, and efficient administration of the laws, without suspicion of personal ends or private interests.'" In July, the Democrats nominated the reformer Cleveland, and *Harper's Weekly* formally endorsed him, claiming that his impartial dedication to justice had won him the hatred of machine politicians. "We love him most for the enemies that he has made," the caption of a Nast cartoon agreed.[41]

Pulitzer's *New York World* had made Cleveland its candidate as early as 1883, and, as a competitor recalled, "flourished like a green bay-tree" when other major New York papers lent their support elsewhere. Pulitzer's *World* begged Congress to investigate corruption scandals to give the Democrats material for the upcoming campaign. It reported the Republican candidate Blaine "represents not only the machine of the Republican party, but the demoralizing and corruptive power of Wall Street, the money interests, the monopolies, corporations, and all protected, privileged, special classes. All that is reprehensible and base in our demoralized political system will naturally rally to his support." The Republicans, it said, stood for "the . . . use of the enormous Federal patronage designedly increased by Republican administrations as a means of perpetuating the power of the party." Led by Carl Schurz and including men like ex-governor Daniel Chamberlain of South Carolina, independent Republicans endorsed Cleveland at their meeting in New York City in July and they met frequently over the summer. In November, the votes of Independents helped to propel Cleveland to victory.[42]

Cleveland's election seemed a great triumph for evenhanded government. He had made no secret of his disdain for the "d——d everlasting clatter for offices," and in his inaugural address he called for smaller government, lower taxes, and a civil service system that would protect citizens from "the incompetency of public employees who hold their places solely as the reward of partisan service, and from the corrupting influence of those who promise and the vicious methods of those who expect such rewards." His peaceful inauguration in March 1885 seemed to promise racial harmony across the Union. In his inaugural address he declared his intention to protect black rights but also to demand African Americans' improvement. "The fact that they are citizens entitles them to all the rights due to that relation and charges them with all its duties, obligations, and responsibilities." This endorsement of the mainstream ideal of success through hard work rather than legislation—along with its refusal to acknowledge that racial discrimination made success illusive for many hardworking Americans—drew the support of the senate of the racist state of Indiana, which resolved that it "heartily concur[red] in [his] sentiments." So, too, did black New Yorker William Gross, who wrote Cleveland to tell him that his references to African Americans had been "well received" in New York and that he hoped his race would benefit from Cleveland's speech, meeting his suggestions for improvement "by their endeavour to become useful and Intelligent Citizens." A Nast cartoon on the cover of

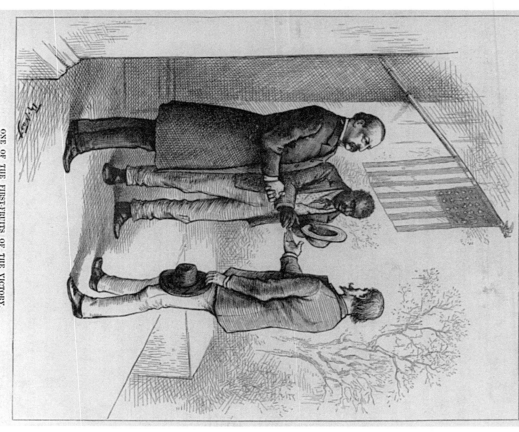

ONE OF THE FIRST-FRUITS OF THE VICTORY.

President-elect Cleveland. "Shake heartily, boys!"

Figure 14. Grover Cleveland's supporters believed that his election would produce clean government and racial reconciliation, as Thomas Nast indicated in this *Harper's Weekly* cartoon from November 1884. Courtesy of Harvard College Library.

Harper's Weekly after the election showed two mainstream men, one black and one white, shaking hands in front of President Cleveland.[43]

In December 1884, this vision seemed on the verge of reality. That month, the World's Industrial and Cotton Exposition opened in New Orleans, a city of about 225,000. It trumpeted the growing industrial strength of the South (despite financial mismanagement that had the fair unfinished for most of its existence) and indicated southern interest in developing trade with Latin America as well as Cuba. Visitors to the fair noted that the South seemed to have put the past behind it. "The mind of the South to-day is on the development of its resources, upon the rehabilitation of its affairs," one visitor commented. Southerners had "the same interest in the general prosperity of the country that exists at the North—the anxiety that the country should prosper, acquit itself well, and stand well with the other nations." Northern visitors saw much to admire in the South. "There is no crowding of population into tenement houses in New Orleans," one noted. "The poorest laborer that rolls cotton-bales on the levee can afford a three-room cottage for his family, where there is plenty of light, air, and shade."[44]

The role of African Americans in the Exposition also revealed a mainstream sensibility. In a dramatic symbolic gesture, the fair organizers had borrowed the Liberty Bell to exhibit at the exposition and had organized a "colored exhibition" for the main hall. The "colored exhibits" garnered widespread approval. The *American Missionary* noted the fine quality of the work there, ranging from "examination papers . . . showing proficiency in penmanship, spelling, arithmetic, algebra, geometry, free drawing, grammar, and translations from the classics," to "cabinet-making; upholstery; tin-smithing; black-smithing; . . . agricultural products, including all the cereals and fruits raised in the country; . . . patented inventions and improvements"; and so on. In the year after the Supreme Court declared civil rights legislation unconstitutional, the *American Missionary* concluded that this creditable showing proved that "the negro race can enter every profession and calling in which the white man is found," and if permitted to work, "in less than half a century there will not be a trade, nor profession, nor calling in which black men will not be found in the front. There will be preachers and professors, and editors, and physicians, and lawyers, and statesmen, and teachers, and bankers, and business men, and artisans, and mechanics and farmers, of African descent." Visiting the exposition, Twain's *Gilded Age* coauthor Charles Dudley Warner agreed and concluded: "With . . . education and with diversified industry, the social question will settle itself, as it does the world over. . . . In New Orleans the street cars are free to all colors; at the Exposition white and colored people mingled freely, talking and looking at what was of common interest." He noted professional African Americans—including "a colored clergyman in his surplice seated in the chancel of the most important white Episcopal church in New Orleans, assisting in the service"—as well as a widespread desire among African Americans for education.[45]

The political significance of the colored exhibits also revealed the darker side of the mainstream vision. Warner's hope about race relations and willingness to accord equality to successful black entrepreneurs was tainted by his belief that "the mass" of African Americans was far from equality. "No one . . . can see . . . the ignorant mass," he wrote, "slowly coming to moral consciousness, without a recognition of the magnitude of the negro problem." Of one thing he was sure; southerners would never permit "black" legislatures to rule them again. Would they disfranchise African Americans? "Well," Warner imagined an answer, "what would you do in Ohio or in Connecticut? Would you be ruled by a lot of ignorant field hands allied with a gang of plunderers?"[46]

The New Orleans exposition was a window not only on mainstream racial ideas, but also on the position of middle-class American women in society. In honor of her presidency of the Woman's Department of a Boston fair in 1882, Julia Ward Howe was invited to preside over "a woman's department in a great World's Fair to be held in New Orleans." Upon arriving in November, Howe found no woman's building, no timber to build one, and no funds to buy timber. Howe and her committee raised money through benefit concerts and lectures, then threw together an exhibit that ran heavily to traditional women's handiwork—beautiful quilts (one with 100,584 pieces of silk), decorated porcelain, and needlework. The exhibit also showed women's work in silk-culture, their "scientific analyses of food adulterations," books, and inventions. Prominent reviewers of the exposition admired the handiwork but thought the women's exhibit did not go far enough. "Woman's work is so entangled with that of man in a thousand lines of effort, that it cannot be separated, ticketed with a feminine label, and put on exhibition," complained one man. "An enormous amount of the labor, skill, and taste employed to carry on the processes of our modern life comes from women's hands and brains. . . . Nine-tenths of the educational exhibit is in reality women's work, and a majority of the fabrics and wares which fill the Main Building have probably received some touch in making or decoration from her hand. If it were possible to present a picture of what woman does to-day in America . . .

and to contrast it with a view of her limited field half a century ago, when closely confined to household duties, none of the revolutions of modern times which have set the world forward would appear so significant and so far-reaching."[47]

As the New Orleans exposition made clear, Americans adhering to the mainstream vision rejected the idea of a government that responded to the needs of special interests, but the exposition also suggested that they might entertain the idea of an active government if it would benefit the "general interest." The growing power of women began to pull the idea of active government into acceptability. Rather than demanding government action for special interests, middle-class women and their husbands began to call for government activism to defend the individualist household, the center, as they saw it, of American society. This argument depended on a critical change in women's activism. The insistence of radical reformers that women had an absolute human right to equality in America had fallen increasingly into disfavor as their cause became associated with both communism and free love at the same time that widespread suffrage seemed to threaten to radicalize American government.

As the call for women's rights based on principles of human rights was weakening, the call for women's rights based on domesticity grew more powerful. Led by women like Julia Ward Howe, the women's club movement of the immediate postwar years accepted the idea that women had special identities as wives and mothers, then argued for societal reforms on the grounds that women could not be good wives and mothers if subjected to the poverty, danger, and immorality of industrial life. Women's clubs had become reform societies by 1874, when the Women's Christian Temperance Union (WCTU) formed to fight for the suffrage and other changes under the rubric of domesticity. These powerful women echoed middle-class values, advocating female suffrage and other reforms as a means to outweigh the political influence of disaffected workers, African Americans, and industrialists.

In the early 1880s, the discovery of germ theory gave a huge push to the idea that women as mothers had special interests in cleaning up society. Once Louis Pasteur established that diseases came not from bad "humors" or night air, but from tiny organisms that multiplied in unsanitary conditions, filth was no longer just an aesthetic problem. "Uncleanly streets, unpleasant odors, a scanty supply of water, defective drains, vice, ignorance, neglect, sweep away old and young," explained *Harper's Weekly*, "but do their work chiefly among children." "Disease hit "the working classes, the industrious and thriving" in "crowded neighborhoods" the hardest, but from there spread "to the homes of the wealthy." Blaming city governments for neglect of sanitation, *Harper's Weekly* insisted that "[it] is the interest of all to unite in demanding from the city officials new and almost undivided attention to the health of the people."[48]

The need to protect what mainstream Americans believed was an ideal home for nurturing good Americans led to the acceptance of social welfare legislation. Samuel Gompers had little patience with the general societal reforms that T. V. Powderly's Knights of Labor backed and worked instead for small gains. With this practical view of labor reform, he joined forces with Theodore Roosevelt to help his workers. Gompers's cigarmakers' union introduced a bill to stop tenement manufacture of cigars. Roosevelt was a member of the committee assigned to investigate conditions in the tenement houses. He was probably put there with the idea that he would oppose Gompers's legislation, for, as he said, "the respectable people I knew were against it; it was contrary to . . . political economy of the *laissez faire* kind; and the business men . . . shook their heads and said that it was designed to prevent a man doing . . . as he had a right to do with what was his own." But he accepted Gompers's invitation to tour the tenements, and the conditions he found there horrified him. Multiple families crowded into a few filthy rooms, where they worked from dawn into the night.

Roosevelt's problem with these conditions was based not on an absolute human right to safety or cleanliness but rather on what such conditions would do to America. They "rendered it impossible for the families of the tenement-house workers to live so that the children might grow up fitted for the exacting duties of American citizenship." Roosevelt became an ardent champion of Gompers's bill and was disgusted when judges overturned it, claiming that the law was "an assault upon the 'hallowed' influences of 'home.'" Roosevelt recalled that the case showed him that the courts "were not necessarily the best judges of what should be done to better social and industrial conditions. . . . The people with whom I was most intimate were apt to praise the courts for just such decisions as this, and to speak of them as bulwarks against disorder and barriers against demagogic legislation. These were the same people with whom the judges who rendered these decisions were apt to foregather at social clubs, or dinners, or in private life. Very naturally they all tended to look at things from the same standpoint." Roosevelt became a staunch advocate of government defense of middle-class America.

Despite his privileged position, Theodore Roosevelt knew the dangers of low health standards in the city. New York City had slashed municipal budgets after the Tweed scandal, leaving the city crowded and dirty, with "a death-rate almost approaching that of St. Petersburg," one man recalled. On February 14, 1884, Roosevelt's mother died of typhoid fever—transmitted by food or water that had been contaminated by sewage—in the family home in New York City. Only two hours later, Theodore's adored wife, Alice Hathaway, died from kidney failure, caused probably by an untreated strep infection that had traveled out of the crowded tenements and into her wealthy home, killing her just two days after she gave birth to the couple's first child. After slashing a black *X* in his diary, a devastated Roosevelt recorded: "The light has gone out of my life." For men like Roosevelt and for their wives, the corrupt politics that prevented officers of the law from cleaning up the city streets (and the adulterated food and other dangers of modern life) literally threatened their home life. Surely the regulation of such things was a legitimate expansion of government power, they thought.[49]

Trying to move on from his wife's death, Roosevelt was a delegate to the Republican National Convention in June, where he fought bitterly against the nomination of Blaine and along with three other independent Republicans tried unsuccessfully to secure the nomination of reform Senator George F. Edmunds. Failing this, he gave up on his normal life. Packing his bags, he set out for the badlands of Dakota Territory to heal his wounds in the great West, a land where, many eastern Americans thought, rural individuals still controlled their own lives. Indeed, in the West, Roosevelt found the true America for which he had been fighting in the East. "It was still the Wild West in those days," Roosevelt recalled, "the West of the Indian and the buffalo-hunter, the soldier and the cow-puncher: "It was a land of vast silent spaces, of lonely rivers, and of plains where the wild game stared at the passing horseman. It was a land of scattered ranches, of herds of long-horned cattle, and of reckless riders who unmoved looked in the eyes of life or of death. In that land we led a free and hardy life, with horse and with rifle. . . . We knew toil and hardship and hunger and thirst; and we saw men die violent deaths . . . but we felt the beat of hardy life in our veins, and ours was the glory of work and the joy of living."[50]

It was the West of a poor man's dream, where individuals could make a fortune, it seemed. The early 1880s were the best of the cattle boom years. In 1883, prime steers sold at $45 to $60, and the cattle fattened on the free grass that grew on federal land, railroad land, or Indian reservations and needed only poorly paid cowboys to get them to market. Newspapers wrote of 40 percent profits in the cattle industry, and books like *Beef Bonanza, or How to Get Rich on the Plains* (1881) induced investors to pour capital into the West, bringing new breeds into the West's stock to develop a fatter animal than the lean Texas longhorns. A series of mild winters in the early 1880s enabled the herds to multiply until by the mid-1880s observers estimated there were 7.5 million animals on the plains north of Texas. Charles Goodnight had taken advantage of the rush of foreign investment in the West, joining with wealthy Englishman John George Adair to carve 25,000 acres out of Palo Duro Canyon to form the J. A. Ranch. By 1882, the clear profits on the enterprise were over half a million dollars.[51]

"I owe more than I can ever express to the West," Roosevelt wrote. There he met his ideal American: hardworking, loyal, helpful, independent. "I could not speak with too great affection and respect of the great majority of my friends, the hard-working men and women who dwelt for a space of perhaps a hundred and fifty miles along the Little Missouri. I was always as welcome at their houses as they were at mine. Everybody worked, everybody was willing to help everybody else, and yet nobody asked any favors. The same thing was true of the people whom I got to know fifty miles east and fifty miles west of my own range, and of the men I met on the round-ups." Roosevelt blessed the people of the West for "the insight which working and living with them enabled me to get into the mind and soul of the average American of the right type." Black cowboy Nat Love shared Roosevelt's vision. "In the history of the frontier there is recorded countless heroic deeds performed, deeds and actions that required an iron nerve, self denial in all that these words imply, the sacrificing of one life to save the life of a stranger or a friend," he wrote. Men were men in the West, unlike wealthy New Yorkers, they "lived and died for a principle, and in the line of duty." "There a man's work was to be done, and a man's life to be lived, and when death was to be met, he met it like a man."[52]

Key to this vision of the ideal American was an absolute equality of individuals according to their individual merits rather than their social status. As an elite easterner, slim and nearsighted to boot, Roosevelt could expect rough westerners to look at him with suspicion. Thanks to his ability to work hard and keep his mouth shut, they did just the opposite, he thought. "They soon accepted me as a friend and fellow-worker who stood on an equal footing with them, and I believe the most of them have kept their feeling for me ever since." For his part, Roosevelt returned the favor, insisting on the equality of his friends in later years when he was president. "No guests were ever more welcome at the White House than these old friends of the cattle ranches and the cow camps—the men with whom I had ridden the long circle and eaten at the tail-board of a chuck-wagon—whenever they turned up at Washington during my Presidency," he recalled. In a later autobiography he wrote of an old friend "who appeared at Washington one day just before lunch, a huge, powerful man who, when I knew him, had been distinctly a fighting character." With the British ambassador on his way to lunch, Roosevelt invited his old friend to join them but warned him: "'Remember, Jim, that if you shot at the feet of the British Ambassador to make him dance, it would be likely to cause international complications,' to which Jim responded with unaffected horror, 'Why, Colonel, I shouldn't think of it, I shouldn't think of it!'"[53]

There was no contradiction between Roosevelt's desire to use government to protect the middle-class family and his celebration of the individualistic West. Indeed, the idealized image of the American West increasingly emphasized individualism, economic opportunity, and political freedom at the same time that mainstream justification for government activism grew. Both were a reaction to popular fears of government as a tool of special interests. The federal government remained critical to western life, but many westerners hated the government and declared themselves its enemies. Roosevelt noted a sharp line in the West "between stealing citizens' horses and stealing horses from the Government or the Indians." Westerners, Roosevelt believed, "recognized their obligations to one another," but to them "both the Government and the Indians seemed alien bodies, in regard to which the laws of morality did not apply."[54]

In the West, long-standing conflicts between gangs and continuing hostility from the war developed into antigovernment convictions that were popularized by gunslingers like Jesse and Frank James and Billy the Kid. The trouble between the James brothers and the law began during the Civil War. Jesse was a guerrilla with Quantrill's Raiders in the violent chaos Missouri suffered during the conflict. When the war was over, Jesse claimed he was persecuted by Union soldiers who were anxious to exact revenge for his wartime activities. They shot him when he tried to get home after the war; they murdered his wartime comrades. They "crep up to my mothers house and hurled a misle of war (a 32-pound shell) in a room among a family of innocent women and cheldren murdering my 8-year-old brother and tore my mothers right arm off & wounded several others of the family, & then fired the house," charged Jesse James in a public letter protesting his persecution at the hands of Republicans. He expected nothing better from the machine politicians who ruled the state with an iron fist but objected to his treatment when Democratic papers also charged him with crimes. "It is enough persecution for the northern papers to persecute us without the papers in the South, persecuting us, the land we fought for four years to save from northern tyranny, to be persecuted by papers claiming to be Democratic, is against reason."[55]

Jesse James died while hiding under the assumed name of Tom Howard in 1882, murdered by comrade Bob Ford, "that dirty little coward who shot Mr. Howard and laid poor Jesse in his grave," as the song goes. In 1882, Frank Triplett's *The Life, Times, and Treacherous Death of Jesse James* revisited James's career. "An angel of light" persecuted by thugs using the mantle of legitimacy given them by the government, Triplett explained, James decided finally that since he was already slandered as a horse thief and bank robber, he might as well have "the game as the name." Anyone could remember, Triplett insisted, that after the war "the entire machinery and control of the government, laws, courts, etc., were in the hands of the enemies of those who fought in the armies of the South. No southern man could vote, hold office, or *sit on a jury*." Their manhood forced men like James to "turn upon that law that hounded them and that society that hunted them, and outrage and defy it." Indeed, James's targets were ones that represented Republican government: banks, railroads, and express companies. Significantly, Triplett recounted James's unwillingness to rob Confederate soldiers, once returning a wallet and watch when a southern veteran identified himself.[56]

According to Triplett, the Republicans, represented by the Pinkerton detectives hired by the express companies robbed by the James gang, responded to James by acting as barbarously as "Cheyennes or Comanches" on the warpath, bombing women and children in James's stepmother's house. Jesse James finally fell to a turncoat coward, coerced and coddled by Missouri Governor T. T. Crittenden himself, who denied Jesse the right to a trial by persuading Bob and Charles Ford to kill him. When the Fords pleaded guilty to the murder and a judge sentenced them to death, Crittenden promptly pardoned them and paid them the bounty that he had placed on Jesse James's head. Democratic newspapers were outraged. The *St. Charles (Mo.) Journal* was happy to be rid of James but protested that the manner of his death was "dastardly, cowardly, and criminal. The State has no right to procure the murder of any man in times of peace." Even Carl Schurz, writing during his brief stint as editor of the *New York Evening Post*, agreed. Crittenden had "hired an assassin," as if he were a potentate. "The Governor's policy . . . was most unpopular," *Scribner's Magazine* noted. "Infinite hatred and scorn were visited upon the betrayers." For many westerners, and easterners, too, Crittenden's actions seemed to confirm the association of government with cowardice, betrayal, and criminality.[57]

Members of the James gang were unquestionably involved in a number of murders and robberies, but opponents of the Republican administration portrayed them as ideal Americans, quite different from tainted politicians and businessmen. Triplett insisted that the signature of Jesse and Frank James's gang was "their coolness in danger, their perfect nerve . . . , their rallying around a disabled comrade, a want of unnecessary brutality, and a desire to avoid the taking of human life." He contrasted these qualities with the continued failures of the railroad detectives, posses, and even the Pinkertons sent to capture the men, who were not up against "ordinary thieves of large cities," but against men "of equal or greater skill, more endurance and overpowering bravery." Jesse James's wife was an ideal woman, too, "a perfect blonde . . . of amiable temper, and loving disposition . . . true and noble," who hated evil but knew that James had been "persecuted and maligned."[58]

This image of western outlaws was widespread. Nat Love claimed to have known Jesse and Frank James well. "They were true men, brave, kind, generous and considerate, and while they were robbers and bandits, yet what they took from the rich they gave to the poor," Love insisted. "That is why they were so popular and hard for the law to capture." "Besides, wrote Love, "if they were robbers, by what name are we to call . . . the great trusts, corporations and brokers, who have for years been robbing the people of this country. . . . The only difference between them and the James brothers is that the James brothers stole from the rich and gave to the poor, while these respected members of society steal from the poor to make the rich richer."[59]

Love also defended Billy the Kid despite the fact that the Kid's story was complicated by overwhelming evidence indicating that he was, in fact, an unstable longtime thief and murderer. The tale that made him famous had the same antigovernment overtones as the James story, with a healthier supply of antimonopoly sentiment thrown in. By the 1880s, a feud between cattle ranchers in remote New Mexico Territory had blossomed into an all-out war that caught the popular imagination as a struggle to establish an economically and politically just society. Like many of the national struggles of the day, the Lincoln County War started with the creation of an economic and political monopoly. Controlling both the lucrative beef contracts for supplying the military at Fort Stanton and the only store in the huge county, cattle ranchers Lawrence G. Murphy and James Dolan and their supporters—a gang locally called "the House of Murphy"—grew powerful. They gathered the reins of politics into their own hands, appointing the sheriffs and controlling the judges. Traveling through the territory in 1877, Teddy Blue was anxious to get away, certain that trouble was brewing.[60]

Lincoln attorney Alexander A. McSween and wealthy newcomer Englishman John Henry Tunstall, backed by cattle baron John S. Chisum, began to challenge this monopoly in 1877 with both lawsuits and guns. The "House" branded the McSween gang's activities illegal. When a sheriff's posse controlled by Murphy men killed Tunstall on February 18, 1878, after he had surrendered his own gun, the group's supporters vowed revenge. Known as "the Regulators," this group included one of Tunstall's employees, nineteen-year-old William H. Bonney, who had left a murder charge and his real name, Henry McCarty, behind in Arizona. "Billy the Kid" joined the Regulators after being arrested by Sheriff William Brady, a member of the House of Murphy, and the Kid was hardly the sort of man to quiet a feud. The Regulators captured the Murphy men who murdered Tunstall, but the accused were killed on the way to jail—probably by the Kid. The Kid was also part of the gang that ambushed and killed Sheriff Brady and his deputy, and by April 1878 the Kid led the Regulators. McSween's murder removed any restraint the Regulators had previously exercised, and they freely stole horses and cattle from the Murphy gang.

Worried by the growing lawlessness in New Mexico Territory, President Rutherford B. Hayes replaced the territorial governor with Civil War veteran Lew Wallace (whose experience in the Lincoln County War would later inform his novel *Ben Hur*). Wallace offered amnesty to the Regulators, but a complicated set of negotiations ultimately excluded the Kid. He went back to rustling cattle and pulling his trigger, preying on Chisum now as well as the Murphy gang, angry that Chisum had not paid him "fighting wages" for the time he spent as a Regulator. He was finally killed by lawman Pat Garrett in 1881.

The popular press lionized western outlaws like Jesse James and Billy the Kid despite their criminal histories, portraying them as representatives of American individualism, family, and loyalty in the face of a large, hostile government tied to business. In 1880, Joseph A. Dacus published *Life and Adventures of Frank and Jesse James and the Younger Brothers, the Noted Western*

Outlaws, which established the outlaws as representatives of a free West, uncorrupted by government. The next year, J. W. Buel published *The Border Bandits: An Authentic and Thrilling History of the Noted Outlaws JESSE AND FRANK JAMES and Their BANDS OF HIGHWAYMEN*, defending the James brothers much as Triplett had done. Billy the Kid was harder to canonize, but cowboy Charlie Siringo managed to do just that in his popular 1885 book, *A Texas Cowboy; Or, Fifteen Years on the Hurricane Deck of a Spanish Pony*, which sold several hundred thousand copies over the next thirty years. Siringo had known the Kid and presented him as a happy-go-lucky youth who fell into crime by accident, stood loyally by his friend Tunstall, was calm and funny in the face of danger, and was well loved by those he helped. He was "one of the coolest-headed, and most daring young outlaws that ever lived," Siringo concluded admiringly.[61]

The image of the West as a land of political and economic freedom enthralled easterners of all backgrounds, but it had special resonance for southern African Americans. When Nat Love thought back on his life in Tennessee, he recalled how very hard he and his family had worked in the South, grubbing in the fields, picking nuts and berries, simply to survive as whites cheated them. In contrast, he remembered the West as a great land of opportunity where his race had not mattered, although in reality it must have. By 1880, for southern African Americans this image gained power as they contrasted it to conditions in the South. In the wake of the elections of 1876, when "reformers" and Democrats like Wade Hampton gained control of southern governments, it was unclear what rights—if any—southern blacks would retain. In 1879 and 1880, more than 20,000 black southerners headed west. There, they thought, they could hold jobs without being cheated of wages and could own land and homes. But for these "Exodusters," the West represented more than economic opportunity. There, they believed, they could vote without harassment from white supremacists, and they could protect their families. They could have "true citizenship" in America, the right to work hard, earn money, accumulate property, and have a say in the government that protected life, liberty, and property. Their rosy dreams overstated the opportunities for African Americans in the depressed prairies and underestimated white prejudices there, but there was certainly more opportunity for African Americans in the West than in the South.[62]

Nat Love had been an impoverished former slave in Tennessee, but out west he had the opportunity to mingle with one of the most famous men of the era: Buffalo Bill. William F. Cody was a fabulous showman, and in 1883, he pulled together former cowboys and Indians to create Buffalo Bill's Wild West Show. The show sought to deliver the drama of the frontier to those who had not seen it. Roping and horse-handling contests had been a natural outgrowth of cattle roundups, and enterprising westerners had begun running local rodeos in the 1870s. Building a following as he portrayed himself on stage and in an 1879 autobiography which promised to tell the story of "Buffalo Bill, the famous hunter, scout and guide," Cody was becoming the face of the West. "He was a good fellow, and while he was no such great shakes as a scout as he made the eastern people believe," Teddy Blue recalled, "still we all liked him, and we had to hand it to him because he was the only one that had brains enough to make that Wild West stuff pay money." Cody cultivated his image carefully. Teddy Blue went on, "I remember one time he came into a saloon in North Platte, and he took off his hat, and that long hair of his that he had rolled up under his hat fell down on his shoulders. It always bothered him, so he rolled it up and stuck it back under his hat again, and Brady, the saloon man, says: 'Say, Bill, why the hell don't you cut the damned stuff off?' And Cody says: 'If I did, I'd starve to death.'"63

Buffalo Bill later wrote that he wanted to keep the frontier alive because it was disappearing. It was true that by the mid-1880s, the plains world of 1865 had been destroyed. By 1884, a writer in *Harper's Weekly* condemned the "buffalo butchers" who had all but exterminated the bison. The free Indians were also a dying breed. In 1885, Sitting Bull joined Buffalo Bill's Wild West Show to earn money for his tribe, for Cody was one of the few people willing to hire Indians and pay them decent wages. Geronimo was the last serious holdout of the western Indians; his raids and the army's search for him were rare enough to earn front page coverage in *Harper's Weekly* and *Frank Leslie's Illustrated Newspaper* in 1886. The cowboys in Buffalo Bill's Wild West Show represented a world of the past. Wet years at the beginning of the 1880s had enabled cattlemen to move too many cattle onto the plains, and a bovine lung disease spreading across state lines made the national government step in to quarantine exposed herds. Then, when drought years reduced forage, cattle went weakened into the terrible winter of 1886–7. In the northern range, cattlemen lost up to 90 percent of their herds. The days of free-ranging cattle were over, and cattlemen settled into ranching, breeding higher-quality beef rather than focusing on quantity.64

The western reality might be one of cattle ranches and reservations, but Cody brought eastern crowds a very different image. He showed them buffalo hunts, Indians and Indian fights, emphasizing the reality of his stories despite how carefully he staged them. But Buffalo Bill's West was not simply a great show, it had a political theme, too. It was a story of the prowess of individual Americans pitted against nature in the form of buffaloes, horses, and Indians. There were no government surveyors in Buffalo Bill's Wild West Show, no railroad grants, no slogging army campaigns, and no railroad barons like Leland Stanford manipulating politics. The audience saw brave men riding, roping, shooting, and challenging the lawless bandits and Indians who stood in their way, and the program assured them that everything they saw was true. The West, the show emphasized, was really America, a land untroubled by the racial and regional tensions of the East. It was a place where individuals used their wits and strength to overcome savagery without the interference of government. It was a heritage every American shared, as all had pushed the frontier across the continent. Ironically, even Cody's Indians seemed to embrace this vision as they adopted roles in a capitalist enterprise for the money it brought. Cody's show was a roaring success. By 1887, Buffalo Bill could boast, "I kick worse than any quartermaster's mule ever kicked if I don't clear a thousand dollars a day."[65]

Nothing made the antigovernment, individualistic theme of the West clearer than a Nast cartoon published in *Harper's Weekly* in 1886. In it, Buffalo Bill holds a theater curtain back for two warlike Indians, a black cowboy, and a white westerner, showing them eastern government. A board of aldermen hands bags of money to a fat politician, who is standing on a "bribery box" dumping it into a jury box. Men in a jury box, watching, sit under a sign announcing "We Do Not Agree!" The caption read: "WELL MAY THE 'WILD WEST' ASK, *IS THIS THE CIVILIZED EAST?*" In the pure West, easterners thought, such scenes of political corruption were unheard of, even to so-called savages.[66]

Theodore Roosevelt brought the western antigovernment image of true citizenship to eastern politics in his 1886 campaign for New York City mayor. He drew on western imagery to prove that he represented a pure, impartial government that was beholden to no special interests and treated all citizens equally. During the campaign, the *New York Times* reprinted a letter purported to be from a settler in Dickinson, Dakota, to the *Newburyport Herald*, telling the story of Roosevelt's capture of three horse thieves. Roosevelt, the author claimed, chased the "roughs" 100 miles down a river, "covered them with his rifles, disarmed them, brought them 150 miles across the country to Dickinson, and turned them over to the Sheriff." The author concluded, "Only such men, men of courage and energy, can hope to succeed in this new,

WELL MAY THE "WILD WEST" ASK, IS THIS THE CIVILIZED EAST?

Figure 15. In Thomas Nast's ironic commentary on government corruption from December 1886, showman Buffalo Bill holds back a stage curtain to show "savage" westerners—including two Indians and what appears to be a black cowboy—the apparent bribery that is passing as "civilization" in the East. Courtesy of Harvard College Library.

beautiful, but undeveloped country." Another letter reprinted from the *Sioux Falls (Dakota Territory) Press* described Roosevelt as "a Dakota cowboy . . . a whole-souled, clear-headed, high-minded gentleman," with such "force of character" that he had once protected stock thieves from a lynch mob by reminding them: "Boys, this isn't right. We have laws and Judges and juries by which these men can be tried and punished if found guilty." With his western fairness, it seemed, Roosevelt would return government to an ideal, old-time purity. "With Mr. Roosevelt in the Mayor's office," an editorial in the *New York Times* read, "all classes would have the security of his integrity, his courage, his justness, and his independence." Another writer even more explicitly connected western life and clean government, claiming that when Roosevelt stopped cowboys "from hanging a couple of cattle thieves whom he himself took to court and had tried and imprisoned for their crime, he showed the spirit in which he would administer the laws—with justice, courage, and energy."[67]

Roosevelt's opponents were special interest politicians, his supporters insisted. Democrat Abram S. Hewitt "distinctly represents the policy of . . . party control, of partisan control in municipal affairs," and his object was "to divide the offices and patronage among the leaders and workers of the party, and to strengthen it as a political organization," claimed the *New York Times*. Labor reform candidate Henry George represented the power of disaffected laborers who wanted to harness the government to pursue their own interest against employers. Workers hoped to stop police officers from interfering in their demonstrations, strikes, and intimidation of those who refused to join them. Roosevelt alone would take on "the task of rooting out abuses, exposing corruption, extirpating fraud, and elevating and purifying the public service; who would make appointments to office with a view solely to efficiency and honesty . . . who would not be swerved by party considerations or party influence from the ends he had in view." He would restore government to those who wanted nothing from it but the evenhanded management of city affairs with special benefits to none.[68] The *Baltimore American* pointed out that electing Roosevelt mayor would save New York City taxpayers several hundred thousand dollars a year.[69]

Roosevelt repeatedly defined an approach to government that echoed mainstream values. "I will faithfully serve every citizen of this great city," he maintained in front of wildly enthusiastic crowds. "I don't care what his creed, his birthplace, or his color. All I ask is, is he trying to fulfill the duties of

American citizenship? If so he is entitled to his full rights, and so far as it is in my power I will see that he shall have those rights protected."[70]

So horrified were New Yorkers at the possibility of Henry George's election most threw their votes behind the traditional Democratic candidate Hewitt, and Roosevelt lost. But his abortive run for mayor was significant. His demand for government purged of special interests and representing all good citizens—lessons Roosevelt took from the West—spoke for middle-class Americans.

In the 1880s, middle-class Americans consolidated their identity around the idea that individuals could rise on their own through hard work. Increasingly, this vision took its contours from popular perceptions of life in the West, where, it seemed, everyone was welcome if only they were willing to put their shoulder to the wheel. This middle-class vision appeared to be inclusive, welcoming African Americans and anyone who embraced these values. At the same time, it explicitly excluded anyone who seemed to belong to a group that argued that there were class interests in society that must be addressed by government. "The mass" of African Americans, labor activists, and activist women were excluded from this mainstream acceptance. It did not matter that Ida B. Wells was a productive, upwardly mobile member of society; she was not welcome to participate equally in society so long as she tried to get the government to protect her right to do so. Mainstream Americans perceived government activism as bowing to those who wanted extra privileges rather than as an attempt to guarantee the same rights to all. This fear, too, was encouraged by increasing attention to the West, where government was hated as a tool of Republicans, businessmen, and special interests. Paradoxically, though, part of the individualist vision included a homemaking wife, who was increasingly calling for activist government to protect her ability to care for her family. Tucked neatly within the middle-class dislike of government activism for special interests was a willingness to use the government to protect the middle-class individualist.

CHAPTER SEVEN

1886–1892

The Struggle Renewed

Julia Ward Howe may or may not have seen Buffalo Bill's Wild West Show. It would have been unlike her to go to such a rowdy public production, where spectators drank and yelled and stamped their boots on the wooden grandstands. But she loved theater so much that her first reaction to Lincoln's assassination was to worry that the actor Booth's "atrocious act, which was consummated in a very theatrical manner, is enough to ruin . . . the theatrical profession." Howe fervently embraced the image that Buffalo Bill portrayed of a society purged of special interests, yet she supported the peculiar expansion of the American government in the 1890s to clean up society. Indeed, women like Howe drove that increasing government activism. "Like so many others, I saw the cruel wrongs and vexed problems of our social life, but I did not know that hidden away in its own midst was a reserve force destined to give precious aid in the righting of wrongs, and in the solution of discords," she once told an audience. Finding their strength, mainstream women began to agitate for government protection of the individualist home.[1]

In 1886, the illumination of the torch of the Statue of Liberty showed optimistic New Yorkers—and other Americans—that the nation could accomplish anything if only the government didn't fall prey to special interests. On the night of November 1, 1886, tugs, sloops, rowboats, sailboats, and even two men-of-war floated in New York Harbor while throngs crowded wharves, rooftops, and bridges to watch the statue light up for the first time. Accompanied by a burst of fireworks, the lights came on and the crowd yelled itself hoarse, unable to be heard over the horns and bells of the tugs. One besotted reporter was less impressed by Liberty's political import than the fact that her lights outshone the stars. "The torch bore eight lamps, which burned as one, with an aggregate power of 48,000 candles. Six other lamps of 6,000 candle power each with parabolic reflectors" illuminated the statue itself, he wrote. The electrical generator was a gift from the American Electric Manufacturing Company and was "probably the largest in the world." A darker symbolism also connected the generosity of the American Electric Manufacturing Company and the symbol of American liberty: interest groups—here in the shape of businessmen—threatened to harness the American government to their own ends. But by now middle-class Americans were willing to increase government power to curb them.[2]

They took as their initial target big business, as it continued to consolidate and exercise more control over the national economy. Large corporations dominated most industries and were a prime illustration of an organized special interest strangling America's individualist ideology as it tried to dictate government policies. Trusts were the order of the day for industrialists, with corporations combining either formally or informally to manage the market. In order to attract business, New Jersey passed general incorporation laws in 1889 that allowed one company to hold stock in other concerns. This permitted the easy establishment of "holding companies," which brought together a number of enterprises under one controlling umbrella organization. There was a legal distinction between trusts and holding companies, but their aim and effect was the same: horizontal integration to control production and prices. The impulse to monopolies ran throughout the national economy, affecting household budgets. In 1895, even the lobstermen in Maine organized to stockpile their catch, create a shortage, and force up the price of this cheap food. On August 3, lobster in New York City cost eight to ten cents a pound, by August 10 it was fourteen cents a pound, and by August 13 had risen to twenty cents a pound, an outrageous sum for a household budget to absorb for what was then seen as an inferior food.[3]

Andrew Carnegie thought consolidation was a good thing, and his justification of it outraged those Americans who were already angry at the businessmen whose practices were manipulating the lives of consumers. In 1883, Carnegie had scooped up yet another competing steel mill in Homestead, Pennsylvania. Although this plant had a history of labor trouble, by 1886, when it was operating fully, it helped push Carnegie's earnings to almost $3 million. When his key manager declined a partnership and asked instead for "a hell of a big salary," Carnegie paid him $25,000 a year, the same paycheck that went into the pocket of the president of the United States. In 1889, Carnegie offered to readers of the *North American Review* his thoughts on industrial America. Promptly retitled "The Gospel of Wealth," the essay became a classic justification of workers' ill treatment by industrialists, although Carnegie clearly meant it to chastise the Jim Fisks and Jay Goulds of the nation as well as striking workers. Carnegie argued that the concentration of wealth and industry in the hands of a few was not only inevitable in an industrial system, but also beneficial so long as the rich used their money wisely. Civilization itself, he wrote, depended on the protection of property. "Individualism, Private Property, the Law of Accumulation of Wealth, and the Law of Competition" were, he said, the highest forms of human society. The wealthy were stewards of society's money, administering it for the common good by using it for libraries, schools, and so on to uplift everyone rather than permitting individuals to squander it in frivolity, Carnegie wrote. Putting his money where his mouth was, he funded libraries and schools across the country to enable workers to study and rise, as he had done. There was no need to worry about business combinations and trusts, he insisted, for competition would always undermine even successful trusts.[4]

Carnegie's breezy solution to the trust question infuriated those watching businessmen lobby for tariff walls to protect their industries from foreign competition, tariffs that led to higher prices for consumers. Even the business-minded *New York Times* took exception to Carnegie's defense of trusts, snapping, "to hold more power than God has allotted to man makes him arrogant, and, attributing to himself a prescience only second to that of his Maker, he becomes unjust." Late nineteenth-century Americans were obsessed with the issue of the tariff, and while historians have explained this focus with complicated examinations of the effects of these import taxes, the true power of the issue lay in how mainstream observers conflated the issue of tariffs with the issue of trusts and saw both as proof that big businessmen controlled government. Because tariffs protected business from foreign competition, the new trusts could fix whatever prices they wanted without fear of being undercut. "It is notorious," claimed the *New York Times*, "that . . . combination[s] to fix prices and maintain them at a certain level with the aid of the tariff [have] been in existence for some years." It set out to educate the people on how businessmen used the tariffs, enacted by the people's own congressmen, against consumers. Once voters understood, the newspaper confidently predicted, the tariffs would be swept away.[5]

Although it was not immediately apparent that the government could go after trusts, it did have a constitutional duty to oversee interstate commerce. On that basis, those who wanted to use the government to curb special interests turned against the businessmen who were snaking their tentacles into political circles and using the legal system and federal legislation to bolster their power. In 1887, Congress created the Interstate Commerce Commission, an independent federal regulatory commission designed to curb shady railroad practices by making sure that railroads adhered to standard rate schedules, for example, across state lines. This would answer Leland Stanford's challenges to state laws that applied to businesses that crossed state lines by allowing the federal government to exercise power over national corporations and insist that they play fairly. In addition to policing the railroads, though, some of the force of the Interstate Commerce Commission came from its power to publicize the previously private actions of corporations. No longer could Carnegie hide his inside deals; they would be broadcast to the public.[6]

The government had also always controlled tariffs, and Americans demanded that the government reduce them in order to curb big business. In 1886, President Cleveland put his call for tariff revision in terms of mainstream American ideas. "We congratulate ourselves that there is among us no laboring class fixed within unyielding bounds and doomed under all conditions to the inexorable fate of daily toil. We recognize in labor a chief factor in the wealth of the Republic, and we treat those who have it in their keeping as citizens entitled to the most careful regard and thoughtful attention," Cleveland announced, invoking the idea of a harmonious society rather than a world of class conflict. Laborers must be cared for not only by advancing industry but also by keeping consumer prices low, he went on. Tariffs were no longer simply protecting industry; they were artificially raising prices, unfairly burdening the American workingman, he suggested. Cleveland's 1887 annual message was much stronger, almost entirely a demand for a lower tariff. The theory of American institutions was to guarantee to every citizen "all the fruits of his industry and enterprise," he insisted, with deductions from that only to support an economical government. More than this "is indefensible extortion and a culpable betrayal of American fairness and justice," taking money from taxpayers to benefit business interests. It meant that money was withdrawn from trade, crippling industry and inviting raids on the Treasury. The Treasury had a surplus, indicating that tariffs were bringing in more money than the government needed; tariff policy was impoverishing consumers to benefit industry.[7]

Having lost his bid for reelection to Republican Benjamin Harrison—who was backed by both businessmen and African Americans—in December 1888, President Cleveland delivered a stinging annual message that sought to recall Americans to their true heritage. He told them that they should be devoted to American citizenship for its own sake and for the nation's advancement, not for "selfish greed and grasping avarice." He mourned, "the Government, instead of being the embodiment of equality, is but an instrumentality through which especial and individual advantages are to be gained. . . . The arrogance of this assumption is unconcealed. It appears in the sordid disregard of all but personal interests, in the refusal to abate for the benefit of others one iota of selfish advantage, and in combinations to perpetuate such advantages through efforts to control legislation and improperly influence the suffrages of the people." There would be a reckoning, he warned. Farmers, laborers, and consumers would insist on fairness. "Communism is a hateful thing and a menace to peace and organized government," he said, "but the communism of combined wealth and capital . . . is not less dangerous than the communism of oppressed poverty and toil."[8]

In 1888, both parties had put antitrust planks in their platforms, and by 1889, middle-class Americans clearly intended to curb big business. That January, the New York courts launched an attack on trusts by dissolving the North River Sugar Refining Company and taking away its charter "for wrongly entering the great Sugar Trust." The attorney representing the people in the case against the company explained happily that the effect of the decision "is to break up this trust, for upon [this] principle . . . every corporation in the 'combine' has forfeited its charter. . . . The principle applies to all . . . trusts and combinations. . . . The principle of law is that any combination to enhance arbitrarily the price of commodities is illegal."[9]

"This decision is a triumph of the people against the mighty tendency of the time toward monopoly and corporate abuses," cheered the *New York Times*. When businesses operating under public charters injured the public, they were acting against their charters and those were, therefore, forfeited, the *Times* argued. During 1889, the pressure to legislate against the trusts grew dramatically. The *New York Times* noted "the intense hostility of the mass of consumers toward all schemes for the suppression of competition." By the end of 1889, Wall Street was "badly shaken," according to the *Times*, with investors pulling their money out of trusts and the value of trust securities plummeting.[10]

Americans were increasingly convinced that tariffs supported trusts by suppressing foreign competition, and by May 1889, even staunchly Republican newspapers were calling for the removal of tariffs on any articles controlled by trusts. The *St. Louis Globe–Democrat* wanted foreign competition to force trusts to lower prices, and while it was willing to use slight duty reductions, it was also willing to use draconian measures. "If the entire removal of duties be necessary, *let the duties be swept away promptly, mercilessly, inexorably.*" It was joined by the *New York Tribune* and the *Cleveland Leader,* among other papers. Even John Sherman, one of the leading architects of postwar protectionism, turned on the trusts that curbed competition, although he defended the protective tariffs that nurtured American enterprise. "If . . . individuals or corporations combine to advance the price of the domestic produce, and to prevent the free result of open and fair competition, *I would, without a moment's hesitation, reduce the duties on foreign goods competing with them in order to break down the combination,*" he announced.[11]

In 1890, Sherman helped to craft a law that would answer popular hatred of the trusts without injuring the principle of protectionism. The Sherman Antitrust Act, as it was known, was a legal codification of the outcry against trusts and was just as broad and vague as that outcry. It made illegal any combination designed to restrain trade or commerce. Anyone whose business or property was injured by illegal trust actions could sue in federal court and could recover costs, attorney's fees, and threefold damages if the case was decided in his favor. Conviction of illegal trust activity meant a fine of up to $5,000 or a year's imprisonment, or both. Unspecified, though, was what exactly "restraint of trade or commerce" meant, an important omission that would strongly influence which combinations were prosecuted and which were not.[12]

Sherman designed the antitrust act to protect the tariff, and it did so, confirming the fears of those who believed business was dictating national policy. Democrats introduced the idea of tariff reform and Congress finally undertook it in 1890, but by the time the House's legislation had made it through the Senate, different business lobbies had demanded so many exceptions that it actually had higher tariff rates than the previous law. The new law, the McKinley Tariff, retained the principle of general protection and raised average tariffs to 49.5 percent. Despite the strength of the iron and steel markets, tariffs on them were not reduced. "Under the McKinley Act the people are paying taxes of nearly $20,000,000 and a much larger sum in bounties to Carnegie, Phipps & Co., and their fellows, for the alleged purpose of benefiting the wage-earners," snarled Pulitzer's *New York World.* It noted that employers cut wages in the months after the passage of the McKinley Tariff and it carefully counted the strikes that followed wage reductions. The McKinley Tariff convinced those who hated the trusts that big business controlled government despite the antitrust act.[13]

As rich businessmen strove to organize the country in their own interests, labor organizations, black rights activists, western agitators, and war veterans threatened violence if their needs were not met. In response, mainstream Americans increasingly perceived them as a menace to the nation. From 1886 to 1893, those advocating an adjustment to the inequities of American industrialism made a strong stand. Between 1880 and 1900, over 23,000 strikes involving more than six and a half million workers erupted. In 1881, Samuel Gompers had begun to draw together craft unions across the country; in 1886, they organized as the American Federation of Labor, looking not for a general reformation of society, as Powderly hoped for, but for short-term gains of better wages, conditions, and benefits. They began their public push for better conditions in February 1886, when Gompers and fellow leaders of the trade union movement revived the push for an eight-hour day that had been laid aside during the Panic of 1873. The call to join together to support an eight-hour day was widely popular with trade union men. As Gompers later recalled, "The eight-hour movement of 1886 was general, but most aggressive in New York, Chicago, Milwaukee, Cincinnati, and Baltimore." On May 1, union men held demonstrations across the country. In Chicago, Gompers recalled, "Forty thousand men were on strike, the railroads were crippled, and many factories closed." Gompers was jubilant that "there seemed to be a probability of trade unions being welded together for united resistance to long hours."[14]

This same circumstance appalled Americans who feared that the doctrine of "socialism" was taking over the nation and who were willing to use force to stop it. On February 27, *Harper's Weekly* ran a Thomas Nast cartoon showing a beefy police officer, holding a pistol and a club marked "U.S." and standing threateningly over a devilish Chicago socialist dragging a "Bloody Red Flag."[15] The fears of many Americans exploded only days after the May 1 demonstrations when an initially peaceful workers' protest meeting in Chicago's Haymarket Square turned deadly. On May 2, strikers at Chicago's McCormick Reaper Works "were ruthlessly clubbed and shot down by the police," Gompers recalled. The next evening, anarchists addressed protesters in Haymarket Square, but drizzling rain that threatened to turn into a downpour dampened interest in the proceedings. People began to drift away, and police moved in to disperse the remaining two hundred or so protesters. As the meeting broke up, a bomb exploded behind the police, killing one officer instantly and wounding six others. Officers charged into the crowd, firing their pistols. When the square was finally quiet, more than sixty people —civilians and police both—lay dead or wounded.[16]

Although what had actually happened in Haymarket Square was unclear, politicians and newspapers trumpeted that the Haymarket Affair proved that disaffected workers were willing to do anything—even bomb cities—to gain control of the country. Popular opinion turned firmly against organized labor, which newspapers across the country equated with anarchy. Chicago's mayor, Carter H. Harrison, issued a proclamation the day after the affair, which castigated "the open defiance of the guardians of the peace by a body of lawless men, who, under the pretense of aiding the laboring men are really endeavoring to destroy all law." Printed on broadsides and pinned up around the city, it assured "the good people of Chicago that . . . the police can protect their lives and property and the good name of Chicago, and WILL DO SO." Knights of Labor leader T. V. Powderly condemned the anarchists at Haymarket, insisting that they had nothing in common with true American workers: "We are attempting to remove unjust laws from the statutes, and are doing what we can to better the condition of humanity. At every step we have to fight the opposition of capital, which of itself is sufficient to tax our energies to the utmost; but at every step we are handicapped by the unwarrantable and impertinent interference of these blatant, shallow-pated men. . . . Our greatest trouble has always been caused by extremists. . . . It is high time for us to assert our manhood before these men throttle it." Powderly was desperately trying to hold on to the idea of organized wage laborers as the heart of America, but his was a losing battle. Most laborers wanted no part of what seemed to be organized radicalism, and membership in the Knights of Labor plummeted from its high of 730,000. For all intents and purposes, it was finished.[17]

The trouble in Chicago seemed symptomatic. Westerners had never trusted eastern cities, but even to easterners cities increasingly seemed to be controlled by criminals, with the law manipulated by those who catered to them. Nowhere was this more obvious than in New York City, where the famous criminal lawyers William F. Howe and his egg-headed little partner Abe Hummel represented prostitutes, murderers, thieves, and corrupt businessmen. Howe and Hummel were often in the news; they were so popular

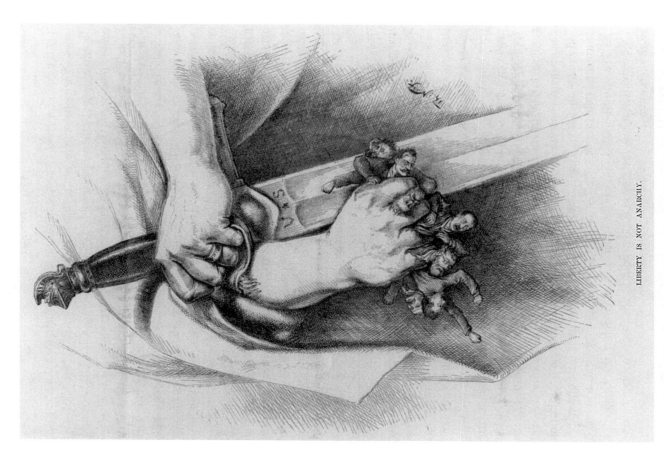

LIBERTY IS NOT ANARCHY.

Figure 16. In this cartoon from September 1886, a powerful America, represented here by Lady Liberty, crushes the Haymarket anarchists while she bares her sword. Liberty's wedding ring reads "Union," indicating that she claims support from all sections. Courtesy of Harvard College Library.

that the *National Police Gazette* sold photographs of them for a dime in their series of famous people, along with Queen Victoria, President Harrison, Buffalo Bill, and other celebrities. In 1871, they defended Jacob Rosenzweig for the murder of Alice Augusta Bowlsby; in 1873, they represented Victoria Woodhull and Tenny Claflin in an obscenity trial; in 1884, when New York City police rounded up seventy-four brothel madams, Howe and Hummel defended every one of them. They represented pickpockets, bigamists, gangs, kidnappers, thieves, arsonists, and the counterfeiter whose copies of U.S. money were so accurate that the U.S. Treasury had to withdraw its own issue of hundred-dollar bills. In 1888, Howe and Hummel published *In Danger; or Life in New York, A True History of a Great City's Wiles and Temptations*, a purported exposé of the New York City underworld. Giving explicit and detailed information about how pickpockets, shoplifters, thieves, and even murderers conducted business, their "exposé" was essentially a how-to manual for would-be criminals. Their book attempted to drum up business by flaunting their success at thwarting the courts and returning their criminal clients to the streets, claims that many Americans believed.[18]

It was not only in cities that ne'er-do-wells seemed to be taking charge of things. Farmers like Luna Kellie were increasingly vocal in their demands that government respond to their needs. "There is something radically wrong in our industrial system," wrote a North Carolina farmer. "There is a screw loose. The wheels have dropped out of balance." Railroads, manufacturing, banking, cities, and professionals were all prospering while agriculture languished, he complained. The drought years of the mid-1880s combined with poor wheat prices to increase interest in the Alliance where it was already established and to continue its spread. In early 1885, farmers in the Dakota Territory organized a branch of the Alliance; Colorado farmers also began to organize locally. In 1887, delegates to a national Alliance convention adopted a permanent constitution and a more radical stance than the organization had previously taken. They called for nationalization of at least one transcontinental railroad line as well as control over railroads in general, demanded the free and unlimited coinage of silver, and approached the Knights of Labor—who were also meeting in Minneapolis in October—to suggest cooperative action.[19]

The organized farmers gained ground quickly in the late 1880s. In 1886, Texas lawyer Dr. Charles Macune took over the Southern Alliance, building it into a strong cooperative that enabled farmers to work together. Pooling their resources, members of the Alliance could buy, sell, mill, and store their products cooperatively, increasing their bargaining power. Unwilling to work with African Americans, the Southern Alliance nonetheless encouraged the organization of the Colored Farmers' National Alliance and Cooperative Union, which attracted a quarter of a million members in five years. As prices continued to fall, the Alliance movement prospered. "The people are aroused at last," cheered an editorial in the *Western Rural*. "Never in our history has there been such a union of action among farmers as now." By the end of 1889, a thousand farmers a week joined the Alliance; they poured in from the poor frontier states like the Dakotas, Minnesota, and Nebraska, with 130,000 from Kansas alone. Refusing to join with traditionally Republican northern farmers, the members of the Southern Alliance had not agreed to ally with the National Farmers' Alliance, but in 1889 issued a statement of their own principles and goals that paralleled that of the northern organization almost entirely.[20]

By 1889, both the Northern and Southern Alliances had declared that they shared the interests of laborers, which to opponents showed the potential for a radical revolution in America. Members of the Northern Alliance announced their sympathy "with the just demands of labor of every grade," and that "many of the evils from which the farming community suffers oppress universal labor, and that therefore producers should unite in a demand for the reform of unjust systems and the repeal of laws that bear unequally upon the people." At the Southern Alliance, Macune had managed to go one better and attract the support of the Knights of Labor. Powderly declined to link the Knights formally with the Southern Alliance, but a committee of the Knights endorsed the platform of the Southern Alliance—newly renamed the Southern Alliance and Industrial Union—and committed the legislative committees of the two organizations to work "in concert before Congress" to secure "the enactment of laws in harmony with [our] demands." "In order to carry out these objects," the committee added, "we will support for office only such men as can be depended upon to enact these principles in statute law uninfluenced by party caucus."[21]

In 1889, North Dakota, South Dakota, Montana, and Washington all became states, adding more western voices to the call for a people's government that, among other things, expanded the currency. In 1890, Idaho and Wyoming won statehood. For westerners who lived in mining states, the demand for free silver offered greater tangible benefits than simply an expanded money supply. For them, silver coinage would mean a dramatic increase in the value of their mines, and their fury at Eastern opposition to free silver increased as the price of silver dropped. By 1890, it had dropped to a 20:1 ratio with gold, and mining westerners joined Farmers' Alliances in pressuring Congress to coin silver.[22]

In June 1890, organizers in Kansas brought the National Farmers' Alliance and the Southern Alliance (now the National Farmers' Alliance and Industrial Union) together to form a new political party. Meeting in Ocala, Florida, they issued the "Ocala Demands," which articulated the popular western sentiment that government acted for rich industrialists. The manifesto called for the abolition of national banks, an increase in paper and silver money to at least $50 a person, an end to corrupt government, the direct election of senators, regulation of railroads or even nationalization of them if necessary, and the reserve of lands "for actual settlers only." Reflecting the organizers' own belief that business interests had co-opted government, it stated faith "in the doctrine of equal rights to all and special privileges to none" and demanded "that our national legislation shall be so framed in the future as not to build up one industry at the expense of another." It called for an end to tariffs on necessities, a graduated income tax, and government loans for farmers. In the "Alliance summer" of 1890, Alliance members like Mary Elizabeth Lease and Tom Watson spread their message of government support to farmers across the plains and the South. It was time, Lease insisted, for farmers to "raise less corn and more hell."[23]

But mainstream Americans clearly did not believe that a systematic problem made western farming a losing battle, for it was precisely to the idea of successful western farming that they turned when trying to find an ultimate solution to the Indian troubles on the Great Plains. In 1887, the Dawes Severalty Act attempted to drag Native Americans into a middle-class vision of American life by allotting 160 acres of land to individual Indian heads of families for farming (single men got 80 acres), thus dramatically reducing the extensive tribal lands that had previously been reserved for a tribe generally. Supporters of this plan—including Carl Schurz, who had advocated it since his time as secretary of the interior—believed it to be benevolent, encouraging Indians to become mainstream Americans. The nation must "teach a grown up Indian to keep," insisted Henry Dawes, the act's sponsor. Thus "the individual is separated from the mass, set upon the soil, made a citizen, and instead of a charge he is a positive good, a contribution to the wealth and strength and power of the nation." The act promised American citizenship to Indians who "adopted the habits of civilized life." In his role as a figure that stood between the wild frontier and the civilized East, Buffalo Bill threw his mighty weight behind the law, arguing that farming and animal husbandry was the best way to enable the Indians to survive. "The scheme of . . . giving a tribe an immense tract to roam over, and feeding and clothing them until they learned to support themselves . . . is foolish. It would ruin white men if it should be applied to them, because it would deprive them of all incentive to work." The Indian population was increasing, Cody told a reporter for *Harper's Weekly*, and ultimately it would mix thoroughly with "the white race."[24]

In July 1890, middle-class Americans fell back on government activism to undercut the silver agitators with the Silver Purchase Act. Although designed to defend the idea of a harmonious economy, this act cut both ways by indicating that western farmers were gaining power in government. The act required the Treasury to buy 4.5 million ounces of silver every month and to issue the same amount of greenbacks in payment. This nodded to those who wanted an expanded currency, but it watered down the proposal of western senators to adopt the silver currency that businessmen worried would force the country off the gold standard. In the end, the Silver Purchase Act only slightly inflated the currency, but its apparent nod to western farmers nonetheless terrified those who worried that free silver agitators were going to force the country off the gold standard. On February 10, 1891, former Democratic President Cleveland lent his weight to the struggle against currency expansion, speaking out against "the dangerous, the reckless experiment of free, unlimited and independent silver coinage."[25]

The September 1890 edition of the *Newark Town Talk* (for the "more intelligent class of readers") recorded under the title "ENTERPRISE" a joke that revealed middle-class concern about western agitators willing to do almost anything to gain control of government, here by inflating their numbers to increase their political representation:

CENSUS ENUMERATOR (aroused at midnight)—What's the matter out thar? What do you want?

PROMINENT KANSAN—Git yer book an hurry down to the creek! The boys air about to string up Alkali Ike, an' fer the good uv the settlement we want him counted before it's ever-lastin'ly too late.[26]

Farmers and miners calling for government to level the economic playing field frightened those who believed that hardworking individuals could rise on their own, but they still seemed less dangerous than those insisting, once again, on improving the lives of African Americans in the South through federal legislation. In 1888, the Republicans gained control of both the House and the Senate for the first time since 1874, and Republican Benjamin Harrison won the White House. With this political control, advocates of black advancement called for new legislation to protect black voting in the South and for nationally funded education for illiterate southern African Americans. Republican platforms in every presidential election since 1872 had promised to protect black voting in the South, but the party had lacked the power to pass legislation fulfilling its pledges. Harrison strongly supported a federal elections bill; his victory made many Americans believe that one was in the offing. Feeding their concerns were Republican proposals for federal funding of public schools, popularly interpreted as an attempt to funnel money into the southern black community since the money would be apportioned according to illiteracy rates.[27]

Americans committed to evenhanded government rose up against the proposed bills. According to an editor of the *New York World*, the federal elections bill "was an attempt of the Republican junta to put . . . 'a bayonet behind every ballot' . . . to turn over [the South's] government to ignorance, spoliation, waste, and greed." Although he admitted that some Republicans honestly wanted to protect African Americans, "designing men in the North were not above cynically using the negro problem as a means of perpetuating the power to tax the people through the tariff." In a passionate article written for the *Forum*, Senator Wade Hampton explained to modern readers "What Negro Supremacy Means." The issue was not social, according to Hampton, but political and economic. Drawing from his skewed version of the early postwar years in South Carolina, when, he said, the lowest elements of society "took control of the government," Hampton explained the evils of an "infusion of [a] large mass of ignorant voters" into the political system. In postwar South Carolina, Hampton inaccurately insisted, demagogues had organized ignorant freedmen as a political base by promising them the confiscation and redistribution of wealth. "Negro Supremacy," he claimed, was the political control of government by the poor and ignorant and would endanger property and prosperity by establishing patronage and legislation that favored workers. This racist southern version of the postwar years grossly misrepresented the southern state governments, of course, but it attracted the support of those across the nation nervous about the corruption of government. They offered a dramatic solution for purifying it. The *New York Times* suggested that "the political evils arising from negro suffrage could be cured if any Southern State could be brought to impose a qualification for voters, which should apply equally to voters of both races. It is ignorance and improvidence that are dangerous, not black ignorance and black improvidence. An educational test or a property test, or a combination of both, would insure the elimination from politics of these dangerous evils, and so long as the tests were impartial and impartially applied, there could be no ground of complaint in the enforcement of such a test."[28]

While the *New York Times* put a principled veneer on racial and class antagonism, in Hampton's own South Carolina, the outcry against African American special interests joined with agrarian agitation to given rise to a new kind of southern politician—brash, crude, and aggressively racist. This new southerner seemed to prove to middle-class observers that the nation was indeed disintegrating into the very worst sort of factionalism. In South Carolina, Benjamin R. Tillman was elected governor in 1890 at the head of a motley group of "reformers" determined to take the state away from "Conservatives" like Hampton, who were more interested in money than in their constituents, they charged. Tillman's inaugural address dripped with racist venom that seemed to reflect the worst of antebellum southern thought, erasing the hard-won emancipation of the Civil War. "The whites have absolute control of the State government, and we intend at any and all hazards to retain it. The intelligent exercise of the right of suffrage . . . is as yet beyond the capacity of the vast majority of colored men. We deny, without regard to color, that 'all men are created equal,' it is not true now, and was not true when Jefferson wrote it." Within a year, Tillman's men in the state legislature refused to reelect Hampton to the Senate—a position most believed he had earned the right to keep until he retired—replacing him with a political hack prone to violence and alcohol. Other state offices went to Tillman's friends and family while the governor himself quickly became embroiled in a scandal about his acceptances of favors from railroad companies. Hampton reported receiving many kind letters after his defeat, "generally deploring what they call the 'disgrace of the State.' I am content, and if the people will rebuke the representatives, who misrepresented their constituents, I shall be satisfied." But in 1892, Tillman was reelected governor. The South Carolina government had fallen into the hands of the worst kind of special interest. In protest, the Senate in 1893 unanimously approved Hampton's appointment as a government railroad commissioner, a well-paying position that would enable the crippled old man to visit the West where he could indulge in his new outdoor passion, fishing.[29]

The calls for a government that catered to political interests were increasingly widespread, making it seem that everyone was looking for a handout.

Veterans were trying to get the pension rolls expanded. After the Civil War, General John A. Logan had taken over the Grand Army of the Republic (G.A.R.) and made it a political organization for veterans. Firmly attached to the Republican Party, it provided a prime example of a special interest affecting politics. No Republican politician in his right mind would challenge the protection of the veterans; the repetition of thanks to veterans in each Republican national platform after the war attested to their importance in the Republican ranks. With a membership of almost half a million in the 1880s, the G.A.R. was not to be trifled with.[30]

Soldiers disabled in the war needed pensions and politicians made it a point to guarantee that those pensions were forthcoming. As the wartime population aged in an era with no social security legislation, the numbers of men who discovered that their disabilities dated from the war expanded dramatically. By the 1880s, pensions had become a big business. Pension agents promised to help veterans collect payments in exchange for a fee, and by 1885, pensions cost the Treasury $56 million every year. By 1888, payments were $89 million. In 1887, under pressure from the G.A.R., Congress passed a dependent pension bill introduced by stalwart Republican Henry W. Blair of New Hampshire, who had also sponsored the federal education bill to benefit African Americans. If enacted into law by Cleveland's signature, this bill would provide pensions for Civil War veterans who were manual laborers and unable to make a living, whether or not they had been disabled during the war.

On February 11, 1887, President Grover Cleveland—the same man who so viciously assailed businessmen's trusts and the tariff—vetoed the dependent pension bill, insisting that it would open the doors to widespread fraud on the Treasury. The bill did not require soldiers or sailors to have been wounded in the war, but only to be "disabled and dependent on their own labor for support." As long as their disability was not "the result of their own vicious habits or gross carelessness" and provided that it "incapacitates them for the performance of labor in such a degree as to render them unable to earn a support," they were to receive a pension payment of $12 a month. This bill had all the hallmarks of a special interest pressure, Cleveland thought, and he insisted that it was an invitation to fraud. It would encourage men to declare themselves unable to work; it would make the government the arbiter of what was adequate support; and it would necessitate continued taxation at a time when Americans clamored for lower taxes.[31]

Not only did veterans demand government aid; increasingly, too, reformers insisted that government redress the inequities between labor and capital. In 1888, Edward Bellamy bitingly critiqued nineteenth-century society in his utopian novel *Looking Backward*. The narrator of this book, a wealthy Boston Brahmin with a sleep disorder, drops into a drug-induced coma on Memorial Day in 1887 and awakens in September 2000. From his new vantage point, the carefully named Julian West can see the nineteenth century clearly and condemns it, comparing it to "a prodigious coach which the masses of humanity were harnessed to and dragged toilsomely along a very hilly and sandy road. The driver was hunger, and permitted no lagging." In the coveted "breezy and comfortable" seats on top of the coach, riders "critically discuss[ed] the merits of the straining team," deluded into thinking that they belonged "to a higher order of beings" than those pulling the cart, despite the fact that sudden jolts of the coach constantly dumped riders to the ground, "where they were instantly compelled to take hold of the rope and help to drag the coach on which they had before ridden so pleasantly."[32]

In contrast to the class conflict of the 1880s, Bellamy's utopia of 2000 had solved all of society's problems by guaranteeing that every individual had "equal wealth and equal opportunities of culture." West's twenty-first-century host explained how this had happened by outlining the history of the nineteenth century in terms that echoed the perceptions of mainstream Americans. When commerce and industry were divided into small concerns with small capital, "the individual workman was relatively important and independent in his relations to the employer," West's host recounted. Since "a little capital or a new idea" could "start a man in business for himself, workingmen were constantly becoming employers and there was no hard and fast line between the two classes." But the concentration of capital reduced a worker "to insignificance and powerlessness . . . against the great corporation," and he could no longer rise. In self-defense, workers organized and fought back against big business, creating the industrial chaos of the late nineteenth century. All it took to solve this situation was to accept that large concerns were more efficient and productive than smaller ones, and to move just a bit further in that direction rather than fighting them. West's host told him, "The nation . . . [was] organized as the one great business corporation in which all other corporations were absorbed; it became the one capitalist in the place of all other capitalists, the sole employer, the final monopoly in which all previous and lesser monopolies were swallowed up, a monopoly in the profits and economies of which all citizens shared." The American people were organized into an "industrial army," trained from childhood into acting for the good of the nation. *Looking Backward* sold 60,000 copies in 1888, over 100,000 the next year, and like Henry George's followers before them, Bellamy enthusiasts joined together in nationalist clubs to promote his vision of state-owned wealth.[33]

But many Americans were shocked by the idea of a national "industrial army" and such sweeping nationalization. Their determination to keep government out of the hands of special interests was illuminated by the rehabilitation of S. S. Cox's image after his death in late 1889. Cox had been vilified during the Civil War and early postwar years for his determination to keep government small and away from Republicans who were trying, he believed, to build a political empire based on special interests. By 1890, he was so honored that Congress published a book of speeches celebrating his greatness. He was moderate, a "true patriot," a great "liberal leader." Honored for defending southern whites after the Civil War, this opponent of the Thirteenth Amendment, military reconstruction, and federal elections measures was described not as a man who opposed human equality, but—astonishingly —as one who "hated oppression." Many eulogists, including Grover Cleveland, spoke feelingly of their admiration for a man who had never been accused of corruption, who put all his energy into acting for the public good. Eulogists claimed: "He realized that labor was the only talisman of success." He was always a friend of labor but never identified himself "with radicalism in any form." Describing Cox as a man who opposed "paternalism in government in all its forms and in all its deceitful disguises," one speaker declared, "He believed that man was capable of self-government and would govern himself better than he would be governed by others; that the people who were governed the least were governed the best . . . and that all governments, national, state, and local, should keep their hands off the citizen as long as he kept his hands off his fellow." Unsurprisingly, Cox had championed the growth of the West, a place that brought representatives into optimal contact with their constituencies. Many of his eulogists also commented on his close relationship with his wife, described as firmly within the domestic sphere. "Like a true woman, her kindly sympathy suggested that her husband might be severe and just and yet be kind even to gentleness." Cox was "a true tribune of the people."[34]

Concerns about big business and black Republicans pushed voters to sweep out of Congress the Republicans they blamed for both the McKinley Tariff and the federal elections bill. In response to the agitation for the latter, Mississippi's revised 1890 constitution disfranchised most poor black voters, and lynching in the South rose dramatically, as opponents of black suffrage sought to purge politics of those who were corrupting true republican government. In the North, many applauded the southern restriction of the suffrage while new registration laws and the nonpartisan secret ballot effectively disfranchised disaffected workers there. In the elections of 1890, Alliance members had backed Democrats who supported their cause, and they elected forty-four congressmen, three senators, and four governors and gained control of eight state legislatures. Mainstream Americans had effectively rebuked the Republicans, who seemed tools of big business and of poor African Americans, but had they simply handed the government over to the agitators on the other side?[35]

In July 1892, two major strikes showed that organized laborers were stronger than ever, and middle-class Americans called on government to suppress the strikers. First, a latent conflict between Carnegie and his workers at the Homestead plant exploded. The plant had had labor troubles, and by 1892 its workers were organized by the Amalgamated Association of Iron and Steel Workers, whose agreement with the Homestead owners was due to expire on July 1, 1892. When he had taken over the plant a few years before, Carnegie determined that it must be nonunion both to enable him to move men around to his various concerns and also to permit him to cut costs. Embarrassed by his past public statements in support of labor organization, Carnegie slipped away to Europe for a vacation shortly before the labor agreement expired, leaving behind his general manager, Henry Clay Frick, with instructions to break the union. Frick reduced wages and then refused to negotiate with a grievance committee appointed to meet with management. He announced that he would close the factory on July 1, reopening it on July 6 with whatever workers turned up. Unable to appeal to Carnegie, who was hiding in a lodge in Scotland, the striking men organized as a military force to surround the plant. Frick quietly hired Pinkertons to open the way for his nonunionized workers to enter the factory. Just before dawn on July 6, as 300 Pinkertons were being towed up the Monongahela River on barges to reach the factory, strikers hidden behind barricades fired on them, ultimately killing seven. The Pinkertons returned the fire, and the battle went on until nightfall, when the chairman of the strikers' advisory committee permitted the Pinkertons to disembark and leave town, although they were attacked repeatedly as they departed. The barges were looted and burned. Local officials sympathized with the strikers, and for the next several days, the strikers controlled the town. On July 12, the Pennsylvania governor called out the state militia to retake Homestead. This action permitted Frick to reopen the plant with nonunion labor, but on July 23, a Russian-born anarchist shot and stabbed Frick in his office. The strike dragged on until November 20.[36]

Many Americans were shocked by these events and perceived the Homestead strikers as launching an attack on society that the government must repel. "Labor War Begun," a headline in the *Philadelphia Evening Bulletin* screamed. *Harper's Weekly* agreed that "Society and civilization are at bay" in Homestead. "A strong mob had been organized and armed, by determined leaders, for the purpose of interfering with property rights, and hindering the peaceful employment of labor; and had threatened death to any man who should assert the rights they wished to destroy." "A mob is in control," it insisted.[37] Pulitzer used the *New York World* to join in condemning the strikers, although he noted that 400 strikes had occurred since the passage of the McKinley Tariff and acknowledged strikers' complaints about Carnegie. "There is but one thing for the locked-out men to do," the *New York World* declared. "They must submit to the law. They must keep the peace. Their quarrel is with their employers. They must not make it a quarrel with organized society. It is a protest against wage reduction. It must not be made a revolt against law and order. They must not resist the authority of the State." When Powderly charged that the Pinkerton guards at Homestead were thugs, bent on stirring up violence, the Pinkerton brothers themselves defended their men in testimony before the Senate. In twenty-six years, the company's men had "been assaulted, stoned, and abused for doing no other act than protecting private property and the lives of non-union laborers," they said. If employers were going to have to stop employing "watchmen" because of the demands of "labor leaders and demagogues . . . we reach the point of anarchy and communism," they growled.[38]

As Homestead was exploding, miners in Idaho rose against the Mine Owners' Protective Association. Like farmers, miners, too, believed they were doing the nation's work, prospecting for gold and precious metals that would feed the government treasury as it made them rich. But the cost of developing a mine made it a common saying that it took a gold mine to develop a silver mine; it was almost impossible for individuals to work claims successfully. Instead, mine owners borrowed money or worked to attract investors, then integrated vertically to smelting and marketing as well as mining. Individual miners worked for companies and bought goods in the company store and were the western counterpart to eastern and southern

Figure 17. In this photograph taken shortly after the Homestead strike of 1892, Andrew Carnegie's Homestead plant dwarfs the worker in the foreground, illustrating just how unrealistic it was to believe that industrial workers and their employers had equal bargaining power in the late nineteenth century. Keystone-Mast Collection, UCR/California Museum of Photography, University of California at Riverside.

unskilled workers. Miners were endangered by cave-ins, fumes, dust, industrial accidents, and the black widow spiders and scorpions that liked the cool entrances to mines. They were also subject to horrid conditions as they worked in the cramped mining tunnels that followed mineral veins. On the Comstock Lode temperatures could be as high as 150 degrees, and men died from the heat or from pneumonia contracted as they shuttled from the hot mines to the cold air outside. Miners had the highest death rate of any occupation; one out of thirty miners was disabled and one out of eighty killed annually in the 1870s. For this brutal work the men received only $2.50 a day—almost twice what unskilled workers in less hazardous jobs made, but still a poor exchange for life or limbs. Like their eastern counterparts, miners organized for better wages and conditions.[39]

After a long strike, war broke out in mining towns stretched through about thirty miles of the canyons along Idaho's Coeur d'Alene River in July 1892. When mine owners obtained federal injunctions to keep strikers from interfering with the operations of the company, including the employment of nonunion labor, strikers marched on mines and took over or destroyed machinery; both union and nonunion men were killed in the struggles. Outsiders looked with horror on the uprising as reports from the region emphasized that strikers were attacking nonunion men, refusing to let them work. "They had driven the non-union men out of the country; the most valuable mines and mills of the district were in their possession and the inhabitants of the principal towns terrorized," one man recalled.[40]

The weight of the government came down on the strikers in Idaho, with the national government now joining forces with state militias. Knowing that local officials sympathized with the miners, the mine owners appealed to the governor for support, and on July 14, 1892, the governor ordered six companies of the Idaho National Guard into the region and declared martial law. He also wrote to President Harrison that he did not have the strength necessary to end the strike. He asked for federal troops. Harrison obliged, avoiding the Posse Comitatus Act by defining the strikers and their supporters as a domestic insurrection. The U.S. Army rushed to the Coeur d'Alene district, where soldiers arrested 300 members of the miners' union and removed the local sheriff from power on the grounds that he "was acting in the interest of his friends, the strikers, to whom he owed his election." The strike and the prosecution of strikers dragged on, and mainstream Americans were given increasingly clear illustrations of the apparent justice of government action against the insurgents. In the fall elections that year, "the hidden vein of Anarchism" resurfaced when, a popular history of the time recorded, letters threatening the nonstrikers surfaced. Addressed to the wife of a foreman was a letter that allegedly read: "I have a wife and daughters myself. Therefore am sorry for you. The day of reckoning is close upon all Scabs. Your husband will be blown into fragments inside of a month and the next fight will not be a milk and water one like the last. The men will be killed, and the women raped. Young and old . . . Get out!!! And leave [your husband] to the fate he deserves." Strikers seemed to have launched an attack on the very fabric of society and its government. In 1893, the Idaho legislature, angry at the overruling of local government by national authority, dismantled the state National Guard by refusing to vote appropriations for it. The man championing this move had been an imprisoned striker during the Coeur d'Alene upheaval.[41]

By the 1890s, mainstream Americans were increasingly willing to use the strong arm of the government to enforce their ideals, and those needing government help to bolster their position were most likely to succeed if they used language that reflected middle-class ideals. One of the most powerful illustrations of this willingness came in the remote West, where large ranchers hurting after the drought of the mid-1880s hid behind federal protection to prop up their industry. Although this story was little different from similar tales of eastern business, the small scale of the Johnson County War brought into stark relief the vital importance of managing to define an interest as speaking for the middle class.

The Johnson County War in Wyoming was much less romantic than the story later told by Owen Wister in his famous novel *The Virginian*, or by Jack Schaefer's *Shane*, or by the many movies based on it. By the early 1890s, the drought, railroads, and settlers had largely ended the cattle drives. Cattlemen began to focus on more intensive farming, developing higher quality herds and tending them more carefully. These herds required extensive grazing land and plenty of water, and big cattlemen bought land to build their headquarters, then ranged their cattle on federal or railroad land nearby. When entrepreneurs tried to push their smaller herds onto the same land, the big cattlemen exploded, accusing them of rustling the cattle the smaller businessmen claimed as their own. Cattlemen's associations sprang up in western states; indeed, Teddy Blue worked for one in Montana and insisted that the smaller cattlemen were the criminals they were portrayed to be, and in his time in the Dakotas, Theodore Roosevelt was most anxious to head out after them.[42]

In 1892, the big ranchers in Johnson County, organized as the Wyoming Stock Growers' Association, decided to clear out the smaller cattlemen once and for all. They hired fifty gunmen in Texas to kill their competitors and gave them a list of the men they wanted dead. The gunmen killed four of the smaller cattlemen after cornering them in a cabin, but outraged Johnson County settlers surrounded the gunmen and threatened to hang them all.

Local law enforcement sided firmly with the small cattlemen—after all, the Stock Growers' men were murdering people—and the Wyoming Stock Growers' Association appealed to the governor for aid in restoring order. The governor, in turn, appealed to President Benjamin Harrison, who sent army troops to rescue the Stock Growers' men from the angry local settlers and lawmen. The expense of keeping the Stock Growers' men imprisoned nearly broke the state. Witnesses became mum, and within months the cases against them fell apart. The Stock Growers had first intimidated and then killed those who tried to break their monopoly on the Wyoming cattle industry, but by appealing to the idea that their opponents threatened middle-class order, the Stock Growers won the support of the federal government and actually got away with murder.[43]

In contrast to the big ranchers in Johnson County, Quanah Parker could not get what he wanted from the government because he did not comfortably fit the middle-class model, despite his dramatic economic and social climb. By 1890, Quanah's stationery announced that he was the "Principal Chief of the Comanche Indians." Building a $2,000, two-story, ten-room house, he carefully cultivated the idea that he had joined mainstream America, but Quanah's ideas and those of white middle-class Americans reached a crisis over the house. Quanah repeatedly asked for government aid to complete the structure, requests in keeping with the government's traditional role in Indian affairs and backed by prominent white men who argued that "he is an Indian who deserves some assistance from the Government." But their advice ran up against Indian commissioner T. J. Morgan, a staunch Baptist who "did not deem it wise for the government to contribute money to assist in building a house for an Indian who has five wives." Morgan declined to provide assistance "unless he will agree, in writing, to make a choice among his wives and to live only with the one chosen and to fully provide for his other wives without living with them." Quanah's "much married condition," as another agent called it, jeopardized his standing as Comanche chief among government agents, but the agent insisted to Morgan that he must not be cast adrift. He had stood with whites against hostile Kiowas and proved "in many ways that he was desirous of walking on 'Washington's' road. He is ambitious and shrewd enough to know that any real progress for himself and his people must be by the white man's way; consequently he can recognize authority and see the wisdom of sometimes combatting the customs and prejudices of his people." Quanah had not quite mastered middle-class values; while he had embraced the economic demands of American life, he had not embraced its ideal family, and his pleas for government funding went unanswered.[44]

In the 1890s, the government enforced the values of mainstream Americans but increasingly refused to protect what they considered special interests. In 1892, a political party of farmers, laborers, and other disaffected Americans challenged the growing association of the government with hard work and economic harmony. Denying that the new middle-class domination of government truly served the nation, they organized and called for a government responsive to what they claimed were "the people." Populist L. Frank Baum later wrote *The Wizard of Oz*, a novel that explained why many Americans felt obliged to demand help. His fictional farmers, Dorothy, Aunt Em, and Uncle Henry, lived in Kansas in a one-room cabin surrounded by "the great gray prairie." Using the word "gray" seven times in his brief description of the lives of his characters, Baum wrote of relentless sun and wind that had baked the ground, weathered the house, and turned Aunt Em from "a young, pretty wife" to a gray woman who was "thin and gaunt, and never smiled . . . [who] . . . looked at [Dorothy] with wonder that she could find anything to laugh at." Like Aunt Em, "Uncle Henry never laughed. He worked hard from morning till night and did not know what joy was. He was gray also, from his long beard to his rough boots, and he looked stern and solemn, and rarely spoke." Torn from her sad relatives by a cyclone, Dorothy was transported to a beautiful and bountiful land where the Wicked Witch of the West and the Wicked Witch of the East held the Winkies and the Munchkins in slavery. Baum's western witch was the drought on the western prairies that undermined even the most diligent farming, his eastern witch was the bankers and corporations that kept farmers in debt. To relieve the sufferers and get home, Dorothy set off on a journey with the tin woodman—a worker whose limbs had gradually been chopped off and replaced by machinery, and who had frozen in a rain that sounded suspiciously like a lock-out—and the scarecrow, a rural hayseed who was terribly wise despite his apparent lack of brains.[45]

In July 1892, the newly formed People's Party held its first national convention in Omaha, Nebraska, to find a way to slay the wicked witches. Nominating a former Union general for president (James B. Weaver) and a former Confederate general for vice president (James G. Field), the Populists announced, "We meet in the midst of a nation brought to the verge of moral, political, and material ruin. Corruption dominates the ballot-box, the Legislatures, the Congress, and touches even the ermine of the bench. . . . The fruits of the toil of millions are boldly stolen to build up colossal fortunes for a few, unprecedented in the history of mankind; and the possessors of these, in turn, despise the Republic and endanger liberty. From the same prolific womb of governmental injustice we breed the two great classes—tramps and millionaires." Populists sought "to restore the government of the Republic to the hands of the 'plain people,' with which class it originated." They declared their solidarity with organized labor and hinted at support for black suffrage by demanding "a free ballot and fair count in all elections," although they opposed federal intervention at the polls. "We believe that the power of government—in other words, of the people—should be expanded . . . as rapidly and as far as the good sense of an intelligent people and the teaching of experience shall justify, to the end that oppression, injustice, and poverty shall eventually cease in the land."[46]

Their platform was a practical agenda to use the government to assist farmers and wage laborers who were not succeeding in the individualist economy. It demanded the coinage of silver at a ratio of 16:1 and the use of greenbacks instead of national bank notes to avoid using "banking corporations." Money must be increased to at least $50 per capita. Demanding a graduated income tax, it asserted that "all State and national revenues shall be limited to the necessary expenses of the government, economically and honestly administered." Government must own the railroads, telegraph, and telephone and reclaim all unused railroad and corporation lands "for actual settlers only." Populists opposed "any subsidy or national aid to any private corporation for any purpose." Supporting the eight-hour day and demanding the suppression of the Pinkertons, party supporters also called for the initiative and referendum, as well as the direct election of senators, to keep big businessmen from buying pet senators to do their bidding.

Middle-class Americans were determined to keep disaffected Americans like the Populists from controlling the government. In the 1892 election reformers introduced at the national level the new secret ballot system pioneered in Australia. It had been brought into local elections in 1888 in an attempt to keep the government from the hands of both the grasping poor and the rich demagogues who hoped to control them. This ballot, printed by government officials, listed all the candidates running in the election, regardless of party. A voter marked this ballot in secret, enabling him to split a ticket and keep his choices invisible to party bosses and employers. The new system revolutionized the electoral process. According to the New York World, the Australian ballot was an effective blow "at the buying of votes and the intimidation of voters," for "the buyer could no longer be certain whether the seller would stay bought, and . . . the intimidator could be fairly sure that his victim would betray him." Until this sort of ballot was adopted, a man trying for reform "was balanced on election day by some poor fellow who for fear of loss of employment or by some knave who for a fee marched to the polls holding in sight the folded ticket the district captain put into his hands." Its adoption promised to purify government.[47]

Critically, the new ballots offered to purify government by limiting the suffrage. The new ballots required that a voter be able to read to choose the candidates he wanted, rather than simply endorsing his party's ticket as a whole. While the new system promised to end the power of political bosses, it also began the process of winnowing out uneducated voters as opponents of the federal elections bill had advocated two years before. And just as they had predicted, it soon severely curtailed black voting in the South and immigrant voting in the North.

Middle-class voters put back in the White House their champion, Grover Cleveland, making him the only man ever elected president in nonconsecutive terms. In a ringing endorsement of reduced taxation, frugality in national expenditure, small government, and self-reliance, Cleveland called for constitutionally possible restraints on business monopolies and for tariff reform. He was not championing the poor against the wealthy but simply trying to restore "the theory of an honest distribution of the fund of the governmental beneficence treasured up for all, . . . a principle which underlies our free institutions." Even as he attacked business, he warned against government "paternalism"— the government pensions that provided benefits to individuals. Paternalism "stifles the spirit of true Americanism and stupefies every ennobling trait of American citizenship," he insisted. Cleveland also demanded that Americans everywhere must in good faith extend equality before the law to every citizen regardless of race. Sounding suspiciously like Roosevelt, he claimed that recognizing this right was a sign of "American manliness and fairness."[48]

Mainstream Americans were beginning to use the government to protect their vision of the nation, and in this atmosphere, women's strong moral role in society and their growing identity as consumers let them demand the expansion of government in dramatic new ways. With the tariff a white–hot issue in 1890, women's interests became the driving force of American politics in that election year. Opponents of the tariff vociferously blamed it for raising the cost of consumer goods, and large business firms sent circulars to customers notifying them that the tariff had necessitated price increases. When Republicans got trounced in the 1890 election, Americans believed their tariff was to blame for their losses. And who had objected to the higher prices created by the tariff? Women. According to Thomas Reed, the prominent Republican Speaker of the House, the party had been defeated by "the Shopping Woman." In a backhanded way, women's power as shoppers also built the power of Pulitzer's reform-minded powerhouse, the *New York World*. The new department stores that catered to women wanted to develop new, eye-catching newspaper advertisements that crossed columns and used different typefaces, but few newspapers would accommodate them at any price. Pulitzer did. He permitted any sort of font and any shape advertisement—at first for a fee but by 1895 for no additional costs—increasing his profits and making his newspaper circulation boom.[49]

Middle-class Americans rejected the idea of special interest legislation when advanced by those who saw a conflict of interest in society between the haves and the have-nots, but female reformers advocated government intervention in the economy with different justification. The postwar mainstream vision had emphasized their societal role as mothers and wives at the same time they had been venturing into new professions and new spheres. These two very different aspects of women's lives came together in the municipal housekeeping movement, in which activist women called for government intervention in society by arguing that they could not be good wives and mothers so long as industry killed their husbands and poisoned their children with tainted goods.

Julia Ward Howe's daughter recalled that thousands of women like her mother, who had worked hard for the Union cause and enjoyed it, had no intention of going back "to the chimney-corner of life" after the war. They formed women's clubs "for self-culture and for public service." When opponents warned that such clubs would take women out of the home where they belonged and might make them strong-minded, Howe privately grumbled that "I would rather be strong-minded than weak-minded!" Beginning as study and social groups to improve women's minds, they quickly involved women in the world around them. One famous Boston reformer joked, "When I want anything in Boston remedied . . . I go down to the New England Woman's Club!"[50]

Western women had seen the way into politics first. As they worked to raise money for schools and then taught in them, it made sense that they should vote on how the money they raised was spent. Then, too, there was the issue of children. "I had been taught it was unwomanly to concern oneself with politics and that only the worst class of women would ever vote if they had a chance," wrote Luna Kellie. But her mind changed when a widowed friend with eight children begged Luna's husband J. T. to vote for a winter school. "Well that started me to thinking," Luna recalled. "She had no vote and no one to represent her. . . . Right then I saw for the first time that a woman might be interested in politics and want nay need a vote. . . . I saw where a decent mother might wish very much to vote on local affairs at least."[51]

As Kellie's reminiscences suggested, women's involvement in politics often began through the issue of schools. By 1885, the Boston and New York school elections were open to women, and *Harper's Weekly* reflected that "the first step toward general suffrage has already been taken. If a woman owning property which is taxed for schools may properly vote upon the expenditure of the tax for that purpose, she may logically vote upon other public expenditures." Indeed, the editor of the magazine took the position that "an immense body of intelligent women in this country . . . do not ask to vote . . . do not wish to vote . . . [and] think it unbecoming to their sex. . . . They have no sympathy with women who demand the suffrage." But these "intelligent women, the cultivated and charming ladies who . . . recoil" at voting, had to face the fact that suffrage was at hand.[52]

In Nebraska, Kellie's husband pressed her to get even more deeply involved in politics. "Why if [a woman] . . . was so interested in her children's school welfare should she not be equally so in having a clean community for them to grow up in? Why not be allowed for instance to vote against the saloon and in favor of clean men to . . . see that the saloons abided by the law." Kellie was not convinced at first. "I still objected that no good woman would or could go to the polls to vote in that drunken, fighting, smoking outfit. Not fit for a woman to be in the town election day or night, say nothing about going near the polls." School elections were different, she thought, because "all were neighbors but in that drunken rowdy element, never."[53]

Rural westerners were not alone in articulating the logic of female involvement in government, for city dwellers felt the lack of government activism most acutely. For a wife and mother, the city was a frighteningly hazardous place. No longer did urban women produce their own food; no longer did they have any control over what was in it, although they were charged with keeping their family healthy. Milk was infamous for carrying tuberculosis; candy wrappers were treated with poisonous dyes that killed children. Only God knew what was in meat, although the smells emanating from the refuse pools outside the factories were so nauseating that one couldn't walk past them without gagging. While streetcars increased city valuable that the punishment for horse theft was the noose. Unable to fight effectively any longer, Comanches drifted toward the reservation, where they surrendered their weapons and horses. Warriors considered most dangerous were imprisoned. Mackenzie sent a negotiator to bring in the Quahadas, and tired and hungry, they agreed to come to the reservation. By June 1875, young Comanche leader Quanah, his wife, and his young daughter had entered Fort Sill reservation in Oklahoma territory, along with most of the remaining free Comanches.[32]

Once there, Quanah realized that the same white blood that was a liability in the Comanche world could be an asset in the white one if he appeared to embrace mainstream values. Right away, he called attention to his ancestry by asking Colonel Mackenzie to find out what had happened to his mother and younger sister. A warrior himself, Mackenzie respected the Quahadi fighters and vowed to "let them down as easily as I can." He let them keep some of their ponies and refused to imprison any of the band. Mackenzie took a liking to Quanah. By the end of 1875, Mackenzie and the reservation's Indian agent had named him head of one of the bands into which the Comanches were divided for the distribution of rations. For his part, Quanah cooperated with the agent and military commander. On one occasion, he negotiated the return of a teenaged captured white boy from the Kiowa-Apaches, eventually adopting the boy into his own family. At another time, he led a band that captured and returned fugitives from the reservation, earning him the praise of Mackenzie for "excellent conduct in a dangerous expedition." He also led sorties against the horse thieves plaguing the region. He steadily gained power and influence until by 1878 he led the ninety-three people who made up the third largest band of Comanches.[33]

Like Quanah, many activist women found that they could use the mainstream image to increase their sphere of action. Rather than insisting on the abstract principle of equal rights for all women that earned ridicule for people like Elizabeth Cady Stanton, they used ideas of domesticity to gain a public voice for wives and mothers. In 1874, Annie Wittenmyer formed the Women's Christian Temperance Union (WCTU) to clean up society through temperance and other reforms (including, eventually, the call for taking the vote away from immigrant men); she insisted she needed the vote to advance her cause. Others argued that women working for the government needed the vote in order to be able to protect their virtue, for without it evil male officials might well require different inducement than the promise of a supportive vote to secure a woman's job. On Thanksgiving Day 1876, Julia Ward Howe dwellers' mobility, the trolleys operated on their own whims, stopping when hailed, charging through streets unbroken by stoplights or crosswalks. Routinely women slipped from them, men lost arms to them, and children fell beneath their wheels. Terrifying, too, were the germs that infested the slops and sewage in the streets and the guns carried by tough boys who used them in fights and sometimes hit bystanders. Everywhere a modern woman turned, it seemed her family was in danger. How could a woman be a good wife and mother when the evils of the outside world came right into her home?[54]

The world was even more frightening for women of color. To their concerns about food safety, sanitation, and urban dangers were added the constant threat of white discrimination and violence, making Ida B. Wells and women like her uncertain whether their male relatives would come home at night or whether they themselves would be treated as middle-class women should be. The *New York Times* recorded a horrifying story of a police officer accosting a respectable black woman for drunkenness. When she protested that she was simply walking home, he broke her jaw in two places and threw her into jail overnight without medical care. In her subsequent trial for disorderly conduct, middle-class white men as well as her husband excoriated the lower-class police officer's attack on a middle-class lady, but this was probably small comfort to a woman who had sat in jail overnight with a broken and dislocated jawbone for the crime of walking home. The South added lynching to violence against blacks. After 1888, lynching rose dramatically in the South, and Wells was determined to end it. While men had tried to stop lynching by claiming—often accurately—that white violence was an attempt to influence politics, newspaperwoman Wells and the African American women's clubs with which she worked put their case differently. By 1892, Wells illustrated the power of women's mainstream justification for political change when she launched her anti-lynching crusade. Instead of attacking lynching on political grounds, as black rights advocates before her had done, she attacked the idea that lynching protected white women from rape. Repeatedly, she published the statistics that showed the lynching of black wives and mothers.[55]

Middle-class girls and women were part of the public sphere in ways they had not been before. The need for money drove many into the workplace, at least temporarily, while the rise of women's education and decline in the birth rate meant that women held professional jobs in unprecedented numbers. At the same time, technological changes meant that tasks previously assigned to household women were now done outside it. Making clothes, preserving food, even baking bread was now cheaper and easier to leave to department stores and food manufacturers. Water was more and more often piped into homes; electricity, coal, and gas reduced the need for candles and firewood; small power motors—invented in 1889—enabled inventors to create household machinery that made traditional tasks easier, the vacuum cleaner, washing machine, and so on. With more free time than ever before, upwardly mobile women turned to public activism to clean up their world. They began to advocate for education, public libraries, an end to child labor, public health laws, oversight of businesses that produced food and drink, reform in marriage and divorce laws, conservation, and a reformed civil service.[56]

Women acting to address the dangers of industrial society drew support from a powerful conservative impulse. Observers of American society worried that the growth of individualism had torn apart the social organization of the nation. They were concerned that "the breach is widening between the rich and cultured and the poor and degraded; brutality and crime are . . . on the increase among us; and political power has . . . been passing steadily into the hands of those who seek and find their support in the more ignorant and lowest classes." The solution, according to many—especially new social scientists—was a return to basic family values, patterned on Christianity. "The cradle of society . . . is the household hearth. Society is made up not merely of so many men, women, and children, but rather of so many families. The single person is not a social unit, but rather a constituent member of an actual, or a potential, or a frustrated family," according to a writer for *Century* magazine. Another identified "the supreme importance of the family in our social problems." These people wanted to use the family to inculcate moral, economic, and religious values in order to bring the poor and degraded to a middle-class lifestyle.[57]

Embracing the belief that women must repair the damage of industrial society to American life, many women added a strong component of religious duty into their public work. Julia Ward Howe was wrenched with despair at the poverty of the industrial world and drew on religion for her determination to ameliorate it. On July 4, 1872, in London, she had seen "a sight of misery, a little crumb of a boy, barefoot, tugging after a hand-organ man, also very shabby. Gave the little one a ha-penny, all the copper I had. But in the heartache he gave me, I resolved, God helping me, that my luxury shall henceforth be to minister to human misery, and to redeem much time and money spent on my own fancies, as I may."[58]

In Illinois, young college woman Jane Addams was equally distraught at what she saw around her in both the city and the country. All her life, those who met Addams commented on her beautiful, luminous eyes, which could not turn away from even the worst scenes of modern life. On a visit to the West she was "much horrified by the wretched conditions among the farmers. . . . The farmer's wife [was] a picture of despair as she stood in the door of the bare, crude house, and the two children behind her . . . their little bare feet so black, so hard, the great cracks so filled with dust that they looked like flattened hoofs . . . appeared but half-human." Addams was even more appalled by the extreme poverty of the industrial cities. She came to believe that "the first generation of college women had . . . departed too suddenly from the active, emotional life led by their grandmothers and great-grandmothers." The only cure for her own sense of helplessness, and probably that of many young women, she thought, was to shun their "sheltered and pampered lives" and recapture their mothers' traditional role as those who relieved suffering and helplessness.59

In 1889, Addams and her friend Ellen Gates Starr bought a decayed mansion on Halstead Street in Chicago and sought to repair their own lives as they launched an experiment using the energy of new womanhood to rebuild America's traditional political economy. Settlement houses—like Hull-House and Lillian Wald's Henry Street Settlement in New York City—were designed to re-create a web of social responsibility in the industrial city as middle-class women moved into a lower-class neighborhood to minister to the people living there. When she opened Chicago's Hull-House, Addams transformed the ideal of economic harmony into a social context. She argued that individuals were fundamentally interrelated and therefore that the government must protect the poor, women, and children, to enable them to contribute to society. "Hull-House was soberly opened on the theory that the dependence of classes on each other is reciprocal."60

At the time, she recalled, Halstead Street was "one of the great thoroughfares of Chicago," lined with butcher shops, saloons, and dry-goods stores. Hull-House had once been on the prosperous fringes of the city, but by 1889 the city had expanded, surrounding it with neighborhoods of immigrants from Italy, Germany, Poland, Russia, Bohemia, Canada, and Ireland. Hull-House brought home to middle-class settlement workers the difficulties of upward mobility in nineteenth-century America. Living in the poor city districts incorporated "the dirty streets, the universal ugliness, the lack of oxygen in the air you daily breathe, the endless struggle with soot and dust and insufficient water supply" into the experiences of settlement house workers. It made "hanging from a strap of the overcrowded street car at the end of your day's work" the act of middle-class settlement house women, who came to understand tenement life when they moved into a poor district and had to "send . . . children to the nearest wretchedly crowded school, and see them suffer the consequences," Hull-House resident Florence Kelley explained.[61]

Hull-House applied women's domestic role to the problems of the city. Women were expected to nurture children, care for the sick, and feed the hungry, and Hull-House residents did this for their neighbors. Even for those "too battered and oppressed" to participate in Hull-House activities, the workers could provide "the bare offices of humanity." As soon as they arrived, Addams recalled, the Hull-House residents were "asked to wash the new-born babies, and to prepare the dead for burial, to nurse the sick, and to 'mind the children.'" Indeed, the needs of the industrial cities seemed to fit naturally into woman's sphere. In the late 1880s, an observer noted, more than a million New Yorkers lived in tenements, and more than 142,000 of them were children less than five years old. Trying to pull these children out of "appalling conditions of ignorance, idleness, and vice," urban women were instrumental in starting the kindergarten movement in America. By 1888, Boston, Philadelphia, and San Francisco all had kindergarten systems, offshoots of the idea of early childhood education, conceived in Germany by Friedrich Froebel and brought to America by none other than Carl Schurz's wife, Margarethe Meyer Schurz, in 1856. Babies seemed to be a woman's province, and it was only natural that women should be in charge of societal reforms that began in babyhood.[62]

From these homelike beginnings, the Hull-House community began to reach into the government to protect home life. Addams's story of how she became involved in politics was a perfect portrait of the larger involvement of women in municipal affairs (although her experiences ultimately made her much more radical than most of her peers). Realizing that her delicate nephew could never visit Hull-House because the stench and germs from nearby garbage boxes would threaten his life, she began an investigation of garbage collection and death rates in the city wards. When it turned out that their ward had the third highest death rate in the city, the Hull-House Woman's Club began to investigate the conditions of the ward's alleys. In two months, they sent the Chicago Health Department 1,037 reports of health violations. "For the club woman who had finished a long day's work of washing or ironing followed by the cooking of a hot supper, it would have been much easier to sit on her doorstep during a summer evening than to go up and down ill-kept alleys and get into trouble with her neighbors over the condition of their garbage boxes," Addams recalled. But they did so, ultimately forcing the city government to transfer three inspectors in a row from the ward because they were not doing their job. The following spring, Addams herself bid for the contract for the ward's garbage removal. Her bid was thrown out on a technicality, but the mayor appointed her the ward's garbage inspector.63

This position was a patronage plum, paying $1,000 a year. It was a difficult job for anyone determined to do it right—getting up at six to make sure the men were at work early, following the wagons to the dump, forcing an unwilling contractor to increase the number of garbage wagons, suing landlords for ignoring garbage laws, arresting tenants who tried to sneak stable trash into the garbage wagons—and the previous inspectors had collected their pay without performing their work. Addams was increasingly frustrated with the machine politics that gave such important jobs to political hacks. "We made desperate attempts to have . . . dead animals removed by the contractor who was paid most liberally by the city for that purpose but who, we slowly discovered, always made the police ambulances do the work, delivering the carcasses upon freight cars for shipment to a soap factory in Indiana where they were sold for a good price although the contractor himself was the largest stockholder in the concern."64

Addams's foray into politics, her "abrupt departure into the ways of men," as she called it, shocked her neighbors, but she explained "that if it were a womanly task to go about in tenement houses in order to nurse the sick, it might be quite as womanly to go through the same district in order to prevent the breeding of so-called 'filth diseases.'" When the ward's death rate dropped dramatically after the Hull-House garbage investigation, the women recognized their potential power. So did the ward boss. Tired of Addams's intervention, he circumvented the civil service law protecting the garbage inspector and got rid of Hull-House oversight of garbage collection by eliminating the job altogether.65

Addams insisted that the government must regulate child labor, women's labor, sanitation, and so on, but she based that claim not on laborers' conviction about economic conflict in society. Rather, she and her associates worked hard to explain that their aim was to protect the home and enable more and more people to enjoy the middle-class dream. Addams insisted that factory women wanted simply to stay home and take care of their children, rather than having to run dangerous machines. Addams recounted her experience comforting a woman whose small son had been killed when he had been blown off a roof. When Addams asked what she could do to help, the woman begged only for a day's wages to enable her to stay home for a day to hold her surviving child.[66]

Addams argued that women needed direct protection so that they could rise in American society. When industrialists defended child labor by claiming that widowed mothers needed their children to bring in money, Addams insisted that, to the contrary, widows supported child labor laws so that their children could stay in school. They assured her, "That is why we came to America, and I don't want to spoil his start, even . . . though his father is dead." Mothers also needed protection from hard work, Addams believed, and she advocated limiting women's work to eight hours a day, six days a week. This was important, she thought, for while men were willing to ignore household work in favor of rest, "a conscientious girl finds it hard to sleep with her mother washing and scrubbing within a few feet of her bed." Women also needed government protection for their daughters. Addams told the story of "a peasant woman straight from the fields of Germany" who earned the money to buy her own country home by working as a laundress at thirty-five cents a day. When her daughters fell "victims to the vice of the city," though, she needed government help, not for charity, "for she had an immense capacity for hard work, but she sadly needed the service of the State's attorney office, enforcing the laws designed for the protection of . . . her daughters."[67]

Most of the men Addams described simply wanted a chance to work. Immigrants were at the mercy of the bosses, who "fleeced them unmercifully, both in securing a place to work and then in supplying them with food," and of the "employment agencies," private businesses that charged them a commission for finding them work. Addams told of a group of Bulgarians who had to walk back to Chicago after an employment agency sent them to Arkansas, where there was no work. The agency promptly sent them off to Oklahoma, costing them both the train fare and another commission to the agency. Even strikers, she insisted, were eager workers who struck only from need. Nothing broke their hearts more than being blacklisted, unable to find employment.[68]

As she described them, Addams's neighbors simply wanted the chance to become middle-class Americans. "I remember one family in which the father had been out of work for this same winter, most of the furniture had been pawned, and as the worn-out shoes could not be replaced the children could not go to school. The mother was ill and barely able to come for the supplies and medicines," she recalled. Two years later Addams was invited back to the house, "which had been completely restored" because the wife could not bear for Addams to believe that they had stayed in their downtrodden condition. "She said that it was as if she had met me, not as I am ordinarily, but as I should appear misshapen with rheumatism or with a face distorted by neuralgic pain; that it was not fair to judge poor people that way." Addams met head-on Carnegie's charge that the working poor wasted their money on frivolities because they didn't share mainstream values; rather, she said, their showy clothes and trinkets were their attempt to mimic mainstream life as closely as they could with what means they had.[69]

The movement that Addams articulated so clearly reached throughout American society as women banded together to improve their communities, whether Hispanic communities in Texas, African American communities in Florida or Chicago, or white communities in rural New Hampshire. Municipal housekeeping was a movement in which women could participate naturally from their homes, as well as through more formal associations like Hull-House. As Addams said, "As society grows more complicated it is necessary that woman shall extend her sense of responsibility to many things outside her own home if she would continue to preserve the home in its entirety." Women established libraries and schools, demanded clean streets, raised money to build playgrounds, and provided aid to the destitute. Always, though, their works reflected their values. They privileged those who shared their own family values of hard work, marriage, religion, and uplift. A church-going widow with children could expect help from a local women's club, but a young unemployed drunkard could go to hell on his own.[70]

Support for women's rights and social legislation on domestic grounds overrode the principle of universal rights that had justified black suffrage and women's suffrage in the immediate postwar years. In 1890, the two estranged women's suffrage associations merged to become the National American Woman Suffrage Association, and two years later its first president, Elizabeth Cady Stanton, resigned when members complained that she was too radical. Suffrage was no longer about individual self-determination; it was now tied into mainstream concerns about good government. Municipal reform "wasn't suffrage, but it was good government, which is about the same thing," Julia Ward Howe commented. "Imposition of taxes, laws concerning public health, order, and morality, affect me precisely as they affect the male members of my family, and I am bound equally with them to look to the maintenance of a worthy and proper standard and status in all of these departments."[71]

In 1890, Julia Ward Howe and others like her organized the General Federation of Women's Clubs, giving the women's club movement national organization. By 1900, it had more than 155,000 members in 2,675 clubs. In 1891, Howe wrote the introduction for *Woman's Work in America*, a book that reviewed the many reforms and professions in which women were participating. As a writer in *Harper's Weekly* commented, "The variety of occupations in which women are now engaged, and the ability and earnestness of their service, will be surprising to those who have a feeling of impatience with any suggestion of such activity, as if it must necessarily involve some sacrifice of womanly character and refinement." The book reviewer for the *Atlantic Monthly* noted the significance of women's postwar activity. "One is struck by the high value which all these women place upon organization," he wrote. They used this organization to advance the cause of home and family. Perhaps encouraged by the election of 1890, when women's anger at high prices was credited with defeating the Republicans, newly organized consumers' leagues sought to use purchasing power to force manufacturers to treat workers fairly and make safer products. They aimed, one Hull-House resident explained, "to educate the purchaser as to her influence in the life of the workers, urging the duty of . . . shopping in conscientiously selected places," places that offered hope of breaking the poverty of the cities by offering to workers a fair wage, reasonable hours, and sanitary conditions.[72]

With women successfully lobbying for government support of the individualist family, it was no accident that, immediately after Cleveland vetoed the Dependent Pension Act, veterans countered with a dramatic new proposal. They promptly suggested a new bill that provided pensions not just to disabled veterans, but to their wives and dependent children. The construction of the pension bill as a welfare program for families, benefiting helpless women and children, made it palatable to a population hostile to providing welfare to individual men. On June 27, 1890, President Harrison signed the Dependent Pension Act, which gave federal pensions to disabled soldiers, their wives, and children, establishing the principle of government responsibility for the welfare of veterans and their families. This groundbreaking act established the idea that government should provide for the American family —wives and dependent children—rather than for individual males. In the five years following the passage of the act, the number of pensioners rose from about 675,000 to 970,000, and the annual appropriation for pensions rose from $81 million to $135 million. By depleting the surplus, the Dependent

Pension Act weakened complaints about the high tariffs that were throwing money into the Treasury, thus linking aid to business with aid to the mainstream family.[73]

Paradoxically, government aid to families did not weaken the middle-class faith in individualism. As the government expanded into social legislation that protected the middle-class household, the idealization of the western image kept the idea of American individualism flourishing. In 1889, the last territorial stronghold of the continental West opened to white settlement. At noon on April 22, 1889, U.S. Army officers fired pistols or signaled for the firing of cannon or the blowing of trumpets to announce to the 50,000 people lined up on the border of Oklahoma territory that they could begin the run to claim a homestead. Horsemen took off in front of the wagon men, who whipped their teams into what were known as the "unassigned lands." These "boomers" had been preceded by "sooners" who had crept across the Oklahoma border before the start of the land rush. Together they settled Oklahoma. When Oklahoma became a Territory in 1890, no unassigned federal lands remained in the continental United States. In his 1890 report, the U.S. census director commented: "There can hardly be said to be a frontier line" any longer. The next year, 900,000 acres of the Sauk, Fox, and Potawatomie lands in Oklahoma were opened to settlement. In 1892, the opening of the Cheyenne-Arapaho Reservation gave away 3,000,000 more acres. The Comanche Reservation was opened, too; even Quanah could not protect it. In 1892 the Jerome Agreement forced Comanches onto 160-acre allotments while the rest of lands guaranteed to them by the Treaty of Medicine Lodge went to white settlers.[74]

Certainly there was no longer significant Indian military resistance to the American conquest. In 1886, General Nelson A. Miles of the U.S. Army had captured the Apache leader Geronimo and ended his final raid from the reservation. Geronimo and his people had fought effectively against Americans from 1874 to January 1884, when Geronimo surrendered and was put back on the same reservation whose poor conditions had sparked his escape. Less than two years later, in May 1885, he made another break for freedom accompanied by a small party of warriors and their wives and children. Geronimo surrendered to an American officer at the Mexican border on May 27, 1886, but bolted before going into American territory, afraid that he would be killed in the United States. Angry army brass sent General Miles to the chase, and newspapers followed the hunting of Geronimo with fascination. Miles caught up with the Apache band in the fall. Promised that he would be returned to Arizona after a prison stay in Florida, Geronimo finally surrendered to Miles on September 3, 1886. The closest he ever got to Arizona again was his incarceration at Fort Sill, Oklahoma. "Once I moved around like the wind," Geronimo had once sadly told an army officer. "Now I surrender to you and that is all." At the end of 1886, President Cleveland proudly told the American public: "There is no such thing as the Indian frontier. Civilization, with the busy hum of industry and the influences of Christianity, surrounds these people at every point. . . . It is no longer possible for them to subsist by the chase and the spontaneous productions of the earth."[75]

The northwestern tribes tried to retain their autonomy, pointedly rejecting the middle-class lifestyle that the Dawes Severalty Act had tried to impose on them in 1887. In 1889, government agents pressed Sioux men for their approval—required under the Treaty of Fort Laramie—of the Sioux Act, which carved six reservations out of the remaining Sioux land and arranged for the disposition of the nine million remaining acres of land to settlers. Furious, Sitting Bull declared, "I would rather die an Indian than live a white man." But his opposition was futile. Negotiators simply claimed they had the requisite votes.[76]

About that year, the Ghost Dance movement for Indian solidarity and a return to traditional native life began with the Paiutes in Nevada. In visions, ancestors of living Indians promised that if their descendants returned to their traditional ways of life and abandoned alcohol, the buffalo would return, whites would be swept from the land, and Indians would once again prosper. In the poverty and degradation of the reservations, the movement quickly gained adherents. By 1890, it had spread across the plains and taken deep root among the Sioux in Montana. Indians at the Pine Ridge and Rosebud reservations there adopted the ceremony, making nervous Indian agents appeal to the U.S. Army for troops to keep the Indians under control.[77]

This last gasp of nineteenth-century Indian resistance to white incursions raised white anxiety. The Ghost Dance movement came to Sitting Bull's reservation, Standing Rock, in fall 1890. Uneasy authorities worried that Sitting Bull would join the Ghost Dancers and, since he was regarded as a spiritual leader, bring the rest of the reservation Indians into the movement as well. The movement "is indicative of greater danger of an Indian war in that region than has existed since 1876," *Harper's Weekly* reported. "Never before have diverse Indian tribes been so generally united upon a single idea." On December 15, 1890, reservation authorities sent forty-three Lakota police officers to Sitting Bull's cabin to bring him into custody. In the ensuing struggle between the officers and Sitting Bull's supporters, seven warriors and six officers died. So did Sitting Bull. A Lakota officer shot him in the head, fulfilling Sitting Bull's own prophecy that he would be killed by his own people.[78]

Sitting Bull's murder only confirmed for the Lakota Ghost Dancers that they must try to recover their lost past. Three hundred and fifty Ghost Dancers—mostly women and children—moved toward the Pine Ridge Reservation, but in the cold their leader contracted pneumonia. When the U.S. Army came after them with the rebuilt Seventh Cavalry, they surrendered without a fight and camped as ordered beside the nearby Wounded Knee Creek. On the morning of December 29, 1890, soldiers came into the camp and demanded the Indians give up their firearms. A Lakota medicine man urged the warriors to resist, claiming that the Ghost Dance shirts they wore would stop bullets. When a soldier tried to disarm a deaf Indian the gun discharged, and firing started on both sides. The Indians ran for cover as the angry soldiers opened fire on them with four Hotchkiss cannons. In an hour, 146 Indians—including 44 women and 18 children—lay dead, along with 25 soldiers, most of whom were probably caught in the crossfire from their own guns.[79]

The real Wild West, with its cowboys and Indian fights, was gone. The buffalo were dead, and in their place rose chimneys and church spires. As Nat Love reflected, "across their once peaceful path now thunders the iron horse, awakening the echoes far and near with bell and whistle, where once could only be heard the sharp crack of the rifle or the long doleful yelp of the coyote." "With the march of progress came the railroad and no longer were we called upon to follow the long horned steers or mustangs on the trail, while the immense cattle ranges, stretching away in the distance as far as the eye could see, now began to be dotted with cities and the towns and the cattle industry which once held a monopoly in the west, now had to give way to the wild and unrestricted life of the boundless plains, the new order of things did not appeal, and many of us became disgusted and quit the wild life for the pursuits of our more civilized brother." Cowboy life "had in a great measure lost its attractiveness" for him, Love concluded. In 1889 he married, and the following year he became a Pullman porter on the Denver and Rio Grande Railroad, running between Denver and Salida, Colorado.[80]

But the idea of the Wild West did not die. It lived, quite naturally, in the

Figure 18. Indians willing to accept middle-class ideals might be able to rise in society, but this image of the victims of the Wounded Knee massacre being piled into a mass grave in December 1890 pointedly illustrated what happened to those who did not. Denver Public Library, Western History Collection, Northwestern Photography, X-31292.

realm of ideology and entertainment where it could represent an idealized economic, political, and social freedom that embodied American individualism without fear of contradiction from the messy details of reality. The West became an image, permanently rural, antigovernment, and wild, untrammeled by the realities of western urbanization and government intervention. In 1887, right after the drought and hard winter of 1886–87 wiped out the cattle herds, Buffalo Bill took his immensely popular show to England for a command performance for the queen. In 1892, Buffalo Bill was back in England, and the artist Frederic Remington commented on how very popular the show was there. "One should no longer ride the deserts of Texas or the rugged uplands of Wyoming to see the Indians and the pioneers, but should go to London." Nowhere was the move from reality to image clearer than in Buffalo Bill's Wild West Show, which after the Battle at Wounded Knee boasted as attractions a number of the warriors from the fight. In May 1891, Cody advertised that he had hired sixty-four new Indians and claimed that twenty-three of them were prisoners of war from Wounded Knee. He advertised them in a London newspaper as "fifty of the worst Indians engaged in the Wounded Knee fight."[81]

Those warlike Indians who were acting in the Wild West Show or who were safely dead could be eulogized as nature's noblemen. After the Wounded Knee massacre, *Harper's Weekly* printed "Hunting-Life in the Rockies," a story in which a mysterious hunting guide assured two British businessmen that "one of the finest men I ever knew was [Sioux] chief, Sitting Bull." The guide showed them "a piece of finely wrought white leather" illustrated with buffalo, deer, and warriors, telling them that Sitting Bull "did that with his own hand; and though it isn't as well done as a picture by a regular artist, I had rather have it than a Raphael." But, remonstrated the businessman, "a Raphael would give you one hundred thousand dollars." "Yes," agreed the guide, "but it would not give me the memories that this bit of skin gives me. . . . When I look at this, I live again the old life with the man who gave it to me, and see the ordered camp, with the ensigns, the spears and shields at the tent doors; the tents of splendid skins . . . the women with their beautiful dresses of bead and leather; the bands of horses; the excitement of the great hunts . . . the kindly chief—the father of his people. . . . By Jove, he was a fine fellow!" He concluded, "I've tried Britain and Europe, and most parts of America, . . . but I never enjoyed a better time than the months I spent with Old Bull."[82]

Americans anxious to keep alive the western heart of American individualism threw their weight behind John Muir's attempt to make Yosemite a national park. In 1864, President Lincoln had given the state of California the land around Yosemite as a park, but by 1890, state management of the property had led to the degradation of its resources by timber companies and sheep-herding enterprises. Tourists who came to view the park's wonders were fleeced by the hotel operators and tour guides who had state-awarded contracts. *Century* magazine featured articles by John Muir, "recognized as the best authority on matters relating to the Sierra," who warned that "Ax and plow, hogs and horses, have long been and are still busy in Yosemite's gardens and groves. All that is accessible and destructible is being rapidly destroyed." George G. MacKenzie agreed, complaining that "the conservation of natural beauty has been outweighed too frequently by the supposed necessity of providing mules, horses, and horned cattle with pasturage and hay at the least possible cost . . . and of . . . the absolutely shocking use that has been made of the wood-chopper's ax."[83]

It was imperative, it seemed, for the government to step in to protect the birthright of free individual Americans from the depredations of avaricious businessmen. In October 1890, Congress passed a law making the area around the state property in Yosemite a federal park, and the military moved in to manage the national park area. This protected the park's natural beauty, and it also guaranteed that San Francisco's growing middle class had healthy drinking water. In March 1891, Congress expanded federal control over pristine western lands. It gave the president the power to "set apart and reserve . . . as public reservations" land that bore at least some timber, whether or not it was of any commercial value. That same year, President Harrison set aside timber land adjacent to Yellowstone National Park. He also set apart over 4 million acres—over 6,000 square miles—south of the original Yosemite National Park, including as much of the "Big Tree" sequoia forests as possible. By September 1893, about 17 million acres of land had been set into forest reserves. Objections to this policy, *Century* claimed, came from "men [who] wish to get at it and make it earn something for them." This was, of course, exactly the meaning of western land to begin with. But now, according to the magazine, "the essential quality [of a public park] is that of a solitude, a wilderness, a place of undisturbed communion with nature in all her primitive beauty, simplicity, and grandeur." Without government protection of the West, private individuals, seeking to make money from the timber, minerals, or even the views of this elemental land, would destroy it for all.[84]

As the struggle intensified between those who believed that government must broker between different groups in society and those who maintained that the government must respond to the American people as a whole, mainstream Americans increasingly pushed their opponents outside of the definition of "the people." So, while the government could not legitimately help self-identified workers, farmers, suffragists, or big businessmen, for example, it could—and should—promote the prosperity of "Americans." It began to do so, tentatively, with the Sherman Antitrust Act. As this transition occurred, mainstream women's activists increasingly encouraged the use of government to promote mainstream values, and it did so with the Dependent Pension Act. It did so much more dramatically in the West, where it seemed the government must take a stand to preserve the pristine land that represented the freedom of the American success story. By the early 1890s, the federal government had become the official protector of American individualism.

1893–1897

The Final Contest

W̲ould the American individualist ideal, supported by an activist government, represent the nation? Or would those who recognized that racial boundaries, economic dislocations, and gender discrimination systematically enforced inequality make Americans recognize that the individualist ideal was not accessible to all? During the 1890s, the fight to control the government became a critical fight over who, in fact, spoke for "the American people." Was it the disaffected, the poor, those who were squeezed by current national policies and who were, in many cases, homeless and starving? Or was it those who were prospering in the American system and who disliked the actions of the disaffected? The fight over who represented "the people" was an important battle of rhetoric that determined the future of American government.

In 1895, it was Atlanta's turn to host an exposition to show the world the industrial progress of America. To demonstrate the racial tolerance of the region (despite the dramatic rise in lynching since 1888) the exposition's white organizers invited Booker T. Washington, the principal and founder of Alabama's Tuskegee Institute, to make a speech at the opening exercises. This was, Washington recalled, "the first time in the entire history of the Negro that a member of my race had been asked to speak from the same platform with white Southern men and women on any important National occasion," and was designed to illustrate that the mainstream would welcome, even honor, any man who shared its dream of self-help. With an audience of "the wealth and culture of the white South," "a large number of Northern whites, as well as a great many men and women of my own race," Washington was well aware of what a white neighbor had jokingly warned him: he was in a "tight place." With Ben Tillman's viciously racist populist movement growing in the South, Washington was not about to waste the chance to gain middle-class white support by declaring African Americans firmly in the self-help mainstream.[1]

Addressing his audience, Washington illustrated just how aptly he has been called "the wizard of Tuskegee." Playing to the mainstream belief in menial labor as the economic foundation of society and individual improvement, he told his audience that "the masses of us are to live by the productions of our own hands, and . . . we shall prosper in proportion as we learn to dignify and glorify common labour and put brains and skill into the common occupations of life." Washington declared himself firmly in the middle-class camp, telling his listeners, who were only too aware of national convulsions over the grievances of workers, African Americans, and farmers in a time of apparent general progress: "It is at the bottom of life we must begin, and not at the top. Nor should we permit our grievances to overshadow our opportunities." In his speech, Washington articulated the latitude and limits of the mainstream vision that had been constructed in the turbulent years after the Civil War. The government would protect the ability of all American individualists— poor or rich, white or black, immigrant or native born, men or women—to participate in it, but it deliberately excluded anyone perceived as emphasizing "grievances" over "opportunities," asking for government aid to right systematic inequalities in America.[2]

This vision had also been broadcast at the 1893 Columbian Exposition of Chicago, a world's fair dubbed the "White City" by one observer. Its organizers designed the Columbian Exposition to celebrate American progress, showing the triumphant march of civilization from ancient Europe to modern America and hinting at glories to come. The discovery of America, the director explained, was "the instrument of human enlightenment and progress. President Grover Cleveland opened the fair, which boasted the most artistic buildings brash Chicago could muster in an attempt to counteract accusations that Americans ignored culture in favor of materialism. To prove the superiority of art in Chicago, Louis Sullivan's brilliant young assistant Frank Lloyd Wright was drafted to help design an imposing gate. Still, technology and progress towered over the art; the brand new Ferris wheel impressed visitors far more than Wright's gate. The story of the Chicago exposition was one of progress and material triumph. Writer Robert Herrick later put the "beautiful city of white palaces on the lake" in a novel, where "its beauty and grandeur" filled his fictional observer with admiration. One evening, the man glided on the lake and looked back at the White City, "The long lines of white buildings were ablaze with countless lights; the music from the bands scattered over the grounds floated softly out upon the water. . . . The toil and trouble of men, the fear that was gripping men's hearts in the market, fell away from me, and in its place came Faith. The people who could dream this vision and make it real, those people from all parts of the land who thronged here day after day—their sturdy wills and strong hearts would rise above failure, would press on to greater victories than this triumph of beauty —victories greater than the world had yet witnessed!"[3]

More than 21 million visitors came to see the exposition, sharing the fair organizers' proud vision of the world's extraordinary progress since the middle of the nineteenth century. "The last four decades . . . have witnessed greater strides than all the previous years of the Columbian epoch combined," the director noted happily. Visitors marveled at the centerpiece of the fair, the Hall of Manufactures and Liberal Arts, which was 1,687 feet long, 787 feet wide, and 236 feet high and covered more than forty acres, an area sufficient to build 500 houses on a 25-by-100-foot lot, enough to house 5,000 people. The American exhibit was "the very embodiment of industrial progress, the substance of material prosperity," one observer boasted. Tiffany & Company provided more than 1,000 pieces valued at over $2 million and displayed a 125-carat diamond worth $100,000. Less showy but also of interest "to all who love to note and study the industrial progress of the United States" were the cotton exhibit, which boasted that the nation produced more than 3.6 billion pounds of cotton in 1890, and the woolen industries exhibit, which claimed an 1892 output worth $400,000 from 250,000 workers. The exhibit of "ready-made" clothing claimed that that industry was worth more than $300 million, expending more than $70 million a year in wages. Other exhibits showed wires, guns, scales, chemicals, ceramics, typewriters, rubber, celluloid, fountain pens, artificial limbs (an important item in the decades after the butchery of the Civil War), and every manufacture necessary to furnish a prosperous American home: wallpaper, toilets, refrigerators, furniture, electric lamp fixtures, sinks, stoves. Prominent, too, were American furs, including, "a robe made of 62,000 pieces of golden otter and seal skin . . . valued at $500." Altogether, the value of the nation's manufactures in 1892 was $7.5 billion, directly employing 3.5 million people and indirectly supporting at least four times that number, an observer noted triumphantly.[4]

Native Americans illustrated the great power of the American system to raise even "savages" to the American middle class. Fair organizers carefully arranged villages of Indians "as an illustration of the primitive life of the aborigines" and then contrasted this image with Indian boys and girls attending school in the government exhibit. A reproduced reservation boarding school, decorated with Indian handicrafts and photographs of Indian leaders and Indian life, and "workshops, school, sitting and dining rooms, dormitories, and kitchen, with apartments for employees," exhibited "boys and girls, studying or reciting, working at trades, or preparing their meals, all as though actually living on reservations, with specimens of their self-taught industries compared with those of civilized nations, and with the methods adopted and the results accomplished." This exhibit was designed to show visitors how government was "civilizing" the Indians. If fair visitors remained unconvinced that the American dream worked for Indians, they could observe one of the assistants to the chief of the Anthropological Building, "a tall, sinewy, finely-featured, full-blooded Apache," related to Cochise and Geronimo, who had gone to night school in New York, been "to Europe on a yacht," and planned to finish his education at Harvard.[5]

If the exposition was designed to show the triumph of human progress in America, it also met head-on the question of who was welcome in American society and the terms on which they could participate. When it created the commission in charge of organizing the fair, Congress also created a separate women's committee, "a striking . . . and gratifying . . . commentary . . . on the change . . . in the condition of women," the director noted. It was a commentary, too, on the role of women in America: they were important in their own sphere but not equally incorporated into a vision of American society. This was not an uncomfortable position for many of the women at the fair. One observer claimed that the Woman's Building, designed by Sophia Hayden, illustrated the elevated position of women in America. Certainly the art at one end of the building was notable. Mary Cassatt, one of the leading American Impressionists, painted a huge mural entitled *Young Women Plucking the Fruits of Knowledge or Science*, using the traditional female task of picking fruit to represent women's education and the modern woman's use of her new-found training to nurture the next generation. In her speech opening the Woman's Building, the president of the Board of Lady Managers made the role of women in society clear: woman's province was to promote the welfare of women and children, protecting them against the evils of modern industry. In tandem with the exposition, organizers planned world's congresses of the "foremost men and women" in the world to be held in the Art Institute, where they could "promote the progress, prosperity, unity, peace, and happiness of the world." The women's congress, where speakers reinforced the idea that women must reform society and needed the ballot to do so, was the most successful of them. "Woman is primarily the mother of the human race," the elderly Julia Ward Howe wrote in her introduction to a history of the Congress of Women, and "has a debt to the human race."[6]

Which workers were welcome in the American White City was clear. While the exposition championed the products of working men and women, there was no place within its walls for disaffected laborers. Paintings in the Hall of Manufactures and Liberal Arts personified different kinds of machinery as a number of beautiful women; workers were "typified by stalwart artisans, with all the accessories of their craft." Employment was easily found in American cities, according to an observer, and wages were two to four times higher than those in European cities. Working families could make more money than they needed to survive, and they spent that money in the community, either in investments or in purchases, keeping the cities healthy. Visitors to the fair noted an exhibit of "a model Philadelphia workingman's house. It is a brick structure, two stories high, of pleasing design, and containing comforts and conveniences such as are found in no other representative dwelling house for workingmen in the world." "Tens of thousands" of these sorts of homes were owned by workers in Philadelphia, an article in the conservative *Manufacturer and Builder* claimed. Philadelphia's "chief glory" is in "the multitudes of small houses in which the man who toils may live with comfort and self-respect, and with the stake in the good government of the community which follows upon the ownership of property." Indeed, it claimed, this was "the best product of advanced American civilization." The fair's Labor Congress was charged with considering the labor question, not "as it is commonly understood, but labor in its highest and broadest sense, as discussed . . . by its sincerest friends and champions." Samuel Gompers, who had been increasingly using middle-class language, was one of the most radical labor leaders invited to speak and, one disgusted observer recorded, "in answer to the . . . question, 'What does Labor want?' said that it wanted the earth and the fullness thereof; and first of all an immediate advance in wages and reduction in time—eight hours a day, with fewer tomorrow and fewer still the next day. But while there was other nonsense of this kind, the discussions of the labor parliament were for the most part of a rational and instructive character, as at times were even the remarks of Samuel Gompers."

Figure 19. *Young Women Plucking the Fruits of Knowledge or Science*, 1893. Impressionist Mary Cassatt turned her fascination with women and children into a mural for the Woman's Building at the Columbian Exposition, using her subjects as an allegory for women's education and its benefit to society. This mural was destroyed when the White City burned, but many of Cassatt's paintings from this period reflect the same themes she explored here. Courtesy of Harvard College Library.

In 1892, the handbook of the American Federation of Labor claimed only 675,117 members. This meant that nonunion workers were far more common than union labor, a fact clearly reflected in the exposition.[7]

How black Americans should fit into the fair was unclear. African Americans wondered whether it would be better for them to have separate exhibits within the exposition or to integrate their products into the general exhibits dominated by white men. For African Americans this question was vital. Since the renewed call for a federal elections bill and a federal education act in 1888–90, and the consequent rise of Tillman's virulently racist populism in the South, the popular press had increasingly denigrated all African Americans as lazy criminals waiting for special treatment from the federal government. In this atmosphere, southern states had been revising their constitutions to curtail black voting, and lynching had risen dramatically. And yet the fair did not reflect this southern pattern; Illinois had a civil rights law and Chicago had integrated its public schools. African Americans differed on how to gain access to a place in mainstream culture and to the fair that represented that culture. Was it better to acquiesce in the plans of the fair's white organizers and showcase the black community's great artists and inventions as part of white exhibits, or was it better to fight the white organizers for equal participation in the fair with events or even days dedicated to black culture and achievements?[8]

Ida B. Wells had no doubt that African Americans must boycott the exposition to call the world's attention to their plight. Despite the vociferous opposition of a number of prominent African American newspapers, whose editors worried that agitation would hurt the black cause by reinforcing the idea that African Americans wanted something for nothing, Wells put together a pamphlet: "The Reason Why the Colored American Is Not in the World's Columbian Exposition." Wells herself wrote three of the pamphlet's six chapters, and as her name was the only one on the pamphlet's cover, her radicalism seemed to speak for all the opponents of black participation in the exposition. Her chapters—"Class Legislation," "The Convict Lease System," and "Lynch Law"—began straight off with a complaint that after the Civil War, "no foot of land nor [agricultural] implement was given" to ex-slaves. From there, Wells went on to marshal evidence that the political, legal, and economic systems of the United States were structured to subordinate African Americans to whites. Supporting her point was the statistic that of the thousands of exposition's employees, only two of the blacks were clerks; the rest were janitors, laborers, and porters (yet other African Americans applauded the organizers' willingness to hire blacks at all).

Wells's pamphlet correctly identified the increasing exclusion of black Americans from middle-class society, but with its demand for government support—one chapter complained that Congress had refused to fund a specific black exhibit at the fair—and its defense of apparent criminals as it attacked lynching and the convict lease system, it also fit perilously within the mainstream image of a grasping, disaffected African American manifesto. In contrast, middle-class Americans looked with complacency on those African Americans who did choose to participate in the fair: Edmonia Lewis, one of the nation's premier sculptors; George Washington Carver, who won honorable mention for his painting *Yucca Gloriosa*; Booker T. Washington, who spoke at the Congress on Labor; the black college exhibitors who provided products for the Palace of Liberal Arts and Education. African Americans were present at the fair, it appeared, and—as the presence of Montana multimillionaire Charles P. Grove indicated—many of them were fitting well into American society without any government action on their behalf.[9]

There was another side to the middle-class acceptance of black achievers. Perhaps the most visible and acceptable African American at the fair was Nancy Green, who had been hired by the R. T. Davis Milling Company to represent the company's new product: the Aunt Jemima pancake mix. Green performed her role by acting as a stereotypical plantation mammy, and the company provided visitors with buttons featuring her picture and the slogan, "I'se in town, honey." A fifty-seven-year-old former slave who had been a servant for a Chicago judge, Green's elevation to fair sensation was in some sense a personal triumph. It was also a fierce reminder of the place of African Americans in mainstream culture. A few Edmonia Lewises were welcome in the elite ranks of society, but most African Americans were popular only when they played the role of happy servants.[10]

This relentlessly determined celebration of the American middle-class dream revealed the fear that America could easily slide away from the individualist ideal to a world in which different interests battled for government benefits. Buffalo Bill's Wild West Show was a feature of the exposition, taking up almost as much space as the buildings themselves. His sister described the show as "a small village" of 600 people where even eating patterns revealed the advance of civilization. "The Indians may be seen eating bundles of meat from their fingers and drinking tankards of iced buttermilk. The Mexicans, a shade more civilized, shovel with their knives great quantities of the same food into [their mouths]. The Americans . . . take time to laugh and crack jokes, and finish their repast with a product only known to the highest civilization—ice-cream." But performing in a city that had sprung from frontier town to host of the White City in decades, and with its cast from the Battle of Wounded Knee, the Wild West Show suggested that the free West was gone. Within its celebration was a question: What would become of American individualism without the wild West?[11]

That worry was pointedly embodied in the presentation of a young historian at the exposition. It was here that Frederick Jackson Turner delivered his famous frontier thesis, wondering if American exceptionalism could survive the loss of the wilderness that the director of the census had noted in 1890. Turner was in town for the twin purposes of delivering his scholarly research to his elders and of seeing the exposition. The American Historical Association had decided to hold its annual meeting in Chicago from July 11 to 13. Hoping both to absorb and to reflect the grandeur of the exposition, the historians determined to keep their meetings short so they could spend as much time as possible at the fair. On the evening of July 12, the young professor from the University of Wisconsin stood to read his paper. Most of the historians did not come to hear Frederick Jackson Turner; his obscurity combined with the summer heat and the lure of the fair to keep his audience small. Even his parents, in town for the fair, did not come to hear his address.[12]

But Turner delivered a bombshell that remains one of the most important essays ever written in American history. His examination of the nation's past, titled "The Frontier in American History," declared that America was exceptional, that it was different—and superior—to any other nation in the world. When European civilization encountered the American environment it created a new, unique American individualism, he argued. The frontier forced society into its most primitive forms, and as individuals relied on their own hands for economic security they created American democracy, where each man protected his economic interests with a voice in the government. "Complex society is precipitated by the wilderness into a kind of primitive organization based on the family. . . . It produces antipathy to any direct control. The tax-gatherer is viewed as a representative of oppression," he explained. "So long as free land exists, the opportunity for a competency exists, and economic power secures political power," Turner wrote.[13]

Turner's vision was not one of unlimited triumph. In it was a profound unease about the nation's future. If the constant rebirth of American society on the frontier was the key to its exceptionalism, what would become of the nation now that its frontier was gone? The census director for 1890 had noted, "Up to and including 1880 the country had a frontier of settlement, but . . . there can hardly be said to be a frontier line" any longer. This "brief official statement marks the closing of a great historic moment," Turner said. The history of America "has been . . . the history of the colonization of the Great West. The existence of an area of free land, its continuous recession, and the advance of American settlement westward," he claimed, "explain American development." Each new wave of the frontier had provided "a new field of opportunity, a gate of escape from the bondage of the past . . . and now, four centuries from the discovery of America, at the end of a hundred years of life under the Constitution, the frontier has gone, and with it going has closed the first period of American history."[14] Turner's thesis was rife with inaccuracies, of course, starting with the fact that its definition of "frontier" and "free land" erased the existence of Indians and proceeding into a remarkably idealized picture of the nation's history. But it identified a central national fear: Was America really different from Europe, a world in which God had provided enough resources so that every hardworking man could rise? Or would the loss of the frontier leave the nation to degenerate into class warfare, a New World copy of Old World struggles?

Turner voiced the deep uncertainty Americans felt about their nation and its exceptional status and role in the world. "I think you have struck some first class ideas, and have put in to definite shape a good deal of thought which has been floating around rather loosely," Theodore Roosevelt wrote to the young historian after reading his address. That uncertainty became full-fledged insecurity in the early summer of 1893 when a looming depression finally hit. The exposition championed the production and success of American workers, but the depression revealed the widening gulf between mainstream workers and those who believed that the government had to broker class conflict. The underlying causes of the depression were overexpansion in industry, but the immediate cause of the crash directly fed the national conflict over political economy. At the center of the 1893 crisis was gold, which was draining out of the U.S. Treasury at a frightening rate for a number of reasons—among them the fact that customs receipts had dropped and the Dependent Pension Act of 1890 had spent the surplus. But middle-class Americans blamed the Panic of 1893 on silver agitators who had pressured Congress into passing the Silver Purchase Act. This act, it appeared, had worried foreign investors, who thought it likely that the United States would soon go off the gold standard and might well pay off securities in depreciated currency rather than gold. They began to unload American securities, drawing gold out of the country. By mid-April, the U.S. gold reserve was below $100 million. On May 5, stocks began to drop, and on June 27, they crashed. To mainstream Americans, it appeared that the demand of disaffected workers for cheap money was visibly destroying the country.[15]

On June 30, 1893, President Cleveland called Congress into a special session to begin August 7. Such a call was rare and used only in times of great emergency, as Lincoln had used it in 1861 after the war broke out. Cleveland justified the call because "the distrust and apprehension concerning the financial situation which pervades all business circles have already caused great loss and damage to our people, and threaten to cripple our merchants, stop the wheels of manufacture, bring distress and privation to our farmers, and withhold from our workingmen the wage of labor." The "present perilous condition," he said, was "the result of a financial policy which," he believed, was "embodied in unwise laws which must be executed until repealed by Congress." Although everyone knew what he meant, when Congress convened he was more explicit. The Silver Purchase Act had to go.[16]

The call, which came when Democrats controlled the House, Senate, and White House for the first time since 1859, guaranteed that the party would split. The House repealed the Silver Purchase Act on August 28 by a vote of 239–108, but it was a desperate fight because it forced Democrats—the party to which many western farmers looked to establish silver money—to take a stand against silver currency. After a vicious fight in the Senate, the repeal passed on October 30 by a vote of 48–37. Cleveland had gotten his repeal, but his victory forced silver Democrats to organize on their own, outside of the party. For the rest of the decade, the division between silver advocates and gold advocates would be the division between those who wanted a government responsive to the needs of different groups in society and those who wanted the government to stay aloof from special interests.

As the recession of 1893 dragged on, agitation for government activism escalated. Squeezed by the crisis, businesses tried to stay afloat by firing workers and cutting wages. Desperately trying to make ends meet, workers responded by striking. In 1893, former journalist Stephen Crane self-published his famous novella *Maggie, A Girl of the Streets*, his indictment of modern industrial society, which painted a daring portrait of an impoverished girl from a New York slum who wanted only to have a safe home and a happy family and who worked hard at a collar factory to achieve that middle-class dream. Her mother's drunken violence forced Maggie to move in with her unsavory boyfriend, who left her for another woman. Driven to prostitution, Maggie died, presumably by drowning herself in despair. Unwilling to accept any blame for the intolerable circumstances of the tenement world that destroyed her, observers, including her drunken mother, self-righteously concluded that she fell into disgrace and death because she was inherently evil. Crane's portrait dramatically described the inaccessibility of the middle-class vision to many locked into poverty. To fight back against the big businessmen they blamed for the recession, Democratic congressmen passed an appropriations bill that included an income tax and reiterated the illegality of business combinations, although they bowed to business pressure to keep tariffs almost as high as they had been under the McKinley Tariff of 1890.[17]

By 1894, the struggle had escalated to the point where it appeared to unsympathetic observers that disaffected workers were trying to destroy America altogether, attacking the very economic and social fabric of the mainstream world. Organized as the Populist Party, farmers and laborers advocated government activism against monopolies and called for government ownership of railroads. Americans who believed in a world of economic harmony blamed the silver agitators for the economic crisis of the 1890s, but westerners and Populists blamed those who opposed the coinage of silver for keeping currency out of the hands of regular people. Desperate farmers and laborers decided to force the government to respond to their needs. In early 1894, Populist Jacob S. Coxey led groups of unemployed men to Washington, D.C., to demand a jobs program. Setting out from Massillon, Ohio, "Coxey's Army," wanted the federal government to issue $500 million in greenbacks to finance road construction and local improvements that would provide jobs. Coxey and four hundred of his army—including his son, Legal Tender Coxey—reached Washington on April 30, but by then they were only the first of many groups calling themselves Industrial Armies or "Commonwealers" that were threatening to come to Washington. In Missoula, Montana, Coxeyites stole a train to go east, and rumors came that Commonwealers from the Coeur d'Alene district would join the movement, too. Eventually, fourteen states and two Territories raised Commonwealers. Coxey was eventually arrested in Washington for trespassing, but while he was in jail he was nominated for Congress from the Eighteenth District of Ohio. Rose Wilder Lane recalled leaving South Dakota with her parents during the Coxey summer. "The whole Middle West was shaken loose and moving. We joined long wagon trains moving south; we met hundreds of wagons going north; the roads east and west were crawling lines of families traveling under canvas, looking for work, for another foothold somewhere on the land. By the fires in the camps I heard talk about Coxey's army, 60,000 men, marching on Washington; Federal troops had been called out. The country was ruined, the whole world was ruined; nothing like this had ever happened before. There was no hope, but everyone felt the courage of despair."[18]

Coxey's Army and the Commonwealers horrified mainstream Americans. The protesters planned to make their way to Washington by relying on the support of sympathizers along their route, but those who disagreed with their cause believed them to be a band of beggars turned loose who would extort food with threats. Some citizens' committees threatened to get rid of them by violence if the law would not. As a sympathetic observer recalled: "Though most of the tramps meant well, their mission was so novel and their destitution so complete that they spread terror all along their line of march. . . . When not supplied by gifts they stole, and arrests for theft much thinned their ranks as they advanced. At points they were violent, and the militia had to be called out to deal with them." Less sympathetic men charged that they were deliberately setting out to enact a violent revolution. When they commandeered trains and fought with law officials, their image as criminals seemed confirmed. A story in the *Atlantic Monthly* bemoaned "a thousand or more men, calling themselves American citizens . . . parading their idleness through the land as authority for lawlessness and crime." It reported a popular song:

The Coxeyites they gathered . . . and stole a train of freight-cars in the morn,

The engine left them standing . . . on the railroad track at Caldwell in the morn.

Very sad it was for Caldwell in the morning to feed that hungry army in the morn.

Where are all the U.S. marshals, the deputy U.S. marshals,
To jail that Coxey army in the morn
That "industrious, law-abiding" Coxey's army
That stole a train of freight-cars in the morn?

In the story, a drunken Coxeyite drowns himself when overwhelmed by the comparison between him and his estranged son, who aspires to be one of the soldiers policing the Coxeyite camp. People called into question the true destruction of the Commonwealers; the *Century* published an article by a man who claimed to have traveled with the tramps and described them as a lazy group of well-paid beggars. A public health officer took a different form of opposition to the Commonwealers; he agreed that they were men who "would take part in any movement which would insure them plenty of food and drink and protection from work" and told the public that they were spreading disease, especially smallpox, from town to town. The marchers profoundly threatened the American mainstream, both by demanding government aid and, striking closer to the hearts of many Americans, by threatening the American home through violence, begging, and disease.[19]

Those opposing the Coxeyites were not simply worried about their laziness or the diseases they might carry; they worried about their insistence that they spoke for "the people" and were demanding government aid in their name. On May 7, the *New York Tribune* insisted: "In spirit and morals, if not yet in law, it is the highest of crimes for any mob in this country to assume to be 'the people.' As it is high treason in a monarchy to assume the power or the titles of the sovereign, so, in this free country, it is an attempt to usurp the sovereignty when any body of men, acting outside of the modes provided for expression of the people's will, pretends that it must be respected and obeyed as the people." The superintendent of the New York Police Department concluded that those marching to Washington were obviously "unable to influence legislation in the legitimate way, by securing enough votes to elect their representatives," or they would do so. Instead, they were "the smallest sort of a minority, and not content to submit to the majority, they propose to get what they want by intimidating Congress."[20] Former abolitionist Major General O. O. Howard also opposed the Coxeyites, and this Civil War veteran's staunch opposition to what he saw as a minority's attempt to control events by claiming to be "the people" revealed one of the reasons that mainstream Americans turned so angrily against this co-option. Many Americans believed the Civil War had broken out when a southern minority had refused to accept the will of the majority and had started a devastating war to try to get their way. With the Commonwealers threatening violence, it seemed perilously like a repetition of the threats that had torn the nation apart thirty years before. Middle-class Americans were determined to stop that division this time, before it got out of hand.[21]

Another component in the politics of the disaffected made it look frighteningly like they were determined to overawe the votes of the mainstream with religious extremism. In 1894, Populist Milford W. Howard—soon to be elected a congressman from Alabama—published *If Christ Came to Congress*, attacking the nation's economic system and lambasting congressmen and businessmen for leading sinful lives. It was a small step from believing that the economic ideas of politicians and businessmen were immoral to believing that elites sinned in other areas, too. Debauched "whoremongers and prostitutes" controlled the nation, Howard wrote, giving government jobs to mistresses and lining the pockets of their friends. "Officials . . . betray the people and keep the commerce of the country paralyzed, while the money power grows stronger and the plutocrats richer and the trusts more powerful and arrogant, and all the while the slaving poor are crying for bread." Even Americans unhappy with various congressmen had a hard time believing that men like well-respected and elderly John Sherman, attacked by name in the book, consorted with prostitutes, or that a drunken president whipped his wife, as Howard reported. This kind of accusation made men like Howard sound either dangerously unbalanced or like demagogues. Howard's endorsement of bombing Congress, looting the Treasury, and trampling the "prostrate bleeding bodies" of "a favored few" hardly made him seem less threatening.[22]

The summer of 1894 only heightened the sense of crisis in America. New trouble began at George Pullman's Palace Car Company outside of Chicago —ironically close to the White City—where the different interests of capitalists and workers came into stark relief. Determined to impose his vision of prosperous, thrifty workers on his employees, Pullman required them to live in a clean, neat, alcohol-free town that he built on the shores of Lake Calumet. Workers resented Pullman's interference in their lives. "The corporation is everything and everywhere," wrote a reporter for the *Pittsburgh Times*, "the corporation does everything but sweep your room and make your bed, and the corporation expects you to enjoy it and hold your tongue." Asserting their independence, many workers aspired to leave the town, even if it meant moving to slums outside it. This conflict was latent while the economy was strong, but it came to the surface when Pullman cut wages five times in 1894 without reducing the high rents for company houses, while leaving officers' salaries intact and with Pullman stock selling above par. Workers at the Pullman Palace Car Company struck.[23]

The Pullman strike rapidly became a national concern. The American Railway Union (ARU), led by Eugene Debs, had formed the year before to oppose the General Managers' Association of the twenty-four railroads in the Chicago area, an employers' organization that made sure wages were kept even across the lines. The ARU's 150,000 members supported the Pullman strikers and refused to handle trains that used Pullman cars. Transportation ground to a halt around the country, "paralyzing nearly every railroad west of Ohio," according to one observer. Although most Pullman workers simply wanted to make enough to live on, their cause was popularly associated with radicals who saw the recent strikes as the sign of an approaching showdown between labor and capital. It was time, announced the Central Labor Federation, for every worker to "cast his ballot for the overthrow of the capitalistic system that is now being bolstered up by the power of arms by the President of the United States, in whom the greedy, grasping monopolies trust, and in whom they have found a willing protector in his capacity of Commander in Chief of the army and navy." When a terrible fire burned the vacant White City on July 5, many Americans blamed the strikers and saw anarchism attacking American progress. War seemed imminent.[24]

Even more than the Coxeyites, the Pullman strikers appeared to threaten every home and family in America, since goods and people moved primarily through train transportation. Jane Addams recalled that during the strike her older sister became seriously ill. Addams made it to the hospital, but "every possible obstacle of a delayed and blocked transportation system interrupted the journey of her husband and children who were hurrying to her bedside from a distant state. As the end drew nearer . . . I was obliged to reply to my sister's constant inquiries that her family had not yet come. . . . How many more such moments of sorrow and death were being made difficult and lonely throughout the land," Addams worried, "and how much would these experiences add to the lasting bitterness, that touch of self-righteousness which makes the spirit of forgiveness well-nigh impossible." While Addams sympathized with the strikers, others were less forgiving. Increasingly, disaffected workers seemed to threaten the well-being of middle-class Americans.[25]

Opposition to the strike was grounds on which mainstream Americans could unite, and they were increasingly willing to use the government to protect their own position in society. As the Coeur d'Alene mine owners had two years before, railroad managers called on the federal government to defend their businesses from disaffected workers. Unlike Idaho's governor, however, Illinois Governor John Peter Altgeld insisted that he could maintain order without the help of federal troops. President Cleveland's attorney general, Richard Olney, a former railroad lawyer, interpreted Altgeld's stand as sympathy for the strikers and, faced with constitutional objections to sending federal troops into a state against the wishes of the governor, he came up with the idea of attaching U.S. mail cars to the Pullman railroad cars. Now when strikers refused to handle the Pullman cars, they were obstructing the U.S. mail. To guarantee the delivery of the mail—a federal responsibility—President Cleveland sent U.S. troops first to Chicago and then to the states along the major railway routes: North Dakota, Montana, Idaho, Washington, Wyoming, California, Utah Territory, and New Mexico Territory. The troops were commanded by Major General Nelson A. Miles, who had hunted down both Sitting Bull and Geronimo. Administration officials were careful to specify that the troops were called out not to break the strike but to defend the functions of the national government.[26]

In 1894, middle-class Americans cheered when Cleveland used federal troops to break the Pullman strike, defending law and order against the mob. In the midst of the strike, the Democratic Chicago Times editorialized that rioting could not be tolerated and must be "averted with powder and ball and cold steel if necessary. Let there be no mistake about that. This nation, this State, this city, will not tolerate vandalism, incendiarism, ruffianism." Pulitzer's New York World agreed, asking the strikers "what just cause of offense it is to them that the Federal and State troops are employed to sustain the law, to guard property against destruction, to protect commerce and the mails." The article continued:

Whom are the troops opposing? Whom are they "oppressing?" Somebody is preventing interstate commerce. Somebody is hindering the transit of mails. Somebody is destroying property. Somebody is assaulting and killing the officers of the law.

These men the troops are called upon to deal with. If there are no strikers among the rioters no strikers will be killed or wounded when the soldiers shoot.

The soldiers are citizens. They seek to oppress no one. They compel no man to work against his will. They seek only to protect men in their natural, necessary, and inalienable right to work.

What grievance is there for honest laborers in this?[27]

Harper's Weekly applauded Olney, whose "cool and steady brain has discovered and given vitality to a doctrine of the authority of the national government, derived from the constitutional provision as to commerce between the States, which may be said seriously to modify and extend that authority." When peace was restored, "the government of the United States will be found clothed with before unsuspected power, and laden with a corresponding responsibility." As for Miles, commanding the troops in Chicago, he "is the right arm of the Federal Executive, now for the first time in our history, extended to enforce the Federal law in the protection of that vast body of interests— . . . the interests of the entire population—known in the Constitution as 'commerce between the States.'" Altgeld, in contrast, according to *Harper's Weekly*, "thinks of himself as the champion of the rights of 'the people' as he understands the people, and, curiously enough, [he] understands the people to be not only the poorest, but those who have the least respect for the rights of property." "He is generally believed to be a demagogue and a 'crank.'" Altgeld "is to-day perhaps the most unpopular and detested man in public life in the United States." In Bristol, Maine, far from Chicago, prosperous farmer and Civil War veteran Joel H. Little made his feelings on the issue clear: when he died in November, "Stand by the flag" was carved into his gravestone.[28]

A wide range of Americans stood up for government protection of the mainstream worldview. In an article in the popular magazine *North American Review*, General Miles explained that his career had been dedicated to defending free labor, first fighting to end slavery during the Civil War and now protecting workers from strikers who threatened the property ownership on which a free labor society depended. Individual property was at the heart of the American system, and it should be protected whether it was owned by the humblest citizen or a corporation, he believed. If it weren't, any citizen's property could be "confiscated, seized, or destroyed by any travelling band of tramps" at any time. This was "revolutionary and dangerous . . . [and] must be met and overcome . . . by the strong arm of the municipal, State, and Federal governments enforcing the guarantee to all the people, from the humblest to the most exalted, of perfect security in life and property," he wrote. "Men must take sides either for anarchy, secret conclaves, unwritten law, mob violence, and universal chaos under the red or white flag of socialism on the one hand; or on the side of established government, the supremacy of law, the maintenance of good order, universal peace, absolute security of life and property, the rights of personal liberty, all under the shadow and folds of 'Old Glory,' on the other."[29]

Miles was a soldier, sworn to defend the flag, and his reaction was to be expected. His mood was widely shared, though, by those who might well have disliked the extension of federal power. Wade Hampton, of all people, now a United States railroad commissioner, believed that "all thoughtful and patriotic citizens . . . deplore the condition of affairs brought about by the disgraceful and dangerous strike recently inaugurated by designing demagogues." Clearly thinking of Tillman and the angry agrarian contingent he commanded in South Carolina, Hampton continued that "the strong arm of the Government" had to maintain the supremacy of the law and repress anarchy and communism. "No one upholds whatever of State's rights is left to us more earnestly than myself," he remarked, but he reminded readers that the president had a constitutional duty to repress domestic violence—a rich statement coming from such a staunch opponent of the Ku Klux Klan laws of the early 1870s. Hampton went on to reveal his understanding of how the developing mainstream vision could reconcile the nation's acceptance of mounting racial discrimination with the long-standing concept of success through hard work. "Every humane man must feel profound sympathy for all honest toilers where labor does not yield proper remuneration," Hampton wrote, "but no legislation, no government, no earthly power, can rectify the immutable law by which the gifts of fortune are distributed with an unequal hand." Invoking the language of old free labor Republicanism that white southerners had scorned immediately after the war, he could solve this problem only by calling for laborers to become landowners, which would make them independent and "conservative, law-abiding citizens."[30]

Hampton's support for national government action against the strikers showed just how clearly the middle-class American viewpoint was defined by 1894. Even labor leader Samuel Gompers felt unable to condemn the government's stand publicly. Instead, in another article in the *North American Review*, Gompers used the language of mainstream values by arguing that workers, who created the wealth of society and were the heart of civilization, were asking only for equality of opportunity. Standing firmly on the idea that middle-class Americans stood between the lazy poor and the grasping rich, Gompers framed the strike as a problem of the wealthy taking control of government for their own interests. The workers were simply trying to protect themselves from being enslaved as Pullman poured out millions of dollars to enlist government on his side to crush them. Workers could no longer hope to reform all of society, as Powderly had advocated, nor even to organize nationally for general labor reforms, as Gompers had originally hoped. From now on, it seemed, successful labor reform would be conducted by arguing that the honest workingman needed protection from businessmen operating in ways that undermined the mainstream ideal.[31]

Not all American workers thought the reinforcement of middle-class attitudes among workers was a bad thing. African American Nat Love also inadvertently weighed in on the Pullman strike. Unwelcome in the American Railway Union, which rejected African American members, Love left no record of sympathy for the strikers. In a memoir that championed the mainstream vision, he carefully ignored the racism that Pullman reinforced by developing an all-black porter staff to serve white riders. Love explained that he had found Pullman a fair employer; and he was, after all, one of the few who hired African Americans and promoted their advancement. Once Love figured out that the company put special agents on trains to report back to the superintendent—inspectors many workers saw as spies—he made up his mind to guarantee that there would never be reason to complain about him. Better service meant better tips, and better money made him like his job. He was given longer and more profitable runs and soon, he boasted, became "one of the most popular porters in Colorado." As the head porter on a run his salary was $40 a month, plus tips and two uniforms a year. He scorned those complaining of poor money, writing, "Naturally the porter that understands his business and gives his whole attention to the passengers in his car and to his work, will make more money than the porter who has not the patience to try and please his passengers." Love had clearly learned his trade well; he boasted of tips from $25 to $50. Love had adopted the message of the individualist dream; the final chapter of his autobiography was entitled: "This Is Where I Shine: Now I Am Out for the Money."[32]

Love recalled that he was on good terms with Pullman himself, as well as other railroad leaders. He claimed to have chatted with Pullman several times, finding him "a fine man, broad-minded in every sense of the word, always approachable and with always a kind word for every one of the large army of his employees that he met on his travels, and he always tried to meet them all." The town of Pullman, Love claimed, "contains fine churches and public buildings, a splendid library and reading rooms and amusement halls. And while I was there I failed to see a single saloon. It seems such places are tabooed there. The shops are the finest in this country, containing all the modern machinery of the finest kind and the men employed there are all past masters of their trades." Implicit in this description, of course, was an accusation that the strikers must be dull drunkards to object to such a community. He went on to claim that Pullman had personally encouraged Love's idea of getting porters to contribute toward the purchase of land to create a retirement home. If they bought 1,000 acres of land, Pullman promised to put up the building on it. By harking back to the idea of productive labor as the foundation of middle-class America, Love equated himself, a black porter, with Pullman, a wealthy man who employed thousands.[33]

Even those who generally hated monopolies and corruption cheered Cleveland's "brave stand against the mob." The *New York Sun* and the *New York World* agreed on this. By 1894, the *New York World* was, according to one observer, one of the top newspapers in the world, with a daily circulation of 400,000, and its opposition to the strikers carried great weight. It was not alone in its equal dislike of both big business and disaffected laborers. Taking a stand between business and the Commonwealers and strikers, in the *North American Review* the secretary of agriculture claimed that America was divided between two classes, "one class representing Industry, Temperance, Frugality, and Self-denial; and is, therefore, self-reliant, and, consequently, self-respecting." These qualities were "the basis of good citizenship." The other class was made up of "the Indolent, the Intemperate, and the Improvident," who lacked "self-reliance, and, therefore, . . . self-respect." Taking their cue from businessmen who had successfully used the government to enrich themselves through the tariff, this class of people was now going to Washington "for the purpose of demanding and securing legislation partial to themselves and in their own interests, regardless of all other interests." "When individuals and classes of individuals evolve the idea of manipulating the machinery of government, so as to prescribe privileges for themselves and taxation and burdens for the masses, the first symptoms of Communism become apparent," he warned.[34]

Nat Love, Better Known as Deadwood Dick, and His Family

Figure 20. By the turn of the century, cowboy turned Pullman porter Nat Love had embraced mainstream ideology, declaring, "Now I Am Out for the Money." He is pictured here with his elegantly dressed wife and daughter. Courtesy of Harvard College Library.

In 1895, the Supreme Court handed down *In re Debs*, which upheld a lower court's injunction ordering Debs to call off the strike and went on to cripple the labor movement by declaring illegal any forcible obstruction of interstate commerce based on the Constitution's provision for federal oversight of interstate commerce. Of course, by 1895 almost all commerce crossed state lines—this very fact had led to the creation of the Interstate Commerce Commission to curb interstate trusts—but this was the first time the court strengthened the federal government by appealing directly to the Constitution. "We hold that the government of the United States . . . [has] . . . jurisdiction over every foot of soil within its territory, and [acts] directly upon each citizen," the Court declared, undermining the ability of sympathetic local officials to shield strikers by asserting their own authority over the area of the strike, as Altgeld had tried to do. In *Harper's Weekly*, John Kendrick Bangs rhapsodized about the relationship between Debs and the government:

> . . . Debs
> When rhymed with Rebs,
> Seems wondrous sensible,
> So reprehensible
> Is Debs.
>
> It goes with ebbs,
> Which shows a tendency
> For the ascendancy
> Of Government o'er Debs . . .
> We're on the brink,
> Some people think,
> Of anarchy;
> But as for me
> I don't believe it. I'll confess
> It sometimes seems so in the press
> The populists
> Would like to govern with their fists;
> But on the whole, from Texas up to Maine,
> The anarchist's distinctly on the wane.
> From Florida to far off Idaho
> The teachings of that tribe have little go;
> And we've enough of people with prepense
> For decent living and for solid sense
> To save the land, including Pennsylvania,
> From what I think is simple Debsomania. . . .[35]

Despite such playful poetry, the battle to make the middle-class vision the dominant worldview was not over yet. Taking a seat in Congress in December 1895, South Carolina's Ben Tillman promised to take a pitchfork to the vipers who refused to monetize silver. Once declaring, "I am a rude man and don't care," "Pitchfork Ben" had won the contempt of mainstream Americans. The *Buffalo Enquirer* scornfully concluded, "Tillman is ignorant and uncouth, his language is vulgar and profane, and his head is full of dangerous and visionary ideas regarding the function of government." Ignoring the senatorial tradition that forbade new senators from making long speeches, on January 29, 1896, Tillman roughly educated his colleagues in his new doctrine. Claiming to be "the only farmer, pure and simple," in the Senate, he insisted that he spoke for the common people. What they wanted, he asserted, was an expanded currency, and if they did not get it, he warned, "the toiling and now downtrodden masses" of the city and country would come together and "agrarianism and communism will join hands." And if industrial workers "some day take a notion to tramp to Washington with rifles in their hands," the farmers "will lift no hand to stay the march, but will join it."[36]

The 1896 presidential campaign turned the question of which vision of America spoke for the American people into a national political fight. In the campaign, Populist/Democratic candidate William Jennings Bryan, who called for a government responsive to the needs of all Americans, ran against Republican William McKinley, who represented individualism and economic harmony. These two ideals of American government were contested on the visible and national scale of a presidential campaign. "Prairie avenger, mountain lion, / Bryan, Bryan, Bryan, Bryan," poet Vachel Lindsay rhapsodized, "Gigantic troubadour, speaking like a siege gun, / Smashing Plymouth Rock with his boulders from the West." Hailing from Nebraska, Bryan was one of the nation's foremost advocates of silver coinage as a way to ease the money supply and put people back to work. In 1895, he and Richard P. Bland of Missouri had framed the "Appeal of the Silver Democrats" in response to Cleveland's determination to keep the nation on a gold standard. They spoke for disaffected workers and farmers when they claimed that coinage of silver at the ratio of 16:1 would redress the inequalities in American society, and they begged the Democratic Party to champion silver coinage.[37]

In 1896, Bryan was the national leader of the silver movement, and in his speech at the Democratic National Convention he framed the silver question as the contest between "the idle holders of idle capital" and "the struggling masses, who produce the wealth and pay the taxes of the country." He demanded that the Democrats side with "the struggling masses" in language that sounded apocalyptic compared to the usual dry convention fare. Cities might demand the gold standard, he said, but cities depended on western farms. "Burn down your cities and leave our farms, and your cities will spring up again as if by magic; but destroy our farms and the grass will grow in the streets of every city in the country." Decrying that business was controlling financial policy when the true producers of the nation—farmers and workers —begged for an expanded currency, Bryan thundered the famous words that secured his presidential nomination: "We will answer their demand for a gold standard by saying to them: You shall not press down upon the brow of labor this crown of thorns, you shall not crucify mankind upon a cross of gold." While Bryan put the aims of the silverites in lofty terms, Tillman, who had been a strong candidate for the nomination, helped to write the platform. Startling observers, his convention speech began: "I come to you from the South . . . from the home of secession," and went on to describe new grounds for sectional warfare. The Democratic platform called for the unlimited coinage of silver, the end of national bank notes, the end of Republican profligacy with the public treasury, stronger antitrust legislation, and it grumbled at the 1895 Supreme Court decision that an income tax was unconstitutional. It also denounced federal interference in "local affairs" as "a crime against free institutions"—there went black voting—and condemned "government by injunction as a new and highly dangerous form of oppression by which Federal Judges, in contempt of the laws of the States and rights of citizens, become at once legislators, judges and executioners." Surprised when the Democrats adopted their main ideas, the Populists simply endorsed Bryan.[38]

McKinley did not inspire poetry. A career politician from Ohio, he was famous primarily for his work on the tariff revision of 1890, which was popularly perceived as a triumph for big business trusts, although McKinley himself worried that trusts were "dangerous conspiracies against the public good." His nomination had been orchestrated by a wealthy businessman, Marcus Alonzo Hanna, who raised the specter of mobs taking over the nation to encourage businessmen to pour money into McKinley's campaign. McKinley's nomination represented hard money men, big businessmen, Republican prosperity, and the downfall of the mobs trying to wrest control of the government away from traditional notions of an expanding economy. At the *New York World*, Pulitzer condemned Hanna's methods as the culmination of big money in politics. "Are the multi-millionaires who have substituted monop-oly for competition in business to apply their method and their money di-rectly to politics, acting in person instead of through agents, as heretofore?" he asked in disgust. The Republican platform simply condemned the Demo-cratic administration by blaming it for the recession that happened on its watch. It also stood firm against silver currency, insisting that Republicans had always kept the American dollar "as good as gold." The platform also nodded to mainstream women by speaking out for temperance and morality and claiming that the Republican Party was "mindful of the rights and inter-ests of women, and believes that they should be accorded equal opportunities, equal pay for equal work, and protection to the home." They hoped women would help them "rescu[e] the country from Democratic and Populist mis-management and misrule."[39]

In this election, mainstream Americans of all parties joined together to put down the apparent radicalism of Bryan and his followers. On August 6, 1896, Charles Henry Dana at the *New York Sun* put the issue clearly. The Democratic platform, he explained, "invites us to establish a currency which will enable a man to pay his debts with half as much property as he would have to use in order to pay them now. This proposition is dishonest." As much as he hated McKinley, Pulitzer had to agree. "Come what may, the first duty of *The World* is to . . . save the public credit, the public honor, the public fame. . . . Later there will be opportunities to promote the reforms for which the Democracy in its pure estate had the mandate and of which democracy has need."[40]

After spending the years from 1889 to 1895 as a civil service commissioner in Washington, Theodore Roosevelt had accepted the post of New York City police commissioner under a Republican reform mayor in 1895, and the fol-lowing year, he campaigned against Bryan across the eastern part of the country. He warned that the Democratic candidate was a "demagogue" who had "attracted the professional laboring man of the type that labors as little as possible, and continually strives to delude such workingmen as are ignorant and foolish enough to be misled into some movement which cannot but end in disaster." Bryan was trying to establish "a government of the mob," he told an audience in Utica, New York, to create a "red welter of lawlessness as fantastic and as vicious as the dream of a European communist." He claimed that "Bryan, Altgeld, Tillman, Debs, Coxey, and the rest have not the power to rival the deeds of Marat, Barrere and Robespierre, but they are strikingly like the leaders of the Terror of France in mental and moral attitude." Their supporters "lie with the ignorant and vicious and also with the weak, who have not the intelligence to see that their failure in life is due not to others but to themselves." Bryan, he insisted, planned to change "a government of the people, for the people, and by the people," with "a government of a mob, by the demagogue, for the shiftless and the disorderly and the criminal and the semi-criminal."[41]

Roosevelt was prone to overblown rhetoric, but his sentiments echoed those of a wide range of Americans. Andrew Carnegie backed McKinley against Bryan, of course, appalled at "the fomenting of strife between the 'Haves,' and the 'Have-nots.'" Unlike Carnegie, Carl Schurz thoroughly disliked McKinley, whom he saw as a tool of business, but even he went on the campaign stump to attack Democrats for threatening to place government in the hands of a mob. Those workers who embraced middle-class ideology also backed McKinley. Samuel Gompers counted McKinley as a personal friend but did not endorse him. Instead, he insisted that unions affiliated with the American Federation of Labor "keep out of partisan politics." Terence V. Powderly went further. Believing that Bryan was a "blatant demagogue," he actively campaigned for McKinley, concentrating on speaking to labor audiences. Booker T. Washington had preferred that another Republican get the nomination, but threw his support behind McKinley once he led the ticket. Although Wade Hampton could not publicly endorse a Republican in the heated climate of southern politics, he loathed the Tillman Democrats that had forced him from power by catering to the racism of the poorest whites in the South. Almost certainly he did not vote for Bryan; his personal secretary sighed, "To vote for Bryan is to vote for a platform imbued with Populism, Socialism, and Tillmanism." Mainstream Americans united against the apparently demagogic Democrats, and in November, McKinley took the White House by the highest margin of victory in twenty-five years.[42]

In 1896, McKinley's victory settled the national decision in favor of the mainstream vision of society. Although only a child, western farm girl Rose Wilder Lane recalled, "I was an ardent if uncomprehending Populist; I saw America ruined forever when the soulless corporations in 1896, defeated Bryan and Free Silver." A Republican congressman, in contrast, was tickled pink: "In the light of . . . the movement of Coxey and his body of tramps, the riots attendant upon the railroad strikes under the leadership of Debs, and the long dispute between coal-mine owners and miners in the various parts of the country . . . the wonder is not that the country has lost so much, but that it has lost so little. . . . It is the strongest tribute that can be paid to the American citizen to note that to-day, notwithstanding the disasters attendant upon these recent events, he is once more enjoying the fruits of a new prosperity full of hope in the future and more strongly than ever a believer in the strength of his government and the wisdom of those who established it."43

That dominance of the individualist vision was secured by the discovery of gold on Bonanza Creek near the Klondike River in the Yukon Territory of Canada in August 1896. The subsequent gold rush, and the ensuing drop in gold prices, eased the money supply and thus the pressure on farmers and laborers, taking the urgency out of the silver currency issue. Also, the strike reinforced the idea that there were riches still to be had for Americans, and that all men were equal—at least in the brutal conditions of the Great Northwest's frozen mountains. More than 100,000 hopeful prospectors took off for the gold fields. The 30,000 of them who actually made it across the deadly mountain passes and through Alaska to Dawson City found that they had little chance of recovering gold from under the permafrost, and few made it rich. Nonetheless, the gold strikes bolstered the individualist ideal. According to gold rush poet Robert Service:

This is the Law of the Yukon, that only the Strong shall thrive;
That surely the Weak shall perish, and only the Fit survive.
Dissolute, damned and despairful, crippled and palsied and slain,
This is the Will of the Yukon,—Lo, how she makes it plain!44

By 1896, mainstream Americans had a clear vision of a world in which hardworking individualists could rise together, protected by an activist government that curbed business and organized labor—as well as any other group trying to harness government—and also protected the individualist family. This vision drew from both the northern and the southern traditional views of American republicanism, filtered through the racial and industrial turmoil of the past three decades. From the North came the idea that any American could improve his lot; from the South came the idea that those who had done so should control the government. In Lincoln's America, everyone could rise to economic security, but by 1896 this openness had been revised. Facing the specter of disaffected Americans trying to control government and use it for their own benefit, mainstream Americans had come to believe that many would fail, that this was their own fault, and that they should be isolated from power before they destroyed society. At the same time, rich businessmen who would buy the government and turn the nation into their own fiefdom must be curbed. Contrasted with the vision of a world in conflict—poor against rich, black against white, women against men—this vision offered hope and peace as it recaptured the midcentury sense that America was God's truly exceptional country.

Roosevelt trumpeted the optimism of this vision; Nat Love internalized it. Love emphasized the democracy of his job as a Pullman porter, in which, he recalled, he met "all manner of people, the business man out for business or pleasure; . . . the wife going to join her sick husband or the husband hurrying home to the bedside of his sick child; . . . the young couple on their honeymoon; the capitalist, the miner, the sportsman and the vast army of people that go to make up the traveling public." Missing from Love's list, of course, were wage laborers, immigrants, or black passengers, few of whom could have afforded to ride in a Pullman car, even if they had been permitted to—and African Americans would not have been. Everyone on the train was equal in being subject to railroad rules, Love noted, emphasizing the equality of the rules rather than the reality that kept black porters and white passengers from mingling on terms of equality. When J. J. Corbett, "a gentleman who was at that time in the height of his career and naturally thought he owned the earth or a large part of it," tried to smoke in a nonsmoking area, Love asked him to move. "So you are Mr. Pullman, are you?" Corbett sneered. "I told him I was not Mr. Pullman, but I was in charge of one of Mr. Pullman's cars, and for that reason I was a representative of Mr. Pullman, and that it was strictly against the rules to smoke in that part of the car, and that if he wished to smoke he would have to go to the drawing room." Had Corbett not left, Love insisted he would have thrown him out, an unlikely boast. Nonetheless, he recounted, the railroad officials "said I had done perfectly right, and what I was paid to do." In his autobiography, Love never mentioned that his race had caused him trouble. When a "cranky individual" handed him two cents and said "that some of us porters needed calling down and some needed knocking down," Love claimed simply to have smiled and "bundled his boxes and satchel out on the platform and left him to follow at his leisure." It is impossible that race was never an issue for a young black man in the late nineteenth-century West, but in an era when all African Americans were increasingly denigrated as an inferior race that belonged at the bottom of society, Love clung tight to the middle-class idea that race never mattered as much as his own ability to rise through his hard work.[45]

Mainstream Americans honored the distinction between hardworking and disaffected Americans. Dramatically, in 1896, Harvard University awarded an honorary degree to Booker T. Washington, public champion of a traditional approach to economic success through self-help. He was the first black man to be so honored, and Harvard's action was widely praised. Washington was unlikely to be turned away from a hotel under the Jim Crow laws; instead, his stays in prominent urban hotels made the society columns of major newspapers. His efforts to educate African Americans into prosperity drew the support of Americans from Julia Ward Howe, who offered her speaking services to raise money for Tuskegee, to Andrew Carnegie, who provided $20,000 for a Tuskegee Library.[46]

Unwelcome in the nation were those who seemed to reject the middle-class worldview and to want government support without having to work. Mainstream Americans had come to believe that African Americans who insisted on voting and civil rights had been pushed forward by demagogic politicians much too fast. Rather than slowly working their way up to property ownership and the corresponding interest in proper government, it seemed to opponents that they had been given government power before they understood that property must be protected for the American system to work. In 1896, planter's daughter Elizabeth Allston Pringle repurchased her family's antebellum plantation home, sold immediately after the war to pay debts, and began a dual career as a rice planter and a writer. Unable to see the systematic economic advantages that permitted her to repossess her plantation while those actually working it remained landless, Pringle wrote columns for the *New York Sun* under the pen name "Patience Pennington," painting a racist picture of lazy, conniving, and stupid black workers whose childishness she patiently tolerated. In *Harper's Weekly*, a southern woman denigrated African Americans' desire for education by asserting that in Atlanta 600 African American children who had tried to enter public schools were homeless, abandoned by their parents—an outrageous claim, even on the face of it. "What the negroes need is not education, not voting privileges," she wrote, "but father, mothers, homes." Blaming those "who thought they were working for the good of the negroes," she insisted that "the way to make them good citizens is to encourage them to buy homes and farms. . . . Let them become tax-payers as well as voters. Representation without taxation is worse than taxation without representation. . . ."[47]

In 1896, the Supreme Court handed down a decision of great historical import, although it was barely noted at the time. On May 19, 1896, the middle of the page-three court column in the *New York Times* read: "Homer Adolph Plessy vs. J. H. Ferguson, Judge, &c.—In error to the Supreme Court of

Louisiana. Judgement affirmed, with costs." This was all the newspaper had to say about the *Plessy v. Ferguson* decision declaring legal the policy of "separate but equal" accommodations that segregated the South until the late twentieth century. The Supreme Court had blessed the idea that hardworking Americans must be protected from those who might insist on government protection for rights they had not earned. The reality of this construction of American ideals, though, belied its rationale. Under the separate but equal doctrine, Pringle, who had never hoed a day, could visit hotels off limits to those who actually worked her fields. And, by its very definition, the pattern was unassailable. The act of agitating for civil rights indicated a person was unworthy of them, making it impossible to challenge increasing segregation and discrimination.[48]

This same pattern was true for Indians. Well known and respected, honored with a visit by British Ambassador Lord Bryce, Quanah was friends with Charles Goodnight and within years would be hosting a wolf hunt for Theodore Roosevelt. Things were not so comfortable for Geronimo, who had been forced onto "the white man's road." After keeping him imprisoned at hard labor for eight years, the War Department gave him special permission in 1894 to sell photographs of himself at fairs and expositions. Until he died, he begged the government to keep its promise to send him and his people to a reservation in their homeland in Arizona.[49]

While the mainstream ideal championed self-sufficiency and individualism, women like Jane Addams were involving government in the prevention of child labor, the spread of disease, and, eventually, in advocating for the rights of laborers in order to prevent the neglect of children by overworked parents. The apparent power of business interests to control government and prevent the reforms that would protect the ideal family added fuel to women's argument that their suffrage would protect the individualist vision and expand it to increasing numbers of Americans. "We have stood for that which was known to be right in theory, and for that which has proved to be right in practice," Julia Ward Howe reflected in a speech at the Massachusetts State House in 1895. Suffragists increasingly advanced their cause by contrasting the purity of middle-class women's votes to the apparently corrupt votes of immigrants and black men. Even as state constitutions restricted voting by black men and white immigrants and disaffected laborers, support for middle-class female voting grew.[50]

The government also had to protect individualism by protecting the West itself, it seemed. In 1896, John Muir was happy to report that federally controlled land in Yosemite had been returned to its natural beauty, but warning that state-controlled land was still a mess, he called for stronger federal control of western lands. "The care of the national reservation by the military has been a complete success," he wrote, while those lands controlled by California were "still being overrun with sheep, and are as dusty, bare, and desolate as ever they were, notwithstanding the Government notices posted along the trails forbidding the pasturing of sheep, cattle, etc., under severe penalties, simply because there is no one on the ground to enforce the rules. One soldier armed with a gun and the authority of the Government is more effective than any number of paper warnings." Muir called for the recession of Yosemite Valley to the federal government, where "it would be under the care of the military department, which would rigidly carry out all rules and regulations, regardless of ever-shifting politics and the small plans of interested parties for private gain." Muir grandly welcomed true settlers to the land to eke an honest living out of it, but he begged for the government to protect the nation's miraculous forests from "tree-killers, wool and mutton men, spreading death and confusion in the fairest groves and gardens ever planted." "Through all the wonderful, eventful centuries since Christ's time—and long before that," he wrote, "God has cared for these trees, saved them from drought, disease, avalanches, and a thousand straining, leveling tempests and floods; but he cannot save them from fools,—only Uncle Sam can do that."[51]

Paradoxically, government's growing interest in legislating individualism did not destroy the power of the individualist idea, thanks to the powerful western image that survived in the American imagination. For Nat Love, the freedom of the cowboy life had translated into a wider American culture. Advising his readers to "See America," he rhapsodized of "the grandeur of our mountains and rivers, valley and plain, canyon and gorge, lakes and springs, cities and towns, the grand evidences of God's handiwork scattered all over this fair land over which waves the stars and stripes." He praised New York's tall buildings, art, and commerce; Pittsburgh's steel works. Go to Kansas City and Omaha, he advised, "and see the transformation of the Texas steer into the corned beef you ate at your last picnic." Go to the plains, think of the dangers that beset the pioneer of 1849, "wonder at the nerve he had, then again let your chest swell with pride that you are an American, sprung from the same stock that men were composed of in those days." "Breathe the pure essence of life," in the Rockies, visit the western mines, see the big trees, seals, and oranges of California, "Then again let your chest swell with pride that you are an American." "This grand country of ours is the peer of any in

Figure 21. This 1892 image of the modern woman bicycling in New York City's Central Park showed active women operating in a public arena. The great popularity of bicycles at the turn of the century prompted city governments to replace cobblestones with smooth paved surfaces for safety. Keystone–Mast Collection, UCR/California Museum of Photography, University of California at Riverside.

the world," Love concluded. "I have seen a large part of America, and am still seeing it, but the life of a hundred years would be all too short to see our country America, I love thee, Sweet land of Liberty, home of the brave and the free."[52]

At the end of 1896, vacationing composer John Philip Sousa was standing on a steamer leaving Italy on its way back to America when a song began to beat in his head. It was, he later recalled, "one of the most vivid incidents of my career."[53] The song he heard, "The Stars and Stripes Forever," became the official march of the United States and was a paean to the American government. Sousa set words to it:

> Let martial note in triumph float
> And liberty extend its mighty hand
> A flag appears 'mid thunderous cheers,
> The banner of the Western land.
> The emblem of the brave and true
> Its folds protect no tyrant crew;
> The red and white and starry blue
> Is freedom's shield and hope.
> Other nations may deem their flags the best
> And cheer them with fervid elation
> But the flag of the North and the South and the West
> Is the flag of flags, the flag of Freedom's nation.

The crisis years in the middle of the 1890s had raised the vital question of who were "the people"—those who believed in individualism bolstered by general government promotion of entrepreneurship, or those who believed in societal conflict that must be adjusted by government. The 1896 election determined that Americans who believed in the mainstream vision of a harmonious economy of hard workers were, in fact, "the people" and that the government would bolster their version of American society. America was an exceptional nation, they agreed, in which anyone was welcome to rise through hard work, while those who called for government aid to specific interests threatened America's successful system. After the election, mainstream Americans could believe that their future was looking better than it had for years.

CHAPTER NINE

1898–1901

Reunion

The election of 1896 settled the dominance of the mainstream vision of American life, but it did not offer sectional reunification on grounds that would enable the nation to move forward as an internationally dominant power. Reunification ultimately came not from a resolution of the disagreements over the nation's political economy, but from the powerful western image that the American people had come to associate with middle-class values. In 1898, they made these values grounds for political action in the Spanish-American War, asserting American individualism in a foreign arena.

At the end of the nineteenth century, Owen Wister wrote *The Virginian: A Horseman of the Plains*, the book that made western novels a respectable genre. This tale of Wyoming from 1874 to the 1890s was the story of "the horseman, the cowpuncher, the last romantic figure upon our soil." He was gone, Wister told readers, but "he will be here among us always, invisible, waiting his chance to live and play as he would like. His wild kind has been among us always, since the beginning: a young man with his temptations, a hero without wings." Wister dedicated the book to Theodore Roosevelt, for whom he expressed his "changeless admiration." Wister had captured the true western American, Roosevelt believed. "I have sometimes been asked if Wister's 'Virginian' is not overdrawn," he recalled. "Half of the men I worked with or played with and half of the men who soldiered with me afterwards in my regiment [in the Spanish-American War] might have walked out of Wister's stories."[1]

A decade after the book's publication, Wister reflected on its dedication. "Ten years ago, when political darkness still lay dense upon every State in the

Union," he wrote, "this book was dedicated to the greatest benefactor we people have known since Lincoln." Roosevelt had inspired Americans to return to honest public men, and after decades of shirking and evasion of their civic duty, Americans had begun "to look at themselves and their institutions straight; to perceive that Firecrackers and Orations once a year, and selling your vote or casting it for unknown nobodies, are not enough attention to pay to the Republic." To celebrate this new, principled America, Wister had written *The Virginian*. "If this book be anything more than an American story, it is an expression of American faith. Our Democracy has many enemies, both in Wall Street and in the Labor Unions. . . . But I believe . . . that, with mistakes at times, but with wisdom in the main, we people will prove ourselves equal to the severest test to which political man has yet subjected himself—the test of Democracy." In 1898, Americans joined together to put themselves to the test in a war for American principles.[2]

Although modern-day Americans tend to forget it, nineteenth-century Americans were very aware that Spain had been the most important European power in the Americas from the time Columbus sailed for Ferdinand and Isabella in 1492. Its power had waned steadily after 1800, when it ceded much of what is now America to Napoleon—who promptly sold it to the United States as the Louisiana Purchase—but it still retained its hold on the valuable island of Cuba, a constant reminder to Americans of its lingering power.

Cuba "lies almost at our door," an American history book read in 1898. About 760 miles long and 30 to 120 miles wide, the book explained, "it is approximately 45,000 square miles, or about one-fourth that of all Spain." Its capital and largest city—boasting about 200,000 people in 1898—was Havana. "The island is mountainous, with a central chain of mountains running down its length while other chains and individual peaks rise elsewhere. Traveling inland and upward, lowlands and marshes on the shore rise gradually toward the regions of great sugar plantations, which in turn give way to the tobacco belt. Above this lies grazing and farming land, and above it are the forests that still cover about half the island." Cuba's sugar crop was even more important than its "world-famous" tobacco, the book explained, for by 1896, the United States secured 96.7 percent of the sugar shipped from Cuba.[3]

Americans had eyed Cuba's rich lands longingly since the early nineteenth century. Americans—especially southerners, who hoped to spread their enterprises onto the slave-holding island—had repeatedly tried to capture or buy Cuba but were repeatedly rebuffed. The island was an object of such curiosity to Americans that when John Muir set out to see the nation after the Civil War, he traveled through the South and went on to Cuba. Landing in Havana on a Sunday afternoon, he was charmed by the tropical island, with its refined and exotically Catholic Spanish and Cuban leaders, its muscled slaves, its flowering vines and cacti, palm trees, seashells, and rosy corals. Muir heard "cathedral bells and prayers in the forenoon, theaters and bull-fight bells and bellowings in the afternoon! Lowly whispered prayers to the saints and the Virgin, followed by shouts of praise or reproach to bulls and matadors! I made free with fine oranges and bananas and many other fruits. Pineapple I had never seen before." During his stay, Muir wandered through the bustling city, its public squares and fine gardens with marble statues providing welcome respite from the narrow dusty and crowded streets of the busy town. More often, he tramped the hills around Havana or walked the coastline, marveling at the strange plants he found. "I was now in one of my happy dreamlands," he recalled, "the fairest of West India islands."[4]

Havana might have looked Spanish, but Spain's relations with Cuba were uncomfortable. The island's plantations produced valuable sugar and tobacco crops, but they did so with the labor of slaves. Landowners wanted more control of the Spanish-dominated government, while slaves wanted freedom. For both groups this translated into hatred of Spanish rule. Their sporadic protests gained momentum after the American Civil War, when the end of slavery in the United States encouraged Cuban slaves to hope for liberty. In 1868, a coup removing Spain's unpopular Isabella II from her throne coincided with a hike in Cuban taxation to prompt a dramatic strike for Cuban freedom. In October 1868, wealthy planter Carlos Manuel de Cespedes issued "The Cry of Yara," complaining of excessive taxation, foreign government, and trade restrictions. In weeks he led an army of 10,000 men, and the Ten Years' War of Cubans against Spanish rule had begun.

The outbreak of war on the island could not help but involve Americans. Southerners greeted the news of the war with eager interest, wondering if at last the rich island would fall into their hands. Northerners were also interested in Cuba now, for they had a political and ideological interest in seeing the republicanism for which they had fought the Civil War triumph over monarchism in the New World. As soon as the Cuban conflict broke out, Americans perceived the struggle between Spanish colonial forces and Cuban insurgents as a republican fight for representative government characterized by low taxation and economic opportunity. They looked approvingly at what they translated as "The Declaration of Independence of Yara," rather than its "Cry," noting its republican language: "Spain has many times promised us Cubans to respect our rights, without further having fulfilled her promises; she continues to tax us heavily, and by so doing is likely to destroy our wealth; as we are in danger of losing our property, our lives, and we want no further Spanish domination." When the rebels wrote a constitution for a republican government, the link between the insurgency and American ideals seemed clear. In 1869, the Cubans abolished slavery and established a president, vice president, cabinet, and legislature. Their army swelled to close to 50,000 men. Unable to resist this fight for freedom, especially when it meant that the rich prize of Cuba might join the United States, American adventurers joined in the Cuban struggle.[5]

This put the American government in an uncomfortable spot. Spanish Cuba was a major American trading partner, and the United States government had no interest in siding against powerful European Spain in favor of a handful of Cuban rebels, especially when many of them were former slaves who would expect power in a new Cuban government and a reborn economy. Still, with its strong interest in a prospering Cuba as a trading partner, the United States wanted the war to end. In 1869, President Grant offered to negotiate between Spain and Cuba. Congress, in contrast, repeatedly talked of recognizing Cuban independence, as Chile, Bolivia, Guatemala, Colombia, and Mexico had already done.

In Congress, Democrats kept up pressure to recognize the Cuban belligerents. In late 1871, S. S. Cox introduced into Congress a joint resolution for the recognition of Cuban belligerents, which would give international status to Cuban rebels. After the Foreign Affairs Committee quietly buried the resolution, Cox gave a speech in February 1872 demanding recognition of the rebellion and demonstrating that, in fact, Spain had virtually forced America to recognize the war by capturing American ships. But Cox did not justify Cuban intervention on economic grounds, instead insisting that America must get involved in the struggle because of Spain's treatment of the Cubans, the "outrages against childhood, humanity, and god . . . by the fiends who . . . make a hell of that Paradise of islands." His speech was curiously dry for Cox, though, and was probably designed to try to keep southern Democrats happy. It didn't matter; the bill had too little support to pass.[6]

Americans less concerned than Grant and Congress about trade sided entirely with the Cubans. Their enthusiasm precipitated a crisis in 1873 that almost took Spain and America to war. The trouble came about over the

Virginius, a ship sailing under American papers. An American had registered the *Virginius* in New York City, swearing that he was the true and only owner of the ship, but he had actually bought the *Virginius* for a group of Cuban rebels who intended to use it to run munitions to the island. Sailing out of the United States with twenty Cubans and a sham cargo of bread and clothing, the *Virginius* picked up from another ship a cargo of "several hundred cases of shot, shell, and ammunition; more than one hundred cases of arms, boxes of leather and other goods, and hardware; six gun carriages and four brass cannons or howitzers." After two successful trips running arms to Cuba, the *Virginius* sailed from Jamaica in October 1873 for yet another trip, this time carrying not arms but a number of relatives of the Cuban leaders and officers of the Cuban army. When the Spanish gunship *Tornado* intercepted "that damned pirate," its officers promptly tried and executed fifty-three of the *Virginius*'s passengers and crew, including the captain, Joseph Fry, a former Confederate navy man who was, of course, a U.S. citizen. Seven other Americans shared Fry's fate.[7]

The *Virginius* crisis linked Cuba's troubles with Americans' growing pride in their role as a world model. They had fought the Civil War to prove that republicanism was "the last, best hope of earth," as Lincoln had said, and with the Union's triumph that role had been transferred to the entire nation. By attacking an American ship—even one registered illegally and carrying Cuban rebels—Spain had challenged America's international status. There was no way Americans were going to stand for that since it attacked the strong national identity for which they had just poured out 600,000 lives and billions of dollars.

At the same time, businessmen and those determined to expand American overseas trade had no interest in going to war with Spain over Cuba. *Harper's Weekly* downplayed the American registration of the *Virginius*, noting instead that the ship was a notorious gunrunner. It also warned readers that once Cuba was free of Spain, it would have to be annexed to the United States to prevent another European power from taking it over. America, *Harper's Weekly* insisted, had enough trouble with racial and ethnic minorities without taking more into the body politic. It did not want Cuba "imposed upon us, and with it all the ferocious and disorderly and chaotic elements which slavery breeds, to add to that part of our own population in which they already exist."[8]

Grant was caught between the need to defend American values and the need to protect trade. He tried to steer between the two by telling the secretary of the navy to put the navy on a war footing, sending a special message to Congress that presented the American view of the crisis at hand, then permitting the Spanish government to remedy the problem with very little effort. The *Virginius* was an American ship, he explained, registered in New York City "as the property of a citizen of the United States, he having first made oath, as required by law, that he was the true and only owner of the . . . vessel." Apparently this had not been the case, but that did not matter, according to Grant. If the ship's papers "were irregular or fraudulent, the offense was one against the laws of the United States, justifiable only in their tribunals."

The solution that calmed the storm over the *Virginius* emphasized the dignity of the United States. Grant demanded that Spain hand over the ship, return the survivors to the United States, and punish the Spanish officers who had captured the ship and shot the eight Americans. The surrender of the miscreants and their ship to the American justice system firmly established the rule of American law over Spanish interests, but Grant went further. He also demanded from Spain "a salute to the flag." Spain demurred at saluting an American flag on what actually appeared to be a Cuban ship. Grant agreed to drop that demand "on the assurance that Spain would then declare that no insult to the flag of the United States had been intended," which the Spanish minister did. Unwilling to cast off European goodwill entirely by siding against Spain, in 1875, President Grant called for joint U.S. and European intervention in Cuba. In February 1878, the treaty of El Zanjon ended the war. It promised a general amnesty for all rebels and reforms in the governance of Cuba.[9]

The Cuban war's terrible costs encouraged American sympathy for the Cuban insurgency. By the time the conflict had worn itself out, the island was ravaged. Crops had been destroyed and trade slashed. As the war's financial costs mounted, the Spanish government demanded higher and higher taxes. By 1878, Cuban taxes had tripled from the 1868 rate that had prompted the "Cry of Yara." The war's human cost was even higher. Brutal fighting combined with disease to make casualties soar. The Spanish lost more than 80,000 of their regular troops. Cuban casualties were harder to gauge, but U.S. estimates put them between 30,000 and 50,000.

Although the war had ended, conditions in Cuba did not improve much. In 1895, Cubans launched a new strike for independence, and, once again, Americans were deeply involved in the struggle. The insurrection was primarily a guerrilla war. In response, Spanish officials used the kind of scorched-earth policies that governments always use to put down guerrillas. In 1896, the

Spanish government fell back on a "reconcentration" policy that forced all Cubans into fortified towns guarded by soldiers and surrounded by barbed wire (indeed, it is likely that the origin of our term "concentration camps" comes from this policy). Cubans who refused to enter the towns—or who did not hear the order—were to be considered rebels and hanged. Death from starvation and disease in the towns rose steadily as the population crowded together.

By the time of McKinley's inauguration in March 1897, the situation in Cuba had deteriorated into a humanitarian crisis. The Spanish reconcentration policy was exacting a terrible toll on Cuban civilians. In January 1898, the Red Cross asked permission from the Spanish government to provide relief. The government agreed, permitting Clara Barton, the founder of the American Red Cross, herself to bring supplies to Cuba. Doubtful that the Red Cross could handle the entire task, the U.S. secretary of state issued a plea to the American people for relief. The needs were simple and heartrending: clothing for women and children, medicine, basic foodstuffs like flour and beans, blankets, and "especially large quantities of condensed milk, as many persons are . . . too feeble for any other nourishment." He also asked for money to provide emergency medicines, food, and transportation for the supplies.[10]

As usual in times of Cuban crisis, American filibustering expeditions sailed to Cuba to aid the insurgents, forcing Americans to jockey around international law. But this time, the American government did not simply let events happen. Before he left office in 1896, President Cleveland had appointed a southerner, Robert E. Lee's nephew Fitzhugh Lee, former governor of Virginia, to become consul general of Cuba. Lee strongly opposed Spanish rule and sent dispatches to his government asserting that Cubans were eager for annexation to the United States. Fueling anti-Spanish sentiment, Lee warned that 600 to 800 American citizens in Cuba were starving because of the reconcentration policy. By the summer of 1897, McKinley was forced to ask Congress for $50,000 to relieve them.[11]

Tension between Spain and America increased as prointerventionists, led by the *New York World* and the *New York Journal*, agitated for war. In February 1898, newspapers published a letter purloined from the Spanish foreign minister assessing the danger of the war agitation; his dismissal of McKinley as a weakling who pandered to the crowd caused such an uproar that the minister, Enrique Depuy de Lome, had to resign. Then, on February 15, 1898, the *U.S.S. Maine*, sent to Cuba to protect Americans there, exploded in

Havana Harbor. Modern-day historians have speculated that the *Maine* blew up when coal dust in the bunker beside the powder magazine spontaneously combusted, but at the time there was good reason to think that Spanish loyalists had planted a mine near the ship. Consul General Lee openly sympathized with Cuban insurgents and had so infuriated the Spanish government that it asked McKinley to recall him. McKinley would not, and Americans could easily believe that Spanish sympathizers were angry enough to launch an attack. Still, the explosion of the *Maine* did not dictate the war with Spain. On March 12, *Harper's Weekly* insisted that "a decent regard for our own dignity demands reticence and self-restraint. The nation cannot consent that the civilized world shall believe that, to please our Jingoes, and in obedience to their noise, we are willing to make war upon a country which has been shown, in a distracting and dangerous crisis, not to have injured us." A letter to the editor of the *New York Times* prayed that the public "shut their eyes from the howling dervishes of journalism who do nothing to serve the public weal, but who want to sell 'extras' and whoop up a circulation." Cautious Americans echoed the president's insistence that no one should draw conclusions about the explosion until a naval committee of inquiry made its report.[12]

The crisis in Cuba fell into an American society primed for just such a struggle. American intervention in the conflict, perceived as unpopular with businessmen and government leaders, appealed to the American mainstream, which saw it as an opportunity to reassert traditional American morality and individualism in a world increasingly controlled by impersonal business forces that circumscribed a man's opportunities. The very fact that business and government seemed to oppose the war increased its attraction to many people. Many middle-class Americans believed that businessmen were attempting to rule the country in the interests of their pocketbooks, to destroy America's classless society, to enervate Americans until they became cogs in an industrial machine. To many, it appeared that hardworking Americans who made up the heart of the nation had to break out of this trap and bring the country back to its fundamental principles.[13]

The competition between two popular newspapers helped to foster the idea that American intervention in the Cuban crisis was a blow against the big business that was corrupting America. In 1894, California newspaperman William Randolph Hearst had come to New York City intent on challenging Pulitzer's *New York World* for national supremacy. Pulitzer's newspaper was designed to be independent of business and political pressure, defending the middle-class American against corruption and monopoly. Hearst claimed to take Pulitzer's independence a step further; he wanted, he wrote, to produce a "sensational" paper that was so wildly popular it could attack business and government at will without worrying about reprisals. (His large collection of fine art, utter ruthlessness, and political ambitions belied this high-minded justification). Locked in a circulation war with Pulitzer, Hearst was willing to make up sensational stories for his *New York Journal* if he needed to (prompting the editor of the *New York Times* to add "All the News That's Fit to Print" to his paper's masthead in 1897). Hearst found the Cuban conflict perfect for his sales, and he tailored his presentation of it to the popular concerns of the day. His writers embellished the Cuban fight into the material of popular romance. They presented lurid stories of the Cuban struggle, emphasizing the torture of Cuban men, the abuse of Cuban women and children, and the brutality of Spanish soldiers, at the same time they rallied Americans to take up arms for the rebels. Pulitzer had little choice but to follow suit. Folding the Cuban situation into his own agenda, he hammered home the idea that businessmen and politicians were preventing good Americans from standing up for suffering humanity in Cuba.[14]

With the help of the two New York newspapermen, Americans interpreted the Cuban struggle through a lens that emphasized contemporary American concerns, focusing on the terrible cost of the war for women and children. The *New York Journal* sensationalized the story of Evangelina Cisneros, for example, a Cuban woman imprisoned by the Spanish after being caught in a failed plot against Spanish officers. Americans took the story to heart. In 1897, Julia Ward Howe and Jefferson Davis's wife joined forces with Consul General Lee in Cuba to appeal to the pope and the queen regent of Spain on behalf of Evangelina Cisneros, described as "a Cuban girl" who was threatened with twenty years' imprisonment at a Spanish penal colony in Africa. The Spanish commander had paid her "gross attentions," *Harper's Weekly* reported; her crime was luring him to a meeting where her brother and fiancé tied him up before his cries brought soldiers. Twenty years at an African penal colony would be "a dreadful fate for a woman," *Harper's Weekly* proclaimed. Howe wrote to the pope that the penal colony was a place "where no woman has ever before been sent, and where, besides enduring every hardship and indignity, she would have for companions the lowest criminals and outcasts." Cisneros was rescued in 1897 by Karl Becker, a newspaper reporter Hearst sent to Cuba for that very purpose; she was taken to New

York and welcomed as a heroine. The Cisneros story was just one of many Cuban romances that hit the presses during the war crisis, and with Hearst and Pulitzer emphasizing the suffering of Cuban women and children at the hands of brutal Spanish soldiers, Americans grew more and more determined to step in.[15]

Westerners impatient with eastern dithering about politics and business interests were anxious to come to the aid of Cuba. Theodore Roosevelt adopted their stance. After Roosevelt's gallant service in the 1896 election, McKinley had appointed the rising New Yorker assistant secretary of the navy, a position which should, in theory, have kept him tucked carefully out of the way. But Roosevelt was never one to be ignored. He later recalled that while the Democrats had been in power, he "had preached, with all the fervor and zeal I possessed, our duty to intervene in Cuba, and to take this opportunity of driving the Spaniard from the Western world." With the Republicans back in power, Roosevelt began to work with others determined to intervene in Cuba, focusing in the House on members "from the West, where the feeling for war was strongest." A war with Spain, Roosevelt believed, "would be as righteous as it would be advantageous to the honor and the interests of the nation."[16]

The crisis in Cuba pushed many Americans to call for intervention, but McKinley preferred not to take the United States into another war, at least not until American citizens were safely out of Cuba. "I have been through one war," the Union veteran remarked. "I have seen the dead piled up, and I do not want to see another." If the nation must fight, he intended to put the crisis off until Americans were not in direct danger. He quietly tried to negotiate a solution to the Cuban crisis, shutting even his own cabinet out of the administration's discussions with Spanish ministers. McKinley's reluctance to go to war and his secret negotiations played directly into the popular conviction that government and business leaders had abandoned morality for money. The McKinley Tariff of 1890 was popularly portrayed as a triumph of the sugar trust, whose members wanted to maintain Spanish rule in Cuba to guarantee the security of their property, and the election of 1896 had cemented McKinley's image as the tool of American business. When McKinley dragged his heels at entering the Cuban struggle, war hawks complained that his reluctance proved the degradation of American values at the hands of eastern businessmen.[17]

While McKinley awaited the results of the naval inquiry into the explosion, popular sentiment built for war. An editor of the *New York World* summed up the situation simply. "In slavery days Southern politicians had cast longing eyes upon Cuba . . . to strengthen the political power of the slave states. . . . When in 1895 a new rebellion broke out and when the Spanish authorities fought it by [the concentration policy] there was no longer any question of the slavery interest. There was simply a feeling that it was time for Spain to leave the continent. The war desire grew gradually for years; with the blowing up of the *Maine*, it burst into sudden flame." War supporters noted that even the English began to call for action. By the end of March, news reports from England were running strongly in favor of American entry into a war with Spain; the *Daily Mail* noted that when the war broke out—as seemed inevitable—"America . . . will earn the world's praise for ridding Cuba of ruthless tyranny." The *Spectator* commented that with the failure of diplomacy, America had only two choices. It could let Spain turn the neighboring island "into a permanent hell upon earth" or go to war to ameliorate the situation. England's support for intervention reinforced the idea that it was a struggle of "Anglo-Saxon" civilization against barbarism.[18]

Tied to war-hungry constituencies, congressmen were much more anxious for war than the president, and during the month of March they pushed more and more strongly for the United States to intervene in Cuba. On March 9, an appropriations bill authorizing the expenditure of $50 million to prepare for war passed the House unanimously. On March 17, Alabama Representative Joseph Wheeler—"Fightin' Joe" Wheeler, who had fought with Wade Hampton under Joseph Johnston—tried to get the House and Senate to agree to a joint resolution that would force the president to get behind the war effort. The proposed resolution demanded that Spain protect American interests on the island and stop the atrocities there.[19]

On that same day, Senator Redfield Proctor of Vermont delivered an important speech to the Senate that swung public opinion toward intervention. Proctor had staunchly favored intervention for more than a year and his "fact-finding" tour of Cuba in early March revealed to him a land that looked much like individualist America would look if overrun by a military government. Proctor's portrait of Cuba was devastating. Outside of Havana, he told the Senate, all was "desolation and distress, misery and starvation. Every town and village is surrounded by a . . . sort of rifle pit" and by "small blockhouses . . . loopholed for musketry, and with a guard of from two to ten soldiers in each." These guards kept reconcentrados in and insurgents out with "every point . . . in range of a soldier's rifle." Soldiers had gone throughout the countryside and rounded up everyone: "farmers, some land-owners, others renting lands and owning more or less stock, others working on estates and cultivating small patches, and even a small patch in that fruitful clime will support a family," he told the Senate. Forced from their farms, these people built huts in the cities, but even barely clad and starving, they were "not beggars." The worst sufferers were women and children. Home life was impossible; people had been "torn from their homes, with foul earth, foul air, foul water and foul food, or none." No wonder half of the reconcentrados had died and a quarter more were too sick to survive. "Little children are still walking about with arms and chests terribly emaciated, eyes swollen and abdomen bloated to three times the natural size," he recorded. In one hospital, Proctor saw "four hundred women and children . . . lying on the stone floors in an indescribable state of emaciation and disease, many with the scantiest covering of rags, and such rags! and sick children, naked as they came into the world." Proctor praised Clara Barton and begged the American people to continue to provide relief for the Cubans. "When will the need for this help end?" Proctor asked. "Not until peace comes and the reconcentrados can go back to their country, rebuild their homes, reclaim their tillage plots . . . in that wonderful soil and clime, and . . . be free from danger of molestation."[20]

Proctor spoke for the interventionists, making sure that the prowar faction was not represented solely by the unpopular jingoes—extremist war hawks—caricatured by the antiwar factions. The *New York Times* made it a point to emphasize that Proctor was a calm conservative from an old New England family, not a hysterical member of a city mob. "It is the general belief in Washington that Senator Proctor's visit to Cuba and his conservative statement of what he saw there have been productive of much good in throwing the clear light of truth upon the actual situation," a reporter remarked. The *New York Commercial Advertiser,* the *Sacramento Bee,* the *Pittsburgh Times,* the *Boston Journal,* the *Chicago Record,* and the *Washington Star* all credited Proctor with swinging the nation behind the movement for war. Eager to distance themselves from unpopular businessmen who appeared to be colluding with McKinley against the war, congressmen swung behind the interventionists. Ohio Democrat John J. Lentz scorned those who called for caution. "This is a free country," he said, "and with the 447 Senators and Congressmen, representatives of a great people, we are better able to decide questions as to the policy of this Government in view of the facts before us, and are better fitted to advise the President, than are those who go at midnight, behind closed doors, to point out the views of the plutocrats and submit them as the voice of the people. This is a Government yet 'by the people and for the people,' and it will remain so." Theodore Roosevelt was more direct. Shaking his fist at powerful Republican operator Mark Hanna at a public dinner, he growled: "We will have this war for the freedom of Cuba in spite of the timidity of the commercial interests!"[21]

After Proctor's speech, the momentum for war picked up. On March 28, the U.S. Naval Court of Inquiry found that a mine had caused the explosion of the *U.S.S. Maine.* The next day, a joint resolution of Congress demanded that Spain leave Cuba, a demand promptly rejected by Spain. On April 4, the *New York Journal* ran a one-million-copy issue calling for American intervention. On April 10, the Spanish governor in Cuba suspended hostilities on the island, but the following day President McKinley asked Congress for authorization to intervene in Cuba without recognizing the insurgent Cuban government. On April 13, Congress approved. Spain then declared that American intervention would threaten Spanish control over the island (as indeed it was intended to) and authorized expenditures for war. On April 19, Congress passed a joint resolution for war with Spain by a vote of 311 to 6 in the House and 42 to 35 in the Senate. On April 20, it was signed by McKinley and sent off to Spain, where officials considered it a declaration of war. On April 23, McKinley called for 125,000 volunteers, and Congress declared war on April 25, 1896.[22]

Mainstream Americans had decided that strong, independent individuals must rise up and restore true republicanism in America by taking control of the country from businessmen and the politicians beholden to them, and they could do so first by establishing a republic in Cuba. The Spanish–American War would be fought for humanity, the American public insisted. Determined to guarantee that businessmen would not somehow manage to scoop up the island with its valuable sugar production, Colorado's Henry M. Teller proposed to codify America's humanitarian impulse. Teller was a Republican silverite who had led the silver Republicans out of the national party in 1896 and was determined to break the hold of business on his party. He proposed an amendment to Congress's joint resolution authorizing intervention reading in part: "The United States hereby disclaims any disposition or intention to exercise sovereignty, jurisdiction, or control over said Island, except for the pacification thereof, and asserts its determination, when that is accomplished, to leave the government and control of the Island to its people." Congress passed the Teller Amendment, establishing that the United States went to war with Spain in Cuba without any interest in keeping the island.[23]

The American people tried to fight the war as individualists. Jesse James's brother Frank offered to lead a cowboy regiment to the war; Buffalo Bill published an article entitled "How I Could Drive Spaniards from Cuba with Thirty Thousand Indian Braves." Roosevelt had been determined to fight in the war for months before it was declared, and he was thrilled when Congress solved for him the problem of how to enlist. Congress authorized the creation of, as Roosevelt recalled, "three cavalry regiments from among the wild riders and riflemen of the Rockies and the Great Plains." Secretary of War Russell A. Alger agreed to offer Roosevelt the command of one of the regiments—the First United States Volunteer Cavalry—but Roosevelt gave the colonelcy to a more experienced friend and took the lieutenant colonelcy for himself. Roosevelt now had permission to raise a "cowboy regiment"; he announced that he needed "men who can ride, fight, shoot, and obey orders." Roosevelt "is very anxious for war to commence in earnest," reported the *New York Times.* "The kind of war that is being played at this time is not serious enough for his nature." Once it began, he would be "found in the front with his dashing band of Western cowboys . . . chosen for their ability to ride, shoot, and fight." These "sturdy frontier heroes" would be ready to fight as soon as they signed up. They "have their own mounts, their own arms, and, what is more, know how to take care of themselves, live under any circumstances, and fight all the time. They need no drilling or inuring to hardship, but can give lessons in endurance and soldierly qualities to the veterans of the regular army," Roosevelt initially objected when the press dubbed his men "rough riders" after the riders in Buffalo Bill's Wild West Show, insisting that his men were real fighters, not showmen. His trip to the West to meet with his regiment got him "thoroughly seasoned and . . . back to his old hardy form when he used to hunt big game in the Rockies," according to a reporter. "He no longer looks like the shrewd, busy, and firm Assistant Secretary of the Navy. He looks like a soldier—a fighting soldier through and through."[24]

The men he had met in the West were "the average American of the right type," Roosevelt recalled. "I made up my mind that the men were of just the kind whom it would be well to have with me if ever it became necessary to go to war. When the Spanish War came, I gave this thought practical realization," he later recalled. Initially asked to raise men only in the Territories, Roosevelt eventually got permission to extend his reach. He later deliberately described the men of his regiment as specimens of the ideal American citizen. The heart of the regiment was formed of southwesterners, "that is, from the lands that have been more recently won over to white civilization, and in which the conditions of life are nearest those that obtained on the frontier when there still was a frontier." But unlike Frederick Jackson Turner, whom he echoed, Roosevelt saw no reason that the frontiersman had to disappear. Cowboys, hunters, and miners had the attributes that true Americans everywhere could have. Roosevelt emphasized that he took his Rough Riders from every walk of life in every part of the country. He took poor frontiersmen and Harvard men, Indian hunters and Indians, northerners and southerners, whites and blacks. All these men needed was discipline and leadership to turn them from a "valueless mob" to the best men in the nation. Their faults were only those of "ignorance," and by simply appealing to "their intelligence and patriotism," their officers quickly turned them into the best possible representatives of Americans.[25]

Individuals from the North, South, and West set out to wrest the nation from the slow poison of big business and strangling government. This was a volunteer war; more than 200,000 volunteers ultimately served in the army, although about 136,000 of them never left U.S. shores. Usually volunteers were unmarried white men—farmers, clerks, common laborers or skilled laborers, with some merchants and professional men thrown in. They enlisted in groups from their hometowns, and they were never integrated with the larger regular army. Roosevelt noted, "The difficulty in organizing was not in selecting, but in rejecting men. . . . We were literally deluged with applications from every quarter of the Union." The men who volunteered, Roosevelt boasted, were not interested in commissions or their social standing in the regiment but were only "endeavoring to show that no work could be too hard, too disagreeable, or too dangerous for them to perform, and neither asking nor receiving any reward in the way of promotion or consideration." Westerners and easterners, northerners and southerners, rich and poor, white, black, and Indian—according to their commander, all simply wanted to do their duty, winning freedom for Cuba, honor for the United States, and glory for themselves.[26]

On June 30, 17,000 U.S. troops landed in Santiago; the next day 7,000 of them—including Roosevelt's Rough Riders—charged up San Juan and Kettle hills to take the high ground around the city. On July 3, when the Spanish fleet tried to run past the American blockade of Santiago Harbor, the U.S. Navy sank all seven Spanish ships, killing 474 Spanish sailors and cutting communication between Cuba and Spain. Isolated and surrounded, the Spanish garrison surrendered on July 17. American Secretary of State John

Figure 22. Camped in Cuba, the Rough Riders indicated their western heritage when they used the army tents as Indian-style tepees. Theodore Roosevelt Collection, Harvard College Library.

Hay wrote to Roosevelt that it had been "a splendid little war; begun with the highest motives, carried on with magnificent intelligence and spirit, favored by that fortune which loves the brave."[27]

Roosevelt deliberately fought the war as an antigovernment escapade. During his brief tenure as assistant secretary of the navy he had bitterly resented the government's inefficiency and lack of preparation for war. Once at the head of his own regiment, he made it a point to cut through red tape and demand that his regiment receive supplies before other troops. Even then, he bellyached about the way government officials wasted time that could have been used to win the war, unable to fathom, for example, why the Ordnance Bureau sent "whatever we really needed by freight instead of express." The corrupt system of army contracting and inefficient officials appointed by patronage meant that some troops were sent to the tropics in wool clothing, that food was often spoiled or missing, and that guns sometimes came from the Civil War era. Roosevelt continually plunged "into and out of the meshes of red-tape," fighting for rifles, tents, clothes, and transportation for his men and horses. At the close of his campaign, Roosevelt wrote a letter to the secretary of war flaying the army for its inability to feed, provision, or transport soldiers adequately.[28]

When government officials actively endangered his men, Roosevelt calmly ditched military protocol and delivered a letter straight to the American press explaining that army inefficiency was murdering soldiers. Only 379 Americans had died in battle during the war, but disease would eventually bring the toll to almost 5,500. By the end of July, yellow fever had begun to spread among the troops, and, stationed in the lowlands, their danger increased as the weather got hotter. Since the "Washington authorities . . . knew nothing of the country nor of the circumstances of the army . . . the plans that were from time to time formulated in the Department . . . for the management of the army would have been comic if they had not possessed such tragic possibilities," Roosevelt recalled. Washington ordered the men first to move camp every few days, then to go uphill, then to move to a region filled with malaria—all options Roosevelt dismissed contemptuously. At the end of July, the commanding officers in Cuba agreed that the army should leave, but "there was naturally some hesitation on the part of the regular officers to take the initiative, for their entire future career might be sacrificed," Roosevelt recalled. "So I wrote a letter." While he prepared his missive, the other officers wrote one of their own; when they were done Roosevelt handed the two letters to an Associated Press reporter. Roosevelt's accusations that his men would soon be "dying like rotten sheep" and that he could not "see our men, who have fought so bravely and who have endured extreme hardship and danger so uncomplainingly, go to destruction without striving so far as lies in me to avert a doom as fearful as it is unnecessary and undeserved" were backed up more moderately by the generals' statement that "this army must be moved at once, or perish." Published in American newspapers, the documents left authorities little choice. Within three days, the army was ordered home.[29]

Northerners, southerners, and westerners had come together on a western quest to bring American individualism to a foreign land. In the aftermath of the war, books about it flew off the presses, each more complimentary than the last. This war was unprecedented, claimed the author of the *Pictorial History of Our War with Spain for Cuba's Freedom*. Other nations fought "for territory and for gold," to hold back "the encroachments of barbarism," "to preserve the integrity of their own empire," or "to fight for holy tombs and symbols." But America had fought Spain for novel reasons: "the happiness of others," "to uproot barbarism and cast it out of its established place," "to set others free," and "to overthrow vicious political systems and regenerate iniquitous government for other peoples." In the past, liberty had grown slowly, the book's author explained, and civilization had been always on the defensive against barbarism. But America had launched a new era in the world. "Now liberty fights for liberty, and civilization takes the aggressive [*sic*] in the holiest war the world has ever known." The "splendid little war" lasted only a few months, but it gave America a seat at the table of international powers. In 1898, old newspaperman Murat Halstead wrote a tremendously celebratory account of American "empire." In *Our Country in War and Our Foreign Relations*, he insisted that "the progress of mankind summons the nation of the United States of North America to exercise the influence belonging to a great people, and participate, as a power, in the affairs of the world."30

Cuba was a great war "for liberty and humanity," but like the rest of the individualist ideal it had an underside, and the dark side of the American system dominated the Philippine theater of the Spanish-American War. This group of islands in the Pacific Ocean to the south of China, halfway around the globe from Cuba, had a long history of resistance to Spanish rule. In the early 1890s, a group of intellectuals had worked hard for reforms in Spanish government; by 1892, a revolutionary society led by poorer men had formed to promote Philippine unity and independence. War broke out between the revolutionaries and Spanish authorities in August 1896. By 1897, Emilio Aguinaldo had emerged as the leader of the rebellion and was harassing Spanish forces. A brief truce in early 1898 sent Aguinaldo into exile in Hong Kong, but the truce quickly fell apart.

With the outbreak of war with Spain, neutrality laws forced the American Asiatic fleet out of Hong Kong; it steamed to Manila, which had valuable coal as well as Spanish naval equipment and which was, as one observer noted, "a splendid base of operations." Ordered to attack the Spanish fleet at Manila as soon as war was declared, Commodore George Dewey attacked the Spanish squadron on May 1, opening the Battle of Manila with the famous line: "You may fire when ready, Gridley." In six hours, the United States sank the entire Spanish fleet. With no land forces, Dewey had to wait until Aguinaldo could rush back to the islands from Hong Kong on an American ship to rally the Filipinos to force out the Spanish once and for all. On June 12, 1898, the Filippinos declared independence. A month later, 12,000 Filippino and 11,000 American men joined forces to drive the Spanish out of Manila. After a brief battle, Spanish forces surrendered on August 13, and the Americans hoisted the U.S. flag in Manila. Spanish power in the Philippines was broken.[31]

The Philippine rebels under Aguinaldo and the American forces cheerfully supported each other against Spain, but with the end of Spanish rule, the accord quickly fell apart. For the Philippines, there was no Teller Amendment promising that Americans would leave the islands. The representative of the Philippine government was not welcome at the peace negotiations in Paris between Spain and America, and the December 1898 Treaty of Paris gave the Philippines to the United States in exchange for $20 million. A firefight between two scouting parties in February 1899 brought the U.S. Army and Aguinaldo's men into open war. Immediately, Americans split over whether or not the United States should launch a career of "imperialism," taking over the Philippines, or stay true to the principles of liberty, humanity, and self-determination that had guided its war in Cuba. One major factor created the difference between the American approaches to Cuba and to the Philippines. While Cuba was economically of interest, it was not strategically important to late nineteenth-century Americans, but the Philippines were a critically important coaling station and refueling stop for both the U.S. navy and trading ships on their way to China and the Orient. With an international race under way for colonies, other nations were eager to snatch the prize of the Philippines if America didn't want it. As Dewey held Manila Harbor, English, French, and German ships steamed into the port, and the German commander made his hostility so clear that Dewey threatened a battle. The German commander backed down only when England promised to support Dewey. Imperial stakes were high in the Philippines.[32]

In order to promote the idea of taking the Philippines in the midst of a war to free Spain's colonies from foreign rule, proannexationists could not simply admit—as European countries did—that they wanted the land for strategic gain. That would undercut the argument that America was different from Europe, that it was God's chosen land spreading the idea of self-government to the world. Instead, they had to justify American acquisition of the islands as an extension of America's unique worldview. To do so, they both trumpeted the superiority of the American system over all others and attacked Filipino government and society as antithetical to the values that made the American system work. They fell back first on the glory of the nation. Having taken the Philippines, how could Americans hand them back to Spain or let them go to another foreign power without reducing the nation's international stature? "Now is the critical time when the United States should strain every nerve and bend all her energies to keep well to the front in the mighty struggle that has begun for the supremacy of the Pacific Seas," wrote John Barrett. If the nation stepped forward now, it would lead forever; but if it failed to accept its leading role in the world, it would never recover. Bartlett applied the doctrine of Darwinism to nations, as William Graham Sumner had applied it to individuals. "The rule of the survival of the fittest applies to nations as well as to the animal kingdom," he wrote. "It is a cruel, relentless competition of mighty forces; and these will trample over us without sympathy or remorse unless we are trained to endure and strong enough to stand the pace."[33]

No one could ignore the huge benefit of controlling the Philippines to business or to the navy that would be necessary to protect that trade. The Philippines were the key to Hong Kong and China, the largest business opportunities of the late nineteenth century. Acquiring the islands would launch America to the forefront of the world's business community. And if business would do well by acquiring the Philippines, what of it? "Is it not a fact that Americans make business and civilization go hand in hand?" wrote a correspondent to *Harper's Weekly*. "It is the instinct of a practical people, and one of the highest tributes to be paid to our commercial giants; and I say now that the American whose heritage is freedom and whose inspiration is liberty will never become aught but the benefactor of these people."[34]

Proannexationists also attacked the Filipinos by claiming they rejected American values. They denied the Aguinaldo government's legitimacy. Brigadier General Thomas A. Anderson insisted that the Filipino leaders were "revolutionary" and that this "self-appointed junta" did not truly represent the people. Indeed, he wrote, in an echo of American political rhetoric, Aguinaldo's men simply wanted to control politics to confiscate wealth. Spanish businessmen in the islands owned valuable property, and the members of Aguinaldo's government planned "to enrich themselves by confiscating . . . railways, tramways, electric plants, water-works, etc." The United States must not permit this, he explained, because it had promised in the Treaty of Paris to protect both private and corporate rights. An Indiana man wrote a vitriolic letter to *Harper's Weekly* insisting that the only civilized Filipinos were those who had asked for United States citizenship. To turn the island over to

Aguinaldo's "half-civilized army" would be like turning "over the entire West to Geronimo and his band of Apache cutthroats when in 1885 they claimed that territory, and pressed their claim, as Aguinaldo is doing to-day, killing, butchering, devastating any and every thing in his path!"[35]

Proannexationist Americans argued that the nation's citizens were duty-bound to govern the Filipinos and lead them to civilization. Despite their long heritage of education and religion, their cities and their agricultural production, Filipinos quickly became perceived as backward savages who "are not equal to independence." Left to their own devices, they would, one annexationist insisted, descend into civil war and foreign powers would have to step in to protect their interests in the islands. Another writer was more blunt: "To speak of the ability of the Filipinos to govern themselves is absurd." It was imperative for Americans to teach them how to be free. The task of "regenerating" the Filipinos had fallen to the Americans. "It is part of 'the white man's burden' which we can not now lay down," one man declared grandly. For those worried about yet more people of color being admitted to citizenship in America, another man suggested that the United States must simply "provide a safe government for the Philippines, without granting that degree of citizenship in such a colony as will permit actual voting powers in the United States."[36]

The deep racial and class biases that underpinned the American main-stream vision were clear in the Philippines. Anderson tried to explain why the Filipinos had come to dislike Americans so, but his casual boys-will-be-boys excuse for his soldiers' treatment of Filipinos was more shocking than the soldiers' actions themselves. "Our soldiers," he explained in a popular maga-zine, "to get what they considered trophies, did a good deal of what the Filipinos considered looting. A number made debts which they did not find it convenient to pay. They called the natives 'niggers,' and often treated them with a good-natured condescension which exasperated the natives all the more because they feared to resent it. Thus it happened that the common people, from at first hailing us as deliverers, got to regarding us as enemies." "A Filipino" who claimed to be one of Aguinaldo's men wrote to the *North American Review* to complain (in his own display of racism): "We have been represented by your popular press as if we were Africans or Mohawk Indians." But, he insisted, Filipinos were civilized men who could govern themselves.[37]

The deteriorating image of the Filipinos from welcome allies who could help defeat Spain to backward savages who rejected mainstream ideals had the same kind of disastrous consequences the deteriorating images of African

Americans, Indians, and organized laborers had back home. In the islands the violence of lynching and the Wounded Knee fight magnified into ferocious warfare, and the suppression of rioting became wholesale suppression of civilians. "War is terrible, but war is a necessity," claimed one observer. "How often have we wasted kindness upon the Indians, and as it failed there so it will fail when extended to the Filipinos. A little spanking with the sword and shell teaches the Indian his place—likewise the Filipino." In the guerrilla warfare of the Philippines, Aguinaldo and the Filipino people were dehumanized, and tactics that both recalled Spanish leaders in Cuba and anticipated Americans in Vietnam became accepted practice. Filipinos were herded into camps while their homes were destroyed; troops killed and tortured indiscriminately. By the time Aguinaldo was captured in 1902, the death toll in the Philippines was about 5,000 Americans, 25,000 Filipino soldiers, and as many as 200,000 civilians.[38]

Those opposed to taking the Philippines revealed the power of mainstream language when they adopted it to stop American imperialism. Many who had been anxious to push the reluctant Republican McKinley into war in Cuba and had insisted that government must not be held in thrall to business interests that opposed the war now just as insistently protested the possession of the Philippines as the outgrowth of the machinations of businessmen. On their side they had American principles of self-determination, fear of the fall of overextended republics, and, finally, racism. Of course Filipinos could govern themselves, insisted a returning soldier; they had done so for the seven months before war with the United States broke out, for America had never held more than Manila during those months and had made no pretense of governing the rest of the country. Wasn't self-determination the principle of the Declaration of Independence, opponents of annexation asked; why not apply the Teller Amendment to the Philippines as well as to Cuba? Those less high-minded worried that the annexation of the Philippines would bring more nonwhites into the Union just as middle-class Americans were losing faith in the ability of African Americans and immigrants ever to become productive members of society.[39]

Carl Schurz and Andrew Carnegie, both outspoken opponents of American acquisition of the Philippines, deliberately used mainstream language to object to imperialism. Schurz condemned the demagoguery that prompted Americans to trample the rights of others, pointing out that wartime opened the door wide to corruption and inflated contracts. Carnegie deplored the potential cost of maintaining a world-class navy and of fighting the wars required to defend Asian possessions. He picked up Julia Ward Howe's old reasoning about war to fight annexation. Human beings were alike everywhere, he insisted, and he bemoaned that "Filipino mothers with American mothers equally mourn their lost sons." To those arguing that Americans would civilize the natives, he insisted that soldiers—adventurers unable to hold a job at home—would only demoralize Filipinos, while there would be "no holy influence flowing from American homes, no Christian women, no sweet children" to raise up the natives. Carnegie offered $20 million to the Philippine government to buy independence.[40]

Opponents of Philippine annexation were arguing against a whirlwind. The growing sense that America must spread its version of liberty across the globe—while it took control of valuable regions—was made manifest in June 1898 when Congress passed a joint resolution annexing the Hawaiian Islands. In Hawaii, a group of American sugar planters had rebelled against native rule in 1894 and asked to join the United States, a move that would permit their sugar to enter America without paying high tariffs. Popular sense that this revolutionary government was illegitimate and that the nation must not acquire foreign territories repeatedly stopped measures designed to admit the Hawaiian Islands to the Union. With Dewey in possession of Manila Harbor and a fight developing about the future of America in the Pacific, however, objections to taking Hawaii fell apart. "As a measure of national protection and advantage, it is the duty of the American people to lay peaceful conquest wherever opportunity may be offered," insisted a member of the Committee on Foreign Affairs. Two years after Hawaiian annexation, in 1900, the Republican's election year platform endorsed the idea of the American duty to impose American freedom on the Philippines. Although the primary factor in American interest in the islands was their critically important position for trading and provisioning the American navy, the Republican platform adopted the language of freedom and duty. "Our authority could not be less than our responsibility," it read, "and wherever sovereign rights are extended, it becomes the high duty of the government to maintain its authority, to put down armed insurrection, and to confer the blessings of liberty and civilization upon all the rescued peoples. The largest measure of self-government consistent with their welfare and our duties shall be secured to them by law."[41]

The rich prize of the Philippines joined together with popular determination to prove that America was "the greatest nation of the earth" ultimately overwhelmed the arguments of antiannexationists. The United States retained control of the Philippines, where it built schools, roads, and factories, gradually transferring power to Filipino elites that supported the United States. Not until July 4, 1946, were the Philippines granted independence.

The lessons of the Spanish-American War translated easily to America. A newly minted war hero, Roosevelt promised to bring the western qualities he had asserted in Cuba to the American government. Roosevelt had brought journalists with him to Cuba, intending for his men to "make themselves famous if an opportunity presents itself. . . . It is predicted by men who have lived on the frontier that where they strike they will leave a mark." Roosevelt's supporters cultivated the image of him as an outsider, aloof from the corrupt machinations of devious politicians who pulled mysterious strings in their shadowy offices. As early as the end of June, Roosevelt was talked of as a candidate for governor of New York, with supporters casually mentioning "Roosevelt the soldier, the man who threw aside every advantage the politicians cherish for the privilege of exposing his life in defense of ideas that he had long advocated." The *Indianapolis Sentinel* remarked that he fought "at the front" in battle, "as composed, as fearless, and as aggressive as if he were charging an army of spoilsmen." The Roosevelt boom built throughout the summer. Illustrating that being a "westerner" was a state of mind, Roosevelt of New York City outshone William Jennings Bryan of Nebraska as a western fighter, since Roosevelt "had a horse shot under him, [and] charged up a hill at the enemy under fire and 'yelling like a Sioux Indian,'" whereas Bryan's trip to the front was delayed by "hitches about his commission . . . having his picture taken . . . [and] speeches . . . at banquets."[42]

Roosevelt described his men at a postwar celebration for the returning soldiers that had been deliberately constructed to appear to be apolitical. After announcing that his regiment had "no politics and no religion" (which he quickly clarified to mean "no religion . . . except as with all good Americans . . . , according to our several creeds, tried to serve God and our country"), he explained what made his regiment a true group of American citizens. His men were "from all walks of life, all standing precisely alike as far as the regiment was concerned. Standing shoulder to shoulder were the man who has left a one-dollar a day job and the man born in wealth and reared in luxury; both good Americans. . . . They demanded only to . . . be judged on their merits. . . . The regiment was American through and through. We had in the ranks Americans who were such by choice as well as by inheritance . . . [and] Americans of the aboriginal blood, as brave and true as the others. It was our good fortune to have . . . the colored cavalry whom the Spaniards

Figure 23. In this image, taken of the Rough Riders on Long Island, New York, during Roosevelt's gubernatorial campaign, the photographer caught Roosevelt unconsciously imitating his young cowboy aide at the same time that he was consciously imitating the western image for his political campaign. Theodore Roosevelt Collection, Harvard College Library.

christened the 'smoked Yankees.' We found them to be a very good breed of Yankees." As Roosevelt insisted, this idealized citizenship cut across traditional party lines. The Democratic *Charleston News and Courier* conceded that he would "make an able Governor and would give the rascals such a shaking up as they have never had."[43]

The government was less successful at managing the war than the Rough Riders had been, Roosevelt told his audience. The regiment was hurried onto transports which then sat for a week at anchor; the baggage did not make the trip with the troops; for three days Roosevelt had neither food nor extra clothing, and "lying in six inches of mud drenched with rain soon takes the gilt edge from the romance of tropical nights." Unlike government bureaucrats, though, Roosevelt had cut through red tape with a machete and held officials accountable for their actions. If elected, he promised he would make government active again and clear out the deadwood that made it seem to be a revenue-sucking beast of inefficiency.[44]

Roosevelt's international vision was the true extension of American exceptionalism, one supporter insisted. His career should teach young men "that there is a higher and nobler ideal than the acquisition of fortune, and that service to one's country is the first duty of patriotic citizenship." His beliefs about foreign policy "breathe a virility and strength of character that stamp him as the true American." Opposed to isolationism, he preached "maintaining the country's honor against the mewling advocates of surrender, National effacement, and 'peace at any price.'" Roosevelt, this staunch expansionist declared, represented "in every sense the highest type of chivalric American manhood.[45]

Roosevelt's image of colorblind, all-inclusive citizenship idealized American life, of course. In turn-of-the-century America, wage laborers and wealthy men did not stand "shoulder to shoulder." That Harvard men fought alongside poor westerners indicated their equal value as soldiers but said little about their unequal access to education, capital, or white-collar jobs. Actual race relations were also quite different from Roosevelt's rosy recollections of the trenches. Lynching and discrimination that prevented black economic and social advancement had increased sharply after 1890 and been codified in the Jim Crow laws. The "smoked Yankees" of whom Roosevelt spoke so fondly in political speeches (elsewhere he accused them of running from battle) were segregated from white troops and complained bitterly about discrimination both in the U.S. Army and in society in general, where the Jim Crow laws kept them out of hotels and restaurants. Native Americans, too, hardly stood on a level playing field with white Americans, however much Roosevelt might hope it was so. Congress had intended the Dawes Act to move Indian families into middle-class life, but the act locked Indians into subsistence farming that was untenable on the dry prairies. ("God Damn a Potato!" one chief reportedly shouted at a government official.) The depression of the 1890s further weakened Indian farmers, even those few willing to abandon their culture and traditions to try the white man's road. In an ironic illustration of the dilemma of American Indians, Roosevelt would soon trot Geronimo out of prison to march in support of his own policies, a role Geronimo accepted in the vain hope of gaining enough favor to get his people back to Arizona.[46]

The idealized image of American citizenship pleased people like Roosevelt, but there was a negative side to the image of a pure American government of individualistic citizens. Those who seemed to support special interests were often purged from government, even if they had won elections fair and square. Their success in winning office simply proved to mainstream Americans that they were corrupting society and strengthened the resolve to get rid of them. In November 1898, for example, the "best citizens" of Wilmington, North Carolina, launched a race riot to purify the city government of the Populist/African American coalition that had won election in 1896. In Wilmington, an observer declared, "ministers, lawyers, doctors, merchants, railroad officials, cotton exporters, and . . . the reputable, taxpaying, substantial men of the city" had to enforce "white supremacy" because "thriftless, improvident" African Americans had had the political clout to raise their coalition with Populists into power. They had, opponents charged, put into office incompetent police officers and magistrates who had permitted their political supporters to commit crimes. Property was not safe, and "highly esteemed" men and women were assaulted on the streets. In November, a citizens' council organized, killed ten black citizens, and forced the coalition members to resign their offices. "We . . . will never again be ruled by men of African origin," white Democrats declared. The new Democratic mayor complacently reviewed the "reform" of Wilmington's government in terms that sounded much like Roosevelt's reform of government in general. "There was no intimidation used. . . . The old government had become satisfied of their inefficiency and utterly hopeless imbecility, and believed if they did not resign they would be run out of town."[47]

The Republican politicos of New York recognized that Roosevelt's wild popularity must be harnessed for the party; if it were not, the Democrats would take the state in the upcoming elections. Reluctantly, they nominated the returning hero for the governorship in 1898. (Ironically, the "colored Republican State Convention" endorsed Roosevelt's candidacy for the governorship and resolved to organize a "colored State Committee" that would act as an auxiliary to the regular Republican State Committee. Colorblind citizenship did not extend to integrated political committees.) Roosevelt crisscrossed the state on a special train, speaking to audiences wherever he found them, and in the fall he won the New York governorship by a decisive 18,000 votes. As governor, Roosevelt strengthened the state civil service laws, enforced legislation that protected workers (inspecting sweatshops himself accompanied by his friend Jacob Riis, whose photographs of New York City tenement life brought the squalor of poverty to the attention of middle-class

Americans). In the face of bitter opposition of businessmen, he forced corporations that acted in a public capacity—streetcars, for example—to pay taxes, thus establishing "the principle that . . . corporations holding franchises from the public shall pay their just share of the public burden."[48]

Finally fed up, New York's Republican establishment concluded to bury Roosevelt in the obscurity of the vice presidency. Roosevelt initially protested this idea, but he came to believe that his national profile and reputation as a straight-dealing reformer would help bring his brand of citizenship to the national arena. He campaigned vigorously for McKinley in 1900, and when McKinley returned to the White House in March 1901, Roosevelt came along. There he discovered just how little an American vice president had to do. His only official duty was to preside over the Senate, which would not be in session until December. Bored almost immediately, he asked the chief justice of the Supreme Court if it would be proper for him to enroll in law school to finish his degree. Aghast at the idea of the sitting vice president in school, the chief justice promised to supervise Roosevelt's studies himself.[49]

An anarchist relieved Roosevelt's boredom by killing President McKinley in September 1901. "It is a dreadful thing to come into the Presidency in this way," Roosevelt noted, "but it would be a far worse thing to be morbid about it." Machine Republicans were less sanguine. "I told McKinley it was a mistake to nominate that wild man at Philadelphia," Republican operator Mark Hanna moaned. "I told him to think what would happen if he should die. Now look. That damned cowboy is president of the United States." As Hanna indicated, Roosevelt brought the western image to the national government. His powerful and comprehensive first message to Congress codified the mainstream vision of America. He talked of a world in which "individual thrift and energy, resolution and intelligence" determined the welfare of each citizen, but embracing the contradiction of mainstream ideology, he announced that government regulation of business and labor combinations would give that individualism fullest scope. At the same time, he insisted on both the extraction of western resources and the preservation of the spirit of the West for the good of the American people. Finally, he called for the fostering of American power to spread the nation's message of independence and prosperity worldwide.[50]

With his famous western novel, *The Virginian*, Owen Wister translated Roosevelt's individualist society into American myth. The novel begins with an eastern dude—said to be modeled on Roosevelt—going west for the first time to visit Judge Henry, a leading rancher in frontier Wyoming. As the train pulls into the town of Medicine Bow, the hero of the novel, an unnamed southerner gone west after the Civil War, dominates the dude's vision. A natural man of quality despite his low birth, the Virginian is a natural leader, handsome, intelligent, honest, hardworking, and loyal. He is "a giant whom life had made 'broad-gauge'" and who left home because he is "more ambitious than my brothers." In the course of the novel, the Virginian rises from a promising youth to a wealthy rancher under the tutelage of his benevolent employer, Judge Henry.[51]

The Virginian demonstrates the nature of true American democracy. His love interest, Molly Wood, had moved west from Vermont, and while Molly's eastern relatives tie themselves in knots about "suitable" acquaintances, her Grandmother Stark—who boasts direct ties to the Revolutionary generation—knows better. She recognizes that despite his roughness, the Virginian is "a man that is a man." But Molly has to have a lesson directly from the Virginian himself. In a chapter entitled "Quality and Equality," the Virginian tells her: "Equality is a great big bluff. . . . I look around and I see folks movin' up or movin' down, winners and losers everywhere. . . . Call your failure luck, or call it laziness . . . and you'll come out the same old trail of inequality." The Virginian points out to Molly that he is "the kind that moves up." In case readers missed the point, Wister spelled it out in the next chapter. "It was through the Declaration of Independence that we Americans acknowledged the *eternal inequality* of man. . . . We decreed that every man should thenceforth have equal liberty to find his own level . . . saying, 'Let the best man win, whoever he is.' That is true democracy." The Virginian rises from cowhand to foreman by proving his worth to his boss, the judge, and manages to master his men even when the discovery of gold threatens to make them take off to the mines.[52]

The Virginian is the ideal individualist; his opposite is also explored in the novel. Wister matches the story of the Virginian's rise with the slow fall of the northerner Shorty, a lost soul who abandons his skill as a horse wrangler for the quick payoff offered by the novel's villain, who promises him more money than he is worth, involves him in cattle rustling, and in the end kills him and steals his horse to escape from a pursuing posse. The Virginian sees Shorty's weakness and tries to stop his fall but believes that he is responsible for his own mistakes. "I reckon man helps them that help themselves," he muses. "As for the universe, it . . . did too wholesale a business to turn out an article up to standard every clip." Harking back to Henry George, Shorty charges the Virginian with having the "luck" to take up land along a creek and then having that land skyrocket in value with him "lifting no finger." The Virginian snaps: "Why did you lift no finger? Did it not stretch in front of yu', behind yu', all round yu', the biggest, baldest opportunity in sight?" Shorty would never be a real man, the Virginian concludes. His lack of foresight and effort to help himself, not circumstances beyond his control, spell his doom.[53]

The Virginian reveals his identity as a western individualist most clearly when he participates in Wister's version of the Johnson County War. When stock starts to disappear from the judge's ranch, the Virginian leads a posse to hunt down the "rustlers." Coming back to Wyoming for a visit, the eastern dude—now a seasoned plainsman—comes upon the posse and its prisoners, who are to be hanged the next morning. He is shocked to find the Virginian's former friend Steve in custody. The easterner shrinks from the necessity of the execution, but his frontier friend has the manhood to do what is right even though hanging his friend so profoundly distresses him that he sobs on the easterner's shoulder after the deed is done. As the Virginian acknowledges to Molly's family, "I have had to live in places where they had courts and lawyers so called but an honest man was all the law you could find in five hundred miles."[54]

In case the justice of the Virginian's actions might be lost on an eastern reader, Wister arranged for the Virginian's employer, a former federal judge, to justify the hanging to Molly Wood. The judge explains that sometimes the law and the right are not the same, and that sometimes a true man must break the law to do right. The judge, who was, after all, the one who sent the Virginian after the rustlers, explains to Molly that he does not approve "of burning Southern negroes in public," but he does approve "of hanging Wyoming cattle-thieves in private." The two acts were completely different, he said (although white southerners justified lynching similarly). "I consider the burning a proof that the South is semi-barbarous, and the hanging a proof that Wyoming is determined to become civilized," the judge says. Southern lynchings stop the legal process from taking place, while western lynchings make sure the legal system works. "In Wyoming the law has been letting our cattle-thieves go for two years. . . . The courts, or rather the juries, into whose hands we have put the law, are not dealing the law. . . . And so when your ordinary citizen sees this, and sees that he has placed justice in a dead hand, he must take justice back into his own hands where it was once at the beginning of all things. Call this primitive if you will. But so far from being a *defiance* of the law, it is an *assertion* of it—the fundamental assertion of self-governing men, upon whom our whole social fabric is based." As terrible as western lynching is, he insisted, it is better than "unchecked theft and murder would be."[55]

Molly Wood also is a lesson in the modern world. She is a daring, modern woman from an old New England family, who leaves home and strikes out for unknown territory to earn her living as a teacher rather than staying safely at home and marrying well, as her silly mother and sister as well as village gossips want her to. She heads for Wyoming in the spirit of her strong Revolutionary era grandmother. But Molly goes west not to become an independent woman; her very first communication with Medicine Bow suggests she is not at all averse to the idea of marriage, and she goes to work in a job that reflects her role as a societal housekeeper. She becomes a schoolteacher and looks after local babies as carefully as their mothers do—sometimes better, as the Virginian sourly notes when she uses the children as an excuse to avoid him early in their acquaintance. Wood finally softens to the Virginian as she plays the role of his civilizer, taming the untutored southerner by introducing him to culture and manners. But he wants no part of her domestic Jane Austen; he admires Shakespeare and Russian novelists and poems about "the world of men" that she doesn't understand. She never masters him; rather, he becomes her "lord." Ultimately, Wood "surrender[s] . . . to her cowpuncher, her wild man" and joyfully becomes his wife and the mother of his children.[56]

The end of this wildly popular book left the adventurous but domestic northern woman and southern individualist together in a western environment that promised riches to the hardworking hero and heroine. After they marry, Judge Henry makes the Virginian a partner, and the young cattleman manages to protect the partnership's herds during the last days of the Johnson County War. Then the railroad builds a line to the Virginian's land, which he had carefully chosen for its coal deposits. "By that time, he was an important man, with a strong grip on many various enterprises, and able to give his wife all and more than she asked or desired." Although Molly sometimes worried that the Virginian's work would kill him, Wister concluded, "strictly between ourselves, I think [he] is going to live a long while."[57]

He did live a long while, for the Virginian represented the final reconstruction of America after the Civil War. From the North, Americans had taken the idea of equal opportunity; from the South, they had taken the idea that not all men could rise. From the racial and industrial troubles of the 1870s, they had taken the idea that those unable to rise and those at the top of society must not be permitted to harness the government to their own interests, for they would destroy America's unique political economy either by redistributing wealth or by circumscribing opportunity. From the strikes and the business consolidation of the 1880s, they had taken the belief that the federal government must be used to protect American individualism both against disaffected workers and against big business. From the women's activism of the 1890s, they had taken the idea that individualism depended on the safety of the middle-class home, and that it must be protected. From the Spanish-American War, they took the mythologized individualism must be expanded internationally. Thanks to the mythologized individualistic hero represented by the Virginian, the nation could use the government to advance individualism without fears of socialism.

The post–Civil War years made Americans define the nation around a peculiar "middle-class" ideology. Hardworking Americans, it seemed, held the great middle against disaffected Americans and unscrupulously wealthy businessmen. While both these outlying special interests seemed to want to hijack the government—and sometimes did—their opponents demanded that the government benefit everyone at once in an evenhanded system that promoted individualism. Since it was the government's job to help Americans, they believed it was the government's job to promote their way of life. It never occurred to them that they, themselves, might be a special interest. "Special interests," they thought, were organized groups that demanded government intervention in society to advance their own particular benefit. Organized labor, big businessmen, African American activists, certain women's rights activists, agrarian groups—all seemed to strike at the heart of America's unique individualism by trying to reduce God's beneficent world to one of struggling interests fighting over a finite set of benefits. If they succeeded in controlling the government, they would create the very limitations mainstream Americans feared, for government benefits would make the lazy stop working while the productive took their abilities elsewhere to keep from being bled dry by taxes. But legislation benefiting the great middle seemed to help the nation as a whole. It enabled more people than ever before to join the ranks of the middle class. It meant better working conditions and more oversight of the workplace. It meant a check on the power of employers. It meant better wages and some financial protection for workplace injury. As the economy rebounded from the depression of the mid-1890s and maintained a healthy level of growth in the early twentieth century, more and more workers identified with the vision of individualism that promised them upward mobility. The belief that labor and capital were naturally at odds lost ground to the idea that individuals could make it on their own.

With Roosevelt in the White House, the Virginian's version of American society had the full weight of the government behind it. Roosevelt endorsed a nation of individuals and used the government to protect that individualism. In the early twentieth century, Roosevelt and the Progressive coalition he represented attacked anarchists and disaffected laborers, put down the trusts, defended the American home, protected the West, and spread the American vision internationally. Supporting the American individual made it imperative to purify the government from the influences of both organized business and organized labor. Given the opportunity, it seemed, either of these groups would harness the government to its own interests, reordering the economy to pour public money into the pockets of its own members. For the same reasons, they thought agitating African Americans, angry western farmers, and other special interests must be kept from participating in government. They must not be given the chance to manipulate the government for their own ends.

Roosevelt and his Progressive coalition defended individualism. On one hand, they attacked certain trusts and monopolies that Roosevelt disliked. This stand was important, for in 1901, Andrew Carnegie helped to create the biggest trust of the age, capitalizing the new U.S. Steel at more than a billion dollars—more money than the entire federal budget that year. Roosevelt envisioned himself as a trustbuster; shortly after taking office he went after J. P. Morgan's Northern Securities Company, a holding company that included the Northern Pacific Railroad and the Great Northern. When a surprised Morgan offered to "fix it up" with the attorney general, Roosevelt informed Morgan that government was no longer a tool of big business. He insisted on enforcing the Antitrust Act, and in 1904, in *U.S. v. Northern Securities Company*, the Supreme Court forced the dissolution of the company. During his tenure, Roosevelt started proceedings against twenty-five major trusts.

On the other hand, Roosevelt and the Progressives came down hard on disaffected Americans. Reformers backing special interests were trying to replace individualism with government paternalism, it seemed, and this, too, must be combated. "Many of those persons who advocated the emancipation of the Southern slave," a writer for the *Forum* explained, and who fought "for his freedom to choose his vocation and enter into competition with the white laborer, now abandon the idea of competition and adopt that of socialism.

They would argue it is better, not only for the colored man, but for the white man, to give up individual adventure, and to accept such an organization of society as would determine the career of each member of it and apportion to him his share of the productions of the whole. A small percentage of the citizens of the United States hold this theory of socialism in the full application of its principle; but very many have adopted some parts of the scheme, perhaps without seeing the drift of the reform which they would introduce into the community." Progressives were pushed to extremes by the fear of anarchy in a time when anarchists were assassinating world leaders: the president of France in 1894, the prime minister of Spain in 1897, the Hapsburg empress of Austria in 1898, the king of Italy in 1900, McKinley in 1901. To protect America from what they saw as the dangerous influences of those attacking individualism, Progressives endorsed new state constitutions across the South that drastically reduced black voting by enacting "grandfather clauses," which permitted any man to vote as long as his grandfather had voted (ruling out those whose grandfathers had been enslaved). They also applauded northern constitutions that imposed property qualifications to curb voting by immigrants and poor whites.[58]

The vision of a free American individual included a domestic home life presided over by a nurturing woman. To fulfill that vision, mainstream Americans turned to the federal government to improve the conditions that threatened the home. This meant regulating the industries that polluted home products and that maimed and killed workers, especially women and children. In 1906, the Pure Food and Drug Act prohibited the manufacture or sale of harmful, mislabeled, or adulterated foods, drinks, or drugs, cutting into the deliberate distribution of dangerous products (although not stopping it). In 1904, the National Child Labor Committee was organized to press for laws to get children out of factories; at the same time, the National Consumers' League worked to get laws reducing the hours of women, arguing that the nation's mothers must be protected in order to guarantee that they produced children who could become healthy and productive citizens. In *Lochner v. New York* (1905), the Supreme Court struck down a law limiting the hours of work for men, but in 1908, the Supreme Court upheld a ten-hour law for women, arguing in *Muller v. Oregon* that women were dependent on men and could not stand independent of them, and that society must protect women. The "Brandeis brief" that presented this case relied not on established legal precedent but on mountains of evidence compiled by Brandeis's sister-in-law Josephine Goldmark of the National Consumer's League, which revealed the harm industrial work did to women. Reviewing this material, the Supreme Court agreed that "as healthy mothers are essential to vigorous offspring, the physical well-being of woman becomes an object of public interest and care in order to preserve the strength and vigor of the race." In 1910, the Mann Act prohibited the transportation of women across state lines for immoral purposes, and reformers campaigned against alcohol to reduce its ravages of the family home. In 1913, Congress adopted a prohibition amendment to the Constitution; it was ratified in 1919 and became the Eighteenth Amendment in 1920. Reforms like temperance emphasized the power of women in society and pushed the idea of women's suffrage to expand the heart of reform. The Nineteenth Amendment providing for women's suffrage was added to the U.S. Constitution in 1920. Since, according to the mainstream view, the government should defend American individualism, it seemed that it must involve itself in social welfare legislation to protect the home life of American individuals.[59]

With his enthusiasm for the West, Roosevelt led the Progressive coalition to protect the region. A friend of John Muir, Roosevelt was determined to use the federal government to keep big business from draining the land of resources. Following Muir's advice, he encouraged the scientific management of the forests and, using the Forest Reserve Act, took 172 million acres of land out of production. He created five new national parks and fifty wildlife refuges. He also created sixteen national monuments—like the Grand Canyon—to protect land of "historic or scientific interest." America's cowboy president was determined to guarantee that the free West did not become dominated by urban business.[60]

Led by Roosevelt, Progressives heavy-handedly exported the American worldview in the name of liberty, commercial opportunity, and national protection. The "Roosevelt Corollary" added to the Monroe Doctrine held that the United States could act in any South American country to forestall intervention by any other power. The nation did so in the Dominican Republic, installing pro-American officials to manage national finances. It did so by refusing to endorse Cuban independence until the new constitution had a provision allowing American intervention if the country fell into disorder or a foreign power threatened it. It did so by supporting a revolution in the part of Colombia that controlled the isthmus of Panama, quickly recognizing the independence of the new nation of Panama and paying it for the right to build and use the Panama Canal (a deal Colombia had refused). When heavy-handed intervention would be disastrous, Progressives used moral suasion and private investment to keep international doors open to the United States. By the end of World War I, America would be the largest and most powerful creditor nation in the world.

By the time Roosevelt sat in the White House, the romantic view of the idealized cowboy was the appropriate symbol of the nation. According to an acquaintance of Charles Goodnight, the old rancher thought that: "No better hands nor finer men ever ate beef out of a skillet than the pioneer cowboys of the Plains. The only code that held them to their places around a herd under any and all conditions was a sense of individual responsibility—pride in an ethic of rugged individualism. No labor union protested their lot; no welfare worker tore his shirt to better cow-camp conditions; no woman's club proposed child labor laws to keep junior cowboys from eating frijoles and taking the trail. Yet somehow they managed to live, and happily." Goodnight added: "They did not only go through all the privations and discomforts of life, and hard work, and exposure . . . but the real hours of the cowboy in actual service, when working on the open range, were about eighteen hours. They performed this with no complaint. They not only did the work as cow-hands, but they served as soldiers and officers as well."[61]

The cowboy image carried with it the ideology of individualism. It was an antigovernment, antiurban, anti-special-interest image. It was one that defined the American individualist around a domestic woman, and one that must be protected by government activism. Finally, it was an expansionist image, for this individualism, deeded to America by God, must spread around the world as the best possible system of human government. Buffalo Bill was determined that this image would never be forgotten. "The West of the old times, with its strong characters, its stern battles and its tremendous stretches of loneliness," he wrote, "can never be blotted from my mind. Nor can it, I hope, be blotted from the memory of the American people, to whom it has now become a priceless possession."[62]

Epilogue

The late nineteenth century defined modern America. Fewer than forty years separated the presidency of Roosevelt from that of Abraham Lincoln, but it is impossible to imagine the two men exchanging eras. Lincoln took the country into the Civil War to protect the idea that opportunity should be open to any man—no matter his race or background. By the time Roosevelt moved into the White House in 1901, the nation had reunited, but its principles were no longer inclusive. Instead of offering a hand to the poor and disfranchised, government dedicated itself to advancing the interests of a new, economically powerful middle class, one that was largely white and unwilling to include in its ranks people of color, the needy, or other "special interests." As their enthusiastic support for the Spanish-American War demonstrated, Americans entered the twentieth century so secure in the values of middle-class individualism that united them that they believed it was their duty to impose those values beyond their borders. From 1865 to 1901, Lincoln's widespread egalitarian vision evolved into a middle-class American dream.

Postwar struggles over the role of government in society drove the transformation of Lincoln's midcentury vision of opportunity for all into the middle-class imperialism of Roosevelt's era. In Lincoln's time, most northerners believed that the establishment of free labor across the nation would enable every individual to achieve prosperity, so long as government avoided disrupting perceived natural economic laws. The example of men like Andrew Carnegie convinced most northerners that hard work guaranteed success. Tremendous postwar technological innovation and economic growth dramatically improved the standard of living for upwardly mobile Americans, cementing their conviction that the free labor system offered universal prosperity. Electric bulbs lit up cities; ready-made clothing filled new chain stores; refrigerated meats and canned foods were widely distributed; cigarettes became a national fad. Economically secure and increasingly comfortable, rising Americans based their ideal image of national life on the traditional idea of an economically self-sufficient father. To this image they added an ideal domestic wife, whose homebound motherhood could erase the war's profound disruption of family life.

But this ideal image of American society immediately came under siege by advocates for government action to protect interests that were threatened, rather than fostered, by the new economy. Industrialists worried by the booms and busts of the market called for beneficial tariffs and tax laws to protect their businesses. Workers earning between $1.25 and $1.50 for ten hours of work in a factory—$2.30 to $2.80 an hour in today's money—demanded that government establish minimum wages and maximum hours. Poor ex-slaves forced into tenant farming and kept there by white supremacists demanded that the government give them land and protect their civil rights. Women agitated for the right to vote; and western farmers, who felt their economic and cultural power slipping away, called for government to regulate railroads and grain companies. To adherents of a free labor ideal, these calls for government support sounded perilously like an admission that certain groups of Americans did not have the initiative to make their own way in the world.

These pleas had the opposite of the desired effect. Rather than responding to them, mainstream Americans—those vocal and powerful men and women who prospered in the dynamic postwar economy—turned against special interest legislation for those on both ends of the economic spectrum, coming to believe that those who could not succeed on their own were not entitled to measures that would protect their access to economic success. Even worse, they seemed to threaten American society. The special interest legislation they coveted would destroy America's system of individual enterprise by inducing the poor to scurry after government handouts while the taxation necessary to pay for government programs would remove the financial incentive for individual effort. By the time Roosevelt gained the White House, middle-class Americans had found means to silence those they saw as special interests. In the North, new suffrage restrictions kept poor workers from the polls. In the South, new state constitutions took the vote away from African Americans, and white southerners increasingly let lynching provide a final solution to the problem of "dangerous" voters. At the same time, national laws sought to break the power of business trusts and their ties to the government.

During the late nineteenth century, opponents of special interest legislation self-consciously coalesced into a middle class, setting aside the idea of opportunity for all in favor of the concept of individualism, personified by the mythologized "self-made man," who pulled himself up by his own bootstraps. This self-made man opposed labor organization, business lobbying, black rights activism, and other special interest agitation. He was independent, hardworking, and opposed to government activism and the taxes that funded it. Regardless of the size of their wallets, Americans who believed they could succeed on their own rallied around this image. Critically, they identified their interests with those of the nation. They believed that what was good for them was good for the country.

Because members of this middle class identified their values with the interests of the country at large, the government could—and did—advance their interests, creating the paradox of a middle class that benefited mightily from government protection while its members espoused self-help and government inaction. At the same time that members of the middle class celebrated individual enterprise, self-reliance, and small government, they promoted certain forms of government action. The need to create taxable property during the war had made them willing to use the government to promote the individual enterprise that lay at the heart of their vision of American life. With fewer and fewer misgivings about government action, they passed a series of laws designed to foster economic growth. After the war, this government activism gradually expanded to government prohibitions on a range of business practices—price fixing, kickbacks, and so on—which threatened the economic security of a developing middle class. In the two decades after 1880, this willingness to use the government to embrace middle-class values stretched further to embrace social welfare legislation demanded by women who insisted that they could not fulfill their roles in the home and community without government oversight of the industrial world. In the belief that it nurtured an ideal individualist society, men who would not tolerate the idea of what they saw as redistributive legislation were willing to back the Progressive movement, in which reformers led by middle-class women supported legislation to regulate business and ameliorate the abuses of industrial capitalism.

Even as government's influence expanded, however, mainstream Americans managed to preserve a myth of individual self-reliance and success that was fueled by the rise of a romantic vision of the American West. In the postwar years, southerners and westerners infuriated by the actions of the federal government in their regions began to celebrate the West as the antithesis of the East. Westerners were portrayed as autonomous and even heroic individuals living in a pristine land. Romantic tales of cowboys and of men like Jesse James and Billy the Kid, who, in spite of their outlaw status, represented loyalty, fairness, antimonopoly, and self-government, permitted mainstream Americans to relocate American individualism to the Far West as it disappeared in the East. In this idealized world, independent individuals rose through their own hard—but often enviable—work in a world unfettered by big government.

By 1898, the powerful image of western individualism had come to define the reuniting nation. When Americans launched the terrifically popular Spanish-American War, they were attempting both to bring the country together and to export economic opportunity and free labor society to Cuba. Popular with neither businessmen nor government leaders, the conflict appealed to the American middle class, which saw it as an opportunity to promote individualism abroad while strengthening it at home. Highlighting the role of the heroic westerner in this overseas crusade, newspaper reporters named the troops that easterner-turned-cowboy Theodore Roosevelt led up San Juan Hill the Rough Riders, after the horsemen in Buffalo Bill's Wild West Show. Emerging victorious from the war, America had won an international identity as a land of rugged individualism. By 1901, when Owen Wister's epic western *The Virginian* described the ideal nation, Americans could accept thoroughgoing government intervention in the economy while still embracing the myth of American individualism. When Theodore Roosevelt —to whom *The Virginian* was dedicated—assumed the presidency in 1901, he could use the government to address the inequities of corporate capitalism feeling confident that socialism could never displace individualism.

The broader patterns of reconstruction echo down to our own time. The wrenching conflicts of the years from 1865 to 1901 forged a new national identity that was based on the needs and expectations of a new middle class, and America entered the twentieth century united around a distinctive ideology of individualism. This ideology made no room for those laborers, African Americans, or advocates for other special interests who organized to demand that government protect their access to economic success. Instead, this American worldview promised economic opportunity for upwardly mobile members of the middle class—professionals, farmers, businessmen, shopkeepers, and those on the make—who rejected the idea of collective action for economic success and instead embraced values of hard work and self-reliance. Even today, taxes and how they are spent define the way we approach political questions as Americans struggle to defend the "middle class" that they see as the heart of the nation. Those who support government programs to address the systematic inequities in American society are much less likely to win popular support than those who speak in the language of mainstream individualism, and those who profess concern for the middle class often garner support even when their programs benefit only a particular group.

Americans' dislike of "special interests" controlling government has meant that twentieth-century politics have swung between, on one hand, opposition to businessmen controlling government and, on the other, a dislike of those laborers, immigrants, advocates for women's rights, and minority activists who call for government protection. During the Progressive Era, the Depression, and the sixties and seventies, Americans protested the businessmen who unfairly stacked the economic deck in their own favor through ties to the government. In these eras, Americans created legislation to protect individuals, disdained business leaders, emphasized government corruption, and worked to curb the power of the wealthy. In the twenties, the fifties, and the conservative revolution of the late twentieth century the pendulum swung the other way, as middle-class Americans argued that the poor refused to work, that calls for women's rights threatened the fabric of society, and that "liberals" calling for legislation to address racial, economic, and gender inequalities were attacking the individualism that made America great.

In the late nineteenth century, the American cowboy came to represent middle-class individualism, and Theodore Roosevelt brought the cowboy image to the White House. Since then, the cowboy has been a powerful talisman for those trying to invoke the idea that they would defend the American individual, especially in the years after the outbreak of the post–World War II cold war between the United States and the USSR. As the United States sought to distinguish its ideology from communism, Americans turned to the western. In the fifties and sixties westerns ruled the television; it was the era of *The Lone Ranger, Gunsmoke,* and *Bonanza.* By the 1970s, western clothing was worn across the nation; 75 million pairs of Levis sold in 1974.[1] Cowboy hats and boots represented America. Elected president in 1980, Ronald Reagan rose to power with a careful evocation of the western image to represent the American mainstream. Shedding jodhpurs for Levis, Reagan continually invoked the western image and declared his California ranch the heart of his inspiration. "I have always believed that this land was placed here between the two great oceans by some divine plan," he told voters. "It was placed here to be found by a special kind of people—people who have a special love for freedom and who had the courage to uproot themselves and leave hearth and homeland and come to what in the beginning was the most undeveloped wilderness possible." He claimed to be a cowboy president who would reduce the size of the federal government to accomplish the will of true Americans. The cowboy image was an irresistible representation of American freedom, equality, and opportunity.[2]

But the upbeat image of the cowboy obscures the systematic inequality and aggressive foreign policies of American society. Cold war westerns shored up the unpopular Vietnam War, and western antigovernment symbols were deployed in the 1970s to protest racial integration of schools and accommodations. Reagan's promises of fairness and small government meant cuts to social programs, but his administration poured federal money into defense contracts offered to favored businessmen. In addition, much like Wister's Virginian, or like the Wyoming cattlemen on whom the Virginian was patterned, Reagan skirted the law to do what he thought was right. Congressional legislation prohibiting aid to the Nicaraguan Contras fighting the leftist Sandinista government in that country did not stop Reagan's men from making a Wild West decision to spread "American values" overseas.

The western image of the American individualist was the key to the map of the 2004 presidential election. George W. Bush promised to be a cowboy president. He vowed to cut through government red tape, cut taxes, slash budgets, take government out of the hands of special interests, and retain America's standing as God's chosen land, even as he spread liberty and humanity abroad. All of these promises had been the rallying cries of first southerners and westerners, and then mainstream Americans in general in the late nineteenth century. Like those invoking the cowboy image before him, Bush carefully painted a picture of his opponents as a godless band of lazy ne'er-do-wells controlling government to garner tax dollars, while he promised to protect morality, the individual, and the American family. Supporters cheered Bush's rhetoric, but opponents recognized that the positive cowboy imagery obscured administration policies that favored the wealthy, challenged racial gains, and threatened women's rights. The western image also obscured important realities of the Iraq War. Saddam Hussein had no significant connection to the terrorists of 9/11, there were no weapons of mass destruction, and the conflict would pour billions of dollars into the pockets of the businessmen who supported the administration. Opponents greeted with skepticism the idea that America was fighting for freedom in Iraq. In 2004, red state voters who championed American individualism and blue state voters who recognized the limitations of that vision both reflected patterns established over a century ago.

At the turn of the twentieth century, Theodore Roosevelt exploded into national prominence as a man who would bring mainstream equality back to America, endorsing western values of individualism and sweeping away special interests at both ends of the economic spectrum that sucked up taxes from those doing the real work of the country. With Roosevelt, the cowboy came to maturity as the symbol of the nation. But the image of the American cowboy has always had two sides. It contains the great hope of American equality of opportunity, of a world where anyone can rise and where no one has special privileges. But it also contains the deliberate repression of anyone identifying racial, gender, or economic inequalities in society, as well as a dangerously self-righteous expansionism. Both sides of the cowboy represent America; both define our nation.

The story of reconstruction is not simply about the rebuilding of the South after the Civil War. This pivotal era defined modern America as southerners, northerners, and westerners gradually hammered out a national identity that united three regions into a country that could become a world power. Ultimately, the story of reconstruction is about how a middle class formed in America and how its members defined what the nation would stand for, both at home and abroad, for the next century and beyond.

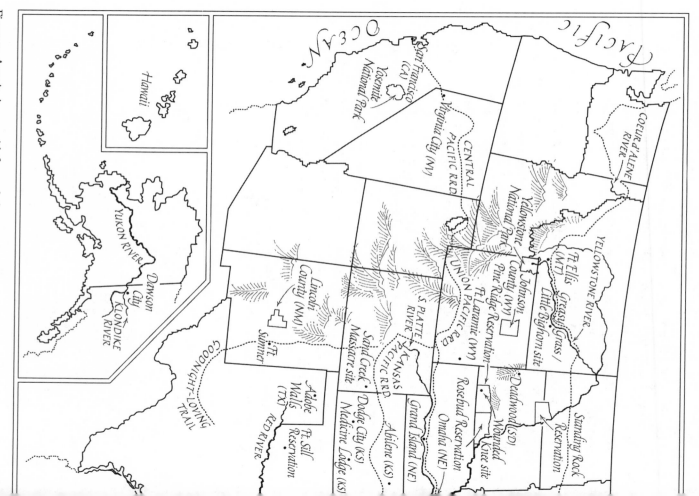

Figure 24. America in 1901 with featured places.

PACIFIC OCEAN

Pacific

COEUR d'ALENE RIVER

San Francisco (CA)

Yosemite National Park

Virginia City (NV)

CENTRAL PACIFIC RRD

Yellowstone National Park

Johnson County (WY)

Pine Ridge Reservation

Ft. Ellis (MT)

Greasy Grass / Little Bighorn site

YELLOWSTONE RIVER

Ft. Laramie (WY)

UNION PACIFIC RRD

Deadwood (SD)

Wounded Knee site

Standing Rock Reservation

Lincoln County (NM)

S. PLATTE RIVER

Rosebud Reservation

Omaha (NE)

Ft. Sumner

Sand Creek Massacre site

KANSAS PACIFIC RRD

ARKANSAS RIVER

Grand Island (NE)

GOODNIGHT-LOVING TRAIL

Adobe Walls (TX)

Ft. Sill Reservation

Dodge City (KS)

Abilene (KS)

Medicine Lodge (KS)

RED RIVER

Hawaii

YUKON RIVER

Dawson City

KLONDIKE RIVER

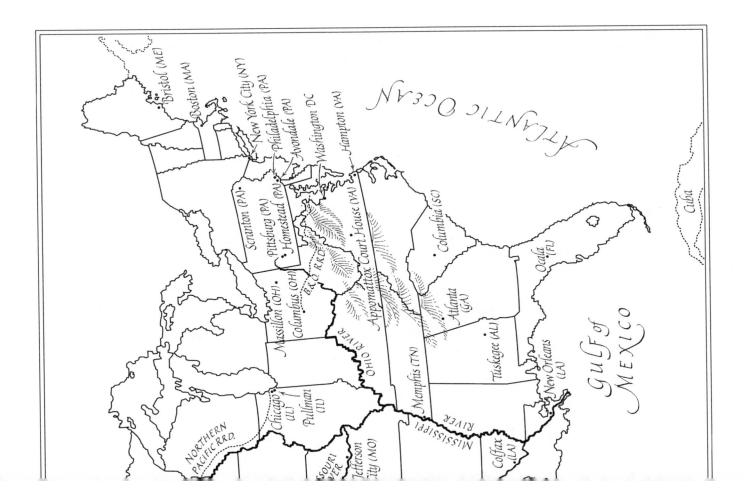

Bristol (ME)

Boston (MA)

New York City (NY)

Philadelphia (PA)

Avondale (PA)

Washington DC

Hampton (VA)

Scranton (PA)

Pittsburg (PA)

Homestead (PA)

Columbia (SC)

ATLANTIC OCEAN

Ocala (FL)

Cuba

Massillon (OH)

Columbus (OH)

B&O RRD.

Appomattox Court House (VA)

OHIO RIVER

Atlanta (GA)

Tuskegee (AL)

New Orleans (LA)

GULF of MEXICO

Chicago (IL)

Pullman (IL)

Memphis (TN)

MISSISSIPPI RIVER

Colfax (LA)

NORTHERN PACIFIC RRD.

MISSOURI RIVER

Jefferson City (MO)

Notes

Introduction

1. Sumeet Sagoo, "Federal Tax Burdens and Expenditures by State," Tax Foundation Special Report No. 132 (December 2004), available online at http://www.taxfoundation.org.

CHAPTER ONE. Spring 1865: The View from the Civil War

1. Ulysses S. Grant, *Personal Memoirs of U. S. Grant*, vol. 2 of *Memoirs and Selected Letters*, selected by Mary Drake McFeely and William S. McFeely (New York: Library of America, 1990), p. 731.

2. Ibid, p. 740.

3. Ibid, p. 744.

4. Manly Wade Wellman, *Giant in Gray: A Biography of Wade Hampton of South Carolina* (New York: Charles Scribner's Sons, 1949), pp. 180, 182–83. This is an old, racist, celebratory biography, but it has good biographical information under the author's agenda. *Montgomery Advertiser*, April 18, 1865, p. 2. Wade Hampton III to ———, May 10 [1865], in Charles E. Cauthen, ed., *Family Letters of the Three Wade Hamptons, 1782–1901* (Columbia: University of South Carolina Press, 1953), p. 114.

5. Edward Alfred Pollard, *Lee and His Lieutenants* (New York: E. B. Treat, 1867), pp. 744–45. Wellman, *Giant in Gray*, pp. 40–42.

6. John Locke, *The Second Treatise on Civil Government* (1690; rpt. Buffalo, N.Y.: Prometheus Books, 1986). Louis Hartz, *The Liberal Tradition in America* (New York: Harcourt, Brace, 1955). Bernard Bailyn, *The Ideological Origins of the American Revolution* (Cambridge: Belknap Press, 1967).

7. Edmund S. Morgan, *American Slavery, American Freedom: The Ordeal of Colonial Virginia* (New York: W. W. Norton, 1975), pp. 295–387. Lacy K. Ford, Jr., *Origins of Southern Radicalism: The South Carolina Upcountry, 1800–1860* (New York: Oxford University Press, 1988), pp. 351–52. [Iveson L. Brookes], *A Defence of Southern Slavery*

(Hamburg, S.C.: Robinson & Carlisle, 1851), pp. 41–45. See also J. Mills Thornton, *Politics and Power in a Slave Society: Alabama, 1800–1860* (Baton Rouge: Louisiana State University Press, 1978), pp. xviii–xix, 206–27. Compare Manisha Sinha, *The Counterrevolution of Slavery: Politics and Ideology in Antebellum South Carolina* (Chapel Hill: University of North Carolina Press, 2000). Stephanie McCurry, *Masters of Small Worlds: Yeoman Households, Gender Relations, and the Political Culture of the Antebellum South Carolina Low Country* (New York: Oxford University Press, 1995), adds the dimension of gender to the justification for white male supremacy.

8. Elizabeth W. Allston Pringle, *Chronicles of Chicora Wood* (1922; rpt. Boston: Christopher Publishing House, 1940), pp. 77–78.

9. Susanna Delfino and Michele Gillespie, eds., *Neither Lady nor Slave: Working Women of the Old South* (Chapel Hill: University of North Carolina Press, 2002). Wellman, *Giant in Gray*, p. 33. The Hampton sisters were unmarriageable because they had been sexually abused by their uncle James Henry Hammond during his tenure as governor. (See Drew Gilpin Faust, *James Henry Hammond and the Old South: A Design for Mastery* [Baton Rouge: Louisiana State University Press, 1982], pp. 241–43.)

10. George Brown Tindall and David Emory Shi, *America: A Narrative History* (New York: W. W. Norton, 1997), 1:432, 446.

11. Pringle, *Chronicles of Chicora Wood*, pp. 6–11, 21–22, 200, 210. Gilbert C. Fite, *Cotton Fields No More: Southern Agriculture, 1865–1890* (Lexington: University Press of Kentucky, 1984), pp. 30–47.

12. Charles Joyner, *Down by the Riverside: A South Carolina Slave Community* (Urbana: University of Illinois Press, 1984). Ira Berlin, "Time, Space, and the Evolution of Afro-American Society," *American Historical Review* 85 (February 1980): 44–78. Ira Berlin, *Many Thousands Gone: The First Two Centuries of Slavery in North America* (Cambridge: Harvard University Press, 1998). Deborah Gray White, *Ar'n't I a Woman? Female Slaves in the Plantation South* (New York: W. W. Norton, 1985). Jacqueline Jones, *Labor of Love, Labor of Sorrow: Black Women, Work, and the Family from Slavery to the Present* (New York: Basic Books, 1985). Pringle, *Chronicles of Chicora Wood*, pp. 13, 53. Nat Love, *Life and Adventures of Nat Love, Better Known in the Cattle Country as "Deadwood Dick," . . .* (Los Angeles: n.p., 1907), p. 13.

13. Alexander H. Stephens, Cornerstone Speech, Savannah, Georgia, March 21, 1861, in Henry Cleveland, *Alexander H. Stephens, in Public and Private: With Letters and Speeches, before, during, and since the War* (Philadelphia: National Publishing Company, 1866), pp. 717–29, online at Making of America, University of Michigan (hereafter MOA-UMich). Ford, *Origins of Southern Radicalism*, pp. 350–73.

14. Ford, *Origins of Southern Radicalism*, pp. 350–73.

15. Wade Hampton, December 10, 1859, quoted in Wellman, *Giant in Gray*, p. 35. Brookes, *Defence of Southern Slavery*, pp. 41–45, quoted in Ford, *Origins of Southern Radicalism*, p. 350. "The Terrors of Submission," *Charleston Mercury*, October 11, 1860, p. 1.

16. Pringle, *Chronicles of Chicora Wood*, p. 173. "Declaration of the Immediate Causes," reprinted in John Amasa May and Joan Reynolds Faunt, *South Carolina Secedes* (Columbia: University of South Carolina Press, 1960), pp. 76–81.

17. James M. McPherson, *Ordeal by Fire: The Civil War and Reconstruction* (New York: Alfred A. Knopf, 1982), p. 476. Wellman, *Giant in Gray*, pp. 50–53, 57–58. Pringle, *Chronicles of Chicora Wood*, pp. 250, 252. Pollard, *Lee and His Lieutenants*, p. 739. U. R.

Brooks, *Butler and His Cavalry in the War of Secession, 1861–1865* (Columbia, South Carolina: State Company, 1909), pp. 370–72.

18. C. Woodward Hutson to Father and Mother, July 22, 1861, in Lily Logan Morrill, ed., *My Confederate Girlhood: The Memoirs of Kate Virginia Cox Logan* (Richmond: Garrett & Massey, 1932), pp. 120–25. Edward G. Longacre, *Gentleman and Soldier: A Biography of Wade Hampton III* (Nashville: Rutledge Hill Press, 2003), pp. 38–43. Wellman, *Giant in Gray*, p. 64. Wade Hampton III to Mary Fisher Hampton, June 3, 1862, and October 5, 1864, in Cauthen, ed., *Hampton Family Letters*, pp. 85–86, 99, 108–9. McPherson, *Ordeal by Fire*, p. 476. Brooks, *Butler's Cavalry*, pp. 64, 150–69, 359–60, 569.

19. George C. Rable, *Civil Wars: Women and the Crisis of Southern Nationalism* (Urbana: University of Illinois Press, 1989). David G. Surdam, *Northern Naval Superiority and the Economics of the American Civil War* (Columbia: University of South Carolina Press, 2001), pp. 55–97. *Richmond Whig*, April 6, 1865, quoted in *Virginia (Nev.) Daily Territorial Enterprise*, April 12, 1865, p. 1. Pringle, *Chronicles of Chicora Wood*, pp. 286–87.

20. Pringle, *Chronicles of Chicora Wood*, pp. 189–91, 221.

21. Mary Boykin Chesnut, *A Diary from Dixie*, ed. Ben Ames Williams (Cambridge: Harvard University Press, 1980), p. 448.

22. Pollard, *Lee and His Lieutenants*, p. 741. McPherson, *Ordeal by Fire*, pp. 471–72. Wade Hampton to William T. Sherman, February 27, 1865, from *Richmond Examiner*, March 9, 1865, reprinted in *New York Times*, March 12, 1865, p. 1. Pringle, *Chronicles of Chicora Wood*, pp. 232–34.

23. McPherson, *Ordeal by Fire*, pp. 475–76. Pringle, *Chronicles of Chicora Wood*, p. 241. Wellman, *Giant in Gray*, p. 168. *Harper's Weekly*, April 15, 1865, p. 228. *Montgomery Advertiser*, April 18, 1865, and April 19, 1865, p. 2.

24. *Montgomery Advertiser*, April 19, 1865, p. 2. *Houston Telegraph*, in *Montgomery Advertiser*, July 22, 1865, p. 3. From *Atlanta New Era*, in *Montgomery Advertiser*, July 23, 1865, p. 1. *New York Times*, March 20, 1865, p. 4, report from *Richmond Whig*.

25. *Montgomery Advertiser*, March 5, 1865. Pringle, *Chronicles of Chicora Wood*, pp. 197, 212. Drew Gilpin Faust, *Mothers of Invention: Women of the Slaveholding South in the American Civil War* (Chapel Hill: University of North Carolina Press, 1994). Jane Turner Censer, *The Reconstruction of White Womanhood, 1865–1895* (Baton Rouge: Louisiana State University Press, 2003). Catherine Clinton, *Tara Revisited: Women, War, and the Plantation Legend* (New York: Abbeville Press, 1995), pp. 79–105.

26. Pringle, *Chronicles of Chicora Wood*, p. 199. Drew Gilpin Faust, "Altars of Sacrifice: Confederate Women and the Narratives of War," *Journal of American History* 76 (March 1990): 1200–28. *Montgomery Advertiser*, March 5, 1865. Clinton, *Tara Revisited*, pp. 191–231.

27. Clarence Mohr, *On the Threshold of Freedom: Masters and Slaves in Civil War Georgia* (Athens: University of Georgia Press, 1986), pp. 99–232. Love, *Life and Adventures*, p. 14. Pringle, *Chronicles of Chicora Wood*, pp. 226.

28. Sidney Andrews, *The South Since the War, as Shown by Fourteen Weeks of Travel and Observation in Georgia and the Carolinas* (1866; rpt. New York: Arno Press, 1969), pp. 113–14.

29. Grant, *Memoirs*, pp. 735, 740.

30. Ibid., p. 741.

31. Eric Foner, *Free Soil, Free Labor, Free Men: The Ideology of the Republican Party*

before the Civil War (New York: Oxford University Press, 1970), esp. pp. 11–39; Gabor S. Boritt, *Lincoln and the Economics of the American Dream* (Memphis: Memphis State University Press, 1978), pp. 155–77; Heather Cox Richardson, *The Greatest Nation of the Earth: Republican Economic Policies during the Civil War* (Cambridge: Harvard University Press, 1997), pp. 15–30; and James L. Huston, *Securing the Fruits of Labor: The American Concept of Wealth Distribution, 1765–1900* (Baton Rouge: Louisiana State University Press, 1998).

32. Carl Schurz, *The Reminiscences of Carl Schurz*, 3 vols. (New York: Doubleday, Page, 1909), 2:3–5.

33. Jeremy Atack and Fred Bateman, *To Their Own Soil: Agriculture in the Antebellum North* (Ames: Iowa State University Press, 1987), pp. 3–4.

34. Abraham Lincoln, address before the Wisconsin State Agricultural Society, Milwaukee, Wis., September 30, 1859, in Roy P. Baseler, ed., *The Collected Works of Abraham Lincoln* (New Brunswick, N.J.: Rutgers University Press, 1953), vol. 3, pp. 471–82; Abraham Lincoln, Message of the President, December 3, 1861, *Congressional Globe*, 37th Cong., 2nd sess., Appendix, p. 4.; Paul E. Johnson, *A Shopkeeper's Millennium: Society and Revivals in Rochester, New York, 1815–1837* (1978; rpt. New York: Hill and Wang, 2002), pp. 15–32, 37–61; Bruce Laurie, *Artisans into Workers: Labor in Nineteenth-Century America* (New York: Hill and Wang, 1989), pp. 15–46.

35. Andrew Carnegie, *The Autobiography of Andrew Carnegie* (Boston: Houghton Mifflin, 1920), pp. 34–39, 45–93.

36. Schurz, *Reminiscences*, 2:37; William E. Gienapp, "The Republican Party and the Slave Power," in Robert H. Abzug and Stephen E. Maizlish, eds., *New Perspectives on Slavery and Race in America* (Lexington: University Press of Kentucky, 1986), pp. 51–78; Leonard L. Richards, *The Slave Power: The Free North and Southern Domination, 1780–1860* (Baton Rouge: Louisiana State University Press, 2000).

37. Schurz, *Reminiscences*, 2:224.

38. Ibid, 2:19–20; Thomas H. Sherman, "Squalid Capital of '60's Recalled," *Washington Evening Star*, March 14, 1835. Compare Richard R. John, *Spreading the News: The American Postal System from Franklin to Morse* (Cambridge: Harvard University Press, 1995).

39. Hannibal Hamlin to Ellie Hamlin, July 7, 1861, Hannibal Hamlin MSS., University of Maine at Orono, on microfilm; Mary Clemmer Ames, *Ten Years in Washington: Life and Scenes in the National Capital as a Woman Sees Them* (Hartford, Conn.: A. D. Worthington, 1873), pp. 70–71; *Atlantic Monthly*, February 1862, p. 145, online at Making of America, Cornell University (hereafter MOA-Cornell).

40. Richardson, *Greatest Nation*, pp. 103–38.

41. Ibid, pp. 31–102.

42. Ibid., pp. 139–69. *Harper's Weekly*, April 22, 1865, p. 256.

43. Richardson, *Greatest Nation*, pp. 103–38. *The Century of Independence: Embracing a Collection from Official Sources, of the Most Important Documents and Statistics Connected with the Political History of America* (Indianapolis: J. R. Hussey, 1876), p. 223, MOA-UMich. Carnegie, *Autobiography*, p. 146.

44. Andrew Johnson, First Annual Message to Congress, December 4, 1865, in James D. Richardson, ed., *Messages and Papers of the Presidents*, 10 vols. (Washington, D.C.: Government Printing Office, 1896–99), 6:353–71. *De Bow's Review* (February 1866): 217–18, MOA-UMich.

45. Carnegie, *Autobiography*, pp. 115–17, 136–41.

46. *Harper's Weekly*, April 1, 1865, p. 194. Julia Ward Howe, Diary, February 16, 1864, Howe MSS. Houghton Library, Harvard University, Cambridge, Mass.

47. Samuel Gompers, *Seventy Years of Life and Labor: An Autobiography*, ed. Nick Salvatore (1925; rpt. Ithaca, N.Y.: ILR Press, 1984), p. 11. *Harper's Weekly*, April 1, 1865, p. 194.

48. Terence V. Powderly, *Thirty Years of Labor, 1859 to 1899* (1890; rpt. New York: Augustus M. Kelley, 1967) p. 35. Grace Palladino, *Another Civil War: Labor, Capital, and the State in the Anthracite Regions of Pennsylvania, 1840–1868* (Urbana: University of Illinois Press, 1990), pp. 95–175.

49. Jeannie Attie, *Patriotic Toil: Northern Women and the American Civil War* (Ithaca: Cornell University Press, 1998). Julia Ward Howe, Diary, January 17, 1864, April 30, 1864, January 28, 1864, March 10, 1864, Howe MSS, Houghton Library, Harvard University.

50. Samuel Sullivan Cox, *Three Decades of Federal Legislation* (Providence: J. A. & R. A. Reid, 1888), pp. 4, 221–27, 363.

51. Julia Ward Howe, quoted in Laura E. Richards and Maud Howe Elliott, *Julia Ward Howe, 1819–1910*, vol. 1 (Boston: Houghton Mifflin, 1915), pp. 219–20. Schurz, *Reminiscences*, 3:137.

52. Lura Beam, *A Maine Hamlet* (1957; rpt. Maine Humanities Council and the Maine Historical Society, 2000), p. 3. Grant, *Memoirs*, pp. 778–79. W. P. Howard to J. E. Brown, December 7, 1864, reprinted in *New York Times*, January 15, 1865, p. 2.

53. Rodman W. Paul, *The Far West and the Great Plains in Transition, 1859–1900* (New York: Harper & Row, 1988), pp. 24–45. John Warner Barber, *All the Western States and Territories, from the Alleghanies to the Pacific* (Cincinnati, Ohio: Howe's Subscription Book Concern, 1867), pp. 491, 519–20, 526, 552, MOA–UMich. *Cincinnati Daily Gazette*, April 2, 1864, p. 3. Carleton quoted in Alvin M. Josephy, Jr., *The Civil War in the American West* (New York: Vintage, 1993), pp. 281–82. Charles F. Browne, *The Complete Works of Charles F. Browne, Better Known as Artemus Ward* (London: Chatto and Windus, n.d. [1868]), p. 386.

54. Barber, *All the Western States*, pp. 506, 510, 530–34; *De Bow's Review* (January 1866):104, MOA–UMich.

55. Walter Prescott Webb, *The Great Plains* (1931; rpt. Lincoln: University of Nebraska Press, 1981), pp. 3–46.

56. *De Bow's Review* (January 1866): 52, MOA–UMich.

57. Surdam, *Northern Naval Superiority*, pp. 26–33, 48, 61–71.

58. J. Evetts Haley, "Charles Goodnight's Indian Recollections," *Panhandle-Plains Historical Review* 1 (1928):3–29. J. Evetts Haley, *Charles Goodnight: Cowman and Plainsman* (Norman: University of Oklahoma Press, 1936), pp. 1–99. Emanuel Dubbs, John A. Hart, et al., *Pioneer Days in the Southwest from 1850 to 1879* (Guthrie, Okla.: State Capital Company, 1909), p. 12.

59. Webb, *Great Plains*, pp. 47–84. Elliott West, *The Contested Plains: Indians, Goldseekers, and the Rush to Colorado* (Lawrence: University Press of Kansas, 1998), pp. 49–57. Ames, *Ten Years in Washington*, pp. 485–86. Thanks to mechanical engineer Klint Rose for confirming that the common nineteenth-century description of arrows going through bison was, in fact, possible. Richard White, *It's Your Misfortune and None of My Own: A New History of the American West* (Norman: University of Oklahoma Press, 1991), pp. 94–95.

60. William T. Hagan, *Quanah Parker, Comanche Chief* (Norman: University of

Oklahoma Press, 1993), p. 11. Brian C. Hosmer, "Quanah Parker," *The Handbook of Texas Online*, http://www.tsha.utexas.edu/handbook/online/articles/view/PP/fpa28.html, accessed November 20, 2003; William T. Hagan, *United States–Comanche Relations: The Reservation Years* (Norman: University of Oklahoma Press, 1990), p. 40.

61. Josephy, *Civil War in West*, pp. 290–91. Robert M. Utley, *Frontiersmen in Blue: The United States Army and the Indian, 1848–1865* (New York: Macmillan, 1967), pp. 211–340.

62. Stanley Vestal, *Sitting Bull, Champion of the Sioux: A Biography* (Boston: Houghton Mifflin Company, 1932), pp. 52, 70. Robert M. Utley, *The Lance and the Shield: The Life and Times of Sitting Bull* (New York: Henry Holt, 1993), pp. 52–70. Josephy, *Civil War in West*, pp. 92–312. White, *Misfortune*, pp. 96–97. Francis Paul Prucha, *The Great Father: The United States Government and the Indians*, 2 vols. (Lincoln: University of Nebraska Press, 1984), 1:411–16.

63. *Virginia (Nev.) Daily Territorial Enterprise*, April 9, 1865, p. 4. *Report of the Joint Special Committee on the Condition of the Indian Tribes* (Washington: Government Printing Office, 1867), p. 2. Josephy, *Civil War in West*, p. 312. Prucha, *Great Father*, 1:467–73 and 1:582–89. White, "The Indian System," *North American Review* 99 (October 1864): 449–64, MOA-Cornell.

64. *De Bow's Review* (January 1866): 3. MOA-UMich.

65. *Harper's Weekly*, April 29, 1865, p. 259.

66. Grant, *Memoirs*, pp. 750–51.

CHAPTER TWO. 1865–1867: The Future of Free Labor

1. Love, *Life and Adventures*, p. 15; Julie Saville, *The Work of Reconstruction: From Slave to Wage Laborer in South Carolina, 1860–1870* (Cambridge: Cambridge University Press, 1994), p. 25. *Augusta Loyal Georgian* (an African American newspaper), January 20, 1866, p. 1. Eric Foner, *Reconstruction: America's Unfinished Revolution, 1863–1877* (New York: Harper & Row, 1988), pp. 124–75.

2. Luna Kellie, *A Prairie Populist: The Memoirs of Luna Kellie*, ed. Jane Taylor Nelson (Iowa City: University of Iowa Press, 1992), p. 111.

3. Andrew Johnson, January 21, 1864, in *Southern Unionist Pamphlets and the Civil War*, ed. Jon L. Wakelyn (Columbia: University of Missouri Press, 1999), p. 265. Andrew Johnson, Annual Message, December 4, 1865, in Richardson, ed., *Messages and Papers*, 6:353–71. *De Bow's Review* (January 1866): 17, MOA-UMich.

4. Wade Hampton had opposed secession but during the war came to represent southern extremism in the minds of northerners.

5. Andrew Johnson, quoted in *Daily Ohio State Journal*, April 24, 1865, p. 2. *Montgomery Daily Advertiser*, July 21, 1865, p. 1. Andrew Johnson, in Richardson, ed., *Messages and Papers*, 6:311–12. McPherson, *Ordeal by Fire*, p. 506. *Philadelphia Daily Evening Bulletin*, January 10, 1867, p. 4.

6. Pringle, *Chronicles of Chicora Wood*, p. 267.

7. Ibid., pp. 265–66, 269–73, 279–80.

8. Ibid., pp. 280, 11. Roger L. Ransom and Richard Sutch, *One Kind of Freedom: The Economic Consequences of Emancipation* (Cambridge: Cambridge University Press, 1977), pp. 56–61.

9. Fite, *Cotton Fields No More*, pp. 30–47. Pringle, *Chronicles of Chicora Wood*, p. 248.

John Muir, *A Thousand-Mile Walk to the Gulf* (Boston: Houghton Mifflin, 1916), p. 278. Andrews, *South Since the War*, pp. 321, 398. *De Bow's Review* (January 1866): 23, MOA-UMich.

10. Roda Ann Childs, in *Augusta Loyal Georgian*, October 13, 1866, p. 3. Andrews, *South Since the War*, pp. 27–28.

11. McPherson, *Ordeal by Fire*, p. 511. *De Bow's Review* (January 1866): 109; (February 1866): 215, MOA-UMich.

12. "Black Republican and Office-Holder's Journal," [August 1865?], Negro Newspapers on Microfilm, reel 2, title 10. This is mislabeled as a black newspaper.

13. Andrews, *South Since the War*, pp. 38–92, 132–73, 237–87.

14. Thavolia Glymph, "Freedpeople and Ex-Masters: Shaping a New Order in the Postbellum South, 1865–1868," in Thavolia Glymph and John J. Kushma, eds., *Essays on the Postbellum Southern Economy* (College Station: University of Texas, Arlington, 1985), pp. 48–73. Saville, *Work of Reconstruction*. Robert Francis Engs, *Freedom's First Generation: Black Hampton, Virginia, 1861–1890* (Philadelphia: University of Pennsylvania Press, 1979), pp. 81–97. Pringle, *Chronicles of Chicora Wood*, pp. 279–80. Ransom and Sutch, *Economic Consequences*, pp. 44–47, 61–64. Love, *Life and Adventures*, pp. 17–21.

15. Love, *Life and Adventures*, pp. 17–21.

16. Ibid, pp. 17–21. Ransom and Sutch, *Economic Consequences*, pp. 186–95. Powell, *New Masters*, p. 146. On scarcities, see *Philadelphia Inquirer*, June 17, 1867, p. 4; *Harper's Weekly*, March 7, 1868, p. 147.

17. Joel Williamson, *After Slavery: The Negro in South Carolina During Reconstruction, 1861–1877* (Chapel Hill: University of North Carolina Press, 1965), pp. 96–102. Love, *Life and Adventures*, pp. 23–24. Andrews, *South Since the War*, pp. 322–23.

18. Engs, *Freedom's First Generation*, p. 104. Armistead L. Robinson, "Worser dan Jeff Davis': The Coming of Free Labor during the Civil War, 1861–1865," in *Essays on the Postbellum Southern Economy*, ed., Glymph and Kushma, pp. 11–47. *New York Daily Tribune*, January 30, 1867, p. 4. *Cincinnati Daily Gazette*, May 24, 1867, p. 2. *New York Herald*, in *Harper's Weekly*, June 1, 1867, p. 339. *Philadelphia Inquirer*, May 21, 1867, p. 1; and cartoon in *Harper's Weekly*, June 1, 1867, p. 341. Report of meeting of National Republican Association of the City of New Orleans, in *New Orleans Times*, quoted in *Montgomery Advertiser*, July 22, 1865, p. 4.

19. Report of meeting of National Republican Association of the City of New Orleans, in *New Orleans Times*, quoted in *Montgomery Advertiser*, July 22, 1865, p. 4.

20. Schurz, *Reminiscences*, 3:158. Carl Schurz correspondence, June 16, 1865–August 27, 1865, in *Speeches, Correspondence and Political Papers of Carl Schurz*, 6 vols, ed. Frederic Bancroft (New York: G. P. Putnam's Sons, 1913), 1:264–70. Schurz, quoted in Carl Schurz, "Report on the Condition of the South," ed. Michael Burlingame (1865; rpt. New York: Arno Press, 1969), pp. iii, 38.

21. Schurz, "Report," pp. 41–42. Richards and Elliott, *Howe*, 1:228.

22. "Letter of General Grant Concerning Affairs at the South," in Schurz "Report," pp. 106–8.

23. Andrews, *South Since the War*, pp. 301–17. *Harper's Weekly*, April 22, 1865, p. 256.

24. *National Intelligencer*, July 12, 1865, p. 2.

25. Andrew Johnson, First Annual Message, December 4, 1865, in Richardson, ed., *Messages and Papers*, 6:353–71.

26. *Philadelphia Inquirer*, April 18, 1867, p. 4, and August 20, 1867, p. 4; *New York*

Times, August 13, 1867, p. 4; *Cincinnati Daily Gazette*, February 27, 1873, p. 4; *Satterthwait's Circular* (London), September 1865, quoted in *De Bow's Review* (January 1866): 24, MOA-UMich. From *Richmond Times*, in *Montgomery Advertiser*, July 22, 1865, p. 4; *Montgomery Advertiser*, July 23, 1865, p. 1; *De Bow's Review* (January 1866): 112, MOA-UMich.

27. Andrew Johnson, Veto Messages, February 19, 1866, and March 27, 1866, in Richardson, ed., *Messages and Papers*, 7:398–405, 405–13; Hans L. Trefousse, *Andrew Johnson: A Biography* (New York: W. W. Norton, 1989), pp. 241–47.

28. "Report of the Special Committee of the House . . . [on the] Riots at Memphis," 39th Cong., 1st sess., H. Rpt. #101, p. 23; James G. Hollandsworth, *An Absolute Massacre: The New Orleans Race Riot of July 30, 1866* (Baton Rouge: Louisiana State University Press, 2001); McPherson, *Ordeal by Fire*, pp. 519–20. George C. Rable, *But There Was No Peace: The Role of Violence in the Politics of Reconstruction* (Athens: University of Georgia Press, 1984), pp. 33–58. Wellman, *Giant in Grey*, pp. 209, 211.

29. Wade Hampton to Andrew Johnson, August 25, 1866, in Cauthen, ed., *Hampton Family Letters*, pp. 123–41. W. A. Carey, "The Federal Union—Now and Hereafter," *De Bow's Review* (June 1866): 588, MOA-UMich.

30. Edward L. Gambill, *Conservative Ordeal: Northern Democrats and Reconstruction, 1865–1868* (Ames: Iowa State University Press, 1981), pp. 61–62, 70–71. *Harper's Weekly*, August 4, 1866, pp. 482–83. *New York Times*, August 7, 1866, p. 5. Edward McPherson, *The Political History of the United States of America during the Period of Reconstruction* (Washington: Solomons & Chapman, 1875), pp. 127–43. MOA-UMich. Andrew Johnson, Message to Congress, July 24, 1866, in Richardson, ed., *Messages and Papers*, 6:395–97. James G. Blaine, *Twenty Years of Congress*, vol. 2 (Norwich, Conn.: Henry Bill Publishing, 1893), p. 216. Trefousse, *Johnson*, pp. 251–54, 262–67.

31. Schurz, *Reminiscences*, 3:240–45.

32. Richardson, *Death of Reconstruction*, pp. 46–48. *Chicago Tribune*, February 23, 1867, p. 2. Thaddeus Stevens, *Congressional Globe*, 39th Cong., 2nd sess., p. 252. Blaine, *Twenty Years*, 2:250–67. Peyton McCrary, "The Party of Revolution: Republican Ideas about Politics and Social Change, 1862–1867," *Civil War History* 30 (December 1984): 330–50.

33. *Charleston Mercury*, March 23, 1867, p. 3. Wade Hampton III to John Mullaly (private), March 31, 1867, in Cauthen, ed., *Hampton Family Letters*, pp. 142–43. Gambill, *Conservative Ordeal*, pp. 89–90.

34. Richardson, *Death of Reconstruction*, pp. 48–51. Mark Wahlgren Summers, *The Press Gang: Newspapers and Politics, 1865–1878* (Chapel Hill: University of North Carolina Press, 1994), pp. 47–49, 205–22. Richard H. Abbott, *For Free Press and Equal Rights: Republican Newspapers in the Reconstruction South* (Athens: University of Georgia Press, 2002), pp. 45–69. Michael W. Fitzgerald, *The Union League Movement in the Deep South: Politics and Agricultural Change during Reconstruction* (Baton Rouge: Louisiana State University Press, 1989). *Harper's Weekly*, June 6, 1867, p. 355. *New York Herald*, July 2, 1867, p. 5.

35. *Augusta Loyal Georgian*, January 20, 1866, p. 3, and January 27, 1866, p. 1. Emma Lou Thornbrough, ed., *Black Reconstructionists* (Englewood Cliffs, N.J.: Prentice-Hall, 1972), pp. 33–34. Robert C. Kenzer, *Enterprising Southerners: Black Economic Success in North Carolina, 1865–1915* (Charlottesville: University Press of Virginia, 1997), pp. 9–34. Thomas Holt, *Black over White: Negro Political Leadership in South Carolina during Reconstruction* (Urbana: University of Illinois Press, 1977). Compare Alwyn Barr, "Black Legislators of Reconstruction Texas," *Civil War History* 32 (December 1986): 340–51. Eric

Foner, *Freedom's Lawmakers: A Directory of Black Officeholders during Reconstruction* (Baton Rouge: Louisiana State University Press, 1996); Howard N. Rabinowitz, ed., *Southern Black Leaders of the Reconstruction Era* (Urbana: University of Illinois Press, 1982); Howard N. Rabinowitz, "Three Reconstruction Leaders: Blanche K. Bruce, Robert Brown Elliott, and Holland Thompson," in *Black Leaders of the Nineteenth Century*, ed. Leon Litwack and August Meier (Urbana: University of Illinois Press, 1988), pp. 191–217.

36. Love, *Life and Adventures*, p. 11. Nell Irvin Painter, *Exodusters: Black Migration to Kansas after Reconstruction* (New York: Alfred A. Knopf, 1977), pp. 15–16, 22–23.

37. Fitzgerald, *Union League*, pp. 16–32; Peter J. Rachleff, *Black Labor in the South: Richmond, Virginia, 1865–1890* (Philadelphia: Temple University Press, 1984), pp. 34–54; John C. Rodrigue, *Reconstruction in the Cane Fields: From Slavery to Free Labor in Louisiana's Sugar Parishes, 1862–1880* (Baton Rouge: Louisiana State University Press, 2001), pp. 86–94. Williamson, *After Slavery*, pp. 102–5. William C. Hine, "Black Organized Labor in Reconstruction Charleston," *Labor History* 25 (1984): 504–17. Jerrell H. Shofner, "Militant Negro Laborers in Reconstruction Florida," *Journal of Southern History* 39 (August 1973): 397–408. Eric Foner, "Black Reconstruction Leaders at the Grass Roots," in *Black Leaders*, ed. Litwack and Meier, pp. 219–34. *Harper's Weekly*, April 6, 1867, p. 211; April 27, 1867, p. 259. *Philadelphia Inquirer*, April 15, 1867, p. 4; May 4, 1867, p. 4. *Washington Chronicle*, April 14, 1867, p. 1. *Chicago Tribune*, April 19, 1867, p. 3. Wellman, *Giant in Gray*, p. 218.

38. Alfreda M. Duster, ed., *Crusade for Justice: The Autobiography of Ida B. Wells* (Chicago: University of Chicago Press, 1970), p. 9. *Clinton (La.) Patriot*, reprinted in *Houston Weekly Telegraph*, September 3, 1867, p. 3. Fitzgerald, *Union League*, pp. 66–71; *New York Herald*, July 18, 1867, p. 11; *Columbus (Ohio) Crisis*, May 22, 1867, p. 132; *Philadelphia Inquirer*, August 29, 1867, p. 4.

39. From Navasota, September 12, 1867, printed in *Houston Tri-Weekly Telegraph*, September 18, 1867, p. 4.

40. John S. Reynolds, *Reconstruction in South Carolina, 1865–1877* (Columbia, S.C.: State Company, 1905), pp. 74–76.

41. *National Intelligencer*, in *Houston Tri-Weekly Telegraph*, September 17 or 18 [paper has both dates on it], 1867, p. 7.

42. Glenn Porter, *The Rise of Big Business, 1860–1910* (Arlington Heights, Ill.: AHM Publishing, 1973), p. 58. *De Bow's Review* (January 1866): 104, MOA-UMich.

43. David Montgomery, *Beyond Equality: Labor and the Radical Republicans, 1862–1872* (New York: Alfred A. Knopf, 1967), pp. 176–96, 227.

44. Hans L. Trefousse, *Benjamin Franklin Wade: Radical Republican from Ohio* (New York: Twayne Publishers, 1963), pp. 285–89.

45. *Harper's Weekly*, July 6, 1867, p. 418; *New York Times*, June 20, 1867, p. 4. See also *Baltimore Sun*, July 9, 1867, p. 2; *New York Herald*, July 8, 1867, p. 4, and July 16, 1867, p. 6; *Cincinnati Commercial*, reprinted in *New York Herald*, July 8, 1867, p. 6.

46. Julia Ward Howe, Diary, April 18, 1864, May 11, 1864, May 29, 1864, Howe MSS, Houghton Library, Harvard University. Julia Ward Howe, *Reminiscences, 1819–1899* (Boston: Houghton, Mifflin, 1900), p. 373. Elizabeth Cady Stanton, *Eighty Years and More: Reminiscences, 1815–1897* (1898; rpt. Boston: Northeastern University Press, 1993), p. 240. Elizabeth Cady Stanton, Susan B. Anthony, and Matilda Joslyn Gage, eds., *History of Woman Suffrage*, 6 vols. (1881; rpt. Salem, N.H.: Ayer, 1985), 11:14–16.

47. *Philadelphia Inquirer*, May 23, 1867, p. 4. See also *Cincinnati Daily Gazette*, April 30, 1867, p. 2. Fitzgerald, *Union League*, pp. 16–23; *New York Times*, May 20, 1867, p. 4.

48. Foner, *Reconstruction*, pp. 317–18.

49. Michael Les Benedict, "The Rout of Radicalism: Republicans and the Election of 1867," *Civil War History* 18 (December 1972): 334–44. Michael Les Benedict, *A Compromise of Principle: Congressional Republicans and Reconstruction, 1863–1869* (New York: W. W. Norton, 1974), pp. 257–78. James G. Blaine to Israel Washburn, Jr., September 12, 1867, in Gaillard Hunt, *Israel, Elihu, and Cadwallader Washburn: A Chapter in American Biography* (New York: Macmillan, 1925), p. 121.

50. Haley, *Goodnight*, pp. 103, 125–26, 131, 142. Randolph B. Campbell, *Grass-Roots Reconstruction in Texas, 1865–1880* (Baton Rouge: Louisiana State University Press, 1997); Carl H. Moneyhon, *Texas after the Civil War: The Struggle of Reconstruction* (College Station: Texas A & M University Press, 2004). Barry A. Crouch, *The Freedmen's Bureau and Black Texans* (Austin: University of Texas Press, 1992). *Montgomery Advertiser*, July 22, 1865, p. 2.

51. Haley, *Goodnight*, p. 105.

52. Hart, ed., *Pioneers*, p. 13. Haley, *Goodnight*, pp. 242–43. Bruce M. Shackelford, "Bose Ikard: Splendid Behavior," in *Black Cowboys of Texas*, ed. Sara R. Massey (College Station: Texas A & M University Press, 2000), pp. 133–40. Campbell, *Reconstruction in Texas*, pp. 230–31.

53. Hart, ed., *Pioneers*, p. 13. Haley, *Goodnight*, pp. 121–22, 127–46.

54. E. C. "Teddy Blue" Abbott and Helena Huntington Smith, *We Pointed Them North: Recollections of a Cowpuncher* (1939; rpt. Norman: University of Oklahoma Press, 1955), p. 6. Haley, *Goodnight*, pp. 249–50.

55. John Warner Barber, *All the Western States and Territories, from the Alleghanies to the Pacific* (Cincinnati: Howe's Subscription Book Concern, 1867), p. 700, MOA-UMich. Abbott and Smith, *We Pointed Them North*, pp. 4, 13.

56. *Harper's Weekly*, May 3, 1873, p. 363. White, *Misfortune*, p. 218.

57. *Helena* (Mont.) *Herald*, in *Houston Weekly Telegraph*, September 3, 1867, p. 3. *Salt Lake Vidette* of August 6, 1867, reprinted in *Houston Weekly Telegraph*, September 3, 1867, p. 3. "Montana," *De Bow's Review* (August 1868): 725–34, MOA-UMich. Browne, *Complete Works of . . . "Artemus Ward,"* pp. 365–68.

58. Haley, *Goodnight*, pp. 183–84.

59. Utley, *Lance and Shield*, p. 35. Sitting Bull quoted in David Rich Lewis, *Neither Wolf nor Dog: American Indians, Environment, and Agrarian Change* (New York: Oxford University Press, 1994), p. v. Indian Commissioner Taylor, November 23, 1868, Annual Report of the Commissioner of Indian Affairs, House Executive Document 1, 40th Cong., 3rd sess., pp. 476–79, reprinted in Paul Francis Prucha, ed., *Documents of United States Indian Policy* (Lincoln: University of Nebraska Press, 2000), pp. 122–25. Sitting Bull quotation in Vestal, *Sitting Bull*, p. 257. *Congressional Globe*, 39th Cong., 1st sess., pp. 569–75. (This is actually a debate over the language used in the Civil Rights Act of 1866, but that language was later imported into the Fourteenth Amendment.)

60. W. McKee Dunn, *Congressional Globe*, 37th Cong., 2nd sess., p. 1701. *Harper's Weekly*, May 13, 1865, p. 304. Donald Worster, *A River Running West: The Life of John Wesley Powell* (New York: Oxford University Press, 2001), pp. 127–260.

61. Robert William Fogel, *The Union Pacific Railroad: A Case in Premature Enterprise*

(Baltimore: Johns Hopkins Press, 1960), pp. 18–23. *Congressional Globe*, 36th Cong., 1st sess., pp. 2332, 2408–9. Richardson, *Greatest Nation*, pp. 170–208.

62. *Houston Weekly Telegraph*, September 18, 1867, p. 2. Center of Military History, U.S. Army, *Winning the West: The Army in the Indian Wars, 1865–1890* (Washington, D.C.: 1989), p. 301, at http://www.army.mil/cmh-pg/books/amh/amh-toc.html, accessed March 5, 2005.

63. Charles J. Kappler, ed., *Indian Affairs: Laws and Treaties* (Washington, D.C.: Government Printing Office, 1904), 2:977–89. The Treaty of Fort Laramie is at 2:998–1007, 1008–15. Francis Paul Prucha, *American Indian Treaties: The History of a Political Anomaly* (Berkeley: University of California Press, 1994), pp. 279–85. Prucha, *Great Father*, 1:488–96.

64. Hagan, *United States–Comanche Relations*, pp. 27–43. Hagan, *Quanah Parker*, pp. 10–12. Vestal, *Sitting Bull*, pp. 108–12, 127–32. Utley, *Lance and Shield*, pp. 77–84. *Harper's Weekly*, October 7, 1871, p. 931.

CHAPTER THREE. 1868–1871: Conflicting Visions

1. I am indebted to Bruce Laurie for helping me describe Gompers. Gompers, *Seventy Years*, ed. Salvatore, pp. 13–14.

2. U. S. Grant, First Annual Message, December 6, 1869, in Richardson, ed., *Messages and Papers*, 7:27–42.

3. Ibid., p. 41. James West Davidson, William E. Gienapp, et al., *Nation of Nations*, 2 vols. (New York: McGraw-Hill, 1990), 2:651. Stanley Buder, *Pullman: An Experiment in Industrial Order and Community Planning, 1880–1930* (New York: Oxford University Press, 1967), pp. 7–8. Harold C. Livesay, *Andrew Carnegie and the Rise of Big Business*, 2nd ed. (New York: Longman, 2000). James Dabney McCabe, Jr., *The Great Republic: A Descriptive, Statistical and Historical View of the States and Territories of the American Union* (Philadelphia: William B. Evans, 1871), pp. 989, 1001, 1008, 1016, 1053, 1075, 1081, 1086, 1116, MOA-UMich.

4. Howe, *Reminiscences*, 374. Richards and Elliott, *Howe*, 1:291. Pringle, *Chronicles of Chicora Wood*, pp. 289–90, 309, 340–41. Censer, *Reconstruction of White Southern Womanhood*, pp. 10–50, 153–274. Jane Addams, *Twenty Years at Hull-House* (1910; rpt. Urbana: University of Illinois Press, 1990), pp. 20, 28, 38. Roger L. Geiger, "The Crisis of the Old Order: The Colleges in the 1890s," in *The American College in the Nineteenth Century*, ed. Roger L Geiger (Nashville: Vanderbilt University Press, 2000), p. 269. Barbara Miller Solomon, *In the Company of Educated Women: A History of Women and Higher Education in America* (New Haven: Yale University Press, 1985), pp. 46–55. Helen Lefkowitz Horowitz, *Alma Mater: Design and Experience in the Women's Colleges from Their Nineteenth-Century Beginnings to the 1930s* (1984; rpt., Amherst: University of Massachusetts Press, 1993), pp. 62–66. Thomas Woody, *A History of Women's Education in the United States*, 2 vols. (1929; rpt. New York: Octagon Books, 1966), 2:256–60. *Harper's Weekly*, January 29, 1870, p. 67.

5. Louisa May Alcott, *Little Women* (1868; rpt. New York: Signet Classics, 2004). Barbara Sicherman, "Reading Little Women: The Many Lives of a Text," in *U.S. History as Women's History: New Feminist Essays*, ed. Linda K. Kerber, Alice Kessler-Harris, and Kathryn Kish Sklar (Chapel Hill: University of North Carolina Press, 1995), pp. 245–66. Jean Webster, *Daddy Long-Legs* (1912; rpt. New York: Grosset & Dunlap, 1964), p. 46.

6. *Overland Monthly*, July 1, 1868, p. 79, MOA-UMich.

7. Harold D. Woodman, "The Reconstruction of the Cotton Plantation in the New South," in Glymph and Kushma, eds., *Essays in the Postbellum Southern Economy*, pp. 95–119. Ransom and Sutch, *Economic Consequences*, pp. 81–106.

8. Pringle, *Chronicles of Chicora Wood*, p. 340. Foner, *Reconstruction*, pp. 319–20.

9. *Atlanta Constitution*, June 17, 1868, p. 2. Wellman, *Giant in Gray*, p. 220.

10. Schurz, *Reminiscences*, 3:282. McPherson, *Political History of Reconstruction*, pp. 261, 269–70, MOA-UMich; Frank Abiel Flower, *Edwin McMasters Stanton: The Autocrat of Rebellion, Emancipation, and Reconstruction* (New York: Western W. Wilson, 1905), pp. 320–43; George C. Gorham, *Life and Public Services of Edwin M. Stanton*, 2 vols. (Boston: Houghton Mifflin, 1899), 2:393–445.

11. *Atlanta Constitution*, June 18, 1868, p. 3, from *Mobile Tribune*. *New York World*, August 16, 1867, p. 2; November 1, 1867, p. 2; May 22, 1867, p. 2. *Columbus (Ohio) Crisis*, May 22, 1867, p. 130. *New York Times*, May 29, 1867, p. 4. *Philadelphia Inquirer*, May 21, 1867, p. 1; August 13, 1867, p. 4.

12. Michael Les Benedict, *The Impeachment and Trial of Andrew Johnson* (New York: W. W. Norton, 1973), pp. 168–80.

13. Thomas H. McKee, *National Conventions and Party Platforms* (Baltimore: Lord Baltimore Press, 1904), pp. 131–36.

14. Wellman, *Giant in Gray*, p. 222.

15. Ibid., p. 223; James D. McCabe, *The Life and Public Services of Horatio Seymour: Together with a Complete and Authentic Life of Francis P. Blair, Jr.* (New York: United States Publishing, 1868). Schurz, *Reminiscences*, 3:286. McKee, *Conventions*, pp. 136–39.

16. V. B. Denslow, "The Situation and the Candidates," *Putnam's Monthly* 2 (September 1868): 373–78, MOA-Cornell. *Philadelphia Inquirer*, August 17, 1868, p. 4; August 10, 1868, p. 4; September 22, 1868, p. 4; Summers, *Press Gang*, pp. 218–22.

17. William E. Parrish, *Missouri Under Radical Rule* (Columbia: University of Missouri Press, 1965), pp. 230–31. Schurz, *Reminiscences*, 3:285.

18. Schurz, *Reminiscences*, 3:287; *Harper's Weekly*, February 22, 1868, p. 115; February 8, 1868, p. 82; April 11, 1868, p. 226. *Chicago Tribune*, March 14, 1868, p. 2.

19. Senator J. W. Patterson, quoted in *Philadelphia Inquirer*, September 29, 1868, p. 8. *New York Times*, June 21, 1868, p. 4. *Philadelphia Inquirer*, September 28, 1868, p. 2. *Chicago Tribune*, July 14, 1868, p. 2. J. M. Ashley, in *New York Times*, August 22, 1868, p. 1.

20. Rable, *There Was No Peace*, pp. 69–80. McPherson, *Ordeal by Fire*, p. 544. "Ku Klux Klan Organization and Principles," in *Documents of American History*, 8th ed., ed. Henry Steele Commager (New York: Appleton-Century-Crofts, 1968) 1:499–500.

21. Schurz, *Reminiscences*, 3:292. McKee, *Conventions*, p. 140. *New York Times*, November 11, 1868, p. 4.

22. Schurz, *Reminiscences*, 3:294–301. Parrish, *Missouri Under Radical Rule*, pp. 232–67.

23. Gompers, *Seventy Years*, ed. Salvatore, p. 23; David Montgomery, *Beyond Equality: Labor and the Radical Republicans* (New York: Alfred A. Knopf, 1967), pp. 197–229. Richardson, *Death of Reconstruction*, pp. 83–89.

24. Laurie, *Artisans into Workers*, pp. 15–46; Johnson, *Shopkeeper's Millennium*, pp. 15–32, 37–61; Robert V. Bruce, *1877: Year of Violence* (Indianapolis: Bobbs-Merrill, 1959), pp. 15–17. Davidson, Gienapp, et al., *Nation of Nations*, 2:672–73.

25. T. V. Powderly, *Path I Trod* (New York: Columbia University Press, 1940), pp. 23–24.

26. Ibid., pp. 24–25. Craig Phelan, *Grand Master Workman: Terence Powderly and the Knights of Labor* (Westport, Conn.: Greenwood Press, 2000), pp. 11–21. Laurie, *Artisans into Workers*, p. 148.

27. Powderly, *Path I Trod*, pp. 50–52. Laurie, *Artisans into Workers*, pp. 141–75.

28. Richard B. Morris, ed., *Encyclopedia of American History* (New York: Harper & Brothers, 1953), p. 446. Jon Gjerde, *The Minds of the West: Patterns of Ethnocultural Evolution in the Rural Middle West, 1830–1917* (Chapel Hill: University of North Carolina Press, 1997). Tyler Anbinder, *Five Points: The Nineteenth-Century New York City Neighborhood That Invented Tap Dance, Stole Elections, and Became the World's Most Notorious Slum* (New York: Free Press, 2001). Kathy Lee Peiss, *Cheap Amusements: Working Women and Leisure in Turn-of-the-Century New York* (Philadelphia: Temple University Press, 1986).

29. Gompers, *Seventy Years*, ed. Salvatore, pp. 14–15. Sicherman, "Many Lives of a Text." Dorothy Richardson, *The Long Day: The Story of a New York Working Girl* (1905; rpt. Charlottesville: University Press of Virginia, 1990), pp. 75–86.

30. Davidson, Gienapp, et al., *Nation of Nations*, 2:694; Jacob A. Riis, *How the Other Half Lives* (1890; rpt. New York: Dover, 1971), pp. 231–33. *New York Times*, July 7, 1871, p. 8.

31. Davidson, Gienapp, et al., *Nation of Nations*, 2:693–94. Riis, *Other Half*, pp. 231–33.

32. William C. Conant, "The Brooklyn Bridge," *Harper's New Monthly Magazine* 66 (May 1883): 925–46, MOA-Cornell. "Here's a Health to the Hard Working Man," songsheet, online at American Memory, Library of Congress, http://memory.loc.gov/ammem/index.html.

33. Iver Bernstein, *The New York City Draft Riots: Their Significance for American Society and Politics in the Age of the Civil War* (New York: Oxford University Press, 1990), pp. 172–90; Karen Sawislak, *Smouldering City: Chicagoans and the Great Fire, 1871–1874* (Chicago: University of Chicago Press, 1995), pp. 85–106; Laurie, *Artisans into Workers.* Richard B. Stott, *Workers in the Metropolis: Class, Ethnicity, and Youth in Antebellum New York City* (Ithaca: Cornell University Press, 1990). Daniel T. Rodgers, *The Work Ethic in Industrial America, 1850–1920* (Chicago: University of Chicago Press, 1974), pp. 22–29.

34. Davidson, Gienapp, et al., *Nation of Nations*, 2:675. Montgomery, *Beyond Equality*, pp. 188, 192.

35. Quotation from *Cincinnati Gazette*, May 22, 1871, p. 2, May 31, 1871, p. 2, rpt. from *New York World. Philadelphia Inquirer*, August 30, 1871, p. 4. Philip M. Katz, *From Appomattox to Montmartre: Americans and the Paris Commune* (Cambridge: Harvard University Press, 1998), pp. 61–84. Richardson, *Death of Reconstruction*, pp. 85–89.

36. Brace quotation in Robert M. Fogelson, *America's Armories: Architecture, Society and Public Order* (Cambridge, Massachusetts: Harvard University Press, 1989), p. 24. Frank Norton, "Our Labor System and the Chinese," *Scribner's Monthly* 2 (May 1871): 62, MOA-Cornell. *New York Times*, April 17, 1871, p. 4.

37. *Chicago Tribune*, February 4, 1870, p. 2. *New York World*, March 19, 1867, p. 4. Albion W. Tourgée, *A Fool's Errand by One of the Fools*, ed. John Hope Franklin (Cambridge: Harvard University Press, 1961; orig. pub. 1879), p. 169.

38. Foner, *Reconstruction*, pp. 365–72; Brown quotation is on p. 369. Charles Sumner, *Congressional Globe*, 41st Cong, 2nd sess., May 13, 1870, p. 3434. *Congressional Globe*, 41st Cong., 2nd sess., July 7, 1870, p. 5314.

39. *Boston Evening Transcript*, February 15, 1871, p. 2. *New York Times*, March 7, 1871, p. 4. *Chicago Tribune*, April 2, 1871, p. 2. *New York World*, January 21, 1871, pp. 1, 4.

40. Carole K. Rothrock Bleser, *The Promised Land: The History of the South Carolina Land Commission, 1869–1890* (Columbia: University of South Carolina Press, 1969). J. Mills Thornton, "Fiscal Policy and the Failure of Radical Reconstruction," in *Region, Race, and Reconstruction: Essays in Honor of C. Vann Woodward*, ed. J. Morgan Kousser and James McPherson (New York: Oxford University Press, 1982), pp. 349–94. Richardson, *Death of Reconstruction*, pp. 89–101.

41. Thomas C. Holt, *Black Over White: Negro Political Leadership in South Carolina During Reconstruction* (Urbana: University of Illinois Press, 1977); and Foner, *Freedom's Lawmakers*. Robert Somers, *The Southern States since the War, 1870–1871* (University: University of Alabama Press, 1965), pp. 41–43. *Charleston Daily Courier*, May 9 through May 15, 1871; see also *Chicago Tribune*, May 11, 1871, p. 2. *Savannah Morning News*, May 10, 1871, p. 2, and *New York Daily Tribune*, May 8, 1871, p. 1.

42. *New York Daily Tribune*, May 1, 1871, p. 1. *Chicago Tribune*, May 8, 1871, p. 2; May 12, 1871, p. 2. *New York Daily Tribune*, May 10–17.

43. William L. Riordon, *Plunkitt of Tammany Hall: A Series of Very Plain Talks on Very Practical Politics* (1905; rpt. New York: Signet, 1995), p. 28.

44. *Scribner's Monthly* 2 (May 1871): 97, MOA-Cornell. *Chicago Tribune*, June 26, 1871, p. 2; June 27, 1871, p. 2.

45. *New York Times*, June 27, 1867, p. 4. Gompers, *Seventy Years*, ed. Salvatore, pp. 19–21. Samuel Gompers, *Seventy Years of Life and Labor: An Autobiography* (New York: E. P. Dutton, 1925), pp. 50–59.

46. *Nation*, October 5, 1871, pp. 221–22. Dale Baum, "The 'Irish Vote' and Party Politics in Massachusetts, 1860–1876," *Civil War History* 26 (June 1980): 117–41.

47. Horatio Alger, Jr., *Ragged Dick: Or, Street Life in New York with the Boot Blacks* (1868; rpt. New York: Penguin Books, 1990), p. 91.

48. Ibid., pp. 8, 10, 40, 54, 185.

49. Allan Nevins, *Hamilton Fish: The Inner History of the Grant Administration* (New York: Dodd, Mead, 1937), pp. 249–78, 497–501.

50. Joseph G. McCoy, *Historic Sketches of the Cattle Trade of the West and Southwest* (Kansas City, Mo.: Ramsey, Millett & Hudson, 1874), available online at the Kansas Collection, http://www.kancoll.org.

51. Carl Schurz, *Congressional Globe*, 41st Cong., 3rd sess., pp. 123–28. Schurz, *Reminiscences*, 3:321–23. John McDonald, *Secrets of the Great Whiskey Ring and Eighteen Months in the Penitentiary* (St. Louis: W. S. Bryan, 1880), p. 70.

52. Schurz, *Reminiscences*, 3:331–33. Grant, Message to Congress, December 4, 1871, Richardson, ed., *Messages and Papers*, 7:142–55.

53. *New York Times*, May 17, 1867, p. 2; July 20, 1867, p. 8.

54. *New York Times*, May 17, 1867, p. 2; July 11, 1867, p. 2.

55. Richards and Elliott, *Howe*, 1:369.

56. Julia Ward Howe, "Appeal to Womanhood throughout the World," in Richards and Elliott, *Howe*, 1:302. *Harper's Weekly*, November 5, 1870, p. 707.

57. *Harper's Weekly*, January 24, 1870, p. 67.

58. *New York Times*, August 27, 1871, p. 1; October 26, 1871, p. 2.

59. Henry Nash Smith, *Virgin Land: The American West as Symbol and Myth* (1950; rpt, Cambridge: Harvard University Press, 2005). M. P. Deady, "Portland-on-Wallamet," *Overland Monthly*, July 1, 1868, p. 43, MOA-UMich. Love, *Life and Adventures*, pp. 37–41. Dubbs, Hart, et al., *Pioneer Days*, pp. 19–20.

60. White, *Misfortune*, pp. 55–59. U. S. Grant, First Annual Message, December 6, 1869, in Richardson, ed., *Messages and Papers*, 7:27–42.

61. S. P. Elkins, in Dubbs, Hart, et al., *Pioneer Days*, p. 275. Haley, *Goodnight*, p. 191.

62. *Atlanta Constitution*, June 18, 1868, p. 3, from *Mobile Tribune*. Haley, *Goodnight*, p. 183.

63. George Fitzhugh, "Liberty and Civilization," *De Bow's Review* (March 1866): 250, MOA-UMich.

64. Muir, *Thousand-Mile Walk*, pp. 177, 225, 232. William Cronon, *Nature's Metropolis: Chicago and the Great West* (New York: W. W. Norton, 1991), pp. 371–85.

65. W. C. Bartlett, "A Breeze from the Woods," *Overland Monthly*, July 1, 1868, p. 10; Deady, "Portland-on-Wallamet," *Overland Monthly*, July 1, 1868, p. 34, MOA-UMich. Eugene P. Moehring, *Urbanism and Empire in the Far West, 1840–1890* (Reno: University of Nevada Press, 2004).

66. Bartlett, "A Breeze from the Woods," *Overland Monthly*, July 1, 1868, pp. 11–12, 16.

67. Ina D. Coolbrith, "Longing," in *Overland Monthly*, July 1, 1868, p. 17, MOA-UMich.

CHAPTER FOUR. 1872: A New Middle Ground

1. U. S. Grant, Fourth Annual Message, December 2, 1872, Richardson, ed., *Messages and Papers*, 7:184–205.

2. Frederic Bancroft and William A. Dunning, "A Sketch of Carl Schurz's Political Career, 1869–1909," in Schurz, *Reminiscences*, 3:339–40.

3. Ibid., 3:341–42. *Harper's New Monthly Magazine* 44 (April 1872): 791, MOA-Cornell. *Harper's Weekly*, April 6, 1872, p. 266. John G. Sproat, *The Best Men: Liberal Reformers in the Gilded Age* (New York: Oxford University Press, 1969). Michael Les Benedict, "Reform Republicans and the Retreat from Reconstruction," in *The Facts of Reconstruction: Essays in Honor of John Hope Franklin*, ed. Eric Anderson and Alfred A. Moss, Jr. (Baton Rouge: Louisiana State University Press, 1991), pp. 53–77.

4. Davidson Gienapp, et al., *Nation of Nations*, 2:620.

5. J. W. De Forest, "The Colored Member," *Galaxy* 13 (March 1872): 293–303, MOA-Cornell.

6. Greeley quoted in *Harper's Weekly*, April 6, 1872, p. 266.

7. Horace White to Lyman Trumbull, quoted in Bancroft and Dunning, "Sketch," in Schurz, *Reminiscences*, 3:342. Everett Chamberlin, *The Struggle of '72* (Chicago: Union Publishing Company, 1872), pp. 334, 363, MOA-UMich.

8. *Harper's New Monthly Magazine* 45 (July 1872): 312, MOA-Cornell. McKee, *Conventions*, pp. 144–47.

9. *Harper's New Monthly Magazine* 45 (July 1872): 312, MOA-Cornell.

10. Ibid. Chamberlin, *Struggle of '72*, p. 364.

11. Adam Smith, *No Party Now* (New York: Oxford University Press, forthcoming). Harper's *New Monthly Magazine* 45 (July 1872): 312, MOA-Cornell. For platform, see *Century of Independence*, pp. 353–55.

12. McKee, *Conventions*, pp. 149–52; *Century of Independence*, pp. 350–53.

13. *Harper's Weekly*, March 9, 1872, p. 195. *Manufacturer and Builder* 4 (December 1872): 281, MOA-Cornell. *Harper's Weekly*, March 16, 1872, p. 211; March 30, 1872, p. 247; January 6, 1872, pp. 14–15; March 16, 1872, pp. 205–206; April 6, 1872, p. 275. Davidson, Gienapp, et al, *Nation of Nations*, 2:708–9.

14. Mark Twain, *Roughing It* (1872; rpt. New York: Oxford University Press, 1996), p. 19. White, *Misfortune*, pp. 218–19.

15. Irving Katz, *August Belmont: A Political Biography* (New York: Columbia University Press, 1968), pp. 195–98. Summers, *Press Gang*, pp. 237–55. *New York Daily Tribune*, April 12, 1872, quoted in Robert Franklin Durden, *James Shepherd Pike: Republicanism and the American Negro, 1850–1882* (Durham: Duke University Press, 1857), p. 189. *New York Daily Tribune*, June 2, 1871, p. 5. William Gillette, *Retreat from Reconstruction: 1869–1879* (Baton Rouge: Louisiana State University Press, 1979), pp. 56–72. Michael Perman, *The Road to Redemption: Southern Politics, 1869–1879* (Chapel Hill: University of North Carolina Press, 1984), pp. 108–26, 145–46. *Boston Evening Transcript*, August 16, 1872, p. 2, and August 17, 1872, p. 8; James M. McPherson, "Grant or Greeley? The Abolitionist Dilemma in the Election of 1872," *American Historical Review* 71 (October 1865): 43–61.

16. Gompers, *Seventy Years*, ed. Salvatore, pp. 21–22. *Harper's New Monthly Magazine* 45 (November 1872): 947, MOA-Cornell.

17. Stanton, Anthony, and Gage, eds., *History of Woman Suffrage*, 1:14–16. *Harper's Weekly*, April 6, 1872, p. 267.

18. Richardson, *Greatest Nation*, pp. 35–36. Schurz, *Reminiscences*, 2:15. Palladino, *Another Civil War*, pp. 121–36.

19. Carnegie, *Autobiography*, pp. 146–47. Joseph Wall, *Andrew Carnegie* (New York: Oxford University Press, 1970), pp. 145–91.

20. Richardson, *Greatest Nation*, pp. 103–38. Rufus P. Spaulding (Ohio) and Josiah B. Grinnell (Iowa) in *Congressional Globe*, 38th Cong., 1st sess., pp. 1876–77; ibid., p. 2515. S. S. Cox, ibid., p. 1858. Justin Smith Morrill, ibid., pp. 1876, 1940. Augustus Frank, ibid., p. 1876.

21. John K. Winkler, *Incredible Carnegie: The Life of Andrew Carnegie* (New York: Vanguard Press, 1931), pp. 75–103.

22. Carnegie, *Autobiography*, p. 135–36, 144–45. Paul F. Paskoff, *Industrial Evolution: Organization, Structure, and Growth of the Pennsylvania Iron Industry, 1750–1860* (Baltimore: Johns Hopkins University Press, 1983), p. 106. Winkler, *Incredible Carnegie*, pp. 110–15.

23. Winkler, *Incredible Carnegie*, pp. 110–12. Buder, *Pullman*, 23; H.J. Gallagher to R. B. Hayes, January 2 [?], 1872, R. B. Hayes MS, Library of Congress, on microfilm.

24. Carnegie, *Autobiography*, pp. 135–36, 144–45. Pauline Maier, "The Revolutionary Origins of the American Corporation," *William and Mary Quarterly* 50 (January 1993): 55–58; Oscar Handlin and Mary F. Handlin, "Origins of the American Business Corporation," *Journal of Economic History* 5 (1945): 1–23; Ronald E. Seavoy, *The Origins of the American Business Corporation, 1784–1855: Broadening the Concept of Public Service during Industrialization* (Westport, Conn.: Greenwood Press, 1982). James K. Medbery, *Men and*

Mysteries of Wall Street (Boston: Fields, Osgood, 1870), pp. 14–24. *History of the New York Stock Exchange . . .* (New York: Financier Company, 1887), p. 9, MOA-UMich.

25. Carnegie, *Autobiography*, p. 135–36, 144–45. Alfred D. Chandler, Jr., *The Visible Hand: The Managerial Revolution in American Business* (Cambridge: Harvard University Press, 1977), pp. 145–205, 240–83. Andrew Carnegie, "The Gospel of Wealth," in *The Gospel of Wealth and Other Timely Essays*, ed. Edward C. Kirkland (Cambridge: Harvard University Press, 1962), p. 16. Prentice Mulford, "The Soul of the Corporation," *Overland Monthly*, January 1872, 87–91, MOA-UMich.

26. *New York Times*, January 8, 1872, p. 1.

27. J. W. Goodspeed, *The Life of Col. James Fisk, Jr., . . . of Miss Helen Josephine Mansfield . . . of Edward L. Stokes . . . and Hon. Wm. M. Tweed . . . with a Sketch of the Grand Duke Alexis, of Russia . . .* (Chicago: J. W. Goodspeed, 1872), p. 21, MOA-UMich.

28. Goodspeed, *Fisk*, pp. 8, 13, 9–10, 15, 39, 40.

29. Goodspeed, *Fisk*, p. 12. *Harper's Weekly*, March 30, 1872, p. 243. Ames, *Ten Years in Washington*, p. 157.

30. *New York Times*, January 8, 1872, p. 1

31. Morrill, quoted in Richardson, *Greatest Nation*, p. 120. Edwin R. A. Seligman, *The Income Tax: A Study of the History, Theory, and Practice of Income Taxation at Home and Abroad* (New York: Macmillan, 1911), pp. 456–68. The bill is HR 2822, 42nd Cong, 2nd sess, passed June 6, 1872.

32. *Boston Globe*, September 16, 1872, p. 4.

33. Richardson, *Greatest Nation*, pp. 206–8, 311–12.

34. *New York Times*, September 27, 1872, p. 8. *Harper's Weekly*, October 19, 1872, p. 803. *New-York Commercial Advertiser*, reprinted in *New York Times*, September 18, 1872, p. 5. *Syracuse Journal*, reprinted in *New York Times*, September 16, 1872, p. 5. *Harper's Weekly*, October 5, 1872, p. 763. T. D. Judah to D. W. Strong, September 1861, in George T. Clark, *Leland Stanford: War Governor of California, Railroad Builder, and Founder of Stanford University* (Stanford: Stanford University Press, 1931), p. 175; William Deverell, *Railroad Crossing: Californians and the Railroad, 1850–1910* (Berkeley: University of California Press, 1994), pp. 13–19.

35. Robert W. Johannsen, "Credit Mobilier of America," at "The American Presidency," Grolier Online, http://ap.grolier.com/article?assetid=0112820-00. Richardson, *Greatest Nation*, pp. 170–208. *New York Times*, December 3, 1872, p. 2.; December 21, 1872, p. 1; December 16, 1872, p. 1; December 4, 1872, p. 1.

36. Mark Twain and Charles Dudley Warner, *The Gilded Age: A Tale of Today* (1873; rpt, New York: Penguin Classics, 2001), p. 200.

37. Ibid, pp. 138, 238, 330, 341, 380–402, 409–15, 428–31, 437.

38. Ibid, p. 452.

39. *Harper's New Monthly Magazine* 45 (November 1872): 947, MOA-Cornell. *New York Times*, September 20, 1872, p. 4; March 6, 1872, p. 1; September 15, 1872, p. 4.

40. *Chicago Tribune*, January 9, 1872, p. 4. *New York Daily Tribune*, January 19, 1872, p. 4.

41. *Harper's Weekly*, April 6, 1872, p. 266; April 13, 1872, p. 282. Wade Hampton to John Mullaly, May 19, 1872, in Cauthen, ed., *Hampton Family Letters*, pp. 143–44. *Cincinnati Daily Gazette*, February 9, 1872, p. 2. *Harper's Weekly*, July 27, 1872, p. 579.

42. *Harper's Weekly*, February 10, 1872, p. 124–26; March 30, 1872, p. 243.

43. *New York Times*, October 14, 1870, p. 4; Aubrey L. Haines, *Yellowstone National Park: Its Exploration and Establishment* (Washington, D.C.: National Park Service, 1974) at http://www.cr.nps.gov/history/online_books/haines/index.htm.

44. *New York Times*, October 26, 1871, p. 2; N. P. Langford, "The Wonders of the Yellowstone," *Scribner's Monthly* 2 (May 1871): 1–17, and N. P. Langford, "The Wonders of the Yellowstone," *Scribner's Monthly* 2 (June 1871): 113–28, both MOA-Cornell. Marguerite Schaffer, *See America First: Tourism and National Identity* (Washington: Smithsonian Institution Press, 2001), pp. 43–46.

45. White, *Misfortune*, pp. 218–19; John Muir, "Yosemite Valley in Flood," *Overland Monthly*, April 1872, pp. 347–50, MOA-UMich. John Muir, "Living Glaciers of California," *Overland Monthly*, December 1872, pp. 547–49, MOA-UMich.

46. *The Gilded Age* pokes fun at a key crook who claims that the West is "the place for a young fellow of spirit to pick up a fortune, simply pick it up, it's lying around loose here" (Twain and Warner, *Gilded Age*, p. 99). F. V. Hayden, "The Wonders of the West—II: More about the Yellowstone," *Scribner's Monthly* 3 (February 1872): 388–96, MOA-Cornell. Pomeroy, deeply committed to the Union Pacific, was probably motivated by a desire to weaken the Northern Pacific.

47. Committee on Public Lands, "The Yellowstone Park," House Report 26, 42nd Cong., 2nd sess.

48. *New York Times*, February 13, 1872, p. 4; July 28, 1872, p. 5.

49. *Nation*, March 7, 1872, p. 153, quoted in Aubrey L. Haines, *Yellowstone: Memorial Addresses on the Life and Character of Samuel Sullivan Cox* (Washington: Government Printing Office, 1890), pp. 66–68, 141.

50. *Harper's Weekly*, December 4, 1869, p. 782.

51. The medal was rescinded in 1917 because, as a civilian, Cody had been ineligible for it. It was restored in 1989 to five civilians from the Indian Wars. For a quick history of the Congressional Medal of Honor, see http://www.cmohs.org/medal/medal_history.htm, accessed January 11, 2005; W. E. Webb, *Buffalo Land: An Authentic Account of the Discoveries, Adventures, and Mishaps of a Scientific and Sporting Party in the Wild West* (Cincinnati: E. Hannaford, 1872), pp. 149, 194–195; MOA-UMich. *Harper's Weekly*, April 13, 1872; July 13, 1872.

CHAPTER FIVE. 1873–1880: Years of Unrest

1. Kellie, *Prairie Populist*, p. 10; David M. Wrobel, *Promised Lands, Promotion, Memory, and the Creation of the American West* (Lawrence: University Press of Kansas, 2002), pp. 19–49.

2. Gompers, *Seventy Years*, ed. Salvatore, p. 31.

3. Lou Faulkner Williams, *The Great South Carolina Ku Klux Klan Trials, 1871–1872* (Athens: University of Georgia Press, 1996). *Boston Globe*, September 15, 1873, p. 1; September 18, 1873, p. 1; September 29, 1873, p. 1; September 1, 1878, p. 4.

4. Foner, *Reconstruction*, p. 437. Richardson, *Death of Reconstruction*, pp. 107–8. *Cincinnati Daily Gazette*, April 16, 1873, p. 1. *New Orleans Picayune*, April 8, 1873, and *Missouri Republican*, April 13, 1873, in *Cincinnati Daily Gazette*, April 17, 1873, p. 4. *Boston Evening Transcript*, April 16, 1873, p. 2. *Chicago Tribune*, June 8, 1874, p. 4, and January 12, 1874, p. 4. *New York Daily Tribune*, January 2, 1874, p. 8, and January 1, 1874, p. 6. *Boston Evening Transcript*, July 30, 1874, p. 4.

5. Harold Evans, *They Made America* (New York: Little, Brown, 2004), pp. 108–13. Eric Arnesen, *Waterfront Workers of New Orleans: Race, Class, and Politics, 1863–1923* (1991; rpt. Urbana: University of Illinois Press, 1994), pp. 44–49. Gompers, *Seventy Years*, ed. Salvatore, p. 32.

6. Gompers, *Seventy Years*, ed. Salvatore, pp. 33–34.

7. Carnegie, *Autobiography*, p. 43.

8. Morris, ed., *Encyclopedia of American History*, pp. 251–52. Ellis Paxton Oberholtzer, *A History of the United States Since the Civil War*, vol. 3 (New York: Macmillan, 1926), pp. 144–61. McDonald, *Whiskey Ring*, pp. 17–18, 139–40, 338–46. *New York Times*, July 12, 1875, p. 4; July 24, 1875, p. 2; November 6, 1875, p. 1; November 20, 1875, p. 4; December 10, 1875, p. 1; February 13, 1876, p. 1.

9. *Bradwell v. Illinois*, 83 U.S. 130 (1873). Susan B. Anthony, "Constitutional Argument," in *Elizabeth Cady Stanton, Susan B. Anthony: Correspondence, Writings, Speeches*, ed. Ellen C. Dubois (New York: Schocken Books, 1981), pp. 152–65. Parrish, *Missouri Under Radical Rule*, pp. 274–78.

10. Susan B. Anthony, "Declaration of Rights for Women by the National Woman Suffrage Association," in *History of Woman Suffrage*, ed. Stanton, Anthony, and Gage, 3:31–34.

11. Thomas A. Woods, *Knights of the Plow: Oliver H. Kelley and the Origins of the Grange in Republican Ideology* (Ames: Iowa State University Press, 1991), pp. 75–93.

12. *Harper's Weekly*, Illinois Central Railroad advertisement, April 22, 1865, p. 256. Wrobel, *Promised Lands*, pp. 19–49. Kellie, *Prairie Populist*, pp. 9–11, 32.

13. Webb, *Great Plains*, pp. 3–44. Kellie, *Prairie Populist*, pp. 4–8.

14. Kellie, *Prairie Populist*, pp. 8–9.

15. Joanna L. Stratton, *Pioneer Women: Voices from the Kansas Frontier* (New York: Touchstone, 1981), pp. 46–56. Sandra L. Myres, *Westering Women and the Frontier Experience, 1800–1915* (Albuquerque: University of New Mexico Press, 1982), pp. 141–211. Cathy Luchetti and Carol Olwell, *Women of the West* (St. George, Utah: Antelope Island Press, 1982).

16. Many thanks to Bill Klein at Sandy Lake Implement Company in Pennsylvania for explaining spring tooth harrows to me. Morris, ed., *Encyclopedia of American History*, p. 481.

17. Fritz Redlich, *The Molding of American Banking: Men and Ideas* (New York: Hafner Publishing, 1951), 2:118–19. *Century of Independence*, pp. 236–37.

18. Kellie, *Prairie Populist*, p. 34.

19. Dubb, Hart, et al., *Pioneer Days*, pp. 20–21. Deverell, *Railroad Crossing*, pp. 32–42.

20. Kellie, *Prairie Populist*, pp. 22–24. Laura Ingalls Wilder, *On the Banks of Plum Creek* (1937; rpt. New York: Harper & Row, 1965), pp. 192–227, 259–67.

21. Hagan, *Quanah Parker*, pp. 12–13.

22. *New York Times*, September 10, 1872, p. 1. Vestal, *Sitting Bull*, p. 62. Utley, *Lance and Shield*, pp. 116–42. Jerome A. Greene, *Battles and Skirmishes of the Great Sioux War, 1876–1877: The Military View* (Norman: University of Oklahoma Press, 1993).

23. Woods, *Knights of the Plow*, p. 80. Kellie, *Prairie Populist*, pp. 10, 122–23. Dubb, Hart, et al., *Pioneer Days*, pp. 20–21.

24. "Report of Special Commissioners J. W. Powell and G. W. Ingalls . . ." reprinted in *The Indian and the White Man*, ed. Wilcomb E. Washburn (New York: Anchor Books, 1969), pp. 377, 381. Haley, *Goodnight*, 184–95. Dubb, Hart, et al., *Pioneer Days*, pp. 20–21.

25. Woods, *Knights of the Plow*, pp. 8–103. Solon Justus Buck, *The Granger Movement* (Cambridge: Harvard University Press, 1913), pp. 40–79. Elizabeth Sanders, *Roots of Reform: Farmers, Workers, and the American State, 1877–1917* (Chicago: University of Chicago Press, 1999), pp. 101–47. *New York Times*, May 23, 1873, p. 2; June 12, 1873, p. 1; July 10, 1873, p. 1; July 26, 1873, p. 4; August 18, 1873, p. 5.

26. Farmers would receive bank notes in exchange for their grain until it sold. This plan, usually associated with Charles McCune in the 1880s, was advanced as early as 1873 by T. R. Allen, the master of the Missouri State Grange. See *New York Times*, August 5, 1873, p. 3. Granger speech in Missouri, printed in *New York Times*, August 5, 1873, p. 4. Buck, *Granger Movement*, pp. 123–237. Augustus M. Burns III, "Munn v. Illinois," in *The Oxford Companion to the Supreme Court of the United States*, ed. Kermit L. Hall (New York: Oxford University Press, 1992), pp. 566–67; Nathan Fine, *Labor and Farmer Parties in the United States, 1828–1928* (New York: Russell & Russell, 1961), pp. 56–62.

27. Walter T. K. Nugent, *The Money Question during Reconstruction* (New York: W. W. Norton, 1967), pp. 49–51, 65–92.

28. *New York Times*, March 12, 1873, p. 7. Platform quoted in Buck, *Granger Movement*. *New York Times*, February 17, 1876, p. 5; Nathan Fine, *Labor and Farmer Parties*, pp. 60–64. On the cultural meanings of gold and silver, see Stanley L. Jones, *The Presidential Election of 1896* (Madison: University of Wisconsin Press, 1964), pp. 3–17.

29. *New York Weekly Herald*, October 29, 1879. *Harper's Weekly*, March 9, 1872, p. 196. Livesay, *Carnegie*, p. 113.

30. *New York Times*, July 13, 1873, see also May 6, 1874, p. 5. *Philadelphia Inquirer*, August 8, 1873; *San Francisco Daily Alta California*, August 16, 1873, p. 2. Engs, *Freedom's First Generation*, pp. 161–82.

31. Henry T. Williams, *The Pacific Tourist* (New York: Henry T. Williams, Publisher, 1876), pp. 70–71, MOA-UMich. Love, *Life and Adventures*, pp. 70–71, 88–91.

32. "Report of Special Commissioners," pp. 377, 38. Haley, *Goodnight*, pp. 187–97. Hagan, *Quanah Parker*, pp. 13–15.

33. Hagan, *Quanah Parker*, pp. 14–15, 21–22. William Thomas Hagan, "Quanah Parker," in *American Indian Leaders: Studies in Diversity* (Lincoln: University of Nebraska Press, 1986), pp. 175–89.

34. Stanton, Anthony, Gage, eds., *History of Woman Suffrage*, 1:14–15, 22. Ames, *Ten Years in Washington*, pp. 380–81. *Harper's Weekly*, December 23, 1876, p. 103. Helen Leah Reed, "Radcliffe College," *New England Magazine* 17 (January 1895): 609–35, MOA-Cornell.

35. *Nation*, January 9, 1873, p. 17; January 30, 1873, p. 66. This was the story of P. B. S. Pinchback, who became governor of Louisiana. Maurine Christopher, *Black Americans in Congress* (New York: Thomas Y. Crowell, 1976), pp. 108–12. Perman, *Road to Redemption*, pp. 142–44. Richardson, *Death of Reconstruction*, p. 105.

36. Durden, *Pike*, pp. 201–2. The articles appeared in the *New York Tribune*, March 29, and April 8, 10, 11, 12, 19, 1873.

37. James S. Pike, *The Prostrate State: South Carolina under Negro Government* (1873; rpt. New York: Loring & Mussey, 1935), pp. 9–16, 105, 137–49, 261–67. Durden, *Pike*, pp. 187–89; Richardson, *Death of Reconstruction*, pp. 106–7.

38. Michael A. Ross, *Justice of Shattered Dreams: Samuel Freeman Miller and the Supreme Court during the Civil War Era* (Baton Rouge: Louisiana State University Press,

2003), 189–210. A Republican legislature had passed the law granting a monopoly to a New Orleans slaughterhouse. If the Supreme Court upheld the plaintiffs, it weakened the legitimacy of the Republican government. If it upheld the law, it weakened civil rights. The racist, Democratic plaintiffs advanced the case with this dilemma in mind. *New York Daily Tribune*, January 2, 1874, p. 8; *Boston Evening Transcript*, July 30, 1874, p. 8. *New York Times*, March 6, 1875, p. 4. Richardson, *Death of Reconstruction*, pp. 140–55.

39. Gompers, *Seventy Years*, ed. Salvatore, p. 34. *Nation*, January 22, 1874, p. 52. *Boston Evening Transcript*, March 30, 1874, p. 8, and May 26, 1874, p. 4. *Philadelphia Inquirer*, March 31, 1873, p. 4, April 4, 1873, p. 4, April 7, 1873, p. 4, June 19, 1873, p. 1, December 24, 1873, p. 4. *Chicago Tribune*, January 5, 1874, p. 4. *Cincinnati Daily Gazette*, April 21, 1873, p. 4. *San Francisco Daily Alta California*, June 1, 1873, p. 2, August 27, 1873, p. 2, November 11, 1873, p. 2. E. Benjamin Andrews, *The History of the Last Quarter-Century in the United States, 1870–1895* (New York: Charles Scribner's Sons, 1896), 1:293–300. Kevin Kenney, *Making Sense of the Molly Maguires* (New York: Oxford University Press, 1998), pp. 213–44.

40. *New York Times*, May 13, 1876, p. 4. *Chicago Tribune*, February 18, 1874, p. 8.

41. *Bradwell v. Illinois*, 83 U.S. 130 (1873). *Minor v. Happersett*, 88 U.S. 162 (1874).

42. *New York Times*, November 29, 1872, p. 4. James Reed, *From Private Vice to Public Virtue: The Birth Control Movement and American Society Since 1930* (New York: Basic Books, 1978), pp. 3–18.

43. *Harper's New Monthly Magazine* 50 (January 1875): 297–98, MOA-Cornell. *Harper's Weekly*, December 12, 1874, p. 1015. Cox, *Three Decades of Federal Legislation*, pp. 628–29. *Cincinnati Daily Gazette*, March 6, 1875, p. 4. *Boston Evening Transcript*, January 1, 1875, p. 4; May 10, 1875, p. 4. Perman, *Road to Redemption*, pp. 135–64, 182–232.

44. *Visitors' Guide to the Centennial Exhibition* (Philadelphia: J. B. Lippincott, 1876), pp. 3–7.

45. Livesay, *Carnegie*, p. 113. Free Library of Philadelphia, "The Centennial Exhibition: Philadelphia 1876," at http://libwww.library.phila.gov/CenCol/, accessed May 29, 2004.

46. Love, *Life and Adventures*, p. 91. Sitting Bull quotation in Vestal, *Sitting Bull*, p. 134. Greene, *Battles and Skirmishes of the Great Sioux War*, pp. 41–62. *The Arikara Narrative of Custer's Campaign*, ed. Orin G. Libby (1920; rpt. Norman, Oklahoma: University of Oklahoma Press, 1998). Utley, *Lance and Shield*, pp. 143–64. *Harper's Weekly*, July 22, 1876, p. 598.

47. McKee, *Conventions*, pp. 173–75.

48. Ibid., pp. 162–68.

49. Ibid., pp. 168–73.

50. Brooks D. Simpson, *The Reconstruction Presidents* (Lawrence: University Press of Kansas, 1998), pp. 199–228.

51. Williamson, *After Slavery*, pp. 405–17. Reynolds, *South Carolina*, pp. 337–407.

52. Rable, *There Was No Peace*, pp. 152–85. Pringle, *Chronicles of Chicora Wood*, p. 38. Edmund Drago, *Hurrah for Hampton: Black Red Shirts in South Carolina during Reconstruction* (Fayetteville: University of Arkansas Press, 1998). Richard Zuczek, "The Last Campaign of the Civil War: South Carolina and the Revolution of 1876," *Civil War History* 42 (March 1996): 18–31. Williamson, *After Slavery*, 408–12.

53. *New York Times*, October 16, 1876, p. 1. Wade Hampton to George M. Johnson, June 9, 1877, in Cauthen, ed., *Hampton Family Letters*, p. 154. I am indebted to historian

Lacy K. Ford for making an educated and well-informed guess for me about the actual vote tallies in this election since the records were largely destroyed. Reynolds, *South Carolina*, pp. 408–62.

54. Hans L. Trefousse, *Rutherford B. Hayes* (New York: Henry Holt, 2002), pp. 65–90. Ari Hoogenboom, *Rutherford B. Hayes: Warrior and President* (Lawrence: University Press of Kansas, 1995), pp. 274–94.

55. Hoogenboom, *Warrior and President*, pp. 284, 290. Cox, *Three Decades of Federal Legislation*, p. 635; John L. Heaton, *The Story of a Page: Thirty Years of Public Service and Public Discussion in the Editorial Columns of the New York World* (New York: Harper & Brothers, 1908), p. 5, MOA-UMich.

56. Bruce, *1877: Year of Violence*. Gompers, *Seventy Years*, ed. Salvatore, p. 47. Allan Pinkerton, *Strikers, Communists, Tramps and Detectives* (1878; rpt., New York: Arno Press, 1969), pp. 19–20. Davidson, Gienapp, et al., *Nation of Nations*, 2:678.

57. Gompers, *Seventy Years*, ed. Salvatore, p. 47. "Preamble of the Constitution of the Knights of Labor," in Commager, ed., *Documents of American History*, 1:546–47.

58. Phelan, *Grand Master Workman*, pp. 28–30.

59. *San Francisco Daily Alta California*, June 3, 1880, p. 2; June 10, 1880, p. 4. *Philadelphia Inquirer*, June 1, 1880, p. 4. *Detroit Evening News*, May 4, 1880, p. 1. *New York Herald*, May 5, 1880, p. 6, and May 10, 1880, p. 6. Deverell, *Railroad Crossing*, pp. 42–56.

60. Henry George, *Progress and Poverty* (1879; rpt. New York: Modern Library, 1938).

61. *Harper's Weekly*, October 2, 1886, p. 639. John L. Thomas, *Alternative America: Henry George, Edward Bellamy, Henry Demarest Lloyd and the Adversary Tradition* (Cambridge: Harvard University Press, 1983), pp. 174–205.

62. Kellie, *Prairie Populist*, p. 104. *Chicago Tribune*, October 15, 1880, in John D. Hicks, *The Populist Revolt: A History of the Farmers' Alliance and the People's Party* (1931; rpt. Lincoln: University of Nebraska Press, 1961), p. 99.

63. *New York Times*, June 11, 1880, p. 5; J. B. Weaver to E. F. Norton et al., July 1, 1880, in *New York Times*, July 3, 1880, p. 5. Fine, *Labor and Farmer Parties*, pp. 70–71.

64. *New York Times*, June 12, 1880, p. 4.

65. Stephen Fiske, *Off-Hand Portraits of Prominent New Yorkers* (New York: Geo. R. Lockwood & Son, 1884), p. 293. MOA-UMich. Trefousse, *Schurz*, pp. 235–52. Frank M. O'Brien, *The Story of the Sun: New York, 1833–1928* (New York: D. Appleton, 1928), pp. 55, 191, MOA-UMich. Schurz, *Reminiscences*, 3:381–82. Hoogenboom, *Warrior and President* (Lawrence: University Press of Kansas, 1995), pp. 298–99, 318–35. Trefousse, *Hayes*, pp. 93–96.

66. *New York Times*, June 9, 1878, p. 1; July 11, 1878, p. 2, October 4, 1878, p. 5, October 6, 1878, p. 1. George S. Boutwell, "The Future of the Republican Party," *North American Review* 131 (December 1880): 480, MOA-Cornell. Rev. H. A. Stimson, "The Indian Question," *American Missionary* 33 (December 1879): 397, MOA-Cornell; *New York Times*, July 4, 1879, p. 1, July 7, 1879, p. 1, Stephen Young, comp., *The Posse Comitatus Act of 1878: A Documentary History* (Buffalo, N.Y.: William S. Hein, 2003).

67. Love, *Life and Adventures*, pp. 91–92, 95.

68. *Harper's Weekly*, April 28, 1877, p. 323. Beth LaDow, *The Medicine Line: Life and Death on a North American Borderland* (New York: Routledge, 2001), pp. 48–49, 65. Benson J. Lossing, *Our Country: A Household History for All Readers, from the Discovery of America to the One Hundredth Anniversary of the Declaration of Independence, 1875–1878*

(New York: Johnson, Wilson, 1875–78), p. 1773, MOA-UMich. Francis Paul Prucha, *American Indian Policy in Crisis: Christian Reformers and the American Indian, 1865–1900* (Norman: University of Oklahoma Press, 1976).

69. *Harper's Weekly*, July 20, 1876, pp. 625–28. Schurz, *Reminiscences*, 3:385–86. Trefousse, *Schurz*, pp. 242–45.

70. McKee, *Conventions*, pp. 182–93, 198–99.

CHAPTER SIX. 1881–1885: Years of Consolidation

1. Heaton, *Story of a Page*, p. 5. Theodore Roosevelt, *An Autobiography* (New York: Macmillan, 1913), pp. 62–63, 70.

2. *New York Times*, November 1, 1881, p. 2. Roosevelt, *Autobiography*, pp. 71–76, 86–87.

3. *Scribner's Monthly* 19 (April 1880): 950, MOA-Cornell. *Harper's Weekly*, September 13, 1884, p. 597; November 7, 1885, p. 727.

4. Carnegie, *Autobiography*, pp. 110–12. Winkler, *Incredible Carnegie*, pp. 153–56. Carnegie, "Gospel of Wealth," pp. 15–16.

5. University of Virginia Geospatial and Statistical Data Center. *United States Historical Census Data Browser*. University of Virginia, available at http://fisher.lib.virginia.edu/census/. Accessed October 1, 2004. Morris, ed., *Encyclopedia of American History*, p. 527.

6. *Harper's Weekly*, July 12, 1884, p. 451; August 30, 1884, p. 565; September 30, 1884, p. 621. Wendy A. Woloson, *Refined Tastes: Sugar, Confectionery, and Consumers in Nineteenth-Century America* (Baltimore: Johns Hopkins University Press, 2002), pp. 88–102. Laura Ingalls Wilder, *Farmer Boy* (1933; rpt. New York: Harper & Row, 1971), pp. 117–18.

7. Donald Dewey and Nicholas Acocella, *The Ball Clubs: Every Franchise, Past and Present, Officially Recognized by Major League Baseball* (New York: HarperPerennial, 1996), pp. 28–46, 121–45, 173–76, 233–35, 271–72, 337–38, 450–52, 572–74. John W. Chadwick, "In Western Massachusetts," *Harper's New Monthly Magazine* 61 (November 1880): 876–77, MOA-Cornell.

8. *Harper's Weekly*, October 23, 1886, p. 679. Grant, *Memoirs*, p. 774.

9. *New York Times*, April 30, 1882, p. 7. Woloson, *Refined Tastes*, pp. 168–186. *Harper's Weekly*, November 28, 1885, p. 775.

10. *Harper's New Monthly Magazine* 60 (January 1880): 302, MOA-Cornell.

11. Laura Ingalls Wilder, *The First Four Years* (New York: Harper & Row, 1971), p. 43. Hicks, *Populist Revolt*, p. 101. Stephan Thernstrom, *The Other Bostonians: Poverty and Progress in the American Metropolis, 1880–1970* (Cambridge: Harvard University Press, 1979), pp. 232–56.

12. *Opening Ceremonies of the New York and Brooklyn Bridge, May 24, 1883* (Brooklyn, N.Y.: Press of the Brooklyn Eagle Job Printing Department, 1883), pp. 8, 20–21, 57. MOA-UMich.

13. Harriet S. Blaine Beale, ed., *Letters of Mrs. James G. Blaine*, vol. 1 (New York: Duffield, 1908), pp. 209–42.

14. *Harper's Weekly*, May 20, 1882, pp. 306–7; March 22, 1879, reprinted in *Harper's Weekly*, July 26, 1884, p. 491. *Harper's Weekly*, September 26, 1885, pp. 638–39; November 21, 1885, p. 753. *Boston Globe*, September 20, 1885, p. 5.

15. William Graham Sumner, *What Social Classes Owe to Each Other* (1883; rpt. New York: Arno Press, 1972), pp. 13–27, 116–52. *Harper's Weekly*, July 12, 1884, p. 447.

16. Sumner, *Social Classes*, pp. 143–44. Porter, *Big Business*, pp. 56–69.

17. Fiske, *Off-Hand Portraits*, p. 293. Don C. Seitz, *The James Gordon Bennetts, Father and Son: Proprietors of the New York Herald* (Indianapolis: Bobbs-Merrill, 1928), p. 70. MOA-UMich. Heaton, *Story of a Page*, pp. 1–2. *Philadelphia Chronicle*, May 14, 1883, in Heaton, *Story of a Page*, p. 11.

18. *New York World*, May 11, 1883, quoted in Heaton, *Story of a Page*, p. 12. Roosevelt, *Autobiography*, pp. 71–73.

19. *New York Times*, June 14, 1882, p. 5.

20. General George Crook, quoted in *Harper's Weekly*, July 5, 1884, p. 427. General George Crook, to Mr. Welsh, reprinted in *Harper's Weekly*, August 30, 1884, p. 565.

21. Utley, *Lance and Shield*, pp. 167–68. Vestal, *Sitting Bull*, pp. 211–37. Testimony of Sitting Bull, 48th Cong., 1st sess., S. Rpt. 283, pp. 79–81. *Boston Globe*, September 20, 1865, p. 12.

22. Hagan, *Quanah Parker*, pp. 30–39. John Burns, American Life Histories: Manuscripts from the Federal Writers' Project, 1936–1940, Manuscript Division, Library of Congress, Washington, D.C., online at American Memory, http://memory.loc.gov/ammem/index.html, accessed October 12, 2004.

23. Hagan, *Quanah Parker*, pp. 30–39. Nat Henderson, American Life Histories: Manuscripts from the Federal Writers' Project, 1936–1940, Manuscript Division, Library of Congress, Washington, D.C., online at American Memory, http://memory.loc.gov/ammem/index.html, accessed October 12, 2004.

24. Hagan, *Quanah Parker*, pp. 35–43.

25. J. Morgan Kousser, *The Shaping of Southern Politics: Suffrage Restriction and the Establishment of a One-Party South, 1880–1910* (New Haven: Yale University Press, 1974), pp. 21–27. Joseph H. Cartwright, *The Triumph of Jim Crow: Tennessee Race Relations in the 1880s* (Knoxville: University of Tennessee Press, 1976), pp. 3–118. Michael W. Fitzgerald, *Urban Emancipation: Popular Politics in Reconstruction Mobile, 1860–1890* (Baton Rouge: Louisiana State University Press, 2002), pp. 198–245. Walter Brian Cisco, *Wade Hampton: Confederate Warrior, Conservative Statesman* (Washington, D.C.: Brassey's, 2004), pp. 270–81. *New York Times*, April 25, 1880, p. 1; July 30, 1880, p. 4. Richardson, *Death of Reconstruction*, pp. 197–201. *San Francisco Examiner*, October 21, 1883, p. 8; *Hartford Weekly Times*, October 18, 1883, p. 2. Lawrence Grossman, *The Democratic Party and the Negro: Northern and National Politics, 1868–1892* (Urbana: University of Illinois Press, 1976), pp. 60–142. Geoffrey Blodgett, *The Gentle Reformers: Massachusetts Democrats in the Cleveland Era* (Cambridge: Harvard University Press, 1966). Gerald W. McFarland, ed., *The Mugwumps, 1884–1900* (New York: Simon & Schuster, 1975).

26. Booker T. Washington, *Up from Slavery* (1901; rpt. New York: Oxford University Press, 1995), pp. 69–77.

27. Robert C. Kenzer, *Enterprising Southerners: Black Economic Success in North Carolina, 1865–1915* (Charlottesville: University Press of Virginia, 1997), p. 49. David M. Katzman, *Before the Ghetto: Black Detroit in the Nineteenth Century* (Urbana: University of Illinois Press, 1973), pp. 135–74. Loren Schweninger, *Black Property Owners in the South, 1790–1915* (Urbana: University of Illinois Press, 1990). Willard B. Gatewood, *Aristocrats of Color: The Black Elite, 1880–1920* (Bloomington: Indiana University Press, 1990). Janette

Thomas Greenwood, *Bittersweet Legacy: The Black and White "Better Classes" in Charlotte, 1850–1910* (Chapel Hill: University of North Carolina Press, 1994). Glenda Elizabeth Gilmore, *Gender and Jim Crow* (Chapel Hill: University of North Carolina Press, 1996), pp. 1–29. *Maryville (Tenn.) Republican* [African American], October 7, 1876. Bernard E. Powers, Jr., *Black Charlestonians: A Social History, 1822–1885* (Fayetteville: University of Arkansas Press, 1994), p. 177. *New York Times*, January 2, 1886, p. 2. George Washington Williams, *History of the Negro Race in America* (New York: G. P. Putnam's Sons, 1883), pp. 527–28, 549–52. William Toll, "Free Men, Freedmen, and Race: Black Social Theory in the Gilded Age," *Journal of Southern History* 44 (November 1978): 571–96.

28. Fite, *Cotton Fields No More*, p. 5. T. W. Higginson, "Some War Scenes Revisited," *Atlantic Monthly*, July 1878, pp. 1–9, MOA-Cornell. *New York Times*, July 31, 1881, p. 6, September 30, 1881, p. 2, November 14, 1881, p. 4, February 20, 1886, p. 3. *Philadelphia Evening Bulletin*, October 16, 1883, p. 4.

29. Article from the *Chicago Tribune*, in *Philadelphia Evening Bulletin*, October 22, 1883, p. 1. *Hartford Courant*, October 19, 1883, p. 2. *Hartford Weekly Times*, October 25, 1883, p. 4. *New York Herald*, May 30, 1880, p. 12. *Cincinnati Daily Gazette*, February 1, 1873, p. 2, *Philadelphia Daily Evening Bulletin*, June 4, 1880, p. 4; October 16, 1883, p. 4.

30. *Philadelphia Daily Evening Bulletin*, October 17, 1883, p. 2. *San Francisco Examiner*, October 17, 1883, p. 2. Richardson, *Death of Reconstruction*, pp. 122–55. Cisco, *Hampton*, pp. 284–91.

31. Alfreda M. Duster, ed., *Crusade for Justice: The Autobiography of Ida B. Wells* (Chicago: University of Chicago Press, 1970), pp. 18–20. *Chesapeake & Ohio & Southwestern Railroad Company v. Wells. Tennessee Reports: 85 Cases Argued and Determined in the Supreme Court of Tennessee for the Western Division, Jackson, April Term, 1887*, p. 615, in *Crusade for Justice*, ed. Duster, p. 20.

32. Hicks, *Populist Revolt*, p. 101. *New York Times*, February 20, 1886, p. 3. Edward Atkinson, "The Food Question in America and Europe," *Century* 33 (December 1886): 238–48, MOA-Cornell. *Boston Globe*, November 21, 1882, p. 2, reprinted from *Century*. See also *Boston Globe*, July 15, 1885, p. 6; *New York Times*, May 6, 1885, p. 1. For a rosy view of western life, see Laura Ingalls Wilder, *Little Town on the Prairie* (1941; rpt. New York: HarperCollins Publishers, 1971). Wilder was staunchly opposed to New Deal legislation and formed her reminiscences to illustrate individualism.

33. Stanford, quoted in Clark, *Stanford*, p. 283. Edward Atkinson, "Economic Pessimism," *North American Review* 144 (May 1887): 540–43, MOA-Cornell. *Harper's Weekly*, February 9, 1884, p. 86. Grover Cleveland, First Annual Message, December 3, 1888, in Richardson ed., *Messages and Papers*, 8: 339–341.

34. Winkler, *Incredible Carnegie*, p. 152. *Harper's Weekly*, November 21, 1885, p. 763. William F. Swindler, "Roscoe Conkling and the Fourteenth Amendment," in Supreme Court Historical Society Publications, 1983 Yearbook, electronic version, http://www.supremecourthistory.org/04_library/subs_volumes/04_c20_a.html, accessed February 26, 2005.

35. *Indianapolis Daily Sentinel*, November 21, 1883, p. 4, quoted in Ian R. Bartky, *Selling the True Time: Nineteenth-Century Timekeeping in America* (Stanford: Stanford University Press, 2000), p. 144.

36. *History of Cincinnati and Hamilton County, Ohio* (Cincinnati: S. B. Nelson, 1894), pp. 367–78.

37. Ibid., pp. 367–78.

38. Since it was hard to portray a violent mob as a group of concerned citizens, *Harper's Weekly* initially insisted that a decorous protest meeting had attracted the criminal classes that had then gone on to riot. *Cincinnati Gazette*, April 5, 1884, p. 2. *Harper's Weekly*, April 12, 1884, pp. 230, 241. *Harper's Weekly*, April 12, 1884, p. 230; see also Nast cartoon, p. 237.

39. McKee, *Conventions*, pp. 201–17.

40. *Harper's Weekly*, March 8, 1884, p. 149. James Pickett Jones, *John A. Logan: Stalwart Republican from Illinois* (Tallahassee: University Presses of Florida, 1982). Mary R. Dearing, *Veterans in Politics: The Story of the GAR* (Baton Rouge: Louisiana State University Press, 1952), pp. 80–112. Stuart McConnell, *Glorious Contentment: The Grand Army of the Republic, 1865–1900* (Chapel Hill: University of North Carolina Press, 1992), pp. 25, 194–95. *Harper's Weekly*, June 28, 1884, p. 406. Simeon E. Baldwin, quoted in *Harper's Weekly*, July 5, 1884, p. 426.

41. Editorial reprinted in Heaton, *Story of a Page*, p. 23. Allan Nevins, *Grover Cleveland: A Study in Courage* (New York: Dodd, Mead, 1932), pp. 94–155. *Harper's Weekly*, June 28, 1884, p. 407. July 5, 1884, p. 426, 429; July 19, 1884, pp. 458, 465.

42. Seitz, *James Gordon Bennett*, p. 359. O'Brien, *Story of the Sun*, p. 192, MOA-UMich. Heaton, *Story of a Page*, pp. 23–25. G. T. C. in *Harper's Weekly*, August 9, 1884, p. 521. *Harper's Weekly*, March 8, 1884, p. 150; April 12, 1884, p. 231. McKelway, quoted in *Harper's Weekly*, July 19, 1884, p. 459. *New York Times*, March 11, 1884, p. 8.

43. H. Wayne Morgan, *From Hayes to McKinley: National Party Politics, 1877–1896* (Syracuse: Syracuse University Press, 1969), p. 253. Grover Cleveland, First Inaugural Address, in Richardson, ed., *Messages and Papers*, 8:299–303. State Senate of Indiana to Grover Cleveland, March 6, 1885, and William Gross [?] to Grover Cleveland, March 6, 1865, both in Grover Cleveland MSS, Manuscript Division, Library of Congress, Washington, D.C., on microfilm. *New York Times*, January 24, 1886, p. 6.

44. Eugene V. Smalley, "In and Out of the New Orleans Exposition," *Century* 30 (June 1885): 185–99, MOA-Cornell. Richard Nixon, "The World's Exposition at New Orleans: Its Scope and Expected Results," *Century* 29 (December 1884): 312–13, MOA-Cornell. Charles Dudley Warner, "Impressions of the South," *Harper's New Monthly Magazine* 71 (September 1885): 548, MOA-Cornell. See also Eugene V. Smalley, "The New Orleans Exposition," *Century* 30 (May 1885): 3–14, MOA-Cornell.

45. Liberty Bell Museum Web site, at http://www.libertybellmuseum.com/Worlds Fair/1885.htm. "The Colored People at the New Orleans Exposition," *American Missionary* 39 (July 1885): 189–91, MOA-Cornell. Warner, "Impressions of the South," pp. 546–52. *Cleveland Gazette*, June 27, 1885, reprinted on Ohio Historical Society Web site, "The African American Experience in Ohio."

46. Warner, "Impressions," pp. 549, 551.

47. Howe, *Reminiscences*, p. 396. Smalley, "In and Out," p. 189.

48. Nancy Tomes, *The Gospel of Germs: Men, Women, and the Microbe in American Life* (Cambridge: Harvard University Press, 1998), 26–47. *Harper's Weekly*, March 1, 1884, p. 139. See also *Harper's Weekly*, July 12, 1884, p. 443.

49. Roosevelt, *Autobiography*, pp. 41–44. Tomes, *Germs*, pp. 23–25. Heaton, *Story of a Page*, p. 4. Dr. Charles A. Garabedian, M.D., unraveled this medical history for me. Theodore Roosevelt, Diary, February 14, 1884, Theodore Roosevelt Papers, Library of Con-

gress, Washington, D.C., available at http://lcweb2.loc.gov/ammem/trhtml/trdiary3.html, accessed September 17, 2004.

50. Heaton, *Story of a Page*, p. 26. Roosevelt, *Autobiography*, pp. 103–4.

51. White, *Misfortune*, pp. 222–23; Charles A. Siringo, *A Texas Cowboy: Or, Fifteen Years on the Hurricane Deck of a Spanish Pony* (1885; rpt. New York: Penguin, 2000), introduction by Richard W. Etulain, pp. 173–92. Haley, *Goodnight*, pp. 295–333.

52. Roosevelt, *Autobiography*, pp. 132–33. Love, *Life and Adventures*, p. 155.

53. Roosevelt, *Autobiography*, pp. 132–33.

54. Ibid, p. 125.

55. Michael Fellman, *Inside War, the Guerrilla Conflict in Missouri during the American Civil War* (New York: Oxford University Press, 1989). T. J. Stiles, *Jesse James: Last Rebel of the Civil War* (New York: Vintage, 2002), p. 387. Jesse James, letter to the editor, July 6, 1875, in *Nashville (Tenn.) Republican Banner*, reprinted in *New York Times*, July 20, 1875. p. 2; all quotations as in the original. *Harper's Weekly*, July 12, 1884, p. 452.

56. Triplett, *Jesse James*, pp. 58, 68.

57. Stiles, *James*, pp. 350, 38–92. Triplett, *Jesse James*, p. 223, 254, 264–66. E. Benjamin Andrews, "A History of the Last Quarter-Century in the United States. VII. Home Agitations and Foreign Problems," *Scribner's Magazine* 18 (October 1895): 477–501, MOA-Cornell.

58. Triplett, *Jesse James*, pp. 66, 81, 90–91.

59. Love, *Life and Adventures*, pp. 156–57.

60. Abbott and Smith, *We Pointed Them North*, p. 47. Robert M. Utley, *High Noon in Lincoln: Violence on the Western Frontier* (Albuquerque: University of New Mexico Press, 1987).

61. *Harper's Weekly*, March 29, 1884, p. 203. Siringo, *Texas Cowboy*, pp. xi–xii, 146–54, 107–21. Robert M. Utley, *Billy the Kid: A Short and Violent Life* (Lincoln: University of Nebraska Press, 1989).

62. *Senate Exodus Reports*, 46th Cong., 2nd sess., S. Rpt. 693. Robert G. Athearn, *In Search of Canaan: Black Migration to Kansas, 1879–1880* (Lawrence: The Regent's Press of Kansas, 1978). Painter, *Exodusters*.

63. Abbott and Smith, *We Pointed Them North*, pp. 51–52.

64. William F. Cody, *An Autobiography of Buffalo Bill* (New York: Cosmopolitan Book Corporation, 1920), pp. 314–328. Kirk Munroe, in *Harper's Weekly*, August 2, 1884, p. 499. Grover Cleveland, First Annual Message, 1885, in Richardson, ed., *Messages and Papers*, 8:355–58. White, *Misfortune*, pp. 222–27. Robert V. Hine and John Mack Faragher, *The American West: A New Interpretive History* (New Haven: Yale University Press, 2000), pp. 325–26.

65. *Harper's Weekly*, October 22, 1887, p. 759. Joy S. Kasson, *Buffalo Bill's Wild West: Celebrity, Memory, and Popular History* (New York: Hill & Wang, 2000).

66. *Harper's Weekly*, December 4, 1886, p. 785.

67. *New York Times*, April 25, 1886, p. 3. *Sioux Falls (Dakota Territory) Press*, quoted in *New York Times*, October 29, 1886, p. 4. *New York Times*, October 31, 1886, p. 8.

68. *New York Times*, October 19, 1886, p. 4.

69. *Baltimore American*, October 21, 1886, reprinted in *New York Times*, October 22, 1886, p. 4.

70. Theodore Roosevelt, quoted in *New York Times*, October 27, 1886, p. 1. Theodore Roosevelt, quoted in *New York Times*, October 28, 1886, p. 2.

CHAPTER SEVEN. 1886–1892: The Struggle Renewed

1. Richards and Elliott, *Howe*, 1:220, 295.
2. *New York Times*, November 2, 1886, p. 1.
3. *New York Times*, August 15, 1895, p. 9.
4. Winkler, *Incredible Carnegie*, pp. 167–68. Carnegie, "Gospel of Wealth." *New York Times*, October 6, 1889, p. 19.
5. *New York Times*, October 6, 1889, p. 19. January 16, 1889, p. 4; March 27, 1889, p. 4.
6. Henry C. Adams, "The Farmer and Railway Legislation," *Century* 43 (March 1892): 780–84, MOA-Cornell.
7. Grover Cleveland, Second Annual Message, December 6, 1886, and Third Annual Message, December 6, 1887, in Richardson, ed., *Messages and Papers*, 8:510–11, 8:580–91. John Sherman, *Recollections of Forty Years in the House, Senate, and Cabinet* (Chicago: Werner, 1895), 2:1004–5.
8. Grover Cleveland, Fourth Annual Message, December 3, 1888, in Richardson, ed., *Messages and Papers*, 8:773–800.
9. *New York Times*, January 10, 1889, p. 4.
10. *New York Times*, January 10, 1889, p. 4; February 2, 1889, p. 4; June 22, 1889, p. 4; November 28, 1889, p. 1.
11. *New York Times*, March 27, 1889, p. 4. See also *New York Tribune*, quoted in *New York Times*, January 16, 1889, p. 4. *St. Louis Globe-Democrat*, quoted in *New York Times*, May 15, 1889, p. 4. *New York Times*, July 19, 1889, p. 4; October 15, 1889, p. 4; November 20, 1889, p. 4.
12. "Sherman Anti-Trust Act," in Commager, ed., *Documents of American History*, 1:586–87.
13. *New York World*, July 1, 1892, in Heaton, *Story of a Page*, pp. 83, 88.
14. Davidson, Gienapp, et al., *Nation of Nations*, 2:678. Gompers, *Seventy Years*, ed. Salvatore, pp. 94–96.
15. *Harper's Weekly*, February 27, 1886.
16. Gompers, *Seventy Years*, ed. Salvatore, pp. 96–97.
17. Mayor's Office, Proclamation to the people of Chicago, May 5, 1886 (Chicago: Jno. B. Jeffrey Printing & Engraving, 1886), available at *Chicago Anarchists on Trial: Evidence from the Haymarket Affair, 1886–1887*, online at American Memory, Library of Congress, http://memory.loc.gov/ammem/index.html, accessed September 11, 2004.
18. Richard H. Rovere, *Howe & Hummel: Their True and Scandalous History* (1947; rpt. New York: Farrar, Straus and Giroux, 1985). *New York Times*, February 1, 1871, p. 2; June 17, 1879, p. 2; July 28, 1880, p. 5; October 27, 1887, p. 1. Howe and Hummel, *In Danger; or Life in New York, A True History of a Great City's Wiles and Temptations* (New York: Red Cover Series, 1888).
19. *Progressive Farmer* (Raleigh, N.C.), April 28, 1887, quoted in Hicks, *Populist Revolt*, pp. 54, 102–3.
20. *Western Rural*, August 20, 1890, quoted in Hicks, *Populist Revolt*, p. 103.

21. Hicks, *Populist Revolt*, p. 125.

22. Robert W. Lawson, *Populism in the Mountain West* (Albuquerque: University of New Mexico Press, 1986).

23. "The Ocala Demands," in Commager, ed., *Documents of American History*, 1:592–93. Lease quoted in Hicks, *Populist Revolt*, p. 160.

24. Henry L. Dawes, Chairman of the Senate Committee on Indian Affairs, speech at Washington, D.C., January 1884, in Francis Paul Prucha, ed., *Americanizing the American Indians: Writings by the "Friends of the Indian," 1880–1900* (Cambridge: Harvard University Press, 1973), pp. 27–30. Prucha, *Great Father*, 2:643–52, 659–73, 686–715. Prucha, *Great Father*, 1:594–96. *Harper's Weekly*, July 14, 1888, p. 507. Francis Paul Prucha, *Documents of United States Indian Policy* (Lincoln: University of Nebraska Press, 1975), pp. 171–74.

25. Sherman, *Recollections*, 2:1061–71. Grover Cleveland to E. Ellery Anderson, February 10, 1891, reprinted in *Boston Globe*, February 12, 1891, p. 2.

26. *Newark (N.J.) Town Talk*, September 6, 1890, p. 6.

27. Richardson, *Death of Reconstruction*, pp. 207–9.

28. Heaton, *Story of a Page*, p. 69. Wade Hampton, "What Negro Supremacy Means," *Forum* 5 (June 1888): 383–95. John T. Morgan, "Shall Negro Majorities Rule?" *Forum* 6 (September 1888): 568–99. *New York Times*, January 21, 1890, p. 4. *Harper's Weekly*, May 24, 1890, p. 399. Washington Gladden, "Safeguards of the Suffrage," *Century* 37 (February 1889): 621–28. MOA-Cornell.

29. Francis Butler Simkins, *Pitchfork Ben Tillman: South Carolinian* (1944; rpt. Gloucester, Mass.: Peter Smith, 1964), pp. 171–90. Wade Hampton to Theodore G. Barker, January 29, 1891, in Cauthen, ed., *Hampton Family Letters*, pp. 159–60. William J. Cooper, Jr., *The Conservative Regime: South Carolina, 1877–1890* (Baltimore: Johns Hopkins University Press, 1968), pp. 143–207. Cisco, *Hampton*, pp. 301–18.

30. McConnell, *Glorious Contentment*, pp. 148–53.

31. Grover Cleveland, February 11, 1887, in Richardson, ed., *Messages and Papers*, 8:549–57.

32. Edward Bellamy, *Looking Backward: 2000–1887*, ed. Daniel H. Borus (1888; rpt. Boston: Bedford Books, 1995), pp. 34–35.

33. Bellamy, *Looking Backward*, pp. 54–57, 106. Thomas, *Alternative America*, pp. 262–82.

34. *Memorial Addresses . . . S. S. Cox*, pp. 89, 60, 109, 212–13, 116, 45, 81–82, 53.

35. Davidson, Gienapp, et al., *Nation of Nations*, 2:775.

36. Winkler, *Incredible Carnegie*, pp. 199–214.

37. *Philadelphia Evening Bulletin*, July 6, 1892, p. 3. *Harper's Weekly*, July 16, 1892, p. 674.

38. *New York World*, July 12, 1892, in Heaton, *Story of a Page*, pp. 84–85, 88. *New York Times*, December 1892, p. 2.

39. White, *Misfortune*, pp. 280–81. Alan Derickson, *Workers' Health, Workers' Democracy: The Western Miners Struggle, 1891–1925* (Ithaca: Cornell University Press, 1988), pp. 28–56. *New York Times*, March 7, 1873, p. 4. Richard E. Lingenfelter, *The Hardrock Miners: A History of the Mining Labor Movement in the American West, 1863–1893* (Berkeley: University of California Press, 1974), pp. 4–30.

40. Lingenfelter, *Hardrock Miners*, pp. 196–218.

41. George Edgar French, First Lieut. U.S. Infantry, "The Coeur d'Alene Riots of 1892," *Overland Monthly* 26 (July 1895): 32–49, MOA–UMich. White, *Misfortune*, pp. 346–47. *New York Times*, July 14, 1892, p. 1; July 15, 1892, p. 3; July 17, 1892, p. 5.

42. Abbott and Smith, *We Printed Them North*, pp. 130–36.

43. Hine and Faragher, *American West*, pp. 326–28.

44. Hagan, *Quanah Parker*, pp. 43–46.

45. L. Frank Baum, *The Wizard of Oz* (1900; rpt. New York: Tom Doherty Associates, 1993). Henry M. Littlefield, "The Wizard of Oz: Parable on Populism," *American Quarterly* 16 (spring 1964): 47–58.

46. McKee, *Conventions*, pp. 278–85.

47. Heaton, *Story of a Page*, p. 7.

48. Grover Cleveland, Second Inaugural Address, March 4, 1893, in Richardson, ed., *Messages and Papers*, 9: 389–93.

49. *New York World*, June 19, 1891, in Heaton, *Story of a Page*, pp. 74–75. *New York Times*, October 3, 1894, p. 12. Seitz, *James Gordon Bennett*, p. 359.

50. Richards and Elliott, *Howe*, 1:293–94. Kathryn Kish Sklar, *Florence Kelley and the Nation's Work: The Rise of Women's Political Culture, 1830–1900* (New Haven: Yale University Press, 1900). Joan Waugh, *Unsentimental Reformer: The Life of Josephine Shaw Lowell* (Cambridge: Harvard University Press, 1997).

51. Myers, *Westering Women*, pp. 213–37. Woody, *Women's Education*, 2:441–44. Kellie, *Prairie Populist*, p. 110.

52. *Harper's Weekly*, October 10, 1885, p. 659; October 24, 1885, p. 691.

53. Kellie, *Prairie Populist*, p. 110.

54. Woloson, *Refined Tastes*, pp. 52–57. Barbara Young Welke, *Recasting American Liberty: Gender, Race, Law, and the Railroad Revolution, 1865–1920* (Cambridge: Cambridge University Press, 2001), pp. 43–136. *New York Times*, July 24, 1893, p. 8. Tomes, *Germs*, pp. 48–67.

55. *New York Times*, December 29, 1886, p. 5. Rosalyn Terborg-Penn, "African-American Women's Networks in the Anti-Lynching Crusade," in *Gender, Class, Race, and Reform in the Progressive Era*, ed. Noralee Frankel and Nancy S. Dye (Lexington: University Press of Kentucky, 1991), pp. 148–61.

56. Alice Kessler-Harris, *Out to Work: A History of Wage-Earning Women in the United States* (New York: Oxford University Press, 1982), pp. 109–16.

57. William Chauncey Langdon, "The Problems of Modern Society," *Century 39* (November 1889): 26–31, MOA–Cornell. Samuel W. Dike, "Problems of the Family," *Century 39* (January 1890): 385–95, MOA–Cornell.

58. Howe, Diary, July 4, 1872, in Richards and Elliott, *Howe*, 1:315.

59. Addams, *Twenty Years at Hull-House*, pp. 44, 48.

60. Ibid., pp. 51, 55.

61. Ibid., pp. 58–61. Florence Kelley, "Hull House," *New England Magazine* 24 (July 1898): 550–66, MOA–Cornell.

62. Addams, *Twenty Years at Hull-House*, p. 65. Angelina Brooks, "Free Kindergartens in New York," *Century* 39 (November 1889): 157–58, MOA–Cornell.

63. Addams, *Twenty Years at Hull-House*, pp. 164–66.

64. Ibid., pp. 166–67.

65. Ibid., pp. 283–90.

66. Ibid., pp. 102–3.

67. Ibid., pp. 120–21.

68. Ibid., pp. 128–30.

69. Ibid., pp. 97–98. Jane Addams, "The Subtle Problem of Charity," *Atlantic Monthly* 83 (February 1899): 163–79, MOA-Cornell.

70. Jane Addams, "Why Women Should Vote," *Ladies Home Journal*, January 1910, pp. 21–22. Frankel and Dye, eds., *Gender, Class, Race, and Reform.*

71. Julia Ward Howe to Maud, May 31, 1894, in Richards and Elliott, *Howe*, 2:196. Julia Ward Howe in Richards and Elliott, *Howe*, 1:370.

72. Kathryn Kish Sklar, "Two Political Cultures in the Progressive Era: The National Consumers' League and the American Association for Labor Legislation," in *U.S. History as Women's History*, ed. Kerber, Kessler-Harris, and Sklar, pp. 36–62. *Harper's Weekly*, March 14, 1891, p. 183. *Atlantic Monthly* 67 (May 1891): 709, MOA-Cornell. Kelley, "Hull House." "Notes and Comments," *North American Review* 166 (February 1898): 250–56, MOA-Cornell Jacob A. Riis, *The Battle with the Slum* (New York: Macmillan, 1902), pp. 196–201. Lawrence B. Glickman, *A Living Wage: American Workers and the Making of Consumer Society* (Ithaca: Cornell University Press, 1997), pp. 116–24.

73. Morris, ed., *Encyclopedia of American History*, p. 261.

74. Prucha, *Indian Treaties*, pp. 319–20. On Jerome Agreement, see Hagan, *United States–Comanche Relations*, pp. 201–61.

75. *Senate Executive Documents*, 49th Cong., 2nd sess., #117. Frederick Turner, ed., *Geronimo: His Own Story . . . as told to S. M. Barrett* (1906; rpt. New York: Penguin, 1996), 39, 171–88. Brian C. Pohanka, ed., *Nelson A. Miles: A Documentary Biography of His Military Career, 1861–1903* (Glendale: Calif.: Arthur H. Clark, 1995), pp. 147–83. Angie Debo, *Geronimo: The Man, His Time, His Place* (Norman: University of Oklahoma Press, 1976), pp. 243–312. Grover Cleveland, Second Annual Message, December 6, 1886, in Richardson, ed., *Messages and Papers*, 8:497–529.

76. Utley, *Lance and Shield*, pp. 268–80.

77. James Mooney, *The Ghost-Dance Religion and the Sioux Outbreak of 1890* (Washington, D.C.: Government Printing Office, 1896), pp. 847–83.

78. *Harper's Weekly*, December 20, 1890, p. 995. Robert M. Utley, *Lance and Shield*, pp. 290–307. James McLaughlin, *My Friend the Indian* (1910; rpt. Lincoln: University of Nebraska Press, 1989), pp. 179–222. Pohanka, ed., *Miles*, pp. 210–11.

79. Hine and Faragher, *American West*, pp. 381–83. Pohanka, ed., *Miles*, pp. 185–224. Mooney, *Ghost-Dance*, pp. 883–86.

80. Love, *Life and Adventures*, pp. 129–30.

81. *Harper's Weekly*, May 9, 1861, p. 339; September 3, 1892, p. 847.

82. "Hunting-Life in the Rockies," *Harper's Weekly*, April 8, 1893, p. 322.

83. "Amateur Management of the Yosemite Scenery," *Century* 40 (September 1890): 797, MOA-Cornell. George G. MacKenzie, "Yosemite Valley: Letters from Visitors," *Century* 39 (January 1890): 476, MOA-Cornell.

84. "Topics of the Time," *Century* 45 (April 1898): 950–52, MOA-Cornell. "Attacks upon Public Parks," *Century* 43 (January 1892): 473–75, MOA-Cornell. Gerald W. Williams, *Early Years of National Forest Management: Implications of the Organic Act of 1897* (Washington, D.C.: USDA Forest Service), available at http://fs.jorge.com/archives/History—National/1897OrganicActESAPaper.htm.

CHAPTER EIGHT. 1893–1897: The Final Contest

1. Booker T. Washington, *Up from Slavery* (1901; rpt. New York: Oxford University Press, 1995), pp. 121–31. Louis R. Harlan, *Booker T. Washington: The Making of a Black Leader, 1856–1901* (London: Oxford University Press, 1972). Louis R. Harlan, *Booker T. Washington: The Wizard of Tuskegee, 1901–1915* (New York: Oxford University Press, 1983).

2. Washington, *Up From Slavery*, pp. 128–29.

3. E. Benjamin Andrews, "A History of the Last Quarter-Century in the United States. XI. Columbus's Deed after Four Centuries," *Scribner's Magazine* 19 (March 1896): 270. Sherman, *Recollections*, 2:1184–85. George R. Davis, "The World's Columbian Exposition," *North American Review* 154 (March 1892): 305–19, MOA-Cornell. Robert Herrick, *The Memoirs of an American Citizen* (1905; rpt. Cambridge: Belknap Press, 1963), p. 147.

4. Andrews, "History of the Last Quarter-Century: Columbus's Deed," p. 289. Davis, "World's Columbian Exposition," pp. 305–19. Hubert Howe Bancroft, *The Book of the Fair* (Chicago: Bancroft, 1893), pp. 136–78, at World's Columbian Exposition of 1893 exhibit, Paul V. Galvin Digital History Collection, Illinois Institute of Technology, Chicago, at http://columbus.gl.iit.edu/.

5. Bancroft, *Book of the Fair*, 122, 663. Frederick E. Hoxie, *A Final Promise: The Campaign to Assimilate the Indians, 1880–1920* (Lincoln: University of Nebraska Press, 1984).

6. Davis, "World's Columbian Exposition," pp. 305–19. Andrews, "History of the Last Quarter-Century: Columbus's Deed," p. 290. Bancroft, *Book of the Fair*, p. 921. *The Congress of Women: Held in the Woman's Building, World's Columbian Exposition* (Chicago: Monarch, 1894).

7. Bancroft, *Book of the Fair*, pp. 139–40, 176–77. "A Model Philadelphia Working-man's House," *Manufacturer and Builder* 25 (September 1893): 213, MOA-Cornell. Bancroft, *Book of the Fair*, p. 948. "Labor Unions of the United States," *Manufacturer and Builder* 24 (June 1892): 129, MOA-Cornell.

8. Christopher Robert Reed, *"All the World Is Here": The Black Presence at the White City* (Bloomington: Indiana University Press, 2000), pp. 1–36. Robert W. Rydell's introduction in Ida B. Wells et al., *The Reason Why the Colored American Is Not in the World's Columbian Exposition*, ed. Robert W. Rydell (Urbana: University of Illinois Press, 1999).

9. Reed, *Black Presence*, pp. 8–14, 57–79

10. Maurice M. Manring, *Slave in a Box: The Strange Career of Aunt Jemima* (Charlottesville: University of Virginia Press, 1998), pp. 18–78.

11. Helen Cody Wetmore, *Buffalo Bill, Last of the Great Scouts: The Life Story of Colonel William F. Cody* (1899; rpt. Lincoln: University of Nebraska press, 1965), p. 279.

12. Miriam Hauss, "An Etching for the AHA," *Perspectives*, September 2004, online at http://www.historians.org/Perspectives/Issues/2004/0409/0409trni.cfm. Wilbur R. Jacobs, *The Historical World of Frederick Jackson Turner* (New Haven: Yale University Press, 1968), pp. 1–4.

13. Smith, *Virgin Land*, pp. 250–60.

14. Frederick Jackson Turner, "The Significance of the Frontier in American History," in *The Frontier in American History* (New York: Henry Holt, 1920), pp. 1–38.

15. Jacobs, *Historical World of Turner*, p. 4. Jacobs points out that Turner had been influenced by Roosevelt's *The Winning of the West*.

16. Grover Cleveland, June 30, 1893, in Richardson, ed., *Messages and Papers*, 9:396. Sherman, *Recollections*, pp. 1186–87.

17. E. Benjamin Andrews, "A History of the Last Quarter-Century in the United States. XII. The Democracy Supreme," *Scribner's Magazine* 19 (April 1896): 469–90, MOA-Cornell.

18. *New York Times*, April 27, 1894, p. 1; May 20, 1894, p. 1. Andrews, "Quarter-Century: Democracy Supreme," pp. 473–74. "Monthly Record of Current Events," *Harper's New Monthly Magazine* 89 (July 1894): 316, MOA-Cornell. Rose Wilder Lane, American Life Histories: Manuscripts from the Federal Writers' Project, 1936–1940, Manuscript Division, Library of Congress, Washington, D.C., online at American Memory, http://memory.loc.gov/ammem/index.html.

19. Rev. Joseph V. Tracy, "A Mission to Coxey's Army," *Catholic World* 59 (August 1894): 666–80, MOA-UMich. Thomas Byrnes, "Character and Methods of the Men," *North American Review* 158 (June 1894): 696–710, MOA-Cornell. Andrews, "Quarter-Century: Democracy Supreme," p. 473. Mary Hallock Foote, "The Trumpeter," *Atlantic Monthly*, December 1894, pp. 721–29, MOA-Cornell. O. O. Howard, "The Menace of 'Coxeyism,'" *North American Review* 158 (June 1894): 689–96, MOA-Cornell. "Josiah Flynt, "Tramping with Tramps," *Century* 47 (November 1893): 99–109, MOA-Cornell. Dr. Alvah H. Doty, "The Danger to the Public Health," *North American Review* 158 (June 1894): 701–6, MOA-Cornell.

20. Byrnes, "Character and Methods," p. 696.

21. O. O. Howard, "Coxeyism."

22. Milford W. Howard, *If Christ Came to Congress* (1894; rpt. New York: Living Books, 1964), pp. 4, 9–10, 315, 323, 350, 296, 339, 358–64. Gene Clanton, *Congressional Populism and the Crisis of the 1890s* (Lawrence: University Press of Kansas, 1998), pp. 14–15.

23. Almont Lindsey, *The Pullman Strike: The Story of a Unique Experiment and of a Great Labor Upheaval* (Chicago: University of Chicago Press, 1942). *Pittsburgh Times*, quoted in William H. Carwardine, *The Pullman Strike* (1894; rpt., Chicago: Charles H. Kerr, 1973), p. 24. Buder, *Pullman*, pp. 148–54. Andrews, "Quarter-Century: Democracy Supreme," p. 474.

24. Andrews, "Quarter-Century: Democracy Supreme," pp. 474–76. Resolutions of the Central Labor Federation, quoted in *New York Times*, July 9, 1894, p. 1. See H. H. Van Meter, *The Vanishing Fair* (Chicago: Literary Art Company, 1894), in Paul V. Galvin Library Digital History Collection, Illinois Institute of Technology, Chicago, at: http://columbus.gl.iit.edu/.

25. Addams, *Twenty Years at Hull-House*, pp. 217–18.

26. Grover Cleveland, "A Proclamation," in *New York Times*, July 10, 1894, p. 1. Testimony of Miles, Chicago Public Library, "Chicago Metro History Fair: 1894, The Pullman Strike," at http://www.chipublib.org/003cpl/hf/pullman_striker.html.

27. *Chicago Times*, July 7, 1894, quoted in Gen. Nelson A. Miles, "The Lesson of the Recent Strikes," *North American Review* 159 (August 1894): 180–88, MOA-Cornell. *New York World*, July 9, 1894, in Heaton, *Story of a Page*, pp. 101–2.

28. *Harper's Weekly*, July 21, 1894, pp. 678–79. Buder, *Pullman*, p. 128.

29. Miles, "Lesson of the Recent Strikes."

30. Wade Hampton, "The Lesson of the Recent Strikes," *North American Review* 159 (August 1894): 188–195, MOA-Cornell.

31. Samuel Gompers, "The Lesson of the Recent Strikes," *North American Review* 159 (August 1894): 201–7, MOA-Cornell.

32. Eric Arnesen, *Brotherhoods of Color: Black Railroad Workers and the Struggle for Equality* (Cambridge: Harvard University Press, 2001), pp. 16–19, 29–30. Love, *Life and Adventures*, pp. 134–36.

33. Love, *Life and Adventures*, pp. 151–52.

34. O'Brien, *Story of the Sun*, p. 193. *The American Cosmopolis: The Foremost City of the World* (Boston: M. King, 1894), p. 60, MOA-UMich. Secretary of Agriculture J. Sterling Morton, "Protection and the Proletariat," *North American Review* 158 (June 1894): 641–46, MOA-Cornell.

35. *In re Debs*, 158 U.S. 564, 599 (1895). William Forbath, *Law and the Shaping of the American Labor Movement* (Cambridge: Harvard University Press, 2001). John Kendrick Bangs, "An Impression," *Harper's Weekly*, July 21, 1894, p. 679. "Reflections on the Latest Strike," *Manufacturer and Builder* 26 (May 1894), MOA-Cornell.

36. Stephen Kantrowitz, Ben Tillman and the Reconstruction of White Supremacy (Chapel Hill: University of North Carolina Press, 2000). Benjamin R. Tillman, quoted in Simkins, *Pitchfork Ben*, p. 2. *Buffalo Enquirer*, September 28, 1894, quoted in Simkins, *Pitchfork Ben*, p. 317. *Congressional Record*, 54 Cong., 1st sess., pp. 1072–80, quoted in Simkins, *Pitchfork Ben*, pp. 319–23.

37. Stanley L. Jones, *The Presidential Election of 1896* (Madison: University of Wisconsin Press, 1964), pp. 18–73.

38. William Jennings Bryan, "Cross of Gold Speech," in Commager, ed., *Documents of American History*, 1:624–28. *New York Times*, July 3, 1896, p. 4. Kantrowitz, *Tillman*, p. 251. Sinkins, *Pitchfork Ben*, pp. 329–42. McKee, *Conventions*, pp. 290–98, 305–10.

39. *New York World*, quoted in Heaton, *Story of a Page*, p. 139. Jones, *Presidential Election*, pp. 276–96. McKee, *Conventions*, pp. 298–305.

40. O'Brien, *Story of the Sun*, p. 194. *New York World*, quoted in Heaton, *Story of a Page*, p. 142.

41. Howard Lawrence Hurwitz, *Theodore Roosevelt and Labor in New York State, 1880–1900* (New York: Columbia University Press, 1943), pp. 177–87.

42. Andrew Carnegie, "Mr. Bryan the Conjurer," *North American Review* 164 (January 1897): 106–19, MOA-Cornell. Schurz, *Reminiscences*, 3:429–32. Gompers, *Seventy Years*, ed. Salvatore, pp. 522–25. Gompers later admitted that he voted for Bryan. Gompers, *Seventy Years* (1925 ed.), p. 378. Hurwitz, *Roosevelt and Labor*, p. 176. Phelan, *Grand Master Workman*, pp. 258–59. See editorial comments in Louis R. Harlan et al, eds., *The Booker T. Washington Papers* (Urbana: University of Illinois Press, 1975), 4:168, online version. C. E. Thomas to Mother, September 30, 1896, quoted in Kantrowitz, *Tillman*, p. 252. Rose Wilder Lane, American Life Histories: Manuscripts from the Federal Writers' Project, 1936–1940, Manuscript Division, Library of Congress, Washington, D.C., online at American Memory, http://memory.loc.gov/ammem/index.html. McKee, *Conventions*, pp. 326–29.

43. Rose Wilder Lane, American Life Histories: Manuscripts from the Federal Writers' Project, 1936–1940, Manuscript Division, Library of Congress, Washington,

D.C., online at American Memory, http://memory.loc.gov/ammem/index.html. James H. Eckels, "Our Reviving Business," *North American Review* 161 (September 1895): 340–48, MOA-Cornell.

44. Robert Service, "The Law of the Yukon," in *Collected Poems of Robert Service* (1907; rpt. New York: Dodd, Mead, 1940), pp. 10–13.

45. Love, *Life and Adventures*, pp. 135, 143–44. 136. Arnesen, *Brotherhoods of Color*, pp. 22–23.

46. Julia Ward Howe to Maud, December 19, 1894, in Richards and Elliott, *Howe*, 2:200. Booker T. Washington, *Up From Slavery*, pp. 190–92.

47. *Harper's Weekly*, June 10, 1899, p. 565.

48. *New York Times*, May 19, 1896, p. 3.

49. Hagan, "Quanah Parker," p. 186. Turner, ed., *Geronimo*, pp. 167–70.

50. Ellis Paxton Oberholtzer, *A History of the United States Since the Civil War*, 5 vols. (New York: Macmillan, 1937), 5:764–65. Julia Ward Howe, Diary, December 31, 1895, in Richards and Elliott, *Howe*, 2:211.

51. John Muir, quoted in "Plain Words to Californians," *Century* 51 (April 1896): 950, MOA-Cornell. John Muir, *Our National Parks* (1901; rpt. Madison: University of Wisconsin Press, 1981), pp. 363–65.

52. Love, *Life and Adventures*, pp. 145–47.

53. John Philip Sousa, *Marching Along: Recollections of Men, Women, and Music* (Boston: Hale, Cushman & Flint, 1928), pp. 157–58.

CHAPTER NINE. 1898–1901: Reunion

1. Owen Wister, *The Virginian: A Horseman of the Plains*, "Rededication and Preface" (1902; rpt. New York: Signet, 1979). Roosevelt, *Autobiography*, p. 133.

2. Ibid., Wister, *Virginian*.

3. J. B. Crabtree, *The Passing of Spain and the Ascendency of America* (Springfield, Mass: King-Richardson, 1898), pp. 194–207.

4. Robert E. May, *The Southern Dream of a Caribbean Empire, 1854–1861* (Baton Rouge: Louisiana State University Press, 1973). Muir, *Thousand-Mile Walk*, pp. 365–81.

5. Grito de Yara, quoted in Crabtree, *Passing of Spain*, p. 230.

6. S. S. Cox, *Congressional Globe*, 42nd Cong, 2nd sess., February 17, 1872, Appendix, pp. 55–56.

7. Crabtree, *Passing of Spain*, pp. 237, 240–41.

8. *Harper's Weekly*, December 6, 1873, pp. 1082–83, 1085–86; December 20, 1873, p. 1135.

9. Crabtree, *Passing of Spain*, pp. 243–46. John H. Latane, "Intervention of the United States in Cuba," *North American Review* 166 (March 1898): 350–62, MOA-Cornell.

10. *New York Times*, January 1, 1898, p. 3; January 2, 1898, p. 3. *New York Times*, January 3, 1898, p. 7.

11. Trumbull White, *United States in War with Spain and the History of Cuba* (Chicago: International Publishing, 1898), pp. 240–91.

12. White, *United States in War*, pp. 291–92. *New York Times*, March 7, 1898, p. 1. *Harper's Weekly*, March 12, 1898, pp. 142–43; March 19, 1898, pp. 266–67. Joel Benton,

"Yellow Journals' and War," *New York Times*, March 2, 1898, p. 6. H. Wayne Morgan, *William McKinley and His America* (Kent, Ohio: Kent State University Press, 2003), pp. 248–87.

13. Gerald F. Linderman, *The Mirror of War: American Society and the Spanish-American War* (Ann Arbor: University of Michigan Press, 1974), pp. 6–7. Morgan, *McKinley and His America*, p. 252.

14. William Randolph Hearst, "Pacific Coast Journalism," *Overland Monthly* 11 (April 1888): 403–5; MOA-UMich.

15. *Harper's Weekly*, September 4, 1897, p. 875. Evangelina Cisneros, *The Story of Evangelina Cisneros Told by Herself [and] Her Rescue by Karl Decker* (New York: Continental Publishing, 1898).

16. Theodore Roosevelt, *The Rough Riders* (1899; rpt. New York: Modern Library, 1999), pp. 3–5.

17. Morgan, *McKinley and His America*, p. 274.

18. Heaton, *Story of a Page*, pp. 159–60. *New York Times*, March 26, 1898, p. 1, 6.

19. *New York Times*, March 18, 1898, p. 3. Morgan, *McKinley and His America*, p. 280.

20. Redfield Proctor, *Congressional Record*, 55th Cong., 2nd sess., pp. 2916–19.

21. Earl D. Berry, "Senator Redfield Proctor," *New York Times*, April 3, 1898, p. SM2. Linderman, *Mirror of War*, pp. 37–59. Lentz, quoted in Murat Halstead, *Our Country in War and Our Foreign Relations* (n.p.: F. Oldach, Sr., 1898), p. 502. Morgan, *McKinley and His America*, p. 277.

22. Morgan, *McKinley and His America*, pp. 288–322.

23. William Jennings Bryan, quoted in *New York Tribune*, quoted in *New York Times*, April 3, 1989, p. 18. "The Point of View," *Scribner's Monthly* 24 (July 1898): 124, MOA-Cornell.

24. David F. Trask, *The War with Spain in 1898* (New York: Macmillan, 1981), p. 156. Roosevelt, *Rough Riders*, p. xxx. *New York Times*, April 28, 1898, p. 1. *New York Times*, May 1, 1898, p. 3; June 3, 1898, p. 2.

25. Roosevelt, *Autobiography*, p. 133. Roosevelt, *Rough Riders*, pp. 7–24.

26. Trask, *War with Spain*, pp. 157–58. Linderman, *Mirror of War*, pp. 60–90. Roosevelt, *Rough Riders*, pp. 7–24.

27. John Hay to Theodore Roosevelt, quoted in Frank Freidel, *The Splendid Little War* (Boston: Little, Brown, 1958), p. 3.

28. Roosevelt, *Rough Riders*, pp. 29–30, 191–98.

29. Ibid., pp. 124–30, 199–202.

30. Trumbull White, *Pictorial History of Our War with Spain for Cuba's Freedom* (n.p.: Freedom Publishing, 1898), p. 27. Halstead, *Our Country in War*, p. 440.

31. White, *Pictorial History*, p. 62. Dewey quotation in Freidel, *Splendid Little War*, p. 22.

32. Ernest R. May, *Imperial Democracy: The Emergence of America as a Great Power* (1961; rpt. Chicago: Imprint Publications, 1991).

33. Ephraim K. Smith, "William McKinley's Enduring Legacy: The Historiographical Debate on the Taking of the Philippine Islands," in *Crucible of Empire: The Spanish-American War and Its Aftermath*, ed. James C. Bradford (Annapolis, Md.: Naval Institute Press, 1993), pp. 205–49. John Barrett, "The Problem of the Philippines," *North American Review* 167 (September 1898): 259–67, MOA-Cornell.

34. Roy Alfred Stacey, "We Will Not Go Back," *Harper's Weekly*, March 16, 1901, p. 296.

35. Brigadier General Thomas M. Anderson, "Our Rule in the Philippines," *North American Review* 170 (February 1900): 272–84, MOA-Cornell. William R. Segeman, "On the Right Path," *Harper's Weekly*, March 16, 1901, p. 297.

36. John Barrett, "The Problem of the Philippines," *North American Review* 167 (September 1898): 259–67, MOA-Cornell. Segeman, "On the Right Path." Charles Bonnycastle Robinson, "We Must Stay," *Harper's Weekly*, March 16, 1901, p. 297. Anderson, "Our Rule," p. 283. Barrett, "Problem of the Philippines," p. 264.

37. Anderson, "Our Rule," pp. 272–84. "A Filipino," "Aguinaldo's Case against the United States," *North American Review* 169 (September 1899): 425–32, MOA-Cornell.

38. Segeman, "On the Right Path." "A Filipino," "Aguinaldo's Case." Davidson, Gienapp, et al., *Nation of Nations*, 2:816.

39. John Hamill, "A Soldier's Solution," *Harper's Weekly*, March 16, 1901, p. 296. Edward Dixon, "Try the Cuban Resolution," *Harper's Weekly*, March 16, 1901, p. 296.

40. Robert L. Beisner, *Twelve against Empire: The Anti-Imperialists, 1898–1900* (New York: McGraw-Hill, 1968), pp. 18–34, 165–85. Andrew Carnegie, "Americanism versus Imperialism–II," *North American Review* 168 (March 1899): 363, MOA-Cornell.

41. Edward P. Crapol, *James G. Blaine: Architect of Empire* (Wilmington, Del.: Scholarly Resources, 2000), pp. 123–28. White, *United States in War*, p. 438. Andrew Carnegie, "Bryan or McKinley: The Present Duty of American Citizens," *North American Review* 171 (October 1900): 495–507, MOA-Cornell.

42. *New York Times*, May 1, 1898, p. 3; June 28, 1898, p. 6; July 10, 1898, p. 16; July 31, 1898, p. 16. *Indianapolis Sentinel*, quoted in *New York Times*, July 4, 1898, p. 7. See, e.g., the *Rochester Post-Express*, reprinted in *New York Times*, August 1, 1898, p. 4.

43. Theodore Roosevelt, quoted in *New York Times*, September 22, 1898, p. 1. *Charleston News and Courier*, quoted in *New York Times*, October 3, 1898, p. 6.

44. Theodore Roosevelt, quoted in *New York Times*, September 22, 1898, p. 1.

45. T. St. John Gaffney, in *New York Times*, August 22, 1898, p. 6.

46. *American Missionary* 52 (September 1898): 106–8, MOA-Cornell. Presley Holliday to *New York Age*, May 11, 1899, in Willard Gatewood, Jr., *"Smoked Yankees" and the Struggle for Empire* (Fayetteville: University of Arkansas Press, 1987), pp. 92–97. William Hilary Coston, *The Spanish-American War Volunteer*, 2nd ed. (1899; rpt. Freeport, N.Y.: Books for Libraries Press, 1971). Willard B. Gatewood, Jr., *Black Americans and the White Man's Burden, 1898–1903* (Urbana: University of Illinois Press, 1975). Lewis, *Neither Wolf Nor Dog*, pp. 169–75. Bonnie Lynn-Sherow, *Red Earth: Race and Agriculture in Oklahoma Territory* (Lawrence: University Press of Kansas, 2004), pp. 106–43. Debo, *Geronimo*, p. 420.

47. Henry Litchfield West, "The Race War in North Carolina," *Forum* 26 (January 1899): 578–91. Col. Alfred M. Waddell, in *Collier's Weekly*, November 26, 1898, reproduced at "For the Record: Representations of the Wilmington Race Riot, 1898," at http://www.mith.umd.edu/courses/amvirtual/wilmington/wilmington.html.

48. *New York Times*, September 29, 1898, p. 3. Roosevelt, quoted in William Roscoe Thayer, *Theodore Roosevelt: An Intimate Biography* (New York: Grosset & Dunlap, 1919), pp. 133–39.

49. Morgan, *McKinley and His America*, pp. 372–81. Thayer, *Roosevelt*, pp. 150–153.

50. Theodore Roosevelt to Henry Cabot Lodge, September 23, 1901, in *Selections from the Correspondence of Theodore Roosevelt and Henry Cabot Lodge, 1884–1918* (New York: Charles Scribner's Sons, 1925), 1:506.

51. Robert G. Athearn, *The Mythic West in Twentieth-Century America* (Lawrence: University Press of Kansas, 1986), p. 165; Owen Wister, *The Virginian* (New York: Grosset & Dunlap, 1904), p. 263.

52. Wister, *Virginian* (1904), pp. 90–91, 144–45, 261.

53. Ibid, pp. 169, 272–74.

54. Ibid., p. 372.

55. William D. Carrigan, *The Making of a Lynching Culture: Violence and Vigilantism in Central Texas, 1836–1916* (Urbana: University of Illinois Press, 2004), pp. 17–47, 132–6.

56. Wister, *Virginian*, pp. 429–36, 468–71.

57. Ibid., p. 504. Nina Silber, *The Romance of Reunion: Northerners and the South, 1865–1900* (Chapel Hill: University of North Carolina Press, 1993), pp. 192–95.

58. W. T. Harris, "Statistics *versus* Socialism," *Forum* 24 (October 1897): 186–99.

59. *Muller v. Oregon*, 208 U.S. 412 (1908).

60. American Antiquities Act, 1906, 16 USC 431–33.

61. Haley, *Goodnight*, p. 447.

62. Cody, *Autobiography*, p. 2.

Epilogue

1. Evans, *They Made America*, p. 113.

2. Hine and Faragher, *American West*, pp. 530–31.

Index